Action Stations Revisited

Action Stations Revisited

The complete history of Britain's
military airfields:
No. 5 Wales and the Midlands

Tim McLelland

Crécy Publishing Limited

First published in 2012 by Crécy Publishing Limited
All rights reserved

© Tiim McLelland 2012
Tim McLelland is hereby identified as the author of this work in accordance with
Section 77 of the Copyright, Designs and Patents Act 1988

A CIP record for this book is available from the British Library

ISBN 9 780859 791113

Printed and bound in
England by MPG Books

Crécy Publishing Limited
1a Ringway Trading Estate, Shadowmoss Road, Manchester M22 5LH
www.crecy.co.uk

CONTENTS

INTRODUCTION

Historians often portray wartime Britain as a fortress, standing defiant against the aggression of Nazi Germany. When America joined the Second World War, this fortress was strengthened and drastically enlarged until the country bristled with military might, most of which had come directly from the other side of the Atlantic. Air power was at the forefront of Britain's posture and as the war progressed more and more airfields were constructed from where Britain and her allies could operate the thousands of defensive fighters and offensive bombers that would be required to achieve victory in Europe. Huge areas of land were requisitioned for development, farmland disappearing, age-old roads and paths suddenly terminated, and houses destroyed, as more and more airfields sprung up across the country. Naturally, the largest number of airfields appeared in the South and East, most notably in East Anglia, where much of America's might was concentrated. The proximity of the enemy's forces just a few miles across the Channel made southern England the primary location for most of the RAF's defensive forces, and this was reflected in the astonishing number of airfields that were created over a period of just a couple of years.

But while so much attention was directed to the southern areas of the United Kingdom, the rest of the country was certainly not forgotten. While it is true that the RAF (and eventually USAAF) concentrated its operational activities in the South and East (thereby positioned as closely to Europe as possible), there was also a huge support structure of second-line activity that needed to be maintained, not least the maintenance and storage of countless aircraft as they were hastily manufactured either here in the UK or delivered from the United States. Likewise, training was a vital task that had to continue and expand, and this was obviously something that could not be conducted in a part of the country where the Luftwaffe was likely to concentrate its attention. Clear air space was a necessity for effective training. The requirement for storage and training facilities resulted in the appearance of new airfields across the West Midlands and Wales, complementing other sites that had survived from the days of the First World War, and complementing the construction of even more airfields created in anticipation of an expanding requirement for even more operational bomber or fighter bases. As the Second World War began, nobody could predict just how long the conflict might last or just how much military power it might consume.

It would be wrong to assume that this region of the country (Wales in particular) was merely a haven for the less-crucial aspects of aerial warfare, however. Although training and support activities were certainly a key part of the region's contribution to the war, the Luftwaffe's enthusiasm for destruction made all of Britain's major cities obvious targets, and in order to defend the region many operational fighter units were based (either in part or as detachments) in Wales and adjacent counties. Likewise, as the German Navy stepped up its activities in the Atlantic, the need for anti-ship and anti-submarine aircraft became vital, and many bases appeared along the western coastline in support of these aircraft. Of course, even training units did not divorce themselves entirely from the war, and many of the bomber Operational Training Units in the region supplied aircraft and crews for a variety of operations, including the famous 'Thousand Bomber' raid on Cologne. Consequently, it would be fair to say that although the record of military activity in Wales and the surrounding area was certainly markedly different from that of the South East, it was by no means any less important. Indeed, it could be argued that without the training and support facilities that existed in Britain's western counties, the war in Europe could not have succeeded.

The origins of military aviation in the region can be traced back to the first balloon flights, some of which took place in Manchester from 1785, similar activity also taking place in Chester.

Ballooning became a popular and familiar sight, but only in the skies around the larger centres of population towards the North West. In Wales, Staffordshire, Worcestershire and adjacent counties, aerial activity was virtually non-existent, and even when fixed-wing flying began to flourish, this part of the country saw virtually none of it. The First World War saw aircraft production get under way in Manchester, but the capabilities of the early warplanes limited them to only short-range flights, and this effectively meant that most found their way to the South of England where they were at least within reach of Europe. With manufacturing to the north and operational activity to the south, Wales and the Midlands remained excluded from military warfare for some time. However, as the war continued, its effects began to spread across the country. Coastal patrols and home defence became a national issue, and as Zeppelin raids started to make their way to targets around the UK from 1916 onwards defences had to be set up in order to counter the threat. Landing grounds for fighters began to appear away from the South, these usually being little more than fields cleared of obstructions to enable fighter aircraft to refuel after having made what would then have been considered as long journeys from bases in the East and South. Airships began to appear too, with stations being built at locations such as Barrow, the Isle of Man, Llangefni on Anglesey and of course Pembroke, and some of these stations and landing grounds survived to reappear as the basis of new airfields when the Second World War began. Training activities also expanded and from 1917 a number of stations began to appear in the region, specifically set up to support training requirements, including Ternhill, Shawbury and Hooton Park, all three becoming established military bases, and two of which remain in military ownership to this day.

When the First World War ended, Wales and the Midlands again became largely silent as Britain's forces rapidly diminished and countless airfields were abandoned. Military aviation gave way to civilian developments, and recreational flying was often the only aerial activity to be seen around the region. But as the dark days of the Second World War approached, even the western reaches of the country were no longer divorced from the military preparations being made across Britain. The Air Ministry had made plans to develop new sites in the area, and many of these were mostly planned as storage facilities, the western regions of the country being judged as the most suitable location for these sites, far away from any threat of danger that might emerge from Europe. In Wales, Hawarden, Sealand, St Athan and Llandow were chosen for development, while in Shropshire, Ternhill, Shawbury and High Ercall were added to the list. When the threat of attack from enemy bombers became real, the North West's areas of population and industry needed to be defended and this resulted in the construction of even more new airfields across the region, capable of supporting aircraft assigned to No 9 Group RAF, tasked with the defence of the area. Meanwhile the Atlantic was an equally important area of action, and protection of convoys soon required more fighter aircraft to come into the region, together with countless anti-submarine aircraft, search and rescue aircraft and other support aircraft tasked with communications, target-towing and training. Airfields appeared at locations such as Dale, Angle, Fairwood Common and Talbenny, all in support of the battle of the Atlantic, while the famous base at Pembroke Dock grew to embrace countless Sunderland and Catalina flying boats, which were littered across Milford Haven. Soon, the once-quiet skies around Wales were buzzing to the sound of warplanes. In addition to operational tasks, training was an even more important requirement than it had been in the previous war, and the region's relative safety (being far away from the European mainland) made it an ideal location for many new training units. In addition to the countless Magisters, Moths, Masters and Oxfords that were scattered among training units, Wellington bombers also became a familiar sight, equipping the Operational Training Units that were set up here. The Wellingtons were soon joined by Lancasters, Halifaxes and Stirlings, and even though the RAF's offensive might was concentrated many miles away to the east, the country's western skies also saw more than enough heavy bombers engaged on training and – sometimes – operational tasks too. The Royal Navy also established a significant presence in the region, many training units being formed here, often at stations that had originally been constructed for the RAF. American forces also appeared as the war progressed and, although most of their units and aircraft went to East Anglia, some of their training operations came to Wales and the Midlands, adding to the growing numbers of aircraft that roamed the skies every day.

A stunning wartime image of a Horsa glider being towed into the air by a Halifax bomber. Such sights were common at a number of airfields featured in this book. (via Tom Greenaway)

By the end of the Second World War, a huge number of airfields had appeared across the western regions of the UK, ranging from fully equipped bomber stations with their standard layout of three concrete runways, to small fields that were no more advanced than the landing grounds that had sprung-up during the First World War. Many of the larger stations had spawned their own designated secondary sites, these being described as Satellite Landing Grounds or Relief Landing Grounds (RLG's), the distinction between the two often being rather indistinct. These sites were sometimes created as facilities for the storage of aircraft so that more space became available at the parent station, or to enable aircraft to be dispersed as a precaution against attack. Other airfields were essentially designed to provide additional facilities for flying training, there often being far too many aircraft and crews to safely operate from just one main site. Some of these airfields eventually developed into significant facilities (eventually replacing their parent fields in some cases) with hangars, runways and support buildings, while others remained undeveloped as simple landing fields, used either infrequently or abandoned when they became surplus to requirements. The result of this ambitious programme was a mosaic of airfields that reached right across the region from the industrial centres of the North West, down to the Welsh coastline and into the lush fields of Gloucestershire, up through Staffordshire, Warwickshire, Worcestershire and into Lincolnshire. The sheer number of sites was so great that many were within easy sight of each other, and flying activities had to be carefully coordinated in order to ensure that aircraft from one site did not conflict with those of another, which might be no more than a couple of miles away.

When the busy days of the Second World War began to draw to a close, military activity slowly began to wind down again, and almost as quickly as the countless airfields had appeared they swiftly fell silent again. Training operations dwindled and, as the requirement for new aircrews slowed down, the many Satellite and Relief Landing Grounds were declared redundant, and were soon abandoned, the least-developed sites often returning to agricultural use, which quickly wiped away any traces of their association with military aviation. Other airfields were retained briefly under Care and Maintenance (which generally meant that the site was simply left unused but retained under military control), but many of these once-busy stations were sold off in the 1950s, some being reborn as sites for private flying, although the majority were simply abandoned, and remain virtually undisturbed even to this day. Some stations enjoyed a brief increase in usage when the RAF began the sad process of aircraft disposal, thousands of aircraft being flown to airfields for storage pending their re-sale (in some rare cases) or (more likely) scrapping.

By the end of the 1950s the majority of the once-active military airfields around Wales and beyond had been returned to civilian ownership. The runways were left to the elements and the hangars and station buildings were often left to crumble. But Britain's military presence in the area didn't end completely, and a great deal of training activities continued to thrive in the region. The Navy also stayed, its base at Brawdy becoming a busy station in post-war years until the RAF took control and established its Tactical Weapons Unit, the last major British home of the magnificent Hawker Hunter. At St Athan, the wartime association with Maintenance Units continued and aircraft servicing and repairs is a function that continues at this base to this day. Shawbury and Ternhill became the RAF's helicopter training centre and in recent years the training of helicopter crews for all three services has been consolidated here; meanwhile, over on Anglesey, the RAF's advanced pilot training is concentrated at RAF Valley, consistently one of the modern RAF's busiest airfields. Further to the south, Lyneham remains as the RAF's main tactical transport base, although its days are now numbered. Just a few miles to the north, Fairford remains in American hands, but for a couple of days every year it is one of the world's busiest airfields, as the home to the Royal International Air Tattoo, attracting visitors from all around the world. But although military aircraft are still a familiar site in the region, the wartime years when the skies were constantly filled with comings and goings are now nothing but memories. The aircraft are long gone, but surprisingly a great many of the airfields survive, and with some research and preparation even the most obscure and long-forgotten airfield sites can still be found, most of which still contain at least a few artefacts to remind any visitor of times when military aircraft were a far more common sight in the skies above Britain. Some sites have undeniably fared better than others, but almost all can still be found – if one knows where to look!

In writing this book, I have attempted to retrace the stories of a long list of military sites that were originally described by David J. Smith, Bruce Barrymore Halpenny and Michael J. F. Bowyer some thirty years ago in the original 'Action Stations' series. Naturally it is impossible to invent history, so the story of each individual site remains unchanged, but in the intervening three decades since the last books were published much has changed, and I have updated each entry to make mention of significant events that have occurred over this period. Most importantly, I have

Now part of a memorial at Lyneham, this C-47 operated for many years on the British civilian register as G-AMPO, most recently with Air Atlantique. (Richard E. Flagg)

described the current status of each site so that the reader can form a reasonable idea of what remains, should he or she propose to pay a visit to any of the locations. To make the task of visiting these sites as simple as possible, I have included map references and GPS coordinates for each site, and a general guide to how each location can be reached by road. Many of the disused airfields are still largely intact and can be accessed easily, while others are now almost impossible to find, having long since merged into the surroundings from which they first emerged. Some, of course, are still actively used, either as a base for private recreational flying (including gliding and microlight flying) or as the home to a major airport (such as Rhoose, Elmdon and Castle Donington). Others are still active RAF bases, Valley, Shawbury and St Athan being the obvious examples. But even these active sites reveal a great deal of their past, and much can be seen from the perimeter roads and tracks that surround them. In the case of the RAF and Army sites, it should be mentioned that security is an ever-present issue and although any casual visitor is entitled to take a look at these facilities from the vantage point of adjacent roads, photography of facilities is sometimes frowned upon, and in view of modern-day terrorist risks nobody should be surprised if one's presence outside a military base encourages the attention of security patrols. Observation of active military sites is generally tolerated, but it should be emphasised that trespassing on Ministry of Defence property can be treated as a serious matter, and these sites should be approached with courtesy and respect. Conversely, disused sites obviously do not raise any such issues, but it is important to remember that almost all of these locations are now on privately owned land. Any explorer should be prepared to pay attention to any prohibition signs, and to avoid causing damage to crops, buildings or equipment that might be encountered. Thankfully, most land-owners (particularly farmers) will happily allow visitors to roam among the remains of a disused airfield providing that this is done carefully, and only if permission is sought. Venturing into areas without permission (particularly those that are clearly not open to public access) is not recommended, not least because it will inevitably make access for others even more difficult.

Hopefully this book will provide the reader with a comprehensive guide to all of the military airfields that fall into the book's designated region. Space obviously precludes an extensive account of each site, but all of the most significant events in each airfield's history have been included together with a description of each site's current status. Many of these sites have now become the subject of more detailed research, with websites and even complete books having been produced, which explore some of the airfields in great detail, and anyone with a more specific interest in any particular site is urged to investigate the growing range of publications that are slowly emerging, some of which explore sites listed in this book. Combined with other volumes in this series, I hope that this book will provide an interesting account of Britain's fascinating military aviation heritage.

The preparation of this book was aided by the generous assistance of many individuals, all of whom were keen to share their interest in the recording of Britain's fascinating aviation history. Space (and memory!) precludes mention of everyone who helped with this task, but the author would like to take this opportunity to thank everyone who has provided contributions, photographs and information. In particular, special thanks must be given to Neil Jedrzejewski, Paul Francis and Richard Flagg, three leading individuals in the field of aviation archaeology and research who selflessly provided many photographs and snippets of information. Mention should also be made of the Airfield Information Exchange, an outstanding online facility dedicated to the subject of airfield architecture, history and archaeology, which actively encourages anyone with an interest in the subject to visit its site and join its fascinating forum where a wealth of information can be found covering all of Britain's airfield locations. Neil, Paul and Richard are all regular contributors to the site and even more examples of their work can be found there. The group's website can be found at: http://www.airfieldinformationexchange.org.

GLOSSARY

AA	Anti-Aircraft
AACU	Anti-Aircraft Co-operation Unit
AAIB	Air Accidents Investigation Branch
AAP	Aircraft Acceptance Park
AAS	Air Armament School
AASF	Advanced Air Striking Force
ABS	Air Base Squadron
(AC)	Army Co-operation
ACHU	Aircrew Holding Unit
AEF	Air Experience Flight
AES	Air Electrical School
AFC	Air Force Cross
AFDU	Air Fighting Development Unit
AFS	Advanced Flying School
AI	Airborne Interception (radar)
ALG	Advanced Landing Ground
AMWD	Air Ministry Works Department
ANS	Air Navigation School
AOC(-i-C)	Air Officer Commanding (-in-Chief)
AONS	Air Observer & Navigator School
AOP	Air Observation Post
APC	Armament Practice Camp
ASP	Aircraft Servicing Platform
ASR	Air Sea Rescue
asl	Above sea level
AST	Air Service Training
ASU	Aircraft Storage Unit
ASV	Air-to-Surface Vessel (radar)
ASWDU	Air Sea Warfare Development Unit
ATA	Air Transport Auxiliary
ATC	Air Traffic Control or Air Training Corps
ATDU	Air Torpedo Development Unit
ATS	Air Training Squadron
AVM	Air Vice Marshal
BADU	Blind/Beam Approach Development Unit
BDTF	Bomber Defence Training Flight

BFTS	Basic Flying Training School
BG	Bomb/Bombardment Group (USAAF)
BW(M) or (H)	Bomb/Bombardment Wing (Medium) or (Heavy) (USAAF)
CAA	Civil Aviation Authority
CAACU	Civilian Anti-Aircraft Cooperation Unit
CACU	Coast Artillery Co-operation Unit
CAF	Canadian Air Force
C&M	Care and Maintenance
C-in-C	Commander-in-Chief
CN&CS	Central Navigation & Control School
CO	Commanding Officer
Co-op	Cooperation
CRO	Civilian Repair Organisation
DCM	Distinguished Conduct Medal
D/F	Direction Finding
DFC	Distinguished Flying Cross
DFM	Distinguished Flying Medal
DFW	Day Fighter Wing
Drem Lighting	Airfield lighting system
DSC	Distinguished Service Cross
DSO	Distinguished Service Order
DZ	Drop Zone
E&RFTS	Elementary & Reserve Flying Training School
E&WS	Electrical & Wireless School
ECM	Electronic Counter-Measures
EFTS	Elementary Flying Training School
ELG	Emergency Landing Ground
EM	Enlisted men (USAAF)
EO	Extra Over Blister hangar
ETPS	Empire Test Pilots School
E/W	East/West
FAA	Fleet Air Arm
FBG	Fighter Bomber Group (USAAF)
FEW	Fighter Escort Wing (USAF)
FEAF	Far East Air Force
FG	Fighter Group (USAAF)
FIDO	Fog Investigation/Intensive & Dispersal Operation
FIS	Flying Instructors School
FIU	Fighter Interception Unit
FPP	Ferry Pilots Pool
FRU	Forward Repair Unit (RAF)
FRU	Fleet Requirements Unit (FAA)
FS	Fighter Squadron (USAAF)
FTS	Flying Training School

FTU	Ferry Training Unit
FW	Fighter Wing (USAAF)
GR	General Reconnaissance
GS	Gliding School or General Service (shed/hangar)
GSU	Group Support Unit
GTS	Glider Training School/Squadron
HCU	Heavy Conversion Unit
HGCU	Heavy Glider Conversion Unit
HD	Home Defence
HE	High Explosive (bomb)
HP	Handley Page
HQ	Headquarters
ITW	Initial Training Wing
LFS	Lancaster Finishing School
LG	Landing Ground
LZ	Landing Zone
MAP	Ministry of Aircraft Production
MoD	Ministry of Defence
MoS	Ministry of Supply
MT	Motor Transport
MU	Maintenance Unit
NAAFI	Navy, Army & Air Force Institute
NCO	Non-Commissioned Officer
'Nickel'	Leaflet-dropping operations
N/S	North/South
OAPU	Overseas Aircraft Preparation Unit
OC	Officer Commanding
OCU	Operational Conversion Unit
OFU	Overseas Ferry Unit
Operation 'Market'	Airborne operation at Arnhem and Nijmegen in September 1944
Operation 'Overlord'	Invasion of Europe in June 1944
ORP	Operational Readiness Platform
OTU	Operational Training Unit
PAC	Parachute and Cable (installation), air defence equipment, 1940
(P)AFU	(Pilots) Advanced Flying Unit
PIR	Parachute Infantry Regiment
PoW	Prisoner of War
PR	Photographic Reconnaissance
PSP	Pierced Steel Planking (metal sectional runway)
Q Site	Decoy site with lighting to simulate an airfield at night
RAAF	Royal Australian Air Force
RADAR	RAdio Detection And Ranging
RAE	Royal Aircraft Establishment
RAF	Royal Air Force

R&SU	Repair & Salvage Unit
RAS	Reserve Aeroplane Squadron
RAuxAF	Royal Auxiliary Air Force
RCAF	Royal Canadian Air Force
RCM	Radio Counter Measures
RDF	Radio Direction Finding
RE	Royal Engineers
Recce	Reconnaissance
RFC	Royal Flying Corps
RFS	Reserve Flying School
RLG	Relief Landing Ground
RNAS	Royal Naval Air Service
RNVR	Royal Naval Volunteer Reserve
ROC	Royal Observer Corps
RS	Reserve Squadron
RS&RE	Royal Signals & Radar Establishment
R/T	Radio Telephony
SAC	Strategic Air Command
SAR	Search and Rescue
SBAC	Society of British Aircraft Constructors (aerospace companies)
SD	Special Duties
SFTS	Service Flying Training School
SHAEF	Supreme Headquarters, Allied Expeditionary Force
SHQ	Station Headquarters
SLG	Satellite Landing Ground
SoAG	School of Aerial Gunnery
SoTT	School of Technical Training
SP	Staging Post
TAC	Tactical Air Command (USAAF)
TBR	Torpedo Bomber Reconnaissance
TCG	Troop Carrier Group (USAAF)
TCS	Troop Carrier Squadron (USAAF)
TCW	Troop Carrier Wing (USAAF)
TDS	Training Depot Station
TDU	Torpedo Development Unit
TEU	Tactical Exercise Unit
TFW	Tactical Fighter Wing (USAF)
THUM	Temperature & Humidity Flight
TS	Training Squadron
TSCU	Transport Support Conversion Unit
TT	Target Towing
TTU	Torpedo Training Unit
UAS	University Air Squadron
USAAC	United States Army Air Corps (from 2 July 1926)

USAAF	United States Army Air Force (from 20 June 1941)
USAF	United States Air Force (from 18 September 1947)
USAFE	USAF Europe
VHF	Very High Frequency
VGS	Volunteer Gliding School
VR	Volunteer Reserve
WAAF	Women's Auxiliary Air Force
WD	War Department
'Window'	Metal foil dropped to disrupt radar systems
WRAF	Women's Royal Air Force
WS	Wireless School

Military Airfields of Wales and the Midlands

The following listing of airfield sites within this volume's designated region is provided in alphabetical sequence. In addition to map and GPS references, additional information is also provided on the recorded details of each airfield's status at the time of completion. It should be noted that the runway data refers to the site's specification at the time of construction; however, many airfields were subsequently improved and modified, and the runways were often extended, sometimes quite considerably. Hangar facilities were also often changed and either expanded or revised.

001 Abbots Bromley	042 Haverfordwest	083 Poulton
002 Aberporth	043 Hawarden	084 Ratcliffe
003 Angle	044 Hells Mouth	085 Rearsby
004 Ashbourne	045 High Ercall	086 Rednal
005 Atcham	046 Hinstock	087 Rendcombe
006 Baginton	047 Hixon	088 Rhoose
007 Balderton	048 Hoar Cross	089 Rudbaxton
008 Battlestead Hill	049 Hockley Heath	090 St Athan
009 Beaumaris	050 Hodnet	091 St Brides
010 Berrow	051 Honiley	092 St David's
011 Bibury	052 Hooton Park	093 Sealand
012 Blakehill Farm	053 Hucknall	094 Seighford
013 Bodorgan	054 Langar	095 Shawbury
014 Bramcote	055 Lawrenny Ferry	096 Shobdon
015 Bratton	056 Lichfield	097 Sleap
016 Braunstone	057 Little Sutton	098 Snitterfield
017 Brawdy	058 Llanbedr	099 South Cerney
018 Bridleway Gate	059 Llandow	100 South Marston
019 Brockton	060 Llandwrog	101 Stoke Orchard
020 Burnaston	061 Long Marston	102 Stormy Down
021 Calveley	062 Loughborough	103 Swinderby
022 Carew Cheriton	063 Lyneham	104 Syerston
023 Castle Bromwich	064 Madley	105 Talbenny
024 Castle Donington	065 Manorbier	106 Tatenhill
025 Chedworth	066 Meir	107 Teddesley Park
026 Chepstow	067 Mona	108 Templeton
027 Chetwynd	068 Montford Bridge	109 Ternhill
028 Church Broughton	069 Newton	110 Tilstock
029 Clyffe Pypard	070 Northleach	111 Tollerton
030 Condover	071 Nuneaton	112 Towyn
031 Cosford	072 Orston	113 Valley
032 Cranage	073 Ossington	114 Warwick
033 Dale	074 Papplewick Moor	115 Watchfield
034 Darley Moor	075 Pembrey	116 Weston Park
035 Defford	076 Pembroke Dock	117 Wheaton Aston
036 Down Ampney	077 Pengam Moors	118 Wigsley
037 Elmdon	078 Penkridge	119 Winthorpe
038 Fairford	079 Penrhos	120 Wolverhampton
039 Fairwood Common	080 Peplow	121 Worcester
040 Halfpenny Green	081 Pershore	122 Wrexham
041 Hardwick Hall	082 Perton	123 Wymeswold

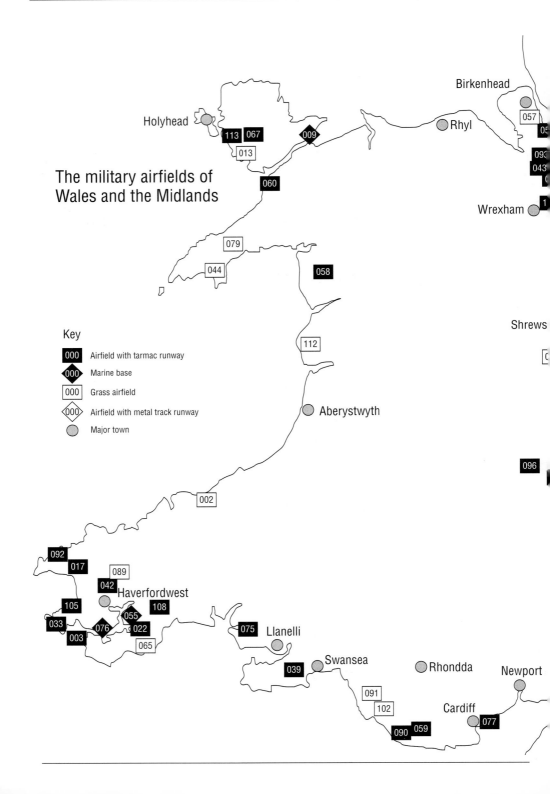

The military airfields of
Wales and the Midlands

Key

000	Airfield with tarmac runway
000	Marine base
000	Grass airfield
000	Airfield with metal track runway
●	Major town

THE AIRFIELDS

ABBOTS BROMLEY, Staffordshire

Grid ref SK075253, Lat 52:49:32N (52.82543) Lon 1:53:22W (-1.88956), 400ft asl. 0.5 miles NW of Abbots Bromley on B5014

Situated just a short distance from the village of Abbots Bromley, close to the junction between the B5014 and B5013, the scattered remnants of this airfield still remain, including a Robin hangar that is now left unused and derelict , having been previously maintained for agricultural storage. Unusually, records suggest that this Robin hangar was actually a subsequent addition to the original compliment of facilities. The site first opened towards the end of 1940 as a Royal Air Force satellite airfield, intended to relieve congestion at the relatively busy Burnaston airfield nearby, where No 16 Elementary Flying Training School was based. The unit's Tiger Moths and Miles Magisters shared their training activities between the two airfields. The airfield was a relatively simple grass facility measuring just 640 by 650 yards, with nine small hangars and a resident groundcrew of just seventy-five personnel, housed in temporary billets. Expansion of the site into a more substantial airfield was ruled out, chiefly because the site was surrounded by roads, all of which would have required expensive diversion. Regular flying operations ended in 1945 and the station became a sub-site for No 21 Maintenance Unit based at Fauld. The Air Ministry also used the site briefly as a Works Depot before the airfield was abandoned in 1949.

Although no traces of the grass airfield are now visible, the former Guard House remains largely intact (although gutted) and the access track leading to the remains of the camp entrance and technical site is now part of a farm, on private land. Little remains of the small technical site apart from one concrete block, which is still used for storage. Apart from the rapidly deteriorating Robin hangar, traces of at least three others can also be seen, their concrete bases and door runners still discernable amongst the vegetation.

Aviation continues in the area thanks to the nearby Yeatshall Farm airstrip, where a small assortment of light aircraft can sometimes be seen, and although this site is sometimes confused with that of Abbots Bromley, no flying has taken place at the former RAF field since the 1940s.

Runways: N/S (650yd) grass, E/W (650yd) grass. *Hangars:* Blister (9). *Hardstandings:* 0.
Accommodation: RAF: 1 officer, 4 SNCOs, 70 ORs; WAAF: 0.

ABERPORTH, Dyfed

Grid ref SN250495, Lat 52:06:58N (52.11614) Lon 4:33:24W (-4.55671), 400ft asl. 5 miles NE of Cardigan on A487

Although this small airfield might give the impression of being rather insignificant, being tucked way close to the Dyfed coast, impressions can certainly be deceptive. In fact, Aberporth has traditionally been involved in a wide variety of vital research and development programmes, which continue to play an important part in modern military operations. On the nearby headland there is a hint of the many and varied activities in which Aberporth has been involved; the former Rocket Research Establishment's facilities are easily visible to passers-by here and they are now part of continuing Government activity in the local area, as the coordination 'hub' for trials work conducted over Cardigan Bay.

The original airfield site at Aberporth (sometimes referred to as Blaenannerch) first opened for RAF use in December 1940 as an Anti Aircraft Cooperation base, supporting the various gunnery ranges situated over Cardigan Bay. Hawker Henleys, Westland Wallaces and De Havilland Queen Bees were among the first aircraft to use the airfield, equipping three component lights of No 1 Anti Aircraft Cooperation Unit. During mid-1942 a handful of Avro Ansons from No 6 Air Observer School (based at Staverton) operated from Aberporth for a few months and in December 1943 the component Flights of No 1 AACU combined to become No 595 Squadron, supporting the Anti Aircraft Practice Camps at Aberaeron and Manorbier, with some of the resident aircraft being detached to Carew Cheriton as necessary. By this stage the unit was operating Miles Martinets, although a rather unhappy association with the less-than-popular Vengeance began in 1944 (the first aircraft being delivered by a female ATA pilot) and lasted until July 1945.

Aberporth's remote location made it an obvious choice for aircrews who occasionally found themselves in difficulty, and a variety of aircraft types found their way to the airfield, often as a matter of urgency. USAAF C-47s took advantage of Aberporth's small grass field on some occasions, and on 22 February 1944 even a USAAF Liberator diverted to the airfield, en route from North Africa to Valley. Two Handley Page Halifaxes also diverted to Aberporth (in July 1942 and February 1944), and it is no surprise to note that both overshot the available space within the landing field before coming to grief outside the airfield boundary. The resident Martinets left Aberporth early in 1946 when No 595 Squadron was transferred to Fairwood Common, but although the unit had no fewer than twenty-four aircraft in total, they departed in formations of six, as this was usually the maximum number of aircraft that could be made serviceable at any given time.

On 15 May 1946 the RAF officially vacated the site and it was placed under Care and Maintenance. It remained inactive for some years until the Ministry of Supply assumed control, reopening in 1959, by which time a small paved runway had been constructed, which remains in use to this day. Most of the aircraft that returned to the site were in the shape of visiting communications types such as the Anson, Devon and Pembroke, and this kind of limited military activity still continues, combined with a variety of many more civilian light aircraft now taking advantage of the airfield facilities. The RAF station was reactivated in order to support the continuing research activities undertaken by the RAE, with a variety of missile trails being conducted on a day-to-day basis, among them the development of the RAF's Bloodhound missile (and the Army equivalent, the Thunderbird). Many test launches were made from the RAE range on the nearby coastal site and the spectacular (and very noisy) tests provided great fascination for both locals and visiting holidaymakers alike. The Bloodhound Support detachment arrived in 1966, tasked with a continuing programme of reliability and improvement programmes for the missile, and providing a facility for missile crews to make live firings against targets over the adjacent range.

Typical of the countless missile launches that have been made from Aberporth, a Mirach target is pictured at launch, off on its short journey to the adjacent range out over the Irish Sea. (QinetiQ)

Bloodhound missiles (and derivatives such as this Swiss example) were regularly launched from Aberporth, the RAF's Bloodhound Support detachment having arrived at the base in 1966. (QinetiQ)

Meanwhile back in 1952 the Royal Naval Trails Unit was established here, tasked with naval acceptance trials, and the provision of facilities for ship firing exercises out at sea. Both the Sea Slug and Sea Cat missile systems were developed at Aberporth prior to becoming part of the Royal Navy's inventory. With facilities scattered around the airfield site and the range area on the coast, Aberporth became a busy base, sprawling across a surprisingly large area of land, even supporting no fewer than two cliff railways dedicated to the transportation of personnel and equipment to and from various facilities. Aircraft movements continued in support of the range operations, albeit on a sporadic basis, the most regular visitors being the RAE's Devon aircraft, resplendent in their 'raspberry ripple' paint schemes in later years.

A surprisingly large number of other trials (many shrouded in secrecy) kept the Aberporth sites very busy through the 1960s and '70s (indeed, the MoD became the largest employer in the area), but when activity began to dwindle the RAF presence ended on 31 May 1984. Today the site is commercially led and renamed 'Parc Aberporth', but despite the presence of various small civilian aircraft much of the airfield's activity is still primarily concerned with military operations, under the control of QinetiQ. Support of the nearby test range facilities continues, but the appearance of any military aircraft is now very rare. More recently, Aberporth was selected as the main base for the Watchkeeper UAV (Unmanned Aerial Vehicle) programme, and UAVs may well become a major part of Aberporth's future activities as technology in this field continues to expand.

Parc Aberporth as seen from the air. Although developed quite significantly, the distinctive shape of an original T2 hangar is very obvious, and the small but much-used runway is visible in the background. (QinetiQ)

Although a variety of modern buildings have been constructed within the small airfield site, the old T2 hangar remains present, providing a link to the airfield's wartime history, and the days when secret Cold War trials were commonplace.

Runways: NNE/SSW (750yd) grass, NE/SW (966yd) grass, NW/SE (755yd) grass. *Hangars:* Bellman (2), Blister (3). *Hardstandings:* 0. *Accommodation:* RAF: 16 Officers, 15 SNCOs, 372 ORs; WAAF: 2 SNCOs.

ANGLE, Dyfed

Grid ref SM858018, Lat 51:40:27N (51.67418) Lon 5:05:55W (-5.09873), 182ft asl. 7 miles W of Pembroke on B4320

Perched on the very edge of the Dyfed coast, it isn't surprising that RAF Angle was a less-than-popular posting for wartime personnel. Although perfectly located for summertime off-duty enjoyment, the airfield was isolated, bleak and forbidding throughout the winter months. First opened in December 1941, the station was under the control of No 10 Group as part of the Fairwood Common Sector, and from April 1942 it became the home of No 263 Squadron, one of only two squadrons operating the twin-engined Westland Whirlwind fighter. At this time the squadron had been dogged with endless difficulties centred on the reliability of the Whirlwind's Peregrine engines, and it is probably fortunate (given the airfield's position so close to the stormy Atlantic seas) that by the time the unit moved to Angle, these problems seem to have largely been resolved. Despite this, the unit did still have some hair-raising moments, not least the delivery of A Flight's armoury, which caught fire in a railway truck while passing through Llanelli. The truck was moved to a siding where the inferno eventually subsided, thankfully before the 20mm shells began to explode.

The squadron's primary task was the air defence of the local coastal region, protecting Allied shipping in the Irish Sea and out towards the Atlantic, occasionally being assisted by a section from No 421 Squadron based at Fairwood Common. The main threat came from Luftwaffe Ju88s, which plagued the area and – much to the frustration of 263 Squadron – often managed to evade the attention of the RAF's fighters. Quite how the Ju88 crews managed to repeatedly avoid interception remained unclear, although the Angle-based crews believed that their Luftwaffe counterparts were able to listen in on radio communications and make their escape accordingly. Eventually, this frustration prompted the RAF to launch a series of direct strikes against the Ju88's home bases on the Brittany coast, and two such missions were conducted by 263 Squadron against Lannion and Morlaix, using Predannack in Cornwall as their forward operating base, assisted by Nos 130, 310 and 234 Squadron's Spitfires. In an effort to intercept the marauding Ju88s, 263 Squadron flew what was to become the longest-ever Whirlwind flight during May 1942 when two aircraft pursued a Ju88 across the Irish Sea as far as the Irish coast near Dublin. A combination of low fuel reserves and poor weather eventually forced the crews to call off their mission but, without sufficient fuel reserves to return to Angle, they managed to get as far as the Lleyn peninsula, from where they immediately headed for the small airfield at Hell's Mouth.

Although the convoy protection patrols continued, no successful interceptions were made, thanks to the difficulty of locating and vectoring the Whirlwinds onto such difficult targets, often in foul weather conditions. Indeed, the closest the squadron came to achieving a successful interception was when two sections of Whirlwinds were accidentally vectored towards each other, the error being realised shortly before the crews prepared to open fire.

The squadron finally moved to Colerne during August 1942, having consistently achieved the highest number of flying hours within No 10 Group. Other units made use of Angle's facilities for varying periods; No 32 Squadron spent five months at the base from June 1941, operating its Hurricanes in support of the convoy patrols before relocating to Manston. The unit was replaced at Angle by No 615 Squadron, its Hurricanes remaining present until January 1942, when it departed for Fairwood Common, its place being taken by the Spitfires of No 312 Squadron, which remained at Angle for three months. No 152 Squadron (with Spitfires) was briefly based at Angle for just one month before departing for Wittering. Hurricanes then reappeared with No 421 Squadron's arrival; it remained until January 1943, when it left for Kenley, with the Kenley-based Hurricanes of No 412 Squadron moving in the other direction to Angle, albeit for just one month before leaving for Fairwood Common. Following No 412's departure, Angle was briefly without any flying units, although a detachment of Whitley bombers and their accompanying Horsa gliders arrived in April 1943 for a week-long exercise with the 9th Parachute Battalion, as did a single Mosquito, tasked with trials of the new 'Highball' bomb (a derivative of the more famous 'Dambusters' weapon).

RAF Angle then briefly switched to Fleet Air Arm operations with the arrival of No 794 Naval Air Squadron in May 1943, tasked with aerial target-towing. The transfer to naval operations was only brief, however, as it was decided that the RAF Coastal Command Development Unit based on the other side of Milford Haven should move to Angle, enabling the naval unit to relocate to Dale. The reason for this was the RAF's operations at nearby Pembroke Dock, where significant numbers of Sunderland flying boats were active both by day and by night. The extended flare path approach to Pembroke Dock ran out into Angle Bay close to RAF Angle, so it was essential that coordination of night activity in the whole area was carefully maintained by the RAF. The CCDU remained at Angle until January 1945, equipped with a pair of Vickers Wellingtons, a Halifax, a Liberator, a pair of Bristol Beaufighters and a Percival Proctor used for communications flying. CCDU trails included a series of flights intended to establish the audibility of approaching aircraft from surfaced submarines. It was established that the Wellington's engine noise was swamped by a combination of wind, sea and diesel noise until the aircraft was remarkably close – often less than a mile – so it was concluded that U-boat crews could not and would not rely on audible detection as a means of safety.

On 29 May 1943 a particularly remarkable incident took place at Angle when the RAF's Short Sunderland made the very first land recovery – albeit somewhat unintentionally. The aircraft (T9114 from No 461 Squadron) had taken off from Pembroke Dock in heavy seas, which had caused some structural damage to the aircraft's hull. The pilot (Gordon Singleton) correctly judged that landing the aircraft back on water would inevitably cause it to sink, so his only option was to head for land, the nearest airfield being Angle. Singleton later remarked that he 'opted for the airfield. I did not aim for the runways but chose an area of grass, which was much more forgiving. Lots of my squadron colleagues rushed out from Pembroke Dock expecting to see a big crash, but instead my CO filmed a smooth landing.' Despite a successful recovery onto land, the aircraft was damaged beyond economical repair and over a period of several days was manoeuvred across 2 miles of fields (six fences being removed in the process) before being returned to Pembroke Dock for use as a ground-based training airframe.

It is perhaps not surprising that other accidents occurred at Angle, one of the most catastrophic being the loss of No 32 Squadron Hurricane Z5222, which collided with ground equipment during a night-flying exercise on 25 August 1941, although the pilot escaped unscathed.

The hapless Sunderland T9114 from No 461 Squadron pictured after its unorthodox arrival at Angle, shortly before its removal to Pembroke Dock. (both via Jim Broadbent)

No 32 Squadron's Hurricane Z5222, which struck a traction engine during a night landing at Angle on 25 August 1941. (via Jim Broadbent)

Following the departure of the CCDU to Thorney Island in 1945, Angle remained inactive and was finally relinquished by the RAF before being eventually returned to agricultural use. Today virtually nothing of the airfield remains apart from a single fighter dispersal close to a farm, and a small stretch of perimeter track adjacent to the eastern end of what was once the main runway. The runways have long since disappeared, although their position can still be determined by the division of the farmland that now covers the site. One footpath leading to the cliffs crosses the traces of the main runway, while a second path runs along the secondary runway's course. It is only from the air that the fields still reveal the precise layout of what was once a relatively large, active and important airfield.

Runways: 290 (1,600yd x 50yd) tarmac and rubber chippings, 230 (1,000yd x 50yd) tarmac and rubber chippings, 162 (1,200yd x 50yd) tarmac and rubber chippings. *Hangars:* T2 (1), Blister (4). *Hardstandings:* 60ft-diameter tarmac (6). *Accommodation:* RAF: 0 Officers, 106 SNCOs, 126 ORs; WAAF: 10 SNCOs, 50 ORs.

ASHBOURNE, Derbyshire

Grid ref SK199454, Lat 53:00:22N (53.00613) Lon 1:42:14W (-1.70387), 600ft asl. 1 mile SE of Ashbourne on A52

The choice of location for what became RAF Ashbourne was less than ideal, being situated high on a 600-foot plateau overlooking the Derbyshire town of the same name, but perilously close to the high ground of the Peak District in an area where fog, low cloud and rain was the prevailing meteorological state for most of the year. The airfield was developed as part of a three-base project, with two satellite fields being constructed at the same time at nearby Church Broughton and Darley Moor. Construction of all three airfields was protracted and ultimately only Ashbourne and Darley Moor were completed.

The first unit to form at Ashbourne was No 81 Operational Training Unit, which came into being on 10 July 1942, although rather perversely the unit didn't receive any aircraft until it had relocated to Whitchurch Heath two months later. It wasn't until October that the first aircraft arrived in the shape of Bristol Blenheims, Armstrong Whitworth Whitleys, Airspeed Oxfords and Avro Ansons, all under the control of No 42 OTU, which arrived from Andover as part of No 70 Squadron and Army Co-operation Command. However, when the latter Command was disbanded in June 1943, Ashbourne was transferred to Fighter Command control. Sadly, by this stage the station had already suffered its first loss when Blenheim N3567 was destroyed shortly after take-off from Ashbourne just before midnight on 7 November. The aircraft suffered engine failure on take-off, stalled and collided with a row of trees less than half a mile from the airfield boundary, before crashing and bursting into flames, resulting in the death of one of the crew.

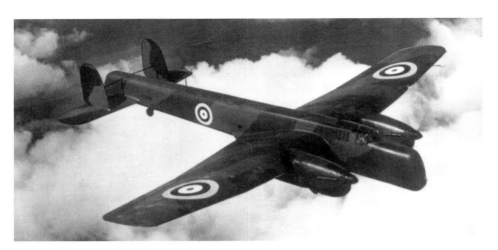

Armstrong Whitworth's ungainly and distinctly unattractive Whitley was, for some years a familiar sight in the skies over Ashbourne. (Ken Billingham collection)

Blenheim flying continued at Ashbourne until July 1943, at which stage Whitleys became the unit's standard aircraft type, their Ansons and Oxfords (belonging to A Squadron) having moved to the satellite airfield at Darley Moor. Training activities at Ashbourne were regularly disrupted by the poor prevailing weather conditions, fog often being the primary cause of the airfield's closure, often for days at a time. Despite this, the airfield's location made it a useful diversion destination under some circumstances, and a variety of unusual visitors were seen on the airfield on some occasions. At least one Halifax (a 102 Squadron aircraft returning from operations during August 1943) diverted to Ashbourne, as did three B-17 Fortresses from the USAAF base at Polebrook, returning from operations over France during September of the same year. Just a few weeks later no fewer than thirteen Fortresses arrived, having diverted from Snetterton Heath. On 5 September 1943 the OTU received its first Albemarle – an unremarkable aircraft for which 42 OTU became the main training unit, prompting a shift in training emphasis and a transfer to No 38 Group for airborne forces training, which included glider-towing. Four of Ashbourne's Albemarles were detached to Hampstead Norris to participate in the D-Day landings; during the operation one of these aircraft went missing, together with its crew.

No 42 OTU finally disbanded on 20 March 1945 with many of the unit's personnel going to Tilstock, where they joined 81 Operational Training Unit. Ashbourne was then transferred to the control of No 28 Maintenance Unit, and some of the airfield's ample runway space was used to store unfused bombs, most of which were subsequently detonated on the nearby moors before the station was abandoned in 1954.

A former airman describes his time at the station:

'The work at RAF Ashbourne was chiefly on the servicing of high-explosive bombs, which were stacked alongside the runways. Being outdoor work made it very pleasant during the summer. We used to check for fuses, paint them up and stencil numbers on them. All unserviceable bombs – that is, ones that were classed as unstable and dangerous – were taken by road to Ashbourne railway station for transportation to South Wales, from where they went by ship for deep-sea dumping in the Atlantic Ocean. We used to throw the bombs onto trolleys, then two or three trolley loads were towed behind a tractor to be loaded onto lorries. We had many exciting trips with the bomb lorries down Derby Road hill into Ashbourne. It could be quite dodgy if the brakes failed, which they did on occasion, although it would probably be diplomatic to try and forget these. I was on one when the brakes went.

Fortunately, we were near the bottom of the hill, so the lorry managed to swerve round the corner at the bottom and come to a halt. There was no health and safety in those days!'

The deserted airfield remained largely untouched until the early 1970s when attempts were made to introduce private flying from the site. Unfortunately a number of locals formed a lobby group to ensure that the plan was subsequently dropped, but only after a fairly significant amount of light aircraft activity had begun. Although the nuisance value of the aircraft was negligible, the site operated largely without incident, apart from one spectacular near-disaster when a parachutist became entangled in the tail assembly of a Cessna 172, which promptly stalled and fell to the ground. The retardation of the attached parachute (and parachutist) served to cushion the impact and both pilot and parachutist suffered only minor injuries.

Despite the termination of regular private flying from Ashbourne, occasional flight activity did continue to take place and still does to this day, despite the deteriorated condition of the remaining runway surfaces, and the gradual destruction of the airfield site. A large industrial estate has been constructed on the western side of the airfield (although this has thankfully resulted in the renovation of the formerly derelict control tower, which is now an office), and JCB now owns a significant part of the airfield, with the company's equipment and building activities slowly destroying portions of the airfield's structure. However, the greater proportion of the airfield has survived, including most of the old main runway (a lane off the A52 now crosses the eastern end), and the base of one of the station's hangars is still visible just to the north of the industrial estate. A couple of industrial buildings have appeared on another portion of one of the secondary runways, but the overall layout of the airfield is still largely intact and, with a couple of the old hangars still in use and most of the runways still visible, Ashbourne still provides visitors with the sights and atmosphere of a once-busy wartime station.

> *Runways:* 323 (2,000yd x 50yd) concrete and wood chippings, 274 (1,400yd x 50yd) concrete and wood chippings, 209 (1,400yd x 50yd) concrete and wood chippings. *Hangars:* T2 23-bay (4). *Hardstandings:* 125ft-diameter frying pan (30). *Accommodation:* RAF: 171 Officers, 454 SNCOs, 1,472 ORs; WAAF: 16 SNCOs, 432 ORs.

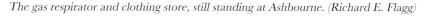

The gas respirator and clothing store, still standing at Ashbourne. (Richard E. Flagg)

ATCHAM, Shropshire

Grid ref SJ570104, Lat 52:41:25N (52.69022) Lon 2:38:13W (-2.63685), 200ft asl. 4 miles SE of Shrewsbury on B4394

An aerial view of Atcham, taken in May 1946. (via Robert Grays)

Although inevitably associated with American operations, Atcham was originally constructed as a standard RAF Fighter Sector Station, designed to accommodate two squadrons. The first of these was No 131 Squadron, which arrived at the base with Spitfires on 27 September 1941. Training activities began almost immediately, often in association with other units, particularly Defiants based at Cranage and Beaufighters from High Ercall (even a Hotspur glider was involved in one exercise). A satellite landing field was also constructed at Condover, although it was not completed until the following year, but 131 Squadron's Spitfires quickly became a familiar site around Shropshire and beyond. Operational activities were rather less intense, the most significant being during 1942 when the Sector Operations Room was responsible for vectoring a Beaufighter (from RAF Valley) onto a marauding Dornier Do 17, the pursuit continuing from North Wales through to Nuneaton, where the aircraft was finally shot down. The Sector Operations Room (originally based at Ternhill) was located approximately a mile beyond Atcham's airfield but under the control of the station. No 131 Squadron (which had been joined by No 5 SFTS operating a Flight of Masters on a temporary basis while the unit's base at Ternhill was equipped with paved runways) moved to Llanbedr during February 1942, its place being taken by No 350 (Belgian) Squadron, which had formed at Valley.

Keen to gain operational experience, the unit's Spitfires were scrambled frequently but poor weather conditions prevented any contact with the Luftwaffe, which had become an increasingly rare sight over the North West by this stage. The unit was briefly joined by No 74 Squadron, which moved north to regroup prior to being assigned to the Middle East after a stay of only two months. No 131 Squadron transferred to Warmswell during April 1942, leaving Atcham with the Spitfires of No 232 Squadron, which arrived in April for a brief one-month stay prior to leaving for Valley. Their time at Atcham was devoted to intensive training, which included high-altitude intercepts, some being conducted against a B-17 Fortress. This American connection provided a taste of Atcham's future, and, with the Luftwaffe having shifted its attention further south, it was decided that the RAF no longer had any requirement for Atcham and it was handed over to American control and the USAAF 8th AF on 15 June 1942, the ground elements of the 31st Fighter Group having transferred from New Orleans.

Fairchild UC-61s quickly became a common site at the station and the air elements of the 31st began to arrive towards the end of June, when the first of around fifty Spitfires appeared, equipping the 307th, 308th and 309th Fighter Squadrons. Spitfires carrying American markings were certainly an unusual sight, but the unit's P-39s were deemed to be unsuitable for long-distance formation ferry flights from the continental USA and the use of British-built Spitfires provided an effective solution. By August the Group was already engaged in operational activity, flying patrols and bomber escort missions, some of these being diversionary tactics. It also supported a joint UK, US, Canadian and French raid on Dieppe on the 19th of that month. However, towards the end of the month the 31st FG moved south to Westhampnett prior to leaving for Algeria. Its place at Atcham was taken by the 14th Fighter Group, which arrived from Hamilton AAF in California on 18 August, equipped with P-38 Lightnings. Comprising the 48th and 49th Fighter Squadrons, the 14th FG was assigned to bomber escort missions, many of their aircraft being detached to bases in the south including Tangmere, Ford and Westhampnett, where they operated in conjunction with the RAF. Little contact with the Luftwaffe was made, and by November 1942 the Group was reassigned to Algeria.

A 14th Fighter Group P-38 Lightning spewing smoke at Atcham. (via Dave Walsh)

Atcham then adopted a new role. Becoming the home of the 6th Fighter Wing's Combat Crew Replacement Center, the airfield quickly becoming home to a mixture of Spitfires and Masters together with P-39 Airacobras. These were gradually exchanged for P-47 Thunderbolts and a small number of Harvards, which remained active at Atcham for a couple of years, tasked with the training and conversion of American pilots who had quickly to come to terms with the operating procedures and weather conditions in the UK, which were a stark contrast to those back in the USA.

P-47D 42-75129 was written off on 9 June 1944 when it was involved in a collision with a P-47C on the ground at Atcham. (via Robert Grays)

An atmospheric picture of two Thunderbolts climbing out from Atcham on a training mission. (via Robert Grays)

The 6th FW disestablished in October 1943 and Atcham became the home of the 495th Fighter Training Group (initially designated the 2906th Observation Training Group), the station's training commitments gradually increasing in line with the enlargement of the IXth AF presence elsewhere in the UK. Training and conversion tasks were developed to include operational roles such as dive-bombing, strafing and ground attack, with the airfield circuit regularly being filled to capacity. During August 1944 the P-38 returned to Atcham when the dwindling training requirement for Lightning pilots was transferred from Goxhill (the latter base having re-equipped with the P-51). This was the last significant change and, as the war drew towards a conclusion, Atcham's training role was slowly wound down, the American presence finally ending on 14 March 1945.

The Royal Air Force then resumed control of the station but with a much-reduced requirement for facilities, making little use of the airfield. Nearby Ternhill used the airfield as a satellite later in 1945, and No 577 Squadron established at detachment at Atcham equipped with Oxfords, Vengeances and Spitfires, tasked with the training of anti-aircraft and searchlight units, but this detachment transferred to Hawarden on 8 April 1946, and the airfield finally fell silent. The RAF's presence ended on 22 October of the same year and the station was sold off in January 1948.

Atcham's control tower (watch office) in 1944. (via Robert Grays)

A fascinating view across Atcham's airfield in 1944. In addition to the Lysander and Thunderbolt, a Royal Air Force Dakota is visible in the distance. (via Robert Grays)

Today very little of this once busy airfield remains. The technical site is still easily found, some of the original buildings having survived (many having been refurbished and re-covered), but there is little to show of much of the airfield's wartime roots. Even the surviving Callender-Hamilton hangar has been re-clad and refurbished and from any distance it appears to be just a simple shed amidst a growing industrial estate. The B4394 road runs along part of the old main runway, but any passing motorist would be forgiven for not even noticing, and a casual visitor would probably be unaware that the area was once a busy American-operated airfield. The only significant remains are sections of two secondary runways and associated taxi tracks, which can still be found in the fields just north of the industrial buildings, but, with farmland and hedgerows slowly covering the area, Atcham's wartime appearance has long since been obliterated.

One unusual survivor of Atcham's military past has survived, however, in the shape of a rare 'mushroom' pillbox, which can be found on the eastern edge of the site. Commanding an excellent view over the airfield and runways, the pillbox provided a secure position for 50mm machine guns and formed part of the station's perimeter defences. A preservation group has now 'adopted' the artefact and it is to be hoped that while the rest of Atcham's remains seem doomed to disappear, this one at least will remain.

> *Runways:* 235 (1,480yd x 50yd) tarmac and rubber chippings, 187 (1,350yd x 50yd) tarmac and rubber chippings, 297 (1,200yd x 50yd) tarmac and rubber chippings. *Hangars:* Callender-Hamilton (3), Blister (8). *Hardstandings:* Banjo (26). Accommodation: USAAF: 319 Officers, 1,333 enlisted.

BAGINTON, Warwickshire

Armstrong-Whitworth's Whitley factory, the forerunner of the company's Baginton plant. (via Spencer Adcott)

Grid ref SP355746, Lat 52:22:07N (52.36858) Lon 1:28:43W (-1.47869), 270ft asl. 4 miles SE of Coventry off A45

Although Coventry Airport's ever-expanding facilities might seem the obvious site of RAF Baginton's origins, it is in fact the nearby Jaguar car plant at Whitley near Coventry where flying first began in this area. Whitley was the home of Armstrong-Whitworth Aircraft (AWA) during the 1920s, its factory being served by a small grass landing field adjacent to the factory. A flying school was also created here, this eventually developing into Air Service Training, which eventually moved to Hamble.

Coventry's City Council was one of many that developed a keen interest in creating a municipal airport prior to the Second World War, and by the mid-1930s a joint plan had been produced to construct a new airfield next to the established Whitley site. This could serve as both an airport and a larger site for AWA's activities, which were gradually shifting towards the production of larger and heavier aircraft. It was also agreed that the site could provide a base for a Royal Air Force Volunteer Reserve unit, but the proximity of both housing and industrial complexes (and chimneys in particular) discouraged the RAF from pursing this plan, and it was No 1 Camouflage Unit that eventually became the first military presence at Baginton during September 1939, its small fleet of aircraft (including Stinson Reliants) being used to examine industrial buildings from the air in order to determine the effectiveness of various types of camouflage.

The airfield site at Baginton has enjoyed a surprisingly long association with all forms of aviation. Even before the advent of fixed-wing flying the site often hosted balloon activities as illustrated by this historic image. (Flight collection)

Production at the Armstrong-Whitworth factory (which included a wide range of pre-war types such as the famous Siskin) eventually ended in 1936. Manufacturing shifted to a new (and much larger) factory on the Baginton airfield site, and the small field at Whitley was slowly wound down and eventually abandoned. When the Second World War began, Baginton was already an active airfield with both Armstrong-Whitworth and the RAF sharing the site. It was clear that Coventry was well within reach of the Luftwaffe's bombers and on 25 September 1940 the airfield was designated as an RAF Fighter Sector Station, with the Hurricanes of No 308 (Polish) Squadron arriving from Speke a few days later. The unit was involved in various encounters with the Luftwaffe, whose attention was directed to both the nearby city and AWA's factory, where the appropriately named Whitley bomber was in production.

In March 1941 No 403 Squadron formed at Baginton with Tomahawks before moving to Ternhill, and No 308 Squadron left for Chilbolton a few weeks later to re-equip with Spitfires. Replacing them was No 605 (County of Warwick) Squadron (flying Hurricanes) and No 457 (RAAF) Squadron, bringing Spitfires to Baginton for the first time. An Army Cooperation Flight was also formed at the station, equipped with Lysanders and Blenheims tasked with the training of troops destined for North Africa. When No 457 Squadron departed for Jurby (to concentrate on weapons training), No 135 Squadron was re-formed at Baginton, with 605 Squadron leaving for Honiley. No 79 Squadron arrived in December 1941 (leaving a year later) and No 135 Squadron following shortly afterwards, both units destined for the Far East.

Throughout this period AWA remained busy with bomber production, conducting test and delivery flights to and from Baginton, while some of its test flying programme was exported to nearby Bitteswell where concrete runways were laid. Conditions at Baginton were poor by comparison, with less available take-off and landing space and only a grass surface, which was prone to flooding. No 79 Squadron's diary records that during 1941 'motor boats are needed to get us from the messes to the

A look inside the Baginton factory shortly after completion. Whitley bombers are pictured under construction for the Royal Air Force. (via Spencer Adcott)

aircraft'. However, the station was undoubtedly a vital part of the RAF's structure during the war, not only as a base for fighters assigned to the defence of the area, but also as a vital training base for countless fighter pilots who went on to operations overseas. Likewise, in addition to the hugely important presence of AWA and its own activities, many other trials and test programmes were conducted at Baginton, including secret testing of jettisonable fuel tanks fitted to Spitfires (with 130 and 234 Squadrons) and Mitchells (98 Squadron). Likewise, engine manufacturer Alvis maintained a presence at the airfield, with various aircraft being present as required by the company.

The last operational RAF unit to arrive at the station, however, was No 616 (South Yorkshire) Squadron, which re-equipped with Spitfires at the base prior to heading north. After its departure, the RAF withdrew from the airfield and the site reverted to a mix of civilian operations combined with AWA activity. Operational and training activities having gone, Baginton remained an active pseudo-military site long after the RAF left, thanks to the presence of AWA. Having completed production of bombers such as the Whitley, Lancaster and Lincoln, post-war programmes embraced the jet age and Baginton was the production site for a series of Meteor variants, which were designed and manufactured at the site. All of the late marks of Meteor night-fighters were produced by AWA, including the bizarre 'prone pilot' Meteor used to investigate the possibility of reconfiguring cockpit seating layouts to enable fighter pilots to withstand the effects of g-forces. Much of the early jet test flying was conducted from the grass airfield (but shifted to Bitteswell when necessary). However, in October 1960 a concrete runway was finally completed at Baginton, enabling both AWA and Coventry Airport to operate efficiently in all weather conditions. In addition to production of the many Meteor variants, some 278 Hunters were manufactured at Baginton together with a staggering 490 Sea Hawks, 133 Javelins and a variety of other designs. The final major project undertaken by AWA was the Argosy transport, seventy-three examples of which were constructed at Baginton, and most of these went on to serve with the RAF for many years, others being sold onto the civilian market.

Countless Meteor night fighter variants were manufactured and test flown from Baginton.
(Author's collection)

The huge AWA factory finally closed in July 1965, activities being transferred entirely to Bitteswell where AWA – as part of the Hawker Siddeley Group – continued work on aircraft refurbishment and modification. This move marked the end of Baginton's permanent association with military aircraft, but the airfield survived and prospered as a base for private flying,

Baginton on 9 July 1960 for the King's Cup Air Race: construction of the new concrete runway
appears to have been completed. The Armstrong-Whitworth factory (to the right of the picture)
is not visible. (Flight Collection)

intermittent scheduled airline services and cargo operations. The airport also held a number of hugely successful air shows, which attracted crowds from across the Midlands, featuring many historic and often unusual aircraft ranging from the mighty Vulcan and the RAF's Canberra display team (a magnificent aerobatic demonstration of four silver-painted T4 trainers), through to a supersonic F-104 Starfighter from the Royal Netherlands Air Force, which successfully operated from Baginton's rather modest (by Starfighter standards) runway.

Much of the airport's traditional civilian activity continues to this day and the airfield is now a much-enlarged and very busy site, the local skies often fully occupied by light aircraft engaged on flying training while larger cargo aircraft (such as the DC-3 and Electra) come and go in pursuit of their commercial duties. Some military connections still remain, however, thanks to the presence of Airbase, which forms the home for more than 30 aeroplanes operated by Air Atlantique Ltd including an airworthy Meteor NF 11, which was manufactured at Baginton, less than a mile from where the aircraft now resides on the opposite side of the airfield. Airbase is gradually developing its operations to enable visitors to see all of its preserved aircraft, including a Shackleton, which, although no longer airworthy, is occasionally run up so that visitors can admire the sound of its four mighty Griffon engines.

An aerial view of Armstrong-Whitworth's Baginton factory, illustrating the size of the sprawling complex. Just visible is an AW Apollo aircraft on the airfield hardstanding. (via Doug Pollard)

Little remains of the AWA factory site, most having being demolished and absorbed into a large industrial estate. The original hangars within the airport have survived, however, and further along the perimeter road the Midland Air Museum is now a popular attraction for visitors, housing an excellent collection of aircraft close to the eastern end of the airport runway, including a Vulcan (which flew in upon retirement from RAF service) and an Argosy and Sea Hawk, both of which were built at Baginton. From the museum's site it is possible to look across the airfield to the old AWA area and imagine the countless bombers and fighters that emerged from the huge factory to play such a significant part in Britain's military history.

Runways: NE/SW (1,730yd) grass, N/S (1,350yd) grass, NW/SE (1,060yd) grass. Hangars: Bellman (2). Hardstandings: 0. Accommodation: RAF: 1 officer, 5 SNCOs, 4 ORs; WAAF: 1 SNCO, 10 ORs.

BALDERTON, Nottinghamshire

Grid ref SK814497, Lat 53:02:21N (53.0392) Lon 0:47:13W (-0.78681), 62ft asl. 2 miles S of Newark, W of A1(M)

Driving along the A1(M) just south of Newark, the flat countryside shows little signs of any connections with military aviation. However, just south of Balderton closer investigation of agricultural land reveals traces of concrete, where the three runways of the former RAF Balderton once lay. The RAF first established a site at this location in June 1941, the new station being part of No 7 Group and acting as a satellite for RAF Finningley, where No 25 OCU operated Hampden bombers. Few facilities were available at the site during the first months of its existence, and the landing surface was little more than a cleared grass field, laid over the local clay. During December of the same year the station transferred to No 5 Group in order to provide a satellite airfield for RAF Syerston, where No 408 'Goose' (Canadian) Squadron was based. This unit eventually made a complete transfer to Balderton, although its Hampdens were unable to fly from the airfield until late the following spring as the grass field was waterlogged and unsuitable for operations. This eventually led to the development of

No 25 Operational Training Unit brought its Hampdens to Balderton when the airfield was designated as a satellite field for its home base at Finningley. However, the poor condition of Balderton's landing field delayed the unit's arrival by many months. (via John Elliott)

the airfield to Class A standard, W. & C. French Ltd being the major contractor for the building programme, which was completed in March 1943. The main runway was 6,110 feet aligned on headings 08/26, with secondary runways of 4,200 feet on a heading of 13/21, and 4,211 feet on a heading of 15/33. Hardstandings were initially in the form of twenty-one frying pan types with thirty-one loop-types added later along a surrounding perimeter track, with a width of 50 feet.

The main support site was comprised largely of Nissen huts of various sizes. Also on the site were the mess facilities, chapel, hospital, mission briefing and debriefing buildings, armoury, life support buildings, a parachute rigging hut, supply warehouses, station and airfield security buildings, a motor pool, and the other ground support functions necessary to support the air operations of the group. These facilities were all connected by a network of single-track support roads. The technical site, connected to the ground station and on the west side of the airfield, originally consisted of a single Blister hangar and two T2 sheds, but in 1943 two additional T2 hangars were erected in order to accommodate thirty-two Horsa gliders that were stored on the airfield. Eventually here were three hangars located around the perimeter track at dispersal loops, and one within the technical site, together with various admin buildings, component and field maintenance shops and accommodation for other personnel necessary for keeping the aircraft airworthy and to quickly repair light and moderate battle damage; aircraft severely damaged in combat were sent to repair depots for major structural repair, with only minor work being carried out at Balderton.

The ammunition dump was located outside the perimeter track on the south side of the field surrounded by large dirt mounds and concrete storage pens for storing the aerial bombs and other munitions required by the combat aircraft. Various domestic accommodation sites were also constructed dispersed away from the airfield, within a mile or so of the technical support site, mostly comprised of clusters of Maycrete or Nissen huts. The huts were either connected, set up end-to-end or built singly, and were made of prefabricated corrugated iron with a door and two small windows at the front and back. They provided accommodation for 2,413 personnel, including communal and sick quarters.

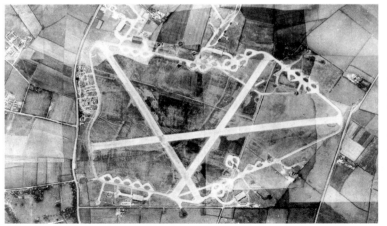

An aerial view of Balderton as seen shortly after completion. The standard triangular runway layout is evident, together with the many bomber-standard 'spectacle' dispersals. (Phil Jarrett collection)

During the site development period No 408 Squadron remained at Balderton, but many of the unit's aircraft were deployed to North Luffenham while runway construction work took place, and the squadron finally moved to Leeming during September 1942. After this date, much of the flying activity at Balderton was undertaken by No 14 (P)AFU's Oxfords, which used the airfield as a Relief Landing Ground. Once the airfield construction was completed, the station was transferred to the Ministry of Aircraft Production (as were other airfields in the region) and the base became a storage facility for more than thirty Airspeed Horsa gliders, which were maintained by a detachment from No 2 Heavy Glider Maintenance Unit. With the airfield largely unused, it provided a suitable base for a Flight Trials Unit equipped with a handful of Meteors, assigned to early jet engine trials being undertaken by Frank Whittle's team.

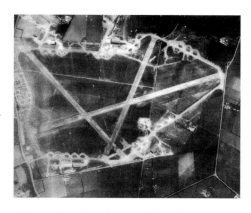

Almost forty aircraft (comprising C-47s and gliders) can be seen at Balderton airfield on 18 April 1944. (via John Elliott)

This work continued until preparations for Operation 'Overlord' dictated that the whole airfield should be assigned to the task. No 1668 HGCU arrived in August 1943 with sixteen Lancasters and sixteen Halifaxes, but departed again three months later, after which the airfield briefly returned to RLG status used by No 12 (P)AFU. On 2 January 1944 the station was transferred to the 9th TCC, USAAF, and the base became Army Air Force Station 482. Just a couple of weeks later saw the first of countless C-47 and C-53 transports arrive at Balderton, the first being from the 437th TCG before being replaced by the 439th TCG. Despite being a storage facility for many American gliders, flying activities remained modest at this stage and it wasn't until mid-1944 that activity increased when No 5 Group (RAF) began using the airfield for training. The 439th TCG returned in September after a five-month absence, and its preparations culminated in the launch of fifty C-47s (each towing a Waco glider) on 17 September, as part of Operation 'Market'. Accompanied by a further thirty aircraft carrying troops and equipment, the whole ensemble set course to Nijmegen in the Netherlands, and successfully returned to Balderton with only one glider being lost during the operation. On the following day the unit's C-47s towed fifty gliders to Groesbeck, and further re-supply missions were flown with formations of fifteen and twenty-five aircraft. American operations then shifted south and Balderton was reassigned to the Royal Air Force.

A C-47 from the 437th TCG receives some attention from one of Balderton's mechanics during 1944. (via John Elliott)

A typical scene at Balderton in 1944 as a C-47 is emptied of its cargo. (via John Elliott)

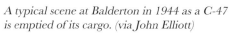

By the end of October 1944 the Lancasters of No 227 Squadron had assembled at the station, joined by the Aircrew Commando School from Scampton. Having been built to bomber standards, Balderton was now able to undertake its designed role, supporting operational missions striking deep into Germany. No 227 remained at Balderton until April 1945, when its Lancasters moved to Strubby, and on 25 April RAF Balderton's active status was removed, the airfield being placed under Care and Maintenance as part of Maintenance Command.

In June 1945 the station was redesignated at No 254 MU and much of the airfield site was used as a storage area for thousands of HE bombs. When these were finally removed in 1954 the airfield was finally abandoned and declared as surplus by the MoD during 1957. The airfield and associated buildings remained virtually unscathed for some years, but when reconstruction of the A1 commenced in the 1960s Balderton's runways provided the source of hardcore for the new road surfaces and the A1 was re-routed across the path of the airfield's eastern perimeter track. Today the runways and taxi tracks are completely removed, although farm tracks still run across parts of the surviving runway structure. Few of the station's domestic and technical site buildings have survived and only the former gymnasium remains intact as a recognisable building (now in private hands and used for storage), but very little remains to suggest that Balderton was once such a large and active site. The only obvious sign of any connection with military aviation now visible in the area is the familiar wreckage of a Lightning interceptor, stranded in a former scrapyard just north of the airfield site on the other side of the A1.

Very little evidence of the former RAF Balderton has survived. The most significant relic is the station's gymnasium, which remains in use as a block of offices. (Richard E. Flagg)

> *Runways:* 085 (2,000yd x 50yd) tarmac, 025 (1,400yd x 50yd) tarmac, 146 (1,400yd x 50yd) tarmac. *Hangars:* T2 (2), Glider (2), B1 (1). *Hardstandings:* Heavy Bomber (50). *Accommodation:* RAF: 69 Officers, 400 SNCOs, 1,041 ORs; WAAF: 9 Officers, 9 SNCOs, 309 ORs.

BATTLESTEAD HILL, Staffordshire

Grid ref SK208236, Lat 52:48:36N (52.80987) Lon 1:41:34W (-1.6928), 300ft asl. 2 miles NW of Burton-upon-Trent, off B5017

One of the smallest and least-documented Royal Air Force sites, Battlestead Hill was created as a Relief Landing Ground under the control of No 16 EFTS at nearby Burnaston. Often referred to as the Burton-upon-Trent RLG, the airfield was almost exclusively assigned to training activities with a mixture of Tiger Moths and Magisters as required by Burnaston, although 30 EFTS at Wolverhampton also used the landing field as required. One former pilot recalls his short stay there:

'In 1944 I was posted to RAF Burnaston south-west of Derby and after a few days elapsed we were then trucked to Battlestead Hill and No 16 EFTS where we were again expected to "keep our hand in" on Tiger Moths. The camp comprised of Nissen huts and outside ablutions with a grass airfield but it was a very happy place. Most of the staff had done their thirty ops ranging from Flight Sergeants to Flight Lieutenants, who I suspect felt sorry for us sprogs who still had to carry on where they had finished. As for flying, we practised the usual low flying, circuits and bumps, etc, but some of us had more experience on the Tiger Moths than the instructors. We also ferried instructors to an airfield near their homes at weekends, a jolly bunch of flak-happy veterans. All in all a very enjoyable month with another forty-five hours on Tiger Moths.'

No significant events took place at the airfield other than the loss of Magister N2789, which stalled while making an approach and crashed just short of the airfield. The assembled Moths and Magisters continued to conduct their mundane but vital task throughout the wartime years. Activity ended during 1945 and the site's grass landing field, hangar and associated buildings were sold off and eventually dismantled. Today there is no trace of the airfield's existence save for a small reminder in the shape of a small road named 'Aviation Lane', which once led to the station's entrance.

> *Runways:* NE/SW (1,100yd) grass, E/W (950yd) grass, N/S (800yd) grass. *Hangars:* Blister (3). *Hardstandings:* 0. *Accommodation:* RAF: 2 Officers, 4 SNCOs, 120 ORs.

BEAUMARIS, Anglesey

Grid ref SH610772, Lat 53:16:25N (53.27373) Lon 4:05:09W (-4.08571), 60ft asl. 1 mile N of Beaumaris on B5109

Although not a recognised military installation, Beaumaris played a significant part in Britain's military aviation history as a home to Saunders-Roe, the famous British design and manufacturing company specialising in seaplane development. It was not surprising that as the Second World War progressed, the company's main plant at Cowes was constantly subjected to the attentions of the Luftwaffe and its East Cowes sites was completely destroyed during a raid in May 1942. The company's ill-fated Lerwick flying boat programme was ultimately abandoned, but when an order for American Catalinas was placed with it as a replacement for the projected RAF order for Lerwicks, Saunders-Roe was contracted to refit the aircraft prior to entering service with RAF Coastal Command. Suitable sites from where the work could be conducted were investigated and the final choice was influenced by the shelter of the Menai Strait, where deep water was available a long way from any significant risk of enemy attack. A small estate at Fryars was purchased as a site for a new production facility and a concrete handling yard and slipway was constructed.

Some 399 Catalinas eventually made their way to Beaumaris (some directly and others via Largs on the Scottish coast) and a significant proportion of the Menai Strait was often packed full with flying boats awaiting modifications, which included the fitment of ASV radar, armament, radio equipment and Leigh lights. The mighty Catalina went on to serve the RAF with distinction, one aircraft being responsible for the crucial detection of the *Bismarck* – a feat that was proudly

Although images of Catalinas at Beaumaris are rare, the type was a daily sight for many years around the location and along the Menai Strait. Although it played a very significant part in the Second World War, the Saunders-Roe factory is probably best remembered for its production of London buses. (via John Elliott)

Few RAF stations could boast a layout and architecture which could compare to that found at Beaumaris. In this rare image a Catalina is visible in the background receiving attention, while a Taylorcraft Auster AOP V is man-handled to the slipway for launch. (Phil Jarrett collection)

recorded by a painting exhibited in the Saunders-Roe works canteen. Other aircraft also occasionally visited Beaumaris, particularly RAF Sunderlands, which often used the site as a bad weather diversion. Perhaps the most unusual aircraft to operate here was the float-equipped Auster V, on trials during 1944 and 1955. Other work conducted by Saunders-Roe included the manufacture of the Shetland flying boat's wing (a project shared with Shorts in Belfast) and the design and initial manufacture of wooden hulls for the Supermarine Walrus, three of these components being built at Beaumaris.

After the end of the Second World War, Saunders-Roe shifted its attention to marine construction and other projects, particularly bus body manufacture, some 300 London Transport RT bodies being built at the site. Flying activities effectively ended when the company shifted its attention away from aircraft, and by the 1950s the sight and sound of flying boats in the Menai Strait was only a memory. Today Beaumaris remains surprisingly intact, although Sanders-Roe is long gone and the site is abandoned and derelict. The two hangars and associated buildings have survived, some still surprisingly close to their wartime state, while others have been substantially modified. However, their condition is deteriorating and it seems likely that they will soon be demolished unless they are purchased and refurbished – a rather unlikely prospect. The slipway remains visible too (together with part of the landing pier) and, although the nearest flying activity is now some miles away to the west at RAF Valley and RAF Mona, it is still easy to picture the magnificent Catalina, Walrus, Coronado and Mariner seaplanes that once could be seen here at rest on the waters, awaiting delivery to their operational units. From the old slipway, the RAF's Hawks

A Taylorcraft Auster AOP V prototype TJ207, complete with Queen Bee floats, pictured adjacent to the slipway at Beaumaris. (Phil Jarrett collection)

occasionally streak overhead, reminding onlookers that although Beaumaris is now merely a reminder of the RAF's past, the RAF is still not very far away.

Runways: 0 (sea surface). *Hangars:* T2 (1), B1 (1). *Hardstandings:* Concrete apron (1). *Accommodation:* Civilian; N/A.

BERROW, Worcestershire

Grid ref SO810339, Lat 52:00:13N (52.00373) Lon 2:16:38W (-2.27732), 320ft asl. 6 miles W of Tewkesbury off A438

One of many small and relatively unknown military sites that are scattered across the country, Berrow (alternatively referred to as Pendock Moor) was established early in 1941 as No 5 Satellite Landing Ground under the control of No 5 Maintenance Unit at Kemble. The site was subsequently transferred to 20 MU at Aston Down, then No 38 MU at Llandow, although when this took place in August 1942 the airfield's limitations became apparent as only one of the two grass strips was judged to be acceptably smooth for Spitfire operations, a factor that limited the airfield's usefulness as a storage facility. In addition to use by these Maintenance Units, RAF Berrow was also occasionally home to other visiting units, among these being No 5 Glider Training School, which flew Hotspur gliders and Miles Master tugs from the airfield at various times. Officialdom eventually prevented a plan for the airfield to be used as a satellite field for Shobdon, and ultimately this same application of Government authority also prevented the Glider Training School from operating here. Flying was subsequently reduced and only occasional movements took place, these being restricted to short stays in order to avoid the possibility of detection by the Luftwaffe. Drawing attention to both the airfield and the local area was avoided as much as possible as the Telecommunications Research Establishment at Defford operated a small facility adjacent to the airfield, which was naturally surrounded by extreme secrecy, although occasional visits to Berrow were still made by aircraft in order to visit the facility as part of ongoing radar and communication trials.

The airfield was finally closed in May 1945 and the few buildings that had been assembled were eventually demolished. Now completely returned to agriculture, there are few signs of military aviation ever having operated here, and the casual visitor would find nothing to suggest the presence of an airfield on this site, the whole area having long since merged into the surrounding countryside.

Runways: 0 (grass field). *Hangars:* 0. *Hardstandings:* 0. *Accommodation:* RAF; N/A.

BIBURY, Gloucestershire

Grid ref SP112091, Lat 51:46:51N (51.7809) Lon 1:50:19W (-1.83873), 521ft asl. 2 miles N of Bibury village off B4425, NE of Cirencester

Situated deep in the Gloucestershire countryside, Bibury is a picturesque village far removed from any visions of war and violence. But just a couple of miles out into the lush countryside there remains evidence of a darker time in Bibury's history. Built on Ablington Down, the airfield was first established in 1939, having been selected in April of that year as a potential relief landing field for the RAF's No 3 SFTS based at South Cerney. By 1940 the airfield was in regular use by that unit's Oxfords, although a brief hiatus occurred when the airfield was temporarily disabled through the liberal scattering of motor vehicles, in order to render the site unusable while the situation in France looked so perilous. However, by the middle of 1940 the airfield was once again active, often acting as a site for night-flying so that the more valuable airfield at South Cerney could hide in darkness, thus avoiding the attention of the Luftwaffe.

On 7 August1940 the first Hurricanes arrived at Bibury when A Flight of No 87 Squadron deployed from Exeter, and was soon thrown into direct confrontation with marauding enemy bombers; indeed, its first encounter took place on the first night after its arrival when an He 111 was successfully intercepted and destroyed. However, by mid-August the Hurricanes made way for Spitfires when No 92 Squadron established a detachment away from its home base at Pembrey. Its stay at Bibury (which included yet more encounters with the Luftwaffe, including one just two hours after the squadron's arrival) was short, although while at Bibury No 92 sustained damage to two of its Spitfires when a Ju 88 from KG51 attacked the airfield during the afternoon of 19 August, killing one airman who was unfortunate enough to be near the aircraft at the time.

When the squadron moved to Biggin Hill, it took its detachment with it, enabling No 87 to return with its Hurricanes of B Flight on 3 September. The squadron maintained a rotational detachment at Bibury until December 1940, but with the Luftwaffe shifting most of its attention to the South East, the squadron's detachment ended on the 18th and its Hurricanes departed for Exeter. From the end of 1940 onwards, Bibury returned to more peaceful activities and the Oxfords of No 3 SFTS returned. Their continual use of the grass field quickly rendered it almost useless and, following a visit from the AOC of No 23 Group, the airfield was extended and upgraded, and in 1942 the two runways were surfaced with Sommerfield tracking.

On 15 April 1943 No 1539 BAT (Blind Approach Training) Flight arrived at Bibury, adding its Oxfords to the established fleet of similar aircraft already present there every day. Despite being upgraded to full Satellite Landing Ground status in November 1943, Bibury's active life quickly came to an end, with 1539 BAT Flight leaving in September 1944, and No 3 (P)AFU shortly afterwards. All flight activity ceased by the end of 1944 and the site was handed to No 7 Maintenance Unit, remaining unused but under RAF control until the site was sold off.

Today the airfield is still recognisable and closer inspection of the agricultural land reveals a small part of a perimeter track and one concrete hardstanding. However, the most obvious signs of the airfield's existence are the T1 hangar, which has been refurbished for storage use, and a smaller Blister hangar, which has been re-clad and now houses agricultural equipment, together with a few smaller buildings within the former technical site such as the old MT shed (now housing farming equipment), a pump house, picket post and a derelict air raid shelter.

A surviving Blister hangar at Bibury, re-clad and now in use as an agricultural shelter. (Neil Jedrzejewski)

A post-war image of Bibury illustrating the two grass runways, which appear to have lost their temporary Sommerfield tracking. (Neil Jedrzejewski)

A long-abandoned picket post at Bibury, still standing amongst the weeds. (Neil Jedrzejewski)

Runways: 040 (1,145yd) Sommerfield track, 100 (1,175yd) Sommerfield track, N/W (2,000yd) Sommerfield track. *Hangars:* T1 (1). *Hardstandings:* 0. *Accommodation:* RAF: 79 Officers, 154 SNCOs, 310 ORs; WAAF: 4 Officers, 3 SNCOs, 93 ORs.

BLAKEHILL FARM, Gloucestershire

Grid ref SU079914, Lat 51:37:18N (51.62175) Lon 1:53:09W (-1.88596), 305ft asl. 2 miles SW of Cricklade, S of B4040

Designed from the outset as a transport aircraft base, the airfield was constructed on the site of Blakehill Farm during 1943 under the control of No 70 Group RAF. The station opened in February 1944 as part of No 46 Group RAF Transport Command, although completion of the airfield facilities continued, often rather more slowly than required. The station quickly assumed a busy casualty evacuation and freight-carrying role; when a fleet of fifty Horsa gliders was gradually deposited on the airfield later in 1944, additional land had to be acquired to accommodate them. The first resident unit was No 233 Squadron, which arrived from Gibraltar during March, freshly re-equipped with Dakotas. Two Field Staging Posts were also established, and the Headquarters Wing of the Glider Pilot Regiment also arrived, tasked with the distribution of glider assets. Further arrivals in March 1944 included the 13th Parachute Company and 1st Canadian Parachute Company. As gliders slowly arrived from Swanton Morley and North Luffenham, 233 Squadron (now fully equipped with thirty Dakotas and forty Horsas) slowly increased the pace of activity, participating in major exercises including leaflet drops over Caen and Alencon.

Dakotas were once a familiar daily sight and sound in the skies above Blakehill Farm. This 1943 image illustrates just one example among the hundreds of similar aircraft that frequented this site. (via John Elliott)

The station's full operational status reached Readiness A condition by 1 June 1944, and preparations were made for Operation 'Tonga', in which No 233 Squadron would be given the unenviable task of making the furthest reach inland to its designated drop zone; many of Blakehill's gliders made their way to Pegasus bridge and a place in history. Blakehill Farm is inevitably most closely associated with Arnhem and D-Day, and the days of summer 1944 were undoubtedly the most significant and busy ones for the station. Resupply and delivery flights to and from France continued throughout the month and into July and August.

No 271 Squadron established a detachment at Blakehill to relieve pressure on its home base at Down Ampney, and No 575 Squadron also occasionally flew from the airfield. More Dakotas arrived in September when No 437 Squadron RCAF arrived, and the station's combined force of Dakotas formed a major part of the famous Operation 'Market Garden'. It was a 233 Squadron Dakota that became the first aircraft to land in a British-controlled area in reoccupied France on 13 June, and one of Blakehill's nurses (who accompanied troops on casualty evacuation flights) who earned the distinction of being the first female RAF aircrew member to fly into the combat zone.

The nose section of one of Blakehill's Dakotas (KG437) survives in the Royal Air Force Museum, whose records illustrate just one of the aircraft's busy days on 21 September 1944 when it was serving with No 437 (RCAF) Squadron at Blakehill Farm:

This solitary example of the ubiquitous Horsa is pictured while being towed to Blakehill's technical site. (via John Elliott)

A C-47 gets airborne, towing a Horsa glider on a training mission. (via Robert Grays)

'KG437 took off at 13:14 hours, loaded with 16 wicker panniers, to be dropped in the "Oosterbeek perimeter", near the HQ of 1st Airborne Division at the Hartenstein Hotel. Out of ten aircraft despatched by the Squadron, five did not return to base. KG437 made it back to Blakehill Farm. Ten aircraft were detailed to convey and drop panniers again in the Arnhem area in an effort to give the airborne elements their supplies, mostly of ammunition, which our guard forces required very urgently. The route taken was Base-Hatfield-Bradwell-North Foreland-5116N 0300E-Ghent-Bourgh Leopold-W of Eindhoven-DZ and return on a reciprocal heading. A total of 40 panniers were successfully jettisoned on or near the DZ. Over DZ visibility was 3-5 miles and 8/10 cloud cover, base of 5,000ft. Enemy reactions were concentrated mainly in the area of DZ and enemy fighters appeared between Eindhoven and DZ on the return journey. The following aircraft did not return: KG387 (F/L Alexander), KG489 (F/O Cressman), FZ656 (P/O Kenny); KG489 (F/O Chambers) landed at B56, engine damaged by flak. 376 (F/O Hagerman) was abandoned when crew baled out. KG427 (F/S Lane) received slight damage from strikes from FW190 just above main plane starboard side. Attacked at 6,000ft 25 miles from DZ on return route. KG410 (F/O Semple) shook off two FW190s by diving into cloud. Crew state at present as follows: KG387 captain and 2nd pilot killed, W/Op returned safely, Navigator believed to be in hospital. 376 2nd pilot and navigator killed, W/Op slightly wounded, pilot safe. KG489 (F/O Chambers) and FZ656 (P/O Kenny) all members of crew are missing.'

Casevac and supply flights continued into the winter, Oxford aircraft often using the airfield for training while Fairford was used as a satellite field when required. Glider flying practice eventually conflicted with operational tasking and the resident Dakota squadrons moved to Birch in Essex in order to participate in Operation 'Varsity', the Rhine crossing. The Canadian unit ultimately moved on to Belgium, while No 233 Squadron relocated to Odiham in June 1945. Its place was taken at Blakehill by No 22 HGCU with a mixed fleet of Albemarles and Waco Hadrian gliders. More Dakotas returned in October 1945 when No 575 Squadron relocated here from Melbourn. The Oxfords of No 1555 RAT Flight arrived from Valley in December, with No 1528's Oxfords shortly afterwards. The station's association with the Dakota ended during January 1946 when 575 Squadron left and Blakehill was transferred to Flying Training Command. The remaining Oxfords gradually departed and flying activity at Blakehill had ended by the end of 1946. Although the station was held in reserve for some time, it was never used for flying again after this period.

The station's huge collection of assorted technical, domestic and support buildings (more than 500 of them) were gradually demolished but the airfield's runways and taxiways survived for some time before being removed. Despite the eventual clearance of the entire site, much of Blakehill is still recognisable (particularly from the air) and the former airfield became the site of a major GCHQ radio monitoring station, evidence of the huge mast erected in the centre of the airfield still

A former compass swing platform at Blakehill Farm. (Richard E. Flagg)

The former gas defence building at Blakehill Farm (Richard E. Flagg)

strikingly visible from the air. Among the surviving buildings are a old gas respirator store and even an old latrine, together with various other unidentified structures. A memorial to the station's heroic exploits is situated on the site and a former Royal Observer Corps underground observation post is now preserved as a haven for bats. Perhaps flying activities at Blakehill haven't ended completely!

> *Runways:* 240 (2,000yd x 50yd) tarmac, 130 (1,400yd x 50yd) tarmac, 190 (1,400yd x 50yd) tarmac. *Hangars:* T2 (2). *Hardstandings:* Loop (46). *Accommodation:* RAF: 224 Officers, 369 SNCOs, 1,990 ORs; WAAF: 6 Officers, 18 SNCOs, 389 ORs.

BODORGAN, Anglesey

Grid ref SH383682, Lat 53:11:12N (53.18661) Lon 4:25:15W (-4.42076), 150ft asl. 8 miles W of Menai Bridge off A4080, SW of Hermon village

The student Hawk pilots making their noisy take-offs from RAF Valley probably have little time to dwell on the nature of the countryside that flashes by beneath them. But just a few miles out under the eastern approach path to Valley's main runway lies the site of a long-forgotten airfield with an unusual history. Opened in September 1940, the site was first known as Aberffraw, although the name was changed to Bodorgan a few months later after continual of postal, rail and freight confusion. The first aircraft to use the site were certainly strange ones; although outwardly almost identical to the ubiquitous Tiger Moth trainer, the Queen Bees operated by Z Flight of No 1 AACU were in fact radio-controlled drones, flown unmanned unless a pilot was required for ferrying or training. The airfield was chosen as being a suitable site for unmanned operations as it was situated in an unpopulated area of countryside close to the coast where the unreliable drones could operate in safety. The gunners at the nearly Ty-Croes range used the Queen Bees as targets whenever possible although aircraft didn't become available until 1941 and the airfield was partially obstructed until December 1940 in order to discourage any potential for enemy landings. The first pilotless flight took place on 2 December, although the Queen Bee (P4804) crashed on landing – the most difficult part of an unmanned sortie. The Queen Bee became a familiar site around Bodorgan, although its difficult and unpredictable nature meant that occasional mishaps still continued.

The troublesome de Havilland Queen Bee, once a common sight at Bodorgan, where the aircraft's often unpredictable (and often hair-raising) qualities were utilised in support of Army gunnery training. (Author's collection)

Lysanders arrived at the airfield in March 1941, with 13 Squadron arriving for night-flying practice, and more Lysanders appeared when the station was designated as a satellite landing ground for Hawarden's 48 Maintenance Unit. Hurricanes were also ferried to Bodorgan and stored on the airfield together with Wellingtons and Swordfish. Squadron pilots were sometimes tasked with the collection of aircraft, and operating safely out of the confines of Bodorgan's small grass site was far from easy. It was eventually decided that aircraft would be ferried out of Bodorgan by MU pilots, prior to their assignment to operational units. The storage of Wellingtons was usually capped at around thirty aircraft so as to avoid the site becoming too much of a tempting target, but despite being a relatively obvious potential target (the regular daily use of the field prevented the employment of any effective camouflage), it was never attacked by the Luftwaffe.

The Queen bees of Z Flight were joined by those of J Flight, these becoming 1606 and 1620 Flights on 1 October 1942, the former unit operating Henleys, Magisters and Tiger Moths while 1620 continued with Queen Bees, their operations being the subject of attention from the USAAC, which visited the station to examine the operation of these unusual aircraft. Other unusual activities included a series of trials with radar-deflecting foil, which ultimately resulted in the widespread use of 'Window' within Bomber Command, as one North Wales local recalls:

'One bright morning, probably early in 1944, we went out to play on Stanley Crescent and met an extraordinary sight. The road and pavements were strewn with vast quantities of "silver paper". It was in the form of coils of fine strips of aluminium foil and it behaved in the same manner as the beginning of a snow storm, the breeze blowing it along so that it formed curious swirls in the road, and accumulated in the gutters. We started gathering it up, to see how much we could collect. Having no use for it, we soon lost interest, and left it to the attention of the street sweepers. What we didn't know until years afterwards was that this was one of the major secrets of the war! It was "Chaff", or "Window". There was a small squadron at RAF Bodorgan devoted to carrying out radar experiments with the foil. They were a success, used with great effect to simulate an armada of aircraft between Dover and Calais on D-Day.'

Hawker Henleys operated from Bodorgan during the 1940s, engaged on target facilities duties. (Author's collection)

When dispersal of stored aircraft became less of a priority at the end of 1944, Hooton Park was selected as a sub-site for storage and Hawarden relinquished its satellite landing grounds, including Bodorgan. The MU had vacated the airfield by the end of December and a detachment from No 577 Squadron arrived with Martinets, joining 650 Squadron, which had arrived a couple of months previously. Flying continued for another nine months, after which the station was closed. As a grass field the site was quickly returned to agriculture. Today little evidence of the airfield remains apart from an area of concrete within a cluster of farm buildings. A handful of huts have survived, together with a rather elaborate pillbox nearby, but amidst the sprawling farmland there is little to remind visitors of the site's colourful history.

Runways: NNE/SSW (1,000yd) grass, E/W (1,000yd) grass, WSW/ENE (960yd) grass. *Hangars:* Bellman (2), Blister (1). *Hardstandings:* 0. *Accommodation:* RAF: 24 Officers, 23 SNCOs, 479 ORs; WAAF: 2 Officers, 4 SNCOs, 124 ORs.

BRAMCOTE, Warwickshire

Grid ref SP410880, Lat 52:29:21N (52.48908) Lon 1:23:48W (-1.39672), 378ft asl. NE of Coventry, off B4114, N of M69

Driving along the M69 motorway, it is easy to head south of Hinckley, surrounded by the rushing traffic, and remain completely unaware that for a few brief seconds you are driving along the course of a disused runway. The presence of tree plantations serves to disguise the presence of the former RAF Bramcote, complete with surviving hangars, control tower and domestic site all looking remarkably similar to the days when they were in operational use more than forty years ago.

Construction of the airfield began in 1939 as part of a pre-war expansion programme that included a series of projected bomber training bases and sites that could be used for dispersal use, should the bomber bases in East Anglia become subject to excessive attention from the Luftwaffe. The first aircraft to arrive were Wellingtons from No 215 Squadron, which used the airfield for two weeks prior to the station officially opening on 4 June 1940. As part of No 6 Group RAF, a decoy airfield was also constructed at nearby Wibtoft. The station's first assignment was the formation of four Polish bomber squadrons. No 300 (Masovian) Squadron with Fairey Battles was the first, followed by 301 (Pomeranian) Squadron (also with Battles), and both moved to Swinderby in August to begin operational service. No 304 (Silesian) was formed on 22 August as the first French-Polish squadron to be created. After initially flying Battles, the unit re-equipped with Wellingtons, as

Polish airmen climb out of the cockpit of Battle L5427 at Bramcote in September 1940. (via John Elliott)

did No 305 (Zeima Wielkopolska) Squadron, which was formed on 29 August, both units transferring to Syerston in December 1940. Six months later the Wellington returned to Bramcote in substantial numbers when No 18 (Polish) OTU arrived from Hucknall and training of Polish crews on the Wellington became Bramcote's primary task, although other units also used the airfield for brief periods. Despite being a training unit, crews and aircraft were provided to take part in the 'Thousand Bomber' raids over Germany, including Cologne, Essen and Bremen.

Hurricanes were much in evidence when No 151 Squadron arrived in November to re-equip with Defiants, while No 605 Squadron established a detachment at the station in May 1941. No 1513 BAT Flight also arrived for a long-term stay with a fleet of Oxfords. During February 1942 nearby Bitteswell was established as a satellite field (Nuneaton was later used for the same purpose). The gradual lack of reserves for training had, by March 1943, brought about the reduction of 18 (Polish) OTU to just one flight, and it was then moved to the training unit at RAF Finningley. Bramcote then took on the training of aircrew for transport flying and the longer flights that such a role would require. This became the task of No 105 OTU, with Bramcote passing from Bomber to Transport Command. In August 1945 No 105 OTU ceased its operations and its duties were taken over by No 1381 (Transport) Conversion Unit. By now Wellingtons were no longer used and the unit was completely equipped with Dakotas. Since 1941 Bramcote had also been the home of 1513 BAT Flight, assigned to Beam Approach Training, and on 16 July 1946 it was replaced by No 1510 Flight, which stayed at Bramcote until November of that year.

This ended the RAF's presence at Bramcote, and on 3 December 1946 the station was handed over to the Royal Navy. Some might have said that the RAF's departure was welcome, as a former airman recalls:

'Bramcote was a very formal permanent camp and the whole place reeked of "bull". The unit was under 44 Group Transport Command and its purpose was to take in aircrew who had completed their bombing missions and convert them to flying transport planes. Most of the aircraft were Vickers Wellingtons from which the armaments were removed, but we later got a couple of Dakotas. There was an airfield but as it was grass, flying was restricted and most of the flying was from RAF Lindley, some 5 miles away on the A5 road, which had concrete runways; it is now the Motor Industries Research Association. There was a large hangar where aircraft that had completed a given number of flying hours were stripped down for servicing; fitters worked on the engines, riggers checked the airframes, and electricians, instrument technicians and wireless mechanics overhauled the equipment. We were issued with a set of tools and it was nice to work in the trade for which we had spent so long in training, but work at the bench was less interesting than working on the aircraft. We had a rota for night work but we were restricted to work as wireless mechanics. In the past somebody had had the brilliant notion that as we had to work with our minds we must not get too tired and therefore wireless mechanics were exempt from all guard and fire duties.'

With the RAF gone, Fleet Air Arm operations soon got under way. As HMS *Gamecock*, the station earned the dubious distinction of being the 'most inland Stone Frigate in the country' – as described by the station's new Commanding Officer. It was indeed the most inland hoisting of the White Ensign that could be possible. As a home to the Royal Naval Volunteer Reserve, the first naval aircraft to arrive were the Seafires of No 1833 RNVR Squadron. These were later replaced by Sea Furies in 1954, later joined by a small number of Fireflies that later formed the nucleus of 1844 Squadron, tasked with anti-submarine operations. The unit moved to Honiley during October 1955 to take advantage of the latter station's concrete runways, and by 1959 RNVR activities had ended, rendering HMS *Gamecock* redundant. The station was transferred to the Army's Royal Artillery, and although flying activity effectively ended at this stage, the station remained virtually intact, although most of the airfield was eventually returned to agriculture, large areas of trees being planted around sports fields in front of the imposing hangars.

A pair of appropriately coded Seafires from No 1833 RNVR Squadron are on final approach to Bramcote in 1953. (via John Elliott)

The Signals Regiment took over the base in 1993 and, as Gamecock Barracks, the station survives in excellent condition. The airfield is gone and only the sports fields remain on the grass where Wellingtons once lumbered into the air. But three of the station's hangars, control tower and technical site remain in good condition, in regular use by the Army. Not many airfields can claim to have been operated by all three services, and few operational stations could expect to have survived in good condition for so long, despite having ended all flying activities nearly half a century ago.

Runways: 030 (1,600yd) Sommerfield track, 130 (1,400yd) Sommerfield track, 090 (1,400yd) Sommerfield track. *Hangars:* C Type (5). *Hardstandings:* Frying pan (30). *Accommodation:* RAF: 174 Officers, 312 SNCOs, 1,187 ORs; WAAF: 8 Officers, 8 SNCOs, 437 ORs.

BRATTON, Shropshire

Grid ref SJ635150, Lat 52:43:54N (52.73174) Lon 2:32:28W (-2.54106), 191ft asl. 2 miles N of Telford off B5063, SW of A442

A relatively small and unknown flying site, Bratton was established in 1939 as a Relief Landing Ground for nearby RAF Shawbury. Weather conditions and the relatively poor condition of many airfields in the area prevented the rapid construction of runways and a great deal of flying training was victim to periods of inactivity when airfields were waterlogged and unfit for use. Shawbury eventually had the advantage of a concrete perimeter track, but Bratton provided a useful additional facility that was used as required until it too succumbed to the weather and was effectively abandoned until the spring of 1941. Oxfords from No 11 SFTS were a regular sight at the field until this time, but after they returned their presence was relatively low-key, with additional relief grounds at Condover and Wheaton becoming available at the same time. Other aircraft types were rarely seen, perhaps the most notable being a Spitfire from No 57 OTU, which force-landed during a snowstorm on 7 December 1941 and skidded through the airfield's perimeter fence.

In January 1944 the airfield was transferred to the control of No 5 (P)AFU at Ternhill, its Miles Masters becoming a familiar presence in company with Oxfords from the Royal Navy's Instrument Training Squadron based at nearby RNAS Hinstock. Later in 1944 the station was transferred to Royal Navy control as a sub-site for Hinstock, but flying ended in 1945 and the airfield quickly reverted to agricultural use. Today virtually nothing remains, save for a handful of small wartime-era huts and remnants of the concrete refuelling apron, which is now built upon.

Runway: NW/SE (900yd) grass. *Hangars:* Blister (5). *Hardstandings:* 0. *Accommodation:* RAF: 2 Officers, 4 SNCOs, 120 ORs.

BRAUNSTONE, Leicester

Grid ref SK538041, Lat 52:37:56N (52.63222) Lon 1:12:22W (-1.20603), 315ft asl. W of Leicester off A47, W of A563

With only a very brief association with military aviation, Braunstone was first developed for aviation use in 1935, having been selected as the site for Leicester's Airport. Some 534 acres of land was purchased and the airfield was opened on 13 July with a fanfare of excitement and plans for the future. Flying began in April of the same year with a grass landing area and a designated runway length of 783 yards. The Leicestershire Aero Club established a presence at the airfield; its clubhouse was situated next to a hangar and support buildings on the western airfield perimeter, and its Tiger Moth and Puss Moths became a familiar sight in the skies over Leicester. Plans were made to develop the airport towards the east with new access from a developing ring road system, but the plans were eventually abandoned as the Second World War approached, and the airfield was transferred to RAF control, as recalled by a local enthusiast:

'On 20 October 1940 Braunstone was requisitioned by the Air Ministry to form a satellite field for 7 Elementary Flying Training School. The airfield continued in this role throughout the war, flying Tiger Moth tandem two-seat single-engine biplanes, although a Stirling bomber visited once. Although far removed from the fast monoplane fighters and bombers of the day, the Moth was a forgiving aircraft and no suitable side-by-side-seat basic trainers were available at this time. Some temporary huts and three Blister hangars were built for the FTS. Inevitably there were mishaps at the airfield, and sometimes, given its small size (800 yards east-west and 600 yards north-south), landing aircraft finished up in the hedge.

Bizarrely, on 10 March 1942 an Instructor, Flt Lt Newbury, actually landed on a soldier, who was killed. Newbury was acquitted at court-martial. Meanwhile, Reid and Sigrist, under Major Reid DFC (actually a Squadron Leader), patented their Turn and Bank instrument, which the firm manufactured at Braunstone for almost all wartime RAF aircraft.

They also repaired Defiant fighters at Desford, but not at Braunstone. As it was satellite to Desford, it is unknown how many people trained at Braunstone. Many pilots received their basic training in Canada or Arizona, where the topography was so different that they needed additional training back here in the UK at Braunstone or elsewhere in Britain to accustom them to European conditions. On 1 December 1944 the establishment was two officers, four NCOs and 120 other ranks, but no WAAFs. At that time there were the three civil hangars, two open Blister hangars, no lighting, some flying control and some radio.'

Little other significant activity took place here, and as the war drew to a close the RAF withdrew, returning the airfield to civilian use. As a relatively small site it was deemed unsuitable for future aviation use; it was never developed any further and was subsequently abandoned. Today all traces of the airfield have gone, the whole site having been buried under a huge industrial complex and road system. A few small remnants of the airfield can be found among the sprawling buildings, but there is virtually nothing left that relates to Braunstone's brief association with military aviation.

> *Runways:* E/W (800yd) grass, N/S (600yd) grass. *Hangars:* Civil type (3), Blister (2). *Hardstandings:* 0. *Accommodation:* RAF: 2 Officers, 4 SNCOs, 120 ORs.

BRAWDY, Dyfed

Grid ref SM848245, Lat 51:52:41N (51.87813) Lon 5:07:37W (-5.12692), 350ft asl. 3 miles E of Solva off A487

Situated out on the bleak Pembrokeshire coast, Brawdy is a remote and often bleak site that has enjoyed a varied and very significant history. Originally created as a satellite field for nearby St David's, Brawdy quickly became the more suitable airfield for flying activities, thanks to longer runways arranged in a better layout in order to take advantage of prevailing winds. Officially opening on 2 February 1942, the airfield had been used prior to this date by No 517 Squadron's meteorological Halifaxes, especially when conditions prevented a fully loaded take-off being possible from St David's. When necessary, the aircraft was ferried over to Brawdy at light weight prior to being fuelled up to full capacity, ready to depart from one of Brawdy's substantially longer runways. When the base officially opened, this practice ended and the squadron relocated from St David's.

The lumbering Halifaxes became a familiar site at Brawdy, their crews being tasked with some of the most perilous flying imaginable. Before the advent of weather radar and weather ships, direct reconnaissance was the only practical means of monitoring weather conditions in 1944, and No 517 Squadron's Halifaxes were obliged to embark upon long sorties far out into the Irish Sea and South Western approaches, often in the most foul of weather conditions. An encounter with the Luftwaffe so far out into the Atlantic was unlikely, although it was believed that should a Luftwaffe Focke-Wulf Condor be spotted, there was an unwritten agreement that neither crew would interfere with the other. It was a combination of bad weather and the remote operating area that made each sortie so dangerous – a number of the squadron's aircraft simply disappeared without trace, although one crew was lucky to survive a ditching and was picked up by a passing ship three days later and returned to Brawdy – via New York.

After the end of the war, No 517 Squadron left Brawdy and headed south to Weston Zoyland. In its place came a detachment from No 595 Squadron, tasked with a series of trials involving gliders being towed by Spitfires. No 8 OTU detached a fleet of thirty Spitfires and Mosquitoes from its base at Haverfordwest during February 1945 for intensive photographic reconnaissance training, and some consideration was given to developing the station for use as a base for the flying of unmanned drone aircraft, but the idea was subsequently abandoned.

Despite assuming the role of HQ station from St David's on 1 November 1945, Brawdy was transferred to naval control just a couple of months later. Initially used as a satellite ground for RNAS Dale, the station was commissioned as HMS *Goldcrest* on 4 September 1952 and became home to Nos 806, 849, 738 and 739 Naval Air Squadrons over subsequent years. Hawker Sea

Hawks became the most familiar sight in the skies over the airfield for many years until 1960, when the airfield was temporarily closed to flying so that the two main runways could be extended. When flying resumed three years later, Brawdy swiftly became home to a large number of FAA Hunters tasked with advanced flying, low-level navigation, ground attack and weapons training. They were joined by the distinctive sight and sound of the Fairey Gannet, and Brawdy once again became a very busy station, day-to-day flying occasionally being interrupted by aerobatic training performed by the home-based 'Rough Diamonds' Hunter team, which enjoyed a brief (but very welcome) presence on the UK air show circuit. The Hunters shared airspace with the buzz of Gannets and the occasional appearance of RAF Vulcans, which now visited the base on practice dispersal exercises, a two-aircraft Operational Readiness Platform (ORP) having been built at the eastern end of one of the runways specifically for this purpose.

A wintry scene at Brawdy as 806 NAS Seahawks are prepared for deployment to HMS Eagle in 1954. (FAA)

A gaggle of Brawdy's resident Fleet Air Arm types have been assembled for the cameraman in 1968. (FAA)

The Fleet Air Arm's presence at Brawdy finally ended in 1971, and the airfield was placed under Care and Maintenance. It was not until 1974 that the base returned to RAF control and reopened as the home to No 1 Tactical Weapons Unit, formed from the now-defunct 229 OCU at Chivenor. A huge number of Hunters returned to Brawdy, this time wearing the markings of the TWU's component RAF squadrons (63, 79 and 234), together with a gaggle of Meteors assigned to target facilities flying. One of these (VZ467) was the RAF's last single-seat Meteor, the last of countless examples that had served the RAF with distinction for more than three decades. No 22 Squadron's D Flight also relocated to Brawdy with its SAR Whirlwind helicopters, these eventually

being replaced by Sea Kings from No 202 Squadron. Intensive weapons training became Brawdy's
main role and Hunter operations once again became its primary activity until the 1980s, when the
venerable Hunter was gradually replaced by new-built Hawk trainers. The Tactical Weapons Unit
remained active until 1992, when a reorganisation of the RAF's training system effectively meant
that the TWU's role was redundant, so Brawdy once again fell silent, save for the occasional sound
of Sea King helicopters, which remained at the base for a further two years until the 202 Squadron
detachment headed back to Chivenor.

*An elevated view of
the Tactical Weapons
Unit flight line in the
early 1980s, with the
typical twin rows of
Hunters accompanied
by one of the TWU's
first Hawks, just
visible to the left of
picture. (N. Potter via
Pete Buckingham)*

*Looking south across part of the
Tactical Weapons Unit flight line,
the station's naval-style layout can
be seen, the main runway just
visible in the distance and the
Pembrokeshire coastline beyond.
(RAF via Pete Buckingham)*

*Assembled for a publicity photograph, Brawdy's fire
section vehicles pose at their base, in front of the airfield
control tower, during 1983. Just visible in the
background are TWU Hawks. Sadly, the tower has
since been demolished. (RAF via Pete Buckingham)*

With the helicopters gone, flying activities ended completely here and Brawdy became Cawdor Barracks, under the control of the Army. The US Navy's Naval (non-flying) facility moved to St Mawgan in 1995 and the station is now home to six units from the Army's Signals Regiment. Although the station's facilities are naturally in daily use, the once-busy airfield is now completely silent, but preserved in remarkably good condition. The runways are intact and the huge aprons still carry their markings for line positioning of Hawks and Hunters. The remaining hangars (of naval design) are also mostly in good condition, but tragically three of these were demolished, together with the long-familiar control tower. It is unlikely that the airfield will ever return to military flying, but having survived so well it is to be hoped that some form of aviation activity returns to this historic site in the future, even though this prospect seems very unlikely.

Runways: 152 (2,010yd x 50yd) concrete and wood chippings, 086 (1,240yd x 50yd) concrete and wood chippings, 029 (2,000yd x 50yd) concrete and wood chippings. *Hangars:* T2 (2). *Hardstandings:* Spectacle (27). *Accommodation:* RAF: 80 Officers, 280 SNCOs, 836 ORs; WAAF: 1 Officer, 20 SNCOs, 165 ORs.

BRIDLEWAY GATE, Shropshire

Grid ref SJ537258, Lat 52:49:43N (52.82852) Lon 2:41:18W (-2.6883), 310ft asl. 1 mile N of Preston Brockhurst on A49

Users of the A49 road today are doubtless seldom aware of Bridleway Gate's association with military aviation. The rolling fields and tree plantations offer no indication that Oxfords once chugged and buzzed around the area or that a Wellington bomber once made a landing here. Only closer inspection of the agricultural land reveals occasional patches of concrete (including an MT ramp) to reveal the former existence of an airfield here.

The ubiquitous Airspeed Oxford was, for many years, the most common aircraft type to operate from Bridleway Gate. (Author's collection)

Bridleway Gate was one of a group of Relief Landing Grounds established in order to relieve traffic congestion at nearby RAF Shawbury. Opening in 1940, the first aircraft to use the site was an Oxford, which made a precautionary landing on 16 January 1941, but after this date the airfield was closed for many weeks due to the weather conditions, which turned much of the landing field into mud. Bridleway was an austere site with few facilities – a local cottage-owner was asked to display a light in an open upstairs window in order to ensure the building's safety during night-flying. Once the state of the airfield enabled regular flying to commence, Oxfords became a familiar site in the area and continued to use the airfield until 1943, when activity gradually shifted to new airfields with concrete runways.

Little remains to indicate that this was once the entrance to Bridleway Gate's airfield. All traces of the site are almost gone and the area has returned to agriculture. (Richard E. Flagg)

On 10 January 1944 the site closed as an RLG and No 245 Maintenance Unit took over the airfield, using it to store huge fuel supplies in drums and cans that were delivered to and from the nearby railway station at Hadnall. In May of the same year, flying activity returned when parachute drop and container dropping exercises began, these continuing on a fairly regular basis throughout the year. Possibly the last aircraft movement at Bridleway Gate was the aforementioned Wellington (NC810) from No 81 OTU, which made a forced landing here on 13 April 1945. After repair, the aircraft departed on 17 April, and after being held in reserve for possible use by No 16 MU, the site was reduced to Care and Maintenance status on 25 October, before being returned to agriculture the following year. Today, the Oxfords are of course long gone and Bridleway has returned to more peaceful times with all but the smallest traces of the RAF's presence gone forever.

> *Runways:* N/S (950yd) grass, NE/SW (985yd) grass, E/W (1,030yd) grass, SE/NW (1,200yd) grass. *Hangars:* Blister (10). *Hardstandings:* 0. *Accommodation:* RAF: 2 Officers, 2 SNCOs, 120 ORs.

BROCKTON, Shropshire

Grid ref SJ723034, Lat 52:37:41N (52.62818) Lon 2:24:35W (-2.40963), 315ft asl. 1 mile N of Sutton Maddock on B4379

Another small and unsophisticated Satellite Landing Ground (SLG), Brockton opened on 30 June 1941 as No 30 SLG, quickly becoming the home to numerous Spitfires and Hurricanes stored by Nos 9 and 29 Maintenance Units away from their main sites. In order to render the airfield (and its contents) as inconspicuous as possible, the entire area was carefully camouflaged with netting and paintwork, even the small Robin hangars being carefully disguised as farm houses. Fake hedges were painted across the grass runways and even cattle were allowed to graze in penned enclosures. From a distance, the airfield gave every indication of being just an innocent part of the countryside. This was of course something of a mixed blessing, as although enemy crews would be unable to locate the airfield unless they were very lucky, the RAF's MU pilots also had a very difficult task in spotting the airfield! Perhaps not surprisingly, flying activity was fairly infrequent and most movements came from the various aircraft that came into and out of storage at the site. Beaufighters were also held at Brockton, as were many FAA aircraft such as Grumman Wildcats. The site gradually became inactive as the requirement for large-scale storage diminished, and by 1945 Brockton was abandoned completely. After having quickly returned to agricultural use, virtually nothing now remains of the RAF airfield, apart from the former watch office, which has been rebuilt as a privately owned bungalow. A concrete stop butt still exists, as do a few other remnants, but only the most careful scrutiny will now reveal any evidence of the RAF's wartime presence here.

> *Runways:* unknown (grass field). *Hangars:* Robin (2). *Hardstandings:* 0. *Accommodation:* RAF; N/A.

BURNASTON, Derbyshire

Grid ref SK292306, Lat 52:52:22N (52.87273) Lon 1:33:59W (-1.56628), 235ft asl. 4 miles SW of Derby adjacent to A38, N of A50

An aerial view of Burnaston, showing the airfield's simple layout and the civil flight shed, which was a familiar sight from the A38 road for decades. (via John Elliott)

Although Burnaston enjoyed a solid connection with military aviation, the site is generally regarded as civilian, having become the home of Derby's Municipal Airport, opening as such on 17 June 1939. By that date the airfield was already established, having first been allocated to the RAF's Volunteer Reserve Training Centre, which had come into being some nine months previously. No 30 Elementary & Reserve Training School was formed on 29 September 1938 (although the unit had been active at Burnaston for some time), operated by Air Schools Ltd, under the leadership of Captain N. Roy Harben DFC, who had also formed the fledgling Derby Aero Club. Shortly after the outbreak of the Second World War, No 30 Elementary Flying Training School was formed, embracing No 27 E&RFTS from nearby Tollerton.

Flying activity at Burnaston was continual throughout the war years, the four grass runways being kept extremely busy with Tiger Moths, Magisters, Hawker Harts and even Fairy Battles being common sites at the airfield, and it is recorded that some of the resident trainer aircraft were equipped with bogus bomb racks during 1940, presumably for either propaganda or counter-espionage purposes. More than 100 trainer aircraft were based at the airfield but the EFTS had an excellent safety record, although some accidents did occur, and four trainee pilots from the Glider Pilot Regiment are buried in a nearby churchyard. The airfield did receive some attention from the Luftwaffe during 1940 and on one occasion a number of incendiaries were dropped successfully, but no major damage to either aircraft or facilities was caused. A great deal of training was conducted on the ground (development of the famous Link Trainer was conducted at Burnaston), but flying activity was still very significant and in order to ease pressure on the often busy airfield a satellite airfield was opened at Battlestead Hill, followed by a second site at Abbots Bromley. The station's training commitments expanded still further in 1942 when trainee Army glider pilots from the Glider Pilot Regiment (part of the Airborne Division) began to arrive to receive basic flying training prior to embarking on many historic wartime glider assaults.

A rare image of No 30 EFTS Tiger Moths making a formation flypast over Burnaston some time in the 1940s. (via John Elliott)

As the Second World War came to an end, training requirements began to dwindle, and by 1953 the RAF's tenure at Burnaston had ended, the station formally closing on 21 July when the last resident unit – No 3 BFTS – departed. By this stage the airfield had already become re-established as a site for civilian flying, with Derby Aviation Ltd having started charter flights during the middle of 1949. Initially the company operated a former C-47 glider tug, which was subsequently joined by KN628, the C-47 that had been used by Field Marshall Montgomery. By 1960 the company's operations had expanded considerably, with more than 35,000 passengers and serving destinations such as Glasgow, Belfast, Isle of Man, Dublin and the Channel Islands. However, the increased activity was rather more than could be handled by a relatively small grass airfield, and although Rapides, Doves and even DC-3s were relatively common sights, the acquisition of DC-4M Argonauts meant that only unloaded flights could be made from the airfield and passengers had to embark at Birmingham. Operations at Burnaston continued for a while until Derby Airways moved to Castle Donington (eventually becoming British Midland Airways) and the airfield reverted to private flying. The last military aircraft at the airfield were probably the motley collection of Mosquito bombers that arrived (mostly from Silloth) in 1955 for refurbishment, prior to embarking on long ferry flights to Canada, where they joined Spartan Air Services.

A passing cyclist is treated to an intimate view of a Mosquito during the type's short stay at Burnaston in 1955, when a handful of aircraft were refurbished prior to delivery to Canada. (Author's collection)

Although most of the flying activity at Burnaston was provided by civil aircraft, a variety of military types were also seen here. Also often seen were former military aircraft under civilian ownership such as this Avro Anson G-AMDA. (Flight collection)

A near-derelict Mosquito TK655/G-AOSS, photographed at Burnaston in 1959. The aircraft was acquired by Roberta Cowell for a record-breaking flight to South America but those plans fell through and the aircraft was later scrapped at Burnaston. (Rod Simpson)

Burnaston's private flying continued for many years and was substantially rejuvenated when the Derby Aero Club and Flying School formed at Burnaston in 1987. However, Burnaston closed to flying in 1990 when the site was sold to car manufacturing giant Toyota in controversial circumstances (the Aero Club eventually relocated to a new site just two miles away near Hilton). Within just a couple of years all traces of the airfield and associated buildings had gone, a huge factory complex being built on the site, and from the busy A38 the once familiar view of the airfield and distinctive hangar is now permanently lost amongst the sprawling concrete jungle of Toyota's massive car-manufacturing facility.

Runways: E/W (1,170yd) grass, NE/SW (1,060yd) grass, SE/NW (1,050yd) grass, N/S (860yd) grass. *Hangars:* Bellman (1), Civil (6), Blister (3). *Hardstandings:* 0. *Accommodation:* RAF; N/A.

CALVELEY, Cheshire

Grid ref SJ596573, Lat 53:06:44N (53.11219) Lon 2:36:16W (-2.60436), 180ft asl. 4 miles NW of Nantwich on A51

This aerial view of the airfield at Calveley was captured shortly after the site was completed. Worthy of note are the various attempts at camouflage which have been applied across the airfield, including some fake hedgerows. (Phil Jarrett collection)

Developed during 1941 as a prospective fighter base, RAF Calveley was allocated to training operations by the time it opened on 14 March 1942, initially serving as a Relief Landing Ground for Ternhill. Miles Master trainers quickly became a familiar sight in the area, especially when an entire course of students was detached to the site to complete their training. During this period one aircraft (W8816) crashed on the airfield during a night training exercise at 03:40 on 16 October 1942. Pilot error was determined as the cause and although the aircraft was written off the two crew members sustained only injuries. No 5 (P)AFU left Calveley for good in May 1943, enabling No 17 (P)AFU to move away from its bases at Watton and Bodney, which, being in East Anglia, were unsuitable for training activities. With an impressive fleet of 174 Masters, Calveley was kept busy, and a satellite airfield was opened at Wrexham in order to ease pressure on the airfield circuit.

More changes took place in 1944 when the AFU departed and No 11 (P)AFU arrived from Shawbury, equipped with 130 Oxfords. Unusually, the unit's aircraft were all transferred on just one day (31 January), and training resumed the next day, with Wrexham being used as a satellite ground together with Cranage, which had also been allocated to the same role. Although concrete runways had been laid, the large number of aircraft also required accommodation, while on the ground and with only limited hangarage available, additional parking space was required and temporary metal tracking was laid in various areas around the airfield to act as hardstandings. Surprisingly, some of this material survives even to this day and can be found within the boundaries of the former airfield.

Sadly, No 11 (P)AFU's stay at Calveley was not without incident. On 12 March 1944 Oxford LX745 was on a night cross-country exercise, the briefed route described as Calveley-Wrexham-

Lichfield-Calveley at a height of 2,300 feet. The Oxford became airborne at 22:22 and headed on the initial short leg from just west of Nantwich to Wrexham. The wireless operator obtained a QDR bearing from the airfield while in the Wrexham area at 22:34 and was heard on radio by another crew at 23:15 trying to contact Calveley from the Lichfield area to obtain a QDM. These calls, although heard by other aircraft, were not received by the ground station and so went unanswered. Nothing further was heard of the crew or aircraft after this point. Five days later wreckage was discovered on the northern reaches of Shining Tor together with the bodies of the three crewmen, who had all been killed instantly when the aircraft impacted. The aircraft had been flying in a southerly direction and in a gentle turn to port when it struck the ground with its port wing before flying through a wall that runs along the Cheshire and Derbyshire boundary. The aircraft then began to disintegrate and was scattered across the moor.

The wireless operator's log was recovered from the wrecked aircraft and he had noted making calls with no specified times, but they were estimated to have stopped around 23:30 (using the log of the other aircraft that had heard calls as a guide). The subsequent Court of Inquiry concluded that the position of the aircraft had been miscalculated while flying in zero visibility with fluctuating wind speeds. It was thought that the drift caused by the weather was not compensated for as the gain in wind strength was unknown to the pilots. The crash occurred roughly at the time the aircraft would have been expected back at Calveley, so it was thought that the pilots had descended through the clouds on ETA over the base. The failure to hear or answer any radio calls was put down to the ground station working with another aircraft at the time when these calls were made, and it was subsequently recommended that crews should maintain regular contact with base, requesting bearings at regular intervals.

Training requirements shifted again in 1944 and the Oxfords were transferred to other AFUs; a small number of Masters arrived, these eventually being replaced or supplemented by fifty-eight Harvards, thirty-nine Hurricanes and four Ansons, supporting a pupil rotation of some 200 personnel, some of which would go to Typhoon or Tempest units, the rest transferring to fighter OTUs. By 1945 the training syllabus had been rationalised so that A and B Flights operated Harvards from Calveley, E, F, G and H Flights flew Harvards from Wrexham, and C and D Flights operated Hurricanes from Calveley. Training activities continued until 31 May when all flying was suspended and the busy airfield (which was often active for up to 22 hours each day) suddenly fell silent. The AFU disbanded on 21 June and the airfield was redesignated as the home of No 5 ACHU (Aircrew Holding Unit). Flying activity remained virtually nil until 22 October, when No 22 SFTS formed at the base with thirty Harvards, but its stay was relatively short and the unit departed for Ouston during May 1946.

Despite a considerable amount of repair and resurfacing work having been conducted on the airfield, all plans for its future use were abandoned and the station closed in October of that year. The last aircraft movement was some years later when a Spitfire Mk.19 from Woodvale's THUM Flight made an emergency landing here following an engine failure. This was an interesting coincidence, as the very first aircraft to land at the airfield had also been an emergency, when Anson K6265 had force-landed on 28 February 1941, before the airfield construction had even been completed.

Today the runways have gone save for small tracks that run along surviving portions, a large patch of trees occupying what was once the south-western threshold of the main runway. Parts of the perimeter tracks are still in evidence and many of the airfield buildings survive, including the remains of the control tower and the gun butts on the far side of the airfield. Likewise, the three T2 hangars are now refurbished and in agricultural use, although the seven Blister hangars appear to have gone. From the air, the airfield is still easily recognisable, but from the ground the site appears to have reverted to agricultural use, even though a great deal of the site remains in recognisable condition, hidden among the fields and foliage.

Runways: 040 (1,400yd x 50yd) concrete, 110 (1,300yd x 50yd) concrete, 170 (1,100yd x 50yd) concrete. *Hangars:* T1 (1), Blister (4). *Hardstandings:* 0. *Accommodation:* RAF: 96 Officers, 238 SNCOs, 777 ORs; WAAF: 6 Officers, 88 SNCOs, 248 ORs.

CAREW CHERITON, Dyfed

Grid ref SN061028, Lat 51:41:26N (51.69057) Lon 4:48:22W (-4.80613), 100ft asl. 4 miles NE of Pembroke on A477

Although this airfield is relatively unknown, Carew Cheriton enjoys a surprisingly varied and interesting history that dates back to 1915 when a Royal Naval Air Station was established at the site, operating various types of non-rigid airships. Originally known as Milton (or sometimes Pembroke), the airships were joined by Sopwith 1½ Strutters and DH6s in 1917. Two large iron-clad hangars were built on the site together with three smaller canvas hangars, and activity continued until March 1920, after which the site was largely abandoned. In 1938 construction of a new airfield on the site commenced, opening as RAF Carew Cheriton, the name having been chosen in order to avoid confusion with nearby Pembroke Dock, and Milton's radar site many miles away. The first unit to arrive was B Flight of No 1 Anti Aircraft Cooperation Unit, its Henley aircraft taking up residence during April 1943, tasked with the provision of towed targets for gunnery units at Aberporth, Towyn and Manorbier. As part of Coastal Command, the airfield became home to the Ansons of 217 Squadron, followed by 236, 248, 254 and 500 Squadrons, flying Blenheims and Beaufighters. They were joined by two Dutch units, Nos 320 and 321 Squadrons, equipped with Ansons and Hudsons.

The RAF's Coastal Command Development Unit spent a year in residence at Carew Cheriton, developing various systems to counter U-boats, and operating various aircraft including Whitley bombers. Its work included the development of radar equipment, the use of depth-charges both by day and night, and even the possibility of using Hudson aircraft as dive-bombers. Not surprisingly the airfield attracted the attention of the Luftwaffe, and a number of raids took place during 1940 and 1941, the most serious occurring on 1 October 1940 when a hangar and various technical site buildings were destroyed, together with a number of Ansons on the airfield. Even more serious in terms of casualties was a raid on 15 April 1941 that destroyed the station's sick bay, killing twelve airmen.

A Lockheed Hudson from No 320 Squadron at Carew Cheriton, one of two Dutch units based there during the Second World War. (via John Elliott)

Other units also operated from the airfield on a shorter-term basis, these including detachments of Beaufighters from Bircham Newton, Blenheims from Aldergrove and Hurricanes from Pembrey. Also No 19 Group's Communications Flight operated from Carew through most of the war, with a variety of aircraft including Lysanders. The station transferred to Technical Training Command in October 1942, and No 10 Radio School began operations, flying Oxfords and Ansons and conducting five-week training courses for wireless operators. Sadly, the unit's stay was marred by the fatal collision of two Oxfords at the intersection of two runways on 3 September 1943. Other incidents are also known to have taken place, one notable event being the unscheduled arrival of a Beaufighter, as described by its pilot, Frederick Lacy:

'Serving in A Flight of No 248 Squadron in 1943, I was tasked on 16 August to fly JM343 from our base at Predannack to Talbenny in Wales, where the squadron's B Flight was on detachment undertaking pilot gunnery training. The aircraft was fully armed with ammunition and all fuel tanks had been filled, totalling some 600 gallons, this being mandatory in wartime in case of a chance in-flight enemy encounter. It was a glorious hot summer's afternoon and after about 20 minutes of flight the aircraft's port engine shuddered to a halt and the blades of its propeller stopped in a coarse cruising flight condition, instead of continuing to rotate or windmill as was normally the case with engine failure. An attempt to restart the engine proved to be unsuccessful and, to my horror, the propeller also refused to feather. This meant that the propeller's paddle blades were face-on to the direction of flight, instead of edge-on, causing considerable drag. In no time the aircraft slowed down from its cruising speed of 180 knots to about 100 knots. I soon discovered, while immediately trying to gain height, that this speed was only a matter of a few knots above the heavily laden aircraft's stalling speed.

I explained the situation to my navigator and, because the mildest of turns was causing the aircraft to shudder on the point of stalling, we agreed to continue to fly ahead towards the airfield at Carew Cheriton, rather than try to return to Predannack. I was able to climb the aircraft very carefully to about 1,000 feet, with the starboard engine roaring flat out and becoming somewhat overheated by dint of our slow forward speed. Fearing that this engine might fail, I decided to attempt a straight-in approach to the north/south runway at Carew Cheriton as it slowly came into view. I selected undercarriage down but needed to lose height rapidly in order to maintain speed above the stall. Increased drag from the lowering undercarriage also began rapidly to consume all remaining height and, to avoid crashing short of the runway, I selected undercarriage up and attempted to go round again. We must have passed along the entire runway about 100 feet up, but as the undercarriage was slow to retract – driven only by the starboard engine's hydraulic pump – the aircraft suddenly became inexorably committed landwards. I aimed towards a field straight ahead and the aircraft landed on its belly and slithered along the ground. Unfortunately, a rural electricity distribution line was in its path and a collision of the port wing with one of the line's wooden poles caused the aircraft to swing sharply left and go sideways through a hedge, over a minor road and through its far hedge into another field, where it came to rest – on fire.

An accident investigation of the aircraft wreckage later discovered the remains of a German cannon shell inside the propeller reduction gear housing of the port engine. How this shell had got into this conical metal covering at the propeller centre, without being subsequently detected, has always been a mystery to me. It had obviously done so during a previous flight in combat off the French Biscay coast when the windscreen was also smashed by a cannon shell. The pilot on that occasion flew the aircraft home safely and my subsequent foreshortened flight was in the nature of a test flight after the fitting of a replacement windscreen. Presumably the offending cannon shell became molten after some 20 minutes of the final flight, then it eventually jammed the intermeshing gears for the propeller blades in such a way as to prevent them from continuing to rotate or from being feathered to reduce drag. In other words, the propeller suddenly seized solid.'

Thankfully, such hair-raising incidents were rare. No 4 APC left in December 1943 after a stay of only a year, a detachment of Martinets arriving to maintain target-towing facilities for the Manorbier range. The station finally closed on 24 November 1945 and remained abandoned for many years. Today most of the airfield's buildings have gone, although the very unusual control tower has survived and is now the subject of a community restoration project. The runways have remained largely intact, the two southern thresholds now being bases for industrial complexes, while the small eastern runway is the foundation of a large caravan site. Go-karting takes place in the centre of what was once the main runway, so the whole site remains accessible from the adjacent A477 road.

This 1946 image of the airfield site at Carew Cheriton clearly illustrates that flying activities had effectively ended by this date – the cross markings on each runway indicating their non-functional status. (Phil Jarrett collection)

An unusual aerial view of Carew Cheriton taken from a passing Sunderland in 1945. (via Spencer Adcott)

Runways: 300 (1,040yd x 50yd) concrete with tar and bitumen, 050 (965yd x 50yd) concrete with tar and bitumen, 340 (765yd x 50yd) concrete with tar and bitumen. *Hangars:* Bellman (2), Bessoneau (2). *Hardstandings:* 0. *Accommodation:* RAF: 74 Officers, 19 SNCOs, 1,019 ORs; WAAF: 4 Officers, 0 SNCOs, 0 ORs.

CASTLE BROMWICH, West Midlands

Grid ref SP136909, Lat 52:31:00N (52.51669) Lon 1:48:03W (-1.8009), 270ft asl. 4 miles ENE of Birmingham, E of A4040 and S of A38

Drivers racing along the M6 motorway north of Solihull might be forgiven for thinking that they are a long way from any links with Britain's aviation heritage. But just a few hundred yards off the motorway, some of the local roads reveal interesting names such as Farnborough Road, Cosford

Crescent and Tangmere Square, which suggest a link that isn't immediately obvious. However, seventy years ago these roads didn't exist, and they now lay across what was once one of the country's most important aviation sites – Castle Bromwich airfield.

Aviation first made an appearance at this site as early as 1909 when Berwood Playing Fields saw the assembly of a rudimentary flying machine built by local mechanic Louis Maxfield. The tentative success of his machine (which first flew – to an altitude of 50 feet – on 27 September) led to the development of what became Castle Bromwich Aerodrome, which became active in 1910, demonstration flights with a Bleriot Monoplane taking place the following year, performed by the distinguished RFC pilot B. C. Hucks. In 1914 the airfield was used as a refuelling base for the London to Manchester Air Race, and civilian activity continued until the outbreak of the First World War, when the site was taken over by the War Office.

The first squadron to be based at Castle Bromwich was No 10 Squadron of the Royal Flying Corps, primarily tasked with the training of the many staff of other squadrons based in France. The training aircraft used at the time were Maurice Farmans, their pilots being accommodated in tents at the edge of the runway, the mess area also being little more than a large marquee. This less-than-satisfactory situation soon changed and the personnel were transferred to Erdington and the jockeys' quarters at the nearby racecourse. With the numbers of personnel increasing all the time, Old Hall Farmhouse was used as an officers' mess, new rooms were built and a line of huts were erected as billets for the remaining staff.

No 5 Reserve Aeroplane Squadron was next to form here followed by No 19 Squadron RFC on 1 September 1915. BE2cs and Caudron GIIIs became common to the area, followed by RE7s when No 55 Squadron formed during April 1916. A succession of RFC units were formed at the station, including Nos 38, 28, 34, 67, 54 and 74 Squadrons. The last to leave was No 54, its aircraft departing in July 1918. By this stage an Airfield Acceptance Park had been established for the testing of locally produced HP 0/400s and SE5s. Commercial development continued; in August 1919 the Air Board acquired the site for development into an airport, and the British Air Transport Company began a London-Birmingham service in September of that year.

Military activity resumed when No 605 Squadron Royal Auxiliary Air Force was established with DH9As in October 1926, Wapitis arriving the following year as replacements. Hawker Harts replaced the Wapitis in 1934 and these were later replaced by Hawker Hinds in 1936. By this stage the airfield had become a very active airport, but the military future of the site had not been overlooked and a new hangar was constructed together with a new RAF headquarters building. Combined civilian and military activity continued in harmony as Lord Nuffield began development of a massive aircraft factory across the Chester Road, adjacent to the airfield. The RAuxAF Squadron (which re-equipped with Gladiators) departed for Tangmere at the beginning of the Second World War and, with nearby Elmdon having been opened, much of the civilian flying had already started to shift to what would become Birmingham International Airport, leaving Castle Bromwich largely inactive. New units did arrive (14 EFTS, 7 AACU and a detachment from No 116 Squadron), although their stay was brief.

The immediate future of the airfield was directly linked to the adjacent factory, and production of Spitfires began there in 1939. Ultimately almost 12,000 Spitfires were manufactured at Castle Bromwich, and if any site can truly claim to be the home of the Spitfire, then this must be the place. The first aircraft to be delivered to the RAF was P7280, which left the airfield on 27 June 1940, and production continued throughout the war, together with the manufacture of Seafires and Lancasters. Test pilot Alex Henshaw (famous for his ability to barrel-roll Lancasters) performed countless test flights from the airfield, and Wellington bombers were also repaired at the factory site.

When the war ended, aircraft production also ceased quite abruptly and Castle Bromwich was reassigned to training operations, No 5 RFS operating Tiger Moths and Ansons, eventually re-equipping with Chipmunks before disbanding on 20 June 1954. By this stage the airfield was relatively inactive, with only 5 RFS, 3606 Fighter Control Unit and No 48 Gliding School (ATC) in residence. By 1958 these units had also left and the station closed on 1 April, after which all flying from the site ended for good. For many years the area remained abandoned, but the huge factory site ultimately became the home of Jaguar Cars, while the airfield disappeared under a new housing estate.

This tranquil 1939 image illustrates a gaggle of Moths assembled in front of one of Castle Bromwich's hangars. In the months to come the relatively peaceful site became one of Britain's most active and vital sites of wartime aircraft production. (AirTeamImages.com)

Spitfires pictured at Castle Bromwich after completion, prior to delivery to the Royal Air Force. (via Dan Hale)

The sprawling Castle Bromwich factory pictured in the early 1940s. (Author's collection)

A Spitfire gets airborne on a test flight at Castle Bromwich; the factory flight sheds are visible in the background. (via Dan Hale)

A gaggle of Chipmunks from No 5 RFS pictured on a training sortie from Castle Bromwich. (via Dan Hale)

Artist David Warrington (responsible for the excellent 'Merlin over the Midlands' painting) recalls Castle Bromwich's wartime days succinctly:

'The Castle Bromwich Aircraft Factory was one of the largest and best-equipped facilities of its kind when erected at a cost of over £4,000,000 between 1938 and 1940. The giant shadow factory was part of Britain's belated efforts to prepare for an air war, and would enable mass-production of the fighters initially designed and built on the South Coast by Supermarine, a subsidiary of the Vickers organisation. The desperate evacuation of Dunkirk was already complete, and what became known as the Battle of Britain about to begin – and not one Spitfire had left the factory at Castle Bromwich. Vickers test pilot Alex Henshaw had been asked to fly the first off the production line and, when it was finally ready in June, he recalled in his book *Sigh For a Merlin* that this was an opportunity to raise diminished morale at the factory, at the same time as showing the performance and ability of the Spitfire. In the brand-new aircraft he executed one of the most precise and breathtaking aerobatic performances in front of the assembled workers. My Dad recalled how he would watch from the perimeter fence as new Spitfires were flight-tested from the Castle Bromwich airfield, and he was sure when it was Henshaw at the controls because "he shot up in a vertical climb off the ground like a bat out of hell".'

The factory was an obvious strategic bombing target, and workers could arrive at stations amid scenes of sickening destruction and loss of life at the end of a night shift.

A Spitfire Vb seen at Castle Bromwich, probably in 1942. (Phil Jarrett collection)

The main, low-rise bulk of the Spitfire factory at Castle Bromwich is partially hidden today by modern retail parks, and recent extensions include the reception and showroom of the present occupiers. It is hard to believe that the plant now "quietly" turning out Jaguars once employed 14,400 people and built what is one of the great icons of British history. I wonder if the Chairman of the Indian conglomerate Tata really appreciates what he bought when he acquired Jaguar Cars.'

A great deal of urban regeneration has taken place in this area over many years, and all remnants of the airfield's military history are now long gone, although the street names remain to remind the occasional visitor of Castle Bromwich's proud history. A rather more obvious reminder of the area's past is a huge Spitfire memorial that has been constructed on a roundabout on the Chester road, adjacent to the old airfield site. The locally named 'Spitfire Roundabout' is a quirky place to stop and ponder how very different British history might have been had it not been for Castle Bromwich.

Today the huge aircraft factories are gone, replaced by an equally extensive car production facility, while housing covers the former airfield. (Jaguar)

A University of Birmingham Tiger Moth pictured on a flight from Castle Bromwich. (University of Birmingham)

Runway: 050 (650yd x 50yd) concrete. *Hangars:* C Type (1), Wooden (3). *Hardstandings:* 0. *Accommodation:* RAF: 23 Officers, 26 SNCOs, 283 ORs; WAAF: 2 Officers, 3 SNCOs, 140 ORs.

CASTLE DONINGTON, Leicestershire

Grid ref SK459259, Lat 52:49:46N (52.82958) Lon 1:19:11W (-1.31982), 290ft asl. SE of Nottingham, W of M1 off A453

The sprawling expanse of East Midlands International Airport is a testament to the success of modern commercial aviation and has little connection with military history. However, the huge airport site is built upon the site of what was once RAF Castle Donington, which first opened on 1 January 1943 as a satellite airfield for nearby Wymeswold. Surveyed in 1941, with work commencing the following year, it was envisaged that the airfield would be assigned to bomber training activities and was suitably equipped with three standard concrete runways for this purpose. No 28 Operational Training Unit operated from the airfield with Wellingtons, Martinets and Masters, Hurricanes eventually replacing the latter two types (which were used for target-towing).

Betty Haywood was a young WAAF posted to Castle Donington, and she recalls the dark days of the Second World War there:

'From here they flew the Wellingtons – the original bombers in the UK. They had a seven-man crew, mostly of our tender age. The poor lads hadn't much chance against the well-organised Luftwaffe. The Luftwaffe were greatly respected for their pin-point bombing even though we were the recipients. I was the first WAAF at Castle Donington. There were 600 airmen building an aerodrome and I was the only qualified driver to start with. There were men drivers but they were doing other jobs. A few days later two more girls arrived and they became my best friends. At the dinner dances around Christmas and New Year the men were queuing up for a dance as the females were in such short supply. I was spoiled rotten! I then got engaged to my first love – Pilot Officer Eric Hawkins. He was a navigator and was shot down (all crew lost) two nights before our wedding. They were coming back from one of the first bombing raids over Italy. I think it was Turin. They went down over the Pyrenees. The Pope sent out people to search for the wreck and it was found 18 months later complete with the skeletons of the crew. I later had a letter from the Papal Office confirming the aeroplane number. By now I was driving a crew bus taking the lads out to the kites. The planes were now the mighty Lancasters. They flew to Germany almost every night – and returned in full what the German bombers had done to us at home. God Bless Bomber Command – we won the war. I am proud to have helped.'

Training for the Pathfinder Force was established here briefly, but attention shifted to transport operations and on 15 October 1944 the bomber OTU was replaced by No 108 OTU equipped with forty Dakota aircraft, the unit subsequently being retitled as No 1382 TCU. The unit's Dakotas were kept extremely busy flying transport routes across Europe and out to the Middle and Far East, but as the Second World War drew to a close the unit's commitments diminished and by 1946 most flying activity at Castle Donington had ended.

The station closed in September of that year and the site was left unused for some time, although it was soon identified as a possible site for a new airport when plans were made to develop a new facility to replace the existing airport at Burnaston, where only a small grass field was available.

Members of No 10 Operational Training Unit pose for the camera in front of one of the unit's Wellingtons at Castle Donington in October 1944. (via John Elliott)

Various airfield sites were considered as potential airports for the area, but Castle Donington's relative size, combined with its close proximity to the new M1 motorway that was then under construction, made it the obvious choice, and work on the airport began in 1964. The old 10/28 transport runway was developed (effectively rebuilt) into a single 5,850-foot civil runway, and adjacent parking and handling facilities were constructed, although most of the original RAF airfield layout remained intact. Further development took place in later years, the runway being extended still further and the main aprons and maintenance facilities growing to embrace all of the former RAF site.

Today virtually nothing remains of RAF Castle Donington, most of the airfield buildings having been demolished many years ago. Oddly, there was never a control tower to preserve, as the station relied on a mobile caravan! The most tangible relics of the former RAF station comprise of a few dispersals that survive on the northern perimeter of the airfield, close to the home of the East Midlands Aeropark where a fascinating collection of preserved aircraft is available for the public to admire; its most recent acquisition is a former RAF Nimrod. Among the busy comings and goings, occasional military aircraft visit, but the day-to-day activities at this once-busy RAF site are now in the shape of airliners.

Undoubtedly the best-known event to have taken place at this airfield was a tragic one. On 8 January 1989 a British Midland Boeing 737 crashed just short of Castle Donington's runway and ploughed into the embankment of the adjacent M1 motorway, resulting in the loss of forty-seven lives. Today all traces of the horrific incident are gone, but as one passes the runway approach lights that straddle the motorway it is not easy to forget that fateful night, and the sometimes cruel events that aviation can create.

> *Runways:* 281 (2,000yd x 50yd) concrete, 235 (1,400yd x 50yd) concrete, 336 (1,100yd x 50yd) concrete. *Hangars:* T2 (1), B1 (1). *Hardstandings:* Heavy Bomber (27). *Accommodation:* RAF: 60 Officers, 212 SNCOs, 644 ORs; WAAF: 2 Officers, 8 SNCOs, 180 ORs.

An aerial photograph of the tragic Kegworth disaster, illustrating Castle Donington's runway and its proximity to the M1 motorway. (Sheffield Newspapers)

A post-crash image of British Midland's 737 being prepared for removal from the M1 embankment. Today no traces of the crash remain and drivers on the M1 motorway are unaware of Castle Donington's proximity, save for a row of approach lights on the motorway embankment. (Sheffield Newspapers)

CHEDWORTH, Gloucestershire

Grid ref SP040126, Lat 51:48:45N (51.81254) Lon 1:56:35W (-1.94295), 826ft asl. 1 mile NW of Chedworth village, 8 miles N of Cirencester on White Way

Chedworth airfield is seen here during construction in 1941; the main runway's path across the east-west road is clearly visible. (via Neil Jedrzejewski)

Officially opened in April 1942, Chedworth was initially established as a satellite ground for nearby Aston Down's No 52 OTU, from where a variety of Spitfires and Masters came on a daily basis. However, by the end of the year AOC Fighter Command had instigated a training system for squadron commanders, a school being created at Chedworth as part of 52 OTU with half of the unit's aircraft being allocated to Chedworth. The first three-week course began in January 1943 and the system was developed into the Fighter Command School for Tactics, although after having been officially created, the unit quickly moved to Charmy Down just weeks later. On 19 February 1943 the station was reassigned to South Cerney's control and Oxfords from Nos 3 and 6 (P)AFUs regularly used the airfield through the summer until the station was reassigned to Honiley on 18 October.

Wellington bombers now became familiar in the airfield circuit, and when No 2 (Air Gunnery) Squadron was forced to move from Honiley it was re-established at Chedworth, joining the air gunnery element of No 60 OTU to become a combined 60/63 Gunnery Squadron, which remained at the airfield until January 1944. No 3 (P)AFU's Oxfords then began to use the airfield, followed by L-5 Sentinels from the US 9th AAF, after the 125th Liaison Squadron was formed here. However, the unit's stay was short and on 17 July 1944 the station was reassigned to Aston Down and P-51 Mustangs from No 3 TEU (later becoming No 55 OTU) arrived a few days later. The OTU's Mustangs were subsequently joined by Hawker Typhoons and the airfield remained active as a training base until 29 May 1945, at which stage flying activity ended and control was transferred to the Admiralty, although no naval flying was ever established at the site. For some time the airfield was retained as an Emergency and Relief Landing Ground for the Central Flying School (at Little Rissington), but no flying took place after 1945 and the site was eventually sold off and returned to agricultural use.

Today the remains of the airfield are easily accessible from Fields Road, which heads north-west out of Chedworth village. The road crosses the remains of the main runway and parts of the surface can still be seen on the northern side of the road. Two smaller roads lead off to the former perimeter tracks, one leading to the secondary runway (which has partially survived), the other passing a Blister hangar that is obscured by trees. A small number of airfield buildings remain and one dispersal remains adjacent to the site of a T2 hangar, which is now covered in trees. More remains can be found in the woodland in the north-western corner of the site where a great deal of the station's support structure was originally located, and if a look into the dark woods isn't creepy enough, perhaps this story from a local is:

> 'Back then when I was a Boy Scout our troop would often hike up to RAF Chedworth and meet up with the Chedworth Scouts for spring camps. Their scout hut was in the old station armoury so a lot of our adventures would be on, in and around the old airfield. We were

More than sixty years later, Chedworth is still remarkably intact and the runways are still visible, although the east-west road has been restored to its former position. (Neil Jedrzejewski)

Hidden in the adjacent woodland, some of Chedworth's buildings are still intact, including this remarkably well preserved Nissen hut. (Neil Jedrzejewski)

Buried in the encroaching foliage, one of Chedworth's air raid shelters still survives. (Neil Jedrzejewski)

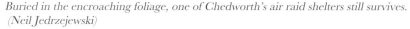

doing a map reading and compass exercise late one night and had to walk on a compass course across the airfield to a gate. We'd just passed where the two runways crossed and were heading over the grass area towards the perimeter track and hangars when the most bizarre thing happened. All three of us felt what can only be described as a wave of energy come at us, pass right under our feet and away. It knocked us off our feet and left us pretty confused for a while. Our first thought was that it must of been a small earthquake or something as it really did feel like something large and heavy moving quickly through the earth under us. When we got to the gate there were about twelve other people there waiting and we mentioned it but no one else felt anything. None of us thought it was anything supernatural but it was certainly very strange.

About six years after that, myself and a few of my ex-Scout mates had a bit of a reunion and decided to go camping one weekend and decided to bivvy on the airfield en route. For some really odd reason we decided to actually roll out our bedding and sleep on the actual runway that night. We pulled together all the old scrap wood that was lying around to make a fire and sat there about 9, just as it was getting dark, keeping warm and talking. Suddenly this enormous blast of air came right through us, blew our kit around and almost blew the fire out. It was only for a second and incredibly powerful. The air had been still all evening prior to this and was still all evening after, just that one massive gust. Again at the time we just thought it was bloody odd rather that ghostly, but many years after someone did comment that it was almost like downwash or prop-blast and that we were actually camped on a runway.'

Runways: 035 (1,400yd x 50yd) tarmac, 115 (1,300yd x 50yd) tarmac. *Hangars:* Blister (2). *Hardstandings:* 25. *Accommodation:* RAF: 21 Officers, 120 SNCOs, 465 ORs; WAAF: 1 Officer, 5 SNCOs, 60 ORs.

CHEPSTOW, Gwent

Grid ref ST528954, Lat 51:39:21N (51.65592) Lon 2:40:57W (-2.68242), 230ft asl. 2 miles N of Chepstow on A466

Famous as the home of a historic racecourse, few of the many thousands of race-goers would be aware that the same site was once littered with Spitfires. Established on 13 May 1941, the racecourse was designated as No 7 Satellite Landing Ground under the control of No 19 MU at RAF St Athan. Although largely inactive, the site did eventually become a temporary home for a large number of Spitfires and other types when No 38 MU at Llandow took over the airfield from 21 February 1942. Aircraft were stored at the site, which was maintained under heavy security provided by locally based Army and Home Guard units. A series of eleven camouflaged hides was constructed from netting, although these were later replaced by more effective hides that were cut into sections of the surrounding woodlands. Numbers of aircraft stored at Chepstow at any given time were modest, the largest total being less than fifty, and in May 1943 records note that some thirty-four Spitfires, Albemarles and Bostons were concealed at the site. Local man Neil Widdas recalls the wartime years at the airfield:

'The aircraft types that I well remember during this time are as follows. Firstly the Defiants. These were picketed on the far side opposite the Administration Offices, the ruins of which still exist by the middle lodge. Hawker Hurricanes were over in the area of the Old House. Supermarine Spitfires were not in residence at this time as the runway was considered too rough for their undercarriages. My Dad had been asked to check out the runway for these aircraft. This he did by driving his car, a 1938 Morris canvas-hooded two-seater, down the runway at its maximum speed. It broke a spring, so the runway was taboo for Spits. Having said this, a Spitfire did come in on one occasion. Dad had a good friend at the time, one Sqn Ldr Freeman, who was one of 'the Few'. He was flying in the area and had some form of engine trouble so was able to quickly land on the racecourse, although knowing of its dislike for the

Spit. He was going to have to prang anyway but this solution at least gave him a chance of a decent landing. The aircraft engine was repaired and it was Freeman who came to collect it.

Whitley Bombers were around at different times, as were Wellingtons. I seem to remember that these were parked across the road at Oakgrove. A section of the wall had been removed along the Monmouth Road and likewise the hedge opposite in order for them to cross the road. Bostons and Havocs were parked over by the house. Some of these were fitted with Turbin Lights. I believe that only three Bothas were ever at Chepstow. They were parked on the grass opposite the walled farmyard under purpose-produced camouflage netting. As with all other aircraft that remained for long periods, their engines were run from time to time. Although I was invited to get up in them while this was being done, I never did because I had a fear of them brought about by the explosion that their engines' Koffman starters gave. Three of the hush-hush high-altitude Wellington bombers were on the racecourse for a short period only. I well remember the arrival of these aircraft for at the time I was in the Lewis gun emplacement not far from the middle lodge.

With regard to Spitfire aircraft, there was a prang, not on the racecourse, but in a field alongside Penterry Lane. Again it was caused by engine failure. The plane was being flown by a young New Zealand pilot. After a pretty good belly-landing, he was just able to get out as the plane burst into flames. The aircraft, while at their various picketing points, were attached to picket blocks. The blocks were made of concrete with a cast-in ring on the top and about the size of a 25-gallon drum. Now at this time the slopes in front of Piercefield House were covered in dense bracken. One day a friend and I realised that these picket blocks would make a very spectacular sight rolling down the slope through the bracken. There happened to be a couple, unused at the time, right at the top of the slope, so we turned them over and off they went in a way even more spectacular than we could possibly imagine. Very recently I made a point of walking down from the front of the Old House to the railings bounding the woods; I did not expect to find anything but it was with almost a shock that lying fairly close to each other were the two picket blocks that we sent on their way sixty years ago. So if any visitors ever wonder … that is what they are!'

As the Second World War ended there was obviously no longer any requirement for aircraft storage, so the site was abandoned on 31 March, returning to more conventional horseracing activities. Today there are no traces of the military activity, although the proportions of the landing site are still maintained by the surrounding woodlands, which once contained so many valuable treasures.

Runways: Unknown (grass). *Hangars:* 0. *Hardstandings:* 0. *Accommodation:* RAF; N/A.

CHETWYND, Shropshire

Grid ref SJ727238, Lat 52:48:43N (52.81185) Lon 2:24:23W (-2.40643), 265ft asl. 2 miles NW of Newport off A41, N of Puleston village

Although a surprisingly small and unremarkable site, RAF Chetwynd has maintained its connection with military flying since the Second World War, and remains active some seventy years later. Completed in 1941, the grass site was assigned to No 5 SFTS, which was then based at nearby Ternhill. When runway construction work at that airfield began, the Miles Masters from E and F Flights were detached to Chetwynd, although flying was often disrupted by weather problems, the grass site being prone to flooding. In addition to normal flying training, various synthetic aids were also employed at the airfield, night-flying being represented by sodium flares, which, when seen through the student's shaded goggles, gave a suitable representation of night-time conditions. Flying continued throughout the war and, with a great deal of training taking place in the area, the site was retained post-1945 in order to continue this role while countless other comparable airfields were abandoned. Ternhill's No 5 SFTS eventually became No 6 Flying Training School and the Masters were replaced by Tiger Moths and Harvards, these eventually being exchanged for Prentices and Provosts.

Aerial view of a No 60 Squadron Griffin crew, busy conducting winch training at Chetwynd. (Author)

When No 6 FTS moved to Acklington, the Central Flying School's helicopters began to operate from the airfield, and through the 1960s and '70s it was regularly used by Skeeter, Sycamore, Sioux, Whirlwind and eventually Gazelle and Wessex crews. Today Chetwynd still survives as an active Relief Landing Ground for RAF Shawbury and helicopter crews regularly use it for handling and load-carrying practice, the black-painted Squirrel and Griffin helicopters being a common sight here on almost a daily basis. Other fixed-wing types are now rarely seen here, although RAF Hercules transports did occasionally use the airfield for rough field training until one hapless crew became firmly stuck in mud; since that unfortunate occurrence, no further landings have been attempted here by the weighty Hercules. No airfield buildings are visible apart from a control hut (and the concrete base of a rather older version), and permanent fixtures comprise only a few concrete hardstandings along the eastern perimeter of the airfield, but remarkably Chetwynd has survived and looks set to remain in business as part of Britain's military helicopter training system.

Only the concrete base of Chetwynd's original control tower/watch office remains. (Richard E. Flagg)

Chetwynd's rather temporary-looking control tower is the only building visible on the airfield. Although small, the tower is busy on most weekdays, handling training traffic from Shawbury. (Richard E. Flagg)

Runways: N/S (1,200yd) grass, E/W (1,150yd) grass. *Hangars:* Blister (7). *Hardstandings:* 0. *Accommodation:* RAF: 1 Officer, 4 SNCOs, 134 ORs.

CHURCH BROUGHTON, Derbyshire

Grid ref SK206323, Lat 52:53:16N (52.88791) Lon 1:41:40W (-1.69438), 225ft asl. 2 miles E of Sudbury on A50 and A511

Construction of this airfield commenced in 1941 and the station opened in August 1942 as a satellite for Lichfield's No 27 OTU, replacing Tatenhill. Wellingtons from B Flight quickly transferred here and conducted training flights from the airfield while No 1429 (Czech) Operational Training Flight (also flying Wellingtons) was also assigned to the airfield, together with No 93 Group's Instructors (Screened Pilots) Pool. Activity continued until 22 June 1945 without any further significant changes or events, after which the RAF's presence ended.

A Vickers Wellington at Church Broughton in 1942, awaiting its crew. (Author's collection)

However, Church Broughton has also played a very significant part in Britain's post-war aviation history as a temporary home for Rolls Royce, when its test-flying activities were moved here from Hucknall in 1944, Church Broughton's concrete runways being more suitable for test flying (Hucknall had yet to acquire a paved runway at this stage). Various aircraft operated from the airfield on engine test flights, including a Wellington engine test-bed, conspicuously painted with yellow undersides – something that caused a great deal of interest among the local inhabitants who were used to seeing Wellingtons in less conspicuous colours. The most significant of these trials conducted at Church Broughton was the development of the Trent turboprop engine, which was fitted to a Gloster Meteor (EE227) and flown for the first time from Church Broughton in September 1945. This historic event was the world's first flight of a turboprop-powered aircraft. The Meteor was intended only as a proof-of-concept aircraft, but the test programme (of some 100 hours) provided valuable data and the bizarre propeller-driven Meteor earned a place in aviation history, even though the airfield from which it operated is rarely credited with any connection to this important development.

The unique Trent turboprop-powered Meteor is seen during trials at Church Broughton. (Rolls Royce)

Avro Lancastrian VM733 was among the Rolls Royce test fleet based at Church Broughton, conducting trials with the Sapphire turbojet. (Rolls Royce)

When both the RAF and Rolls Royce vacated the airfield, only civilian glider flying took place in subsequent years until all activity ended and the entire site was finally abandoned. Today a considerable proportion of the airfield still survives, adjacent to the busy A55 road. The secondary runway is gone but parts of the main runway are intact, and major portions now provide the base for industrial and agricultural buildings, the site being dominated by a huge distribution shed close to the A50. The south-western corner of the airfield has been developed quite significantly, with this large industrial complex and associated access roads obliterating all traces of the runway and taxiways here. However, the west and north perimeter tracks are still present, together with a number of dispersals, airfield buildings (the control tower was demolished some years ago) and a hangar. The woodland to the west (Pennywaste Wood) was used as a camouflaged hide for aircraft during the war and traces of the dispersals and connecting tracks can still be seen in this area.

> *Runways:* 015 (1,400yd x 50yd) concrete and tarmac, 064 (1,900yd x 50yd) concrete and tarmac. *Hangars:* T2 (1), B1 (1). *Hardstandings:* Heavy Bomber (27). *Accommodation:* RAF: 109 Officers, 157 SNCOs, 1,008 ORs; WAAF: 2 Officers, 4 SNCOs, 150 ORs.

CLYFFE PYPARD, Wiltshire

Grid ref SU070759, Lat 51:28:57N (51.48253) Lon 1:54:01W (-1.90016), 660ft asl. 9 miles SW of Swindon, 1 mile S of Clyffe Pypard village

A small flying field was created at this site in 1941, No 29 EFTS being formed at the station on 8 September. Operated by Marshall's Flying School, the unit comprised up to forty officers, 440 airmen and a supporting staff of 200 civilians. The grass field was relatively modest with two 1,100-yard strips and a smaller third runway of 830 yards, although a concrete perimeter track was laid to link the strips, complete with turning circles placed every 600 yards. Frank Lund was one of countless servicemen posted to the base:

> 'Clyffe Pypard turned out to be a private flying training school (part of the Marshall's Flying School group) and was still maintained and managed by civilian staff and mechanics. The aircraft were the veteran twin-seat Tiger Moths and the pupils were Fleet Air Arm cadets. The

No 29 EFTS operated the faithful de Havilland Tiger Moth from Clyffe Pypard starting in September 1941 when the airfield first opened for flying. (Author's collection)

kitchen and mess staff were WAAFs so, all in all, it was a somewhat cosmopolitan set-up. It was a lovely station with a great camaraderie right across the board. The CO was the managing Director of Marshall's Flying Schools and held the rank of Wing Commander. Clyffe Pypard was about 8 miles south of Swindon, overlooking Wootton Bassett, and the local bus service was virtually non-existent. As well as being the senior navigation and meteorological instructor, I was allocated two other appointments, Education Officer and officer in charge of bicycles! Everyone wanted a service bicycle; some were old (probably almost First World War vintage) and many were new Hercules with three-speed Sturmey Archer gears. Being in charge I was able to take my choice, after the CO, and I had one of the new ones. We cycled everywhere; when going on leave we cycled the 8 miles to Swindon where an enterprising soul had taken over a small warehouse near the railway station where cycles could be safely left for a small fee during your absence (I think the charge was sixpence a day).'

The Tiger Moths and Magisters at the station were assigned to No 1 Course, taking students directly from No 7 ITW at Newquay and No 1 ITW at Duxford. Facilities at the station were few and the airfield's remote location was emphasised in January 1942 when heavy snow caused deep drifts to cover the airfield and cut it off from the main Swindon road.

In 1942 the station began to accept Army glider pilots for basic training and, although training activities were significant, few aircraft types other than the trusty Magister and Tiger Moths were seen, although on 18 October 1942 a Liberator made an emergency landing on the field after experiencing engine difficulties en route from Prestwick. The crash-landing was probably the most spectacular event to take place at the airfield, but the crew survived unscathed. Unfortunately two instructors were less fortunate when their aircraft crashed some miles away after having taken off in poor weather conditions; both were killed. Likewise, a Stirling Bomber crashed close to the airfield after suffering engine failure, although the crew bailed out and were recovered to the station.

The remains of Clyffe Pypard's northern taxiway, looking towards the former technical site. (Richard E. Flagg)

The 25-yard range at Clyffe Pypard, still standing among the weeds. (Richard E Flagg)

From November 1942 No 29 EFTS adopted Manningford and Alton Barnes as Emergency and Relief Landing Grounds respectively, enabling training operations to be increased; in addition to the RAF and Army pilots, some Navy personnel were also introduced. Activities continued beyond the wartime years and it wasn't until 11 October 1947 that the unit finally disbanded, the training commitment being transferred to Booker. The station then closed and quickly reverted to agricultural use.

Today the grass landing field shows no trace of any connections with aviation, although most of the concrete perimeter track is still intact, together with the unusual turning circles. A T2 hangar survives, the concrete bases of the many Blister hangars can still be found surrounding the site, and a pillbox lurks in woodland to the north, together with a scattering of small station buildings that are now used for agricultural storage or simply abandoned. Perched on a hill, the sprawling acres of RAF Lyneham can be seen in the distance.

Runways: N/S (1,100yd) grass, NE/SW (1,160yd) grass, E/W (1,333yd) grass, NW/ES (1,050yd) grass. *Hangars:* Bellman (4), Blister (15). *Hardstandings:* 0. *Accommodation:* RAF: 48 Officers, 98 SNCOs, 482 ORs.

CONDOVER, Shropshire

Grid ref SJ507042, Lat 52:38:01N (52.63371) Lon 2:43:44W (-2.72894), 420ft asl. 3 miles S of Shrewsbury, off A49, 2 miles SE of Condover village

Created as a satellite airfield for Atcham, Condover was equipped with three concrete runways, the first aircraft arriving before construction was complete when Atcham's Station Commander visited to inspect progress on 17 October 1941, flying a Miles Magister. However, by the time Condover's construction was completed, Atcham had been transferred to American control and it was decided that Condover could act as a satellite airfield for nearby RAF Shawbury, also acting as an RLG for Ternhill. On 5 August 1942, just before the station opened, Supermarine Spitfire Mark Vb AA928 of No 411(F) Squadron, RCAF, made a wheels-up crash-landing at Condover following a catastrophic engine failure. The formal RAF enquiry later noted:

'Category B damage in a flying accident on 5 August 1942, wheels-up landing following an engine failure. Failure of big-end bearings in No 2 and 5 pistons. Pilot unable to select wheels down until a suitable landing ground found and then undercarriage selector lever stuck and he had neither time nor height to free it. Successful recovery under difficult situation. Aircraft landed at Condover field in Shropshire, which was still under construction at the time.'

The station formally opened on 21 August 1942 and No 11 (Pilot) Advanced Flying Unit arrived from Bridleway Gate shortly afterwards with a fleet of Oxfords. When the unit moved to Calveley the station was assigned to Ternhill, Miles Masters from No 5 (P)AFU arriving thereafter. Flying activities were suspended in the summer of 1944 while the runways were resurfaced, the resident aircraft moving to Atcham and Bratton for some weeks. When flying resumed, the Masters were largely replaced by Harvards during 1945, and when the USAAF left Atcham it was decided that these aircraft would move there, enabling Condover to be reduced to Care and Maintenance status. Closure was postponed until mid-1945, however, as the Fleet Air Arm was actively seeking an aircraft storage site, but with only one T1 hangar and nine Blister hangars the site was hardly suitable, and by the end of 1945 the site had largely been abandoned, although it was not sold until 1960. Despite being a relatively large airfield, Condover was undoubtedly under-utilised and, apart from the regular training activities, other movements were confined to only occasional visitors and emergency diversions, mostly in the shape of Spitfires, Hurricanes, Stirlings and Lancasters.

Few significant events took place at this site, although a Pathfinder Force Lancaster made a wheels-up crash-landing on the airfield in November 1942 while night-flying was in progress; the aircraft was towed clear of the runway so that training could continue. Likewise, a Tiger Moth made a spectacular crash-landing here on 8 May 1945, the aircraft being written off (the pilot escaped with only minor injuries).

Although greatly modified, the former parachute store at Condover is still recognisable. (Richard E. Flagg)

Avro Lancaster RF5852 crashed on its way back to Condover on 10 September 1942. (via Dean Ashley)

During the latter part of the war a prisoner-of-war camp was established at the western end of the station and the former WAAF accommodation hutting used to house German prisoners, mostly shot-down and captured Luftwaffe airmen (the entrance to the camp site was at OS Map Ref SJ 4908 0423, with the main camp on the northern side of the road). The German prisoners were still housed there awaiting repatriation until early 1947. They were utilised as farm labourers in the local area and several remained in the Shrewsbury area after the war and settled in the UK.

Long abandoned, Condover's control tower is still standing, although its condition suggests that it may not survive for much longer. (Richard E. Flagg)

Today the airfield is mostly gone and the secondary runways have been removed, although small parts of the main runway survive. Virtually all of the perimeter track is still in situ, and the control tower still stands in good condition. Although few buildings remain and virtually all of the runway surfaces are gone, the wartime presence of a surprisingly large airfield is still evident although it is perhaps sad to note how a site with such potential was largely unused.

Runways: 180 (1,330yd x 50yd) concrete and wood chippings, 110 (1,380yd x 50yd) concrete and wood chippings, 050 (1,145yd x 50yd) concrete and wood chippings. *Hangars:* T1 (1), 65ft Blister (4), 69ft Blister (5). *Hardstandings:* Rectangular concrete (2). *Accommodation:* RAF: 67 Officers, 101 SNCOs, 493 ORs; WAAF: 8 Officers, 1 SNCOs, 89 ORs.

COSFORD, Shropshire

Grid ref SJ789044, Lat 52:38:15N (52.63754) Lon 2:18:43W (-2.31185), 260ft asl. 1 mile N of A464, 1 mile SW of A41, NW of Albrighton

Now part of the Royal Air Force Museum, Cosford is a familiar name to historians and enthusiasts both in the UK and beyond. Housing the RAF's largest collection of fascinating military aircraft, the station plays host to thousands of visitors every year, although few people pay much attention to the relatively small and quiet airfield that lies adjacent to the museum's display hangars. But despite being a small airfield, Cosford is in fact a large RAF station hosting a variety of units.

Construction at the site began in 1937 and No 2 School of Technical Training was established here on 15 July 1938. By the outbreak of the Second World War more than 3,500 trainee fitters, mechanics, riggers and armourers were undergoing instruction. No 9 Maintenance Unit was formed here on 15 March 1939 and countless aircraft were temporarily stored among the airfield's many hangars, including Spitfires, Battles, Lysanders, Blenheims, Ansons, Wellingtons and even a pair of Gauntlets, which were supplied to the Finnish Air Force. Additional Robin hangars were constructed in 1940, scattered around the airfield perimeter to house Spitfires, although these were subsequently dismantled.

A detachment of Masters from Ternhill arrived in February 1941 (their home base being waterlogged), although Cosford's grass field was barely an improvement, and it was not until the end of 1941 that construction of a 3,600-foot concrete runway was commenced, a Spitfire making a crash-landing on it before it was finally completed in July 1942. Just a week later the first of many Horsa gliders was successfully towed into the air (by a Halifax) from the small runway, followed by many Hotspurs in subsequent weeks, towed by Lysanders. A Tug and Glider Flight was formed in April 1942 to handle the ferrying flights and testing operations, which were often intensive; some sixty Horsas were delivered in just one month during 1943. In order to handle the many Spitfire deliveries, No 12 Ferry Pilots Pool was formed in July 1941 as a branch of its main site at Castle Bromwich, eventually becoming an independent unit and the first all-woman ferry pool within the ATA.

When the war ended, activity dropped significantly and attention turned to the scrapping of many surplus airframes, particularly the Horsa and Hadrian gliders that were still stored on the airfield. No 9 MU disbanded in 1959 to be replaced by No 236 MU, which itself disbanded in 1966, but No 2 SoTT remained active together with the RAF Hospital, which had been established during 1940 and remained in use until 1977. The RAF School of Photography arrived in 1963 and the RAF School of Physical Training arrived in 1977. As No 1 SoTT at Halton wound down, responsibilities shifted to Cosford and the station eventually became the RAF's main base for technical training, joined in 1999 by No 1 Radio School from Locking. Today these units remain in business, albeit under different names and structures.

The Defence College of Aeronautical Engineering (DCAE) now embraces technical training, and the huge C Type hangars contain a fascinating collection of former operational aircraft that are now used for ground instruction, including a large fleet of Jaguars that arrived by air when the type was withdrawn from operational service. Out on the airfield, former 6 FTS Dominies can often be seen, sometimes moving under their own power, resplendent in their former Training Command colours. Flying activities are largely confined to the Tutor aircraft operated by the University of Birmingham Air Squadron (and No 8 AEF) and the gliders flown by 633 Volunteer Gliding School, together with various civil aircraft (including those operated by the Cosford Flying Club), although the West Midlands Air Ambulance can often be seen parked next to the unique Fort-type control tower that has survived since the Second World War and is still used on a daily basis. The many Lamella, B1 and Bellman hangars littered around the airfield's perimeter also remain intact, and the small runway occasionally provides an opportunity for aircraft destined for the RAF Museum's collection to arrive intact; even the huge Belfast freighter made a safe arrival here before being placed on display.

Since the war an astonishing variety of aircraft have safely landed at Cosford, a Flight of Varsities being based here briefly, and even Shackletons often making practice approaches. Other aircraft to have landed at Cosford include the Tornado, VC10, Hercules, Harrier, Canberra,

This image illustrates the main technical and admin site at RAF Cosford and the sprawling complex of buildings, many of which still survive today. (RAF Cosford)

Hunter, Vulcan, Hastings and many more, and the last airworthy Varsity made its final landing here. With some of the former SoTT hangars now providing accommodation for the large and impressive museum collection (including the magnificent TSR2 XR220), a huge purpose-built display hall now dominates the site; this is the Cold War Museum, housing a thrilling collection of post-war aircraft ranging from examples of all three V-Bomber types, through to the Belfast, Hastings, York and American F-111.

B1 hangars at Cosford, now in use as museum display halls as part of the Royal Air Force Museum. (Richard E. Flagg)

Hangar No 4 at Cosford is a D Type, and is still in use as part of the station's technical training activities, with one of the resident Jaguars visible outside. (Richard E. Flagg)

Cosford Station Flight Chipmunks fly over the station and airfield complex. A Vulcan B1 and Victor B1 can be seen adjacent to Cosford's familiar railway station, and a light aircraft can also be seen on the nearby sports pitch. (via John Elliott)

Cosford's vintage watch office, still in use every day as a modern control tower. (Richard E. Flagg)

As if the large museum facility wasn't enough to entertain any enthusiast, Cosford is now the home to an annual air show, which attracts a huge audience from around the country. In 2009 (when Vulcan XH558 made a flying appearance) the show's capacity was exceeded and countless visitors were turned away, such was the popularity of the event. The future of RAF Cosford as a military site is certainly secure, although the RAF's presence may soon diminish, as Cosford has announced:

'The formation of federated Defence Training Colleges, such as the DCAE, was and is an important step in the migration to a partnered solution for Defence Training. On 17 January 2007 the Secretary of State for Defence, as part of a broad statement about the whole of the DTR, announced that a PPP contract route had been chosen to take forward Phase Two (generic trade training) within the UK's Armed Forces. Metrix Consortium was selected as the Preferred Bidder for Package One and Two. Subsequently, it was decided that Package One training streams would, subject to final ministerial approval, migrate to the Metrix-proposed Defence Training College at MoD St Athan in South Wales. That is the situation at present, with the following key milestones in position: Financial Closure Autumn 2010, Start of Construction Autumn 2010, Service Commencement Date/Vesting Day Spring 2011, New Service Commencement date 2014-2015. Thus there is no anticipated move from Cosford to St Athan for DCAE and No 1 RS staff and trainees before 2014-15 at the earliest. For those other training schools, headquarters and units at present at Cosford, decisions have yet to be made about their future location. RAF Cosford remains the preferred estate solution for 102 Logistics Brigade on its return from Germany. The Brigade will move to Cosford when the DCAE and No 1 RS have migrated to St Athan. Given the strong likelihood that the DCAE would migrate to St Athan (ie a tri-Service AE college would not eventually be built at Cosford) the decision was taken in early 2009 to resume calling the site RAF Cosford.'

Although RAF Cosford is still an active site, flying activities have dwindled considerably over the past couple of decades. Most of the station's flying activity is now conducted by Tutor trainer aircraft which regularly buzz around the airfield circuit, particularly at weekends. (Author's collection)

Thus it seems that the RAF's long association with this site will continue, but in a much smaller capacity (chiefly through the UAS and Museum). But it seems certain that the station will survive.

> *Runway:* 073 (1,200yd x 50yd) asphalt. *Hangars:* Various (storage and maintenance types) (38). *Hardstandings:* 0. *Accommodation:* RAF: 1,023 Officers, 300 SNCOs, 7,591 ORs; WAAF: 91 Officers, 25 SNCOs, 787 ORs.

CRANAGE, Cheshire

Grid ref SJ734694, Lat 53:13:18N (53.22168) Lon 2:23:54W (-2.39845), 150ft asl. N of Byley village on B5081

Constructed as a grass landing field, RAF Cranage was created as a home for No 2 School of Air Navigation, which was formed there on 21 October 1940, equipped with Ansons. The unit was subsequently renamed as the Central Navigation School, eventually operating a total of fifty-eight Ansons, later supplemented by Wellingtons. The airfield's strategic position close to Merseyside prompted the arrival of fighter aircraft that could support the defence of Liverpool and Manchester, once the attention of the Luftwaffe turned towards them. On 18 December 1940 No 96 Squadron was formed at Cranage, flying Hurricanes, although its unsuitability for night defence led to the introduction of Defiants some weeks later. Eventually, A Flight was detached to Squires Gate at Blackpool while B Flight remained at Cranage, taking up residence in a dispersal area hidden in woodland that lined part of the airfield boundary.

Hangar facilities were somewhat unusual, with eight Bellman hangars being assembled in two parallel rows of four along the northern perimeter, adjacent to fairly rudimentary technical and domestic buildings. Plans to build fighter pens were never realised, nor were pleas to construct concrete runways, although American steel planking was eventually laid in order to give the station a better all-weather capability. By mid-1941 No 96 Squadron was operational with both the Defiant and Hurricane, and Heinkel He 111s and Ju 88s were becoming regular targets for the unit's pilots, who scored a number of victories in the skies over Cheshire and Merseyside. As 1941 progressed the Luftwaffe's presence dwindled markedly until most of 96 Squadron's patrols proved fruitless. Many were extended to cover the West Midlands, with aircraft detached to Ternhill and High Ercall when necessary, but on 21 October the squadron moved en masse to Wrexham, leaving No 2 SAN in isolation at Cranage.

After being renamed as the CNS, the arrival of some Wellingtons led to the possibility of Halifaxes and Lancasters also being allocated to the unit, but the facilities at Cranage were barely capable of supporting the existing aircraft types, and in order to operate larger and heavier aircraft the CNS was moved to Shawbury where concrete runways, large hangars and permanent accommodation was available. In exchange, No 11 (P)AFU moved out from Shawbury to Calveley, adopting Cranage as a satellite field, although the unit's aircraft were also repaired and maintained at the station when necessary. The station came under the control of No 90 ITW (a ground unit) by May 1944, and the USAAF's 14th Liaison Squadron arrived with Stinson L5 aircraft, before leaving again on 29 June. No 90 ITW disbanded on 28 October, returning the station to the control of 11 (P)AFU, but as the unit began to standardise on single-engined aircraft it proved practical to undertake all servicing at Calveley, so Cranage was transferred to No 12 (P)AFU as a satellite field for that unit's Beauforts and Blenheims. No 11 (P)AFU's Beam Approach Training Flight (which had remained as a lodger unit since 1942 with Oxfords) finally disbanded on 1 June 1945.

Operational and training activity at Cranage ended by mid-1945, but the proximity of a Vickers-Armstrong shadow factory at nearby Byley enabled aircraft to be completed at the factory before being towed to Cranage for delivery by air. The factory was later taken over by the Ministry of Supply and various airframes were stored at nearby Cranage until the mid-1950s, including a Cierva Air Horse helicopter and an Avro Tudor fuselage. The last flying unit to use the airfield was No 190 Gliding School, which arrived in May 1945 and left two years later. When a USAAF support (storage) unit departed in 1957, followed by the Ministry of Supply the following year, Cranage was abandoned.

Today the airfield is still vaguely recognisable, although the trees that once housed No 96 Squadron's Hurricanes and Defiants have mostly gone. The M6 motorway cuts along what was once the eastern boundary of the airfield, but traces of the RAF's presence survive, the winding perimeter track still being evident, together with the access tracks around the hangar complex, which has long since been demolished and replaced by trees and shrubs. The short concrete lead-in to the old main (grass) runway has survived among the fields, and an industrial area has intruded into the northern corner of the site, but in all other respects Cranage remains visible as testament to the darks days when the Luftwaffe brought the Second World War into the skies of the North West. For the future, plans are being made to develop a huge gas storage facility on the site of the former airfield, pumping vast quantities of gas underground into a geological fault line. Local opposition might delay or defeat the plans (the prospect of sitting on so much potentially explosive power is naturally a worry to many people), but if it goes ahead it may well help to ensure that the existing remains of RAF Cranage survive still longer, as they are unlikely to be affected by the development and its presence here may well ensure that any more significant development of the site is deferred indefinitely.

Runways: 160 (1,090yd) steel matting, 230 (1,263yd) steel matting, 280 (1,283yd) steel matting. *Hangars:* Bellman (8), Blister (4). *Hardstandings:* 0. *Accommodation:* RAF: 6,216 Officers, 202 SNCOs, 899 ORs; WAAF: 8 Officers, 10 SNCOs, 368 ORs.

DALE, Dyfed

Grid ref SM799063, Lat 51:42:46N (51.71278) Lon 5:11:11W (-5.18649), 270ft asl. 5 miles W of Milford Haven on B4327

Perched on the very edge of Pembrokeshire's coastline, RAF Dale opened on 1 June 1942, designed as a satellite airfield for Talbenny. However, the station quickly became quite active and just two weeks later Wellingtons from No 304 Squadron arrived from Tiree, assigned to the support of No 311 Squadron (also operating Wellingtons) at Talbenny. Less than a month later the station scored its first victory against Germany when one of 304 Squadron's Wellington crews spotted a U-boat and laid depth-charges. Operational activity continued with anti-submarine, convoy patrols and even bombing raids over occupied France, although the squadron's losses and accidents were all ultimately due to mechanical failures or weather difficulties, which afflicted Dale quite frequently. Perhaps the most tragic accident took place on 11 August 1942 when Wellington HX384 failed to get safely airborne after attempting to take off on a secondary runway (the main runway into the wind being out of service), and the aircraft, together with its crew, went over the adjacent cliff edge into the sea, killing all on board.

A Wellington from No 304 Squadron taxies out at Dale, ready to embark on a mission out over the Atlantic. (Ken Bowman collection)

In March 1943 the squadron moved to Docking in Norfolk and a month later the Coastal Command Development Unit arrived from Tain with a varied fleet of aircraft, joined briefly by No 303 FTU, which deployed to the airfield while a lighting system was installed at Talbenny. The RAF relinquished control of the station on 5 September 1943 and the Fleet Air Arm arrived from Angle, Dale becoming HMS *Goldcrest*. The first unit to arrive was No 794 Squadron with a fleet of Defiants, Fulmars, Masters and Martinets, all assigned to the target facilities role, although the unit's stay was brief, lasting only a matter of weeks, after which their aircraft moved to Henstridge. However, in April 1944 No 762 Squadron arrived, equipped with Blenheims and Beaufighters, together with Mosquitoes and Wellingtons, which arrived later.

An atmospheric image of RNAS Dale looking out to sea as a Mosquito gets airborne while a second aircraft taxies to the runway. (Ken Bowman collection)

An aerial photograph of RNAS Dale taken in 1946, illustrating the complex layout of the airfield and the numerous hangars and dispersals scattered across the site. (Ken Bowman collection)

No 790 Naval Air Squadron Mosquitoes are seen at rest in front of one of Dale's hangars. (Ken Bowman collection)

Increasing use of larger multi-engine aircraft by the FAA required an airfield with good runways and Dale was an ideal site for operations. No 790 Squadron was established there on 30 August 1945 as a Fighter Direction School, operating in association with a ground training unit at nearby Kete. Fireflies and Ansons joined the growing numbers of resident aircraft when No 784 Squadron was established on 1 February 1946, assigned to night-fighter training. After disbanding again on 1 October 1946 it became B Flight of 790 Squadron, moving south to Culdrose, and on 13 December 1947 RNAS Dale was closed down.

Brian Jepson remembers his time at the base:

'Life at Dale was good; at least it was in the summer when the weather was often nice and you could enjoy the conditions. In winter the station was always cold, damp and often windy, and fog would often cover the whole area sometimes for days on end or so it seemed. It was miserable then, and you couldn't really get away from it as you were out in the middle of nowhere. As for the aircraft, I remember the Mosquitoes most of all as they seemed to be the most busy type when I was there. They used to take off and remain quite low usually, rumbling off over the fields and usually went off out to sea.'

Since then the airfield has been abandoned, although it remains preserved in remarkably good condition, considering that seventy years have passed since it was last used. The Pentad and smaller Mainhill hangars are long gone, although the concrete bases on which they stood are still evident. From the air, the layout of the hangar complex looks remarkably similar to the HAS sites found on many modern military airfields in the UK. The runways are intact and much of the technical site remains too, and a walk along the coastal path embraces a number of dispersals that are positioned precariously close to the cliff edges. Some of the land is gradually being reclaimed, but it seems likely that Dale will remain in recognisable form for many more years to come.

Runways: 040 (1,140yd x 50yd) tarmac, 110 (1,410yd x 50yd) tarmac, 160 (1,280yd x 50yd) tarmac. *Hangars:* 185ft x 110ft (5), 60ft x 84ft (9), storage (6). *Hardstandings:* Lare Aircraft Standings (11). *Accommodation:* RN: 50 Officers, 250 ORs; WRNS: 25 Officers, 171 ORs.

DARLEY MOOR, Derbyshire

Grid ref SK172420, Lat 52:58:31N (52.97521) Lon 1:44:39W (-1.74404), 580ft asl. 3 miles S of Ashbourne on A515

Constructed as a satellite airfield for nearby Ashbourne, RAF Darley Moor's first resident unit was a detachment from No 81 OTU, which stayed only briefly before moving to Whitchurch Heath in September 1942. The airfield then remained dormant until 12 June 1943 when it reopened for business and A Flight of No 42 OTU moved in, equipped with ten Ansons, nine Oxfords, two Martinets and a pair of Lysanders. Training activities were fairly routine although a demonstration was arranged for 13 August that informed and entertained both the unit's personnel and locals who were invited to the event. A pair of Blenheims laid a smoke screen across a representative Drop Zone (assisted by a Mile Master 'fighter'), after which three Whitleys flew over in a line-astern formation to drop containers in front of the assembled audience. Another demonstration was staged on 18 October involving Horsa gliders towed by Whitleys and Hotspur gliders towed my Masters.

Although somewhat unorthodox in appearance, the Armstrong Whitworth Whitley was respected by the countless air crews who flew the machine. Darley Moor was home to numerous Whitleys during the Second World War. (Ken Billingham collection)

The more regular training activities were often hampered by bad weather, which plagued both this airfield and Ashbourne just a few miles away. Although as a training base Darley Moor had no direct connection with operations, the students from the OTU progressed to 38 Group's Albemarle, Stirling and Halifax squadrons and many former personnel took part in the Normandy invasion. A rather more quirky connection with wartime conditions was the capture of an Italian prisoner of war who escaped from a local PoW camp and was caught on the airfield attempting to steal an aircraft in which he proposed to fly home to Italy.

No 42 OTU was absorbed into No 81 OTU in February 1945 and, with the aircraft having moved to Tilstock, the airfield's flying activities ended, the station officially closing on 10 February. Despite having had a relatively short and uneventful service history, Darley Moor is a large airfield and today the three runways remain intact, a large portion having now become a motorbike racing circuit. Some private flying (mostly connected with air sports) takes place from the southern portion of the airfield and virtually all of the perimeter track and dispersals can still be seen, together with the crumbling remains of the domestic and technical site, which can still be found in various areas on either side of the A515 road.

The former Link trainer building at Darley Moor now forms part of a private residence and is maintained in a reasonably good condition. (Richard E. Flagg)

Still standing at Darley Moor, the station's former lubricant and inflammables store. (Richard E. Flagg)

Runways: 200 (1,800yd x 50yd) concrete and wood chippings, 269 (1,400yd x 50yd) concrete and wood chippings, 319 (1,400yd x 50yd) concrete and wood chippings. *Hangars:* 0. *Hardstandings:* 125ft frying pan (27). *Accommodation:* RAF: 60 Officers, 267 SNCOs, 735 ORs; WAAF: 8 Officers, 40 SNCOs, 135 ORs.

DEFFORD, Worcestershire

Grid ref SO901441, Lat 52:05:44N (52.09548) Lon 2:08:44W (-2.14564), 63ft asl. 1 mile W of Besford village off A4101, E of M5

Looking across the site of the former RAF Defford, one might be forgiven for thinking that military aviation was still present there, with a fenced complex, aerial masts and 'golf ball' antennae dominating the centre of the airfield. But this complex is chiefly concerned with satellite communications although, as part of QinetiQ's many activities, it does at least suggest that Defford still retains a small pseudo-military connection even to this day.

The airfield first opened in September 1941 as a satellite to Pershore, although its development lagged behind that of the parent airfield and most equipment was fairly rudimentary, with no facilities for night-flying and only a mobile trailer unit to act as a control tower. The Wellington bomber crews had barely begun to become accustomed to the local area when the Ministry of Aircraft Production took over the site and No 23 OTU was obliged to abandon its satellite station. A recent raid on the French coast, which had enabled scientists to successfully capture parts of Germany's new Wurzburg radar, led to the conclusion that similar raids might be conducted against British facilities and, with the Telecommunications Research Establishment located in Swanage, it was clear that moving to a safer location would be a wise decision and Malvern was chosen as the TRE's new home, with its Telecommunications Flying Unit being allocated to Defford. The move was achieved quickly, so much so that most of the TFU's personnel were obliged to live in tents for some time, although a total of 2,500 personnel were eventually accommodated at the station.

A great deal of secret development and trials work was conducted at Defford, the TRE's aircraft fleet (which sometimes approached 100 aircraft in total) including Blenheims and Beaufighters engaged in AI radar development, radar-controlled tail turrets fitted to Lancasters and Wellingtons, and ASV

(Air-to-Surface Vessel) work utilising a Swordfish. The all-important H2S ground-mapping radar was created at Defford, with a variety of Halifax and Stirling bombers assigned to the programme. A USAAF Fortress (42-5793) was fitted with the radar at Defford in May 1943, and many more aircraft passed through the airfield in order to be similarly equipped, making Defford's parking facilities full to capacity – and beyond. Sadly, development of H2S also saw Defford experience its worst accident when Halifax V9977 crashed on 7 June 1942, killing all the crew and scientists on board.

Halifax bombers were regularly seen at Defford, engaged on radar trials, the best known temporary resident being V9977, which crashed during a trials flight on 7 June 1942. (via Ken Cooper)

The TRE's naval section also operated a variety of aircraft including Barracudas, Fireflies, Avengers and a Martlet, although the most unusual aircraft to be seen at Defford was probably DZ203, a Boeing 247D that was used for blind approach experiments before being returned to the US in June 1944 for fitment with an all-electric autopilot and automatic approach equipment, after which it returned to the TFU for further work. Many other vital projects emerged from Defford including the use of 'Window' radar decoy material; other less well-known programmes were also conducted, including the concept of displaying radar and flight information directly onto the windscreen of a Mosquito (DZ301) – effectively creating the forerunner of today's Head Up Display systems.

Countless other systems were developed and Defford undoubtedly played a vital part in the Allied successes of the Second World War. The TRE was suitably rewarded by being renamed as the Royal Radar Establishment after the end of the war, the TFU becoming the Radar Research Flying Unit in 1953. However, as even larger and heavier aircraft emerged (particularly the V-Force, which naturally required a great deal of associated radar development), Defford's runways were no longer able to cope; the RRFU moved to Pershore in 1957, and the airfield quickly fell silent.

One of the runways was used occasionally for private flying, but today the airfield is no longer active, and most of the site is abandoned with just small portions of the perimeter track surviving, together with various crumbing buildings scattered around the former technical and domestic sites. However, the runways have survived and QinetiQ maintain two fenced compounds in the centre of the airfield, laid across parts of two runways. The site now belongs to West Mercia Constabulary and is therefore unlikely to be developed, which means that the remains of Defford's very significant history look set to remain for the foreseeable future.

Slowly disappearing into the growing woodland at Defford, the former station mortuary and garage is still standing. (Richard E. Flagg)

As mentioned, the most notable accident in the history of the unit involved Halifax V9977, which crashed in 1942. In 2002, exactly sixty years later, a Royal Air Force Defford Memorial was unveiled by Sir Bernard Lovell on the village green of Defford. It commemorates those who lost their lives in accidents while carrying out scientific research. It reads: 'Dedicated to the memory of those Royal Air Force Air Crew, Scientists, Engineers and Civilian Personnel who lost their lives in the furtherance of Radar Research while flying with The Telecommunications Flying Unit (TFU) later the Radar Research Flying Unit (RRFU) from RAF Defford 1941-1957. Requiescant In Pace.'

> *Runways:* 216 (2,000yd x 50yd) asphalt, 284 (1,400yd x 50yd) asphalt, 166 (1,350yd x 50yd) asphalt. *Hangars:* T2 (14-bay) (2), T2 (24-bay) (4), Blister (8). *Hardstandings:* 59. *Accommodation:* RAF: 110 Officers, 216 SNCOs, 1,738 ORs; WAAF: 11 Officers, 18 SNCOs, 434 ORs.

DOWN AMPNEY, Gloucestershire

Grid ref SU114964, Lat 51:40:02N (51.66712) Lon 1:50:08W (-1.83566), 265ft asl. 6 miles SE of Cirencester, NW of A419

Despite being active for less than three years, RAF Down Ampney enjoyed a busy and varied operational existence. The first personnel arrived from Broadwell on 7 February 1944 and the first aircraft touched down on 18 February, this being a Proctor flown by AOC 46 Group. The first unit to be based at the station was No 48 Squadron, which arrived ten days later, followed by No 271 Squadron after a further five days. Equipped with Dakotas and eventually a large fleet of Horsa gliders, the two squadrons arrived before much of the airfield infrastructure had been completed, and as the numbers of Dakotas and gliders began to swell it soon became clear that the airfield had insufficient dispersals and hardstandings on which to accommodate them.

No 91 SP arrived on 19 March and training exercises got under way immediately. In April, for example, a formation of thirty-five Dakotas flew a night navigational tour around the Cotswolds, and intensive glider-towing quickly became a common site in the local area. On 28 April no fewer

An aerial view of Down Ampney during construction in 1942. (via Neil Jedrzejewski)

that forty Dakotas got airborne from Down Ampney, each towing a Horsa and all airborne in just 27 minutes, although even this achievement was subsequently bettered. Of course, training was ultimately geared towards D-Day, and Down Ampney played a pivotal part in the event, delivering thirty-seven Horsas across the English Channel in Operation 'Mallard'. Casualty evacuation was also an important task for the two squadrons, and large numbers of casualties were brought directly back to Down Ampney for subsequent transfer to hospital, as recalled by airman Tom Greenwell:

'At its busiest there were Dakotas coming in and out of the aerodrome almost continually and there always seemed to be quite a large number of them out on the airfield. It was a busy time and the transfer of casualties just seemed to go on and on like it would never stop and for a while it was our main preoccupation to the exclusion of almost everything else. When the flights started to become less frequent it was a real relief as we all felt as if we'd seen the worst of it.'

By the end of June 869 casualties had been handled. Such was the huge task of caring for so many wounded people that HM Queen Mary made a visit to the station to meet personnel, talk to casualties and inspect 271 Squadron's KG419, which was presented on the airfield. By August more than 20,000 injured personnel had been evacuated to Down Ampney, but the situation was expected to get even worse with the risk of as many as 1,000 casualties being brought to the station in just one day – far more than Down Ampney's facilities could cope with. Broadwell and Blakehill were therefore brought in to share the task, additional support coming from Nos 24, 511 and 525 Squadrons, among others.

The legendary Douglas Dakota was by far the most common aircraft type to be seen operating from Down Ampney during the Second World War. Illustrated is a Royal Air Force example preparing to embark on a night mission. (Author's collection)

The next major operation was the Arnhem landings, and on 17 September a total of forty-nine Dakotas were each assigned to a Horsa glider, and thirty-nine of the aircraft were released over the Drop Zone, a second wave of fifty gliders being despatched the next day, followed by resupply flights, which continued through the month. Casualty evacuation flights continued with depressing regularity (HRH the Duchess of Kent visited Down Ampney in December in order to raise morale), and supply flights to France were also maintained, together with more specialised transport tasks such as the transfer of vital blood supplied to and from various bases in the area.

Dakota KG545 brings a casualty evacuation flight to Down Ampney in August 1944. (via Ron Clarke)

In 1945 the pace of the activities began to slow, the last major operation being the launch of sixty aircraft (from Gosfield) on 24 March, towing more Horsas into Europe for the Rhine crossing. In July the Dakotas from No 48 Squadron were progressively fitted with glider-towing snatch gear, and their departure was accompanied by the Dakotas of No 271 Squadron, which transferred to Odiham in August. However, Dakota operations continued, and Nos 435 and 436 Squadrons from the Royal Canadian Air Force arrived towards the end of the year, and maintained transport operations into and out of Europe until 1946, at which stage they too left Down Ampney, the last ten Dakotas leaving for Leeming on 22 April; the final aircraft to depart was KN256.

After this date the skies over Down Ampney fell silent and the airfield was swiftly returned to agricultural use. Today its layout is still very evident, the three runways still surviving in various areas, while tracks and trees denote the runway positions elsewhere. The dispersals that once housed countless Horsas and Dakotas are gone but, having mostly been replanted with trees, their

Down Ampney's runway 15/33 is now barely recognisable, forming part of the agricultural landscape. (Richard E. Flagg)

distinctive shapes are still unmistakable, especially if viewed from the air. The hangars and technical site are all long gone, just a few farming buildings littering the site. The road running east out of Down Ampney village cuts across the threshold of the two main runways and from this point is its possible to look across the rolling fields and picture the busy scene when the skies were filled with tugs and gliders bound for Europe.

At the southern end of the main runway a memorial has been erected, which reads: 'From this Airfield in 1944-5 Douglas Dakotas from 48 and 271 Squadrons RAF Transport Command carried the 1st and 6th Airborne Division units of the Air Despatch Regiment and Horsa gliders flown by the Glider Pilots regiment to Normandy, Arnhem and on the Crossing the Rhine Operations. We Will Remember Them.'

> *Runways:* 030 (2,000yd x 50yd) concrete, 090 (1,400yd x 50yd) concrete, 150 (1,400yd x 50yd) concrete. *Hangars:* T2 (2). *Hardstandings:* Loop (50). *Accommodation:* RAF: 249 Officers, 510 SNCOs, 1,386 ORs; WAAF: 12 Officers, 20 SNCOs, 252 ORs.

ELMDON, West Midlands

Grid ref SP177836, Lat 52:27:01N (52.45025) Lon 1:44:22W (-1.73953), 362ft asl. 7 miles ESE of Birmingham on A45

Birmingham International Airport is of course a very popular and busy regional facility that enjoys a long association with aviation going back to pre-war days, when the local Council first identified a site at Elmdon suitable for development into an airport. Construction began in June 1936 and almost

A rather poor-quality image taken over Elmdon during the airfield's first years of existence. The small site bears little resemblance to the major airport that now operates here. (via John Elliott)

A historic image of Elmdon's rather elaborate terminal building under construction. (Author's collection)

immediately the Air Ministry expressed an interest in establishing a Volunteer Reserve centre at the airfield once completed. The first aircraft to arrive at the site, however, was Dragonfly G-AEDH from Western Airways, on 1 May 1939. The Airport was officially opened by HRH the Duchess of Kent on 8 July of that year, the Volunteer Reserve School having duly arrived two months previously, as No 44 E&RFTS under No 53 Group. The component units amalgamated to form No 14 EFTS (as part of 51 Group) in September, and during the same month the training activities were interrupted by the arrival of No 99 Squadron's Wellington bombers, which were dispersed to Elmdon for a week.

After the unit departed, most of Elmdon's regular military activity was confined to the resident Tiger Moths, although the presence of No 27 MU (from October 1940 until November 1941) and No 48 Maintenance Unit (from February until October 1941) occasionally saw the arrival of aircraft from operational units. The more significant activity at Elmdon was the pseudo-military presence of numerous Lancaster and Stirling bombers, which were manufactured at the nearby Austin works at Longbridge, assembled at the Marston Green shadow factory and finally towed to Elmdon for test-flying and eventual delivery to the RAF.

When the Second World War ended the airfield was no longer of any interest to the Air Ministry; control was handed to the Ministry of Civil Aviation on 8 July 1946 and more regular civil flying was quickly re-established at the site. Connections with military flying were subsequently severed, although occasional appearances by military aircraft did still take place, with various types using the airport for practice approach flying or the collection and delivery of personnel and supplies.

Elmdon's runway 33 as seen from the viewpoint of an airliner captain. The crew of a wartime Wellington would now doubtless be unable to recognise the airfield and its surroundings. (Richard E. Flagg)

The modest proportions of the original airfield have long since gone, but the original concrete runways (both just over 4,000 feet in length and built in order to safely accommodate Lancaster and Stirling test flights) are still very much in evidence, the main runway having now been strengthened and doubled in length. A huge terminal facility has been constructed on the eastern side of the airfield, contrasting with the more modest and undoubtedly more interesting site of the original terminal to the south. The busy daily comings and goings of airliners, cargo aircraft and lighter types ensure that there is always something to see at Elmdon, but military visitors are now fairly rare, and among the parade of Airbus and Boeing customers it is difficult to imagine the lumbering Stirling bombers and tiny Tiger Moths that were once so common here.

> *Runways:* 060 (1,344yd x 50yd) concrete, 150 (1,363yd x 50yd) concrete. *Hangars:* Bellman (2), Civil (2), Blister (11). *Hardstandings:* Apron (1). *Accommodation:* RAF: 28 Officers, 61 SNCOs, 251 ORs.

FAIRFORD, Gloucestershire

Grid ref SU150982, Lat 51:40:59N (51.68299) Lon 1:47:00W (-1.78339), 260ft asl. Off A417, 2 miles S of Fairford village

Situated in the glorious Gloucestershire countryside, Fairford is of course a familiar name to aviation enthusiasts throughout the country and far beyond. As the annual home of the Royal International Air Tattoo, Fairford hosts what is undoubtedly the world's biggest and best air show, attracting predominantly military aircraft from across the globe. But Fairford also has a fascinating history that makes the airfield a site of great interest, regardless of its modern connections with air shows.

Authorisation for an airfield on this site was first obtained in 1943, as a potential base for USAAF transport and air observation aircraft, but when the station opened on 14 January 1944 it was assigned to RAF operations, and Stirlings from No 620 Squadron arrived from Leicester East during March of that year, joined just days later by more aircraft from No 190 Squadron. Horsa gliders then followed, these being towed by the Stirlings, and both aircraft types became a familiar sight in the skies around the Cotswolds. Sadly, not all of the station's activities proceeded without incident, and on 17 April Horsa LJ623 crashed into the airfield control tower, killing the pilot. Another catastrophic accident occurred near the airfield over Kempsford when two of the resident Stirlings (towing Horsas) collided in mid-air, killing the crews.

On 5 June 1944 a formation of forty-five Stirlings set off to Europe carrying paratroops as part of Operation 'Tonga', and on the following day thirty-six aircraft and glider combinations participated in Operation 'Mallard', the Normandy landing. The Arnhem landings saw another forty-three Horsas towed from Fairford, after which both of the resident squadrons flew regular supply flights to the area, seven of their aircraft being shot down by Luftwaffe fighters on 21 September. Nos 190 and 620 Squadrons departed for Great Dunmow during mid-October and Fairford became a satellite field for Keevil, where No 22 Heavy Glider Conversion Unit operated Albemarles, together with Horsa and Hadrian gliders. The unit moved to Blakehill Farm in June 1945 and Fairford then became a satellite for that airfield until 21 October, when it was placed under Care and Maintenance.

It wasn't until January of the following year that flying resumed when Nos 1529, 1556 and 1555 Radio Aids Training Flights operated from the base with a fleet of Oxfords, the latter unit staying for the longest period, until August 1947. When No 47 Squadron returned from Europe in September 1946, Fairford became the main airborne forces base, and Halifax aircraft became the main resident aircraft type, joined by aircraft from 113, 295 and 297 Squadrons; the base had become the home for twenty-five Halifaxes, five Hamilcars, one Oxford and one Tiger Moth by this stage. These units all departed towards the end of 1948 and at the end of that year the base was again placed under Care and Maintenance.

In June 1950 Fairford was reactivated, finally coming under the command of the USAF as had originally been intended, and when the base reopened on 1 July 1951 it had been transformed; the original bomber runways had been abandoned, and the main runway strengthened, widened and

The sight of the ungainly Hamilcar glider under tow was relatively routine in the skies over Fairford from 1946, when a small number of these aircraft were based there. (via John Elliott)

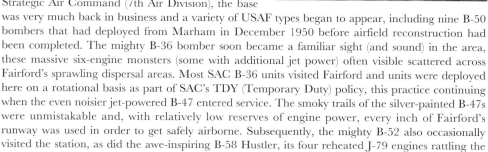

extended to an impressive 10,000 feet. Now part of Strategic Air Command (7th Air Division), the base was very much back in business and a variety of USAF types began to appear, including nine B-50 bombers that had deployed from Marham in December 1950 before airfield reconstruction had been completed. The mighty B-36 bomber soon became a familiar sight (and sound) in the area, these massive six-engine monsters (some with additional jet power) often visible scattered across Fairford's sprawling dispersal areas. Most SAC B-36 units visited Fairford and units were deployed here on a rotational basis as part of SAC's TDY (Temporary Duty) policy, this practice continuing when the even noisier jet-powered B-47 entered service. The smoky trails of the silver-painted B-47s were unmistakable and, with relatively low reserves of engine power, every inch of Fairford's runway was used in order to get safely airborne. Subsequently, the mighty B-52 also occasionally visited the station, as did the awe-inspiring B-58 Hustler, its four reheated J-79 engines rattling the windows of the picturesque village houses in nearby Fairford village.

When SAC ended its operations at Fairford, the RAF resumed control, with C Flight of the Central Flying School arriving in June 1964. From early 1965 until the following year, Fairford was the home of the Red Arrows, their scarlet-painted Gnats undoubtedly a welcome break from the rowdy presence of SAC's bombers. When nearby Brize Norton's runway was resurfaced, its VC10s and Belfasts operated from Fairford, and from February 1968 No 47 Squadron began Hercules operations from the base, joined by No 30 Squadron three months later. The sound of turboprops was occasionally interrupted by the roar of reheated Olympus engines when the station was selected as the testing base for Concorde development, and through the early 1970s the Concorde test fleet operated from here, the unique Canberra PR9 prototype (complete with long nose probe and dayglo paint) acting as a chase plane.

Concorde 002 arriving at Fairford on 9 April 1969. The same vantage point is now hugely popular with enthusiasts every July when Fairford stages the Royal International Air Tattoo. (John Graves)

An unusual aerial view of Fairford in 1969, shortly after Concorde 002's arrival at the base. The resident RAF Hercules transports are visible between the hangars. (John Graves)

The RAF's Hercules operations ended on 30 April 1971 and Fairford was redesignated as a Relief Landing Ground for Brize Norton, although Concorde operations continued until 1977. A year later the USAF was back, this time with KC-135 refuelling tankers, and over successive years various tanker units were assigned to the base either on a temporary or a longer-term basis. In 1986 Fairford supported KC-135 and KC-10 tankers, which were used as part of the bombing missions staged against Libya. In 1991 the base became a major part of the Gulf War, with many long-range bombing missions being staged from the there, the mighty B-52 having returned to Gloucestershire skies after an absence of nearly thirty years. Fairford supported similar missions during the second Gulf War, with numerous B-52, KC-135 and B-1B aircraft being assigned to the base for the duration of these conflicts. In subsequent years the USAF's presence has continued, various deployments and exercises taking place here, with the U-2 and even the B-2 operating from Fairford (a new hanger having been constructed specifically for B-2 operations).

Rather perversely, after a huge and expensive improvement programme had been completed in 2008, the USAF announced that it was to withdraw from Fairford by 2011 and, with the airfield closed for most of the year, its future looks set to be relatively peaceful, acting as a standby base that will be activated only occasionally for exercise periods. But Fairford will still remain the home of the Royal International Air Tattoo, and for just one weekend every year will be busier than any other military site in Europe, the tiny Cotswold lanes jammed full of cars as the enthusiasts gather at this, one of the country's most fascinating centres of aviation.

> *Runways:* 230 (2,000yd x 50yd) concrete and asphalt, 280 (1,400yd x 50yd) concrete and asphalt, 330 (1,400yd x 50yd) concrete and asphalt. *Hangars:* T2 (2). *Hardstandings:* Spectacle (52). *Accommodation:* RAF: 172 Officers, 648 SNCOs, 1,562 ORs; WAAF: 8 Officers, 6 SNCOs, 302 ORs.

FAIRWOOD COMMON, West Glamorgan

Grid ref SS566911, Lat 51:36:02N (51.60053) Lon 4:04:18W (-4.07164), 272ft asl. 4 miles W of Swansea on A4118

Created as a fighter station, Fairwood Common opened on 15 June 1941, No 79 Squadron arriving from Pembrey with Hurricanes just two days later. Beaufighters quickly followed when No 600 Squadron moved in, but their stay was short and their presence was replaced by No 317 Squadron from Colerne, flying Spitfires. A detachment of Lysanders also appeared at Fairwood, these providing air-to-surface radar cover for the area. 317 Squadron took part in a raid on Le Havre, providing fighter cover, and two enemy intercepts were credited to the squadron. In July 1941 the unit successfully intercepted a Ju 88 just 10 miles from the airfield and shot it down. A week later the squadron left Fairwood, and No 504 Squadron arrived on 21 July, its Spitfires playing a significant part in the attacks on Brest on the 24th of that month. No 79 Squadron also participated and remained at the station until December 1941, when No 125 Squadron arrived, by which stage Fairwood was an established Sector Station.

Nos 312 and 615 Squadrons were the next units to move in, both flying Hurricanes and Spitfires, and No 263 Squadron arrived in February 1942, equipped with Westland Whirlwinds. A Luftwaffe raid on Bath (26 April 1942) saw aircraft from 125 Squadron operating from Fairwood, and several enemy interceptions were achieved. A Ju 88 was shot down by a Beaufighter pilot from 125 Squadron and two Do 217s were successfully destroyed during another enemy raid.

Squadrons continued to rotate through the station providing convoy protection over the Irish Sea and fighter sweeps for the local area. Most operated Spitfires, although on 28 October 1942 No 536 Squadron arrived with Turbinlite Havocs. Mosquitoes first appeared in April 1943 when No 307 (Polish) Squadron was formed at the station, eventually making way for 264 Squadron, which flew defensive missions over Plymouth on 11 August. No 456 Squadron – also operating the Mosquito – arrived in November 1943, leaving for Ford in February of the following year. The departure of 68 Squadron in June 1944 saw the station shift from operational to training duties, a

Westland Whirlwinds were operated from Fairwood Common by No 263 Squadron for two months, from February 1942. They returned again during January 1944 for an Armament Practice camp. (via Neil Robinson)

role that it had first embraced in October 1943 when No 11 APC was formed here. A total of twenty-nine squadrons visited the APC, which had a specially built stretch of railway track constructed, complete with a driverless train, which enabled crews to practise the art of train-busting. No 18 APC also formed here in August 1944, but both units subsequently disbanded in July the following year after the last visiting unit (609 Squadron with Typhoons) departed. A detachment from No 595 Squadron was established early in 1945 for target-towing duties and a few weeks later the whole squadron moved in from Aberporth in order to be closer to the School of AA at Manorbier; however, with relatively poor domestic accommodation at Fairwood, the unit moved to Pembrey in October 1946 and the RAF's presence at the airfield ceased at the end of that year.

Another ten years passed before the RAF handed over the site to Swansea Corporation and construction of an airport for the local area began. Although relatively successful, with various airlines operating medium-sized airliners on charter and scheduled services, the airport subsequently down-sized; no scheduled services have operated there since 2004, and the airfield is

An aerial photograph of Fairwood Common in 1946. (MoD)

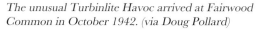

The unusual Turbinlite Havoc arrived at Fairwood Common in October 1942. (via Doug Pollard)

now mostly used for private flying. Although there are still plans to expand the airport's facilities in the future, local opposition suggests that any expansion might be modest, and it seems likely that the airfield will maintain its basic structure for the foreseeable structure.

The original runways are intact (the main and secondary ones still in use) and traces of dispersals, technical and domestic buildings are still to be found around the airfield's perimeter. Sadly, any connections with military aviation have long since departed, save for a Volunteer Gliding School, and the appearance of occasional 'warbirds'.

> *Runways:* 231 (1,650yd x 50yd) tarmac, 290 (1,350yd x 50yd) tarmac, 338 (1,350yd x 50yd) tarmac. *Hangars:* Bellman (3), Blister (8). *Hardstandings:* 24. *Accommodation:* RAF: 98 Officers, 206 SNCOs, 1,770 ORs; WAAF: 12 Officers, 8 SNCOs, 397 ORs.

HALFPENNY GREEN, Staffordshire

Grid ref SO824910, Lat 52:31:02N (52.51721) Lon 2:15:36W (-2.26001), 270ft asl. 3 miles SW of Wombourne

The less-than-popular Blackburn Botha arrived at Halfpenny Green during 1941. Its replacement by the Avro Anson was welcomed by air and ground crews alike. (via John Morley)

Situated literally at the junction of the Shropshire, Staffordshire and Worcestershire borders, Halfpenny Green originally opened in 1941 as RAF Bobbington, although the station's name was changed to Halfpenny Green on 1 September 1943 in order to avoid phonetic confusion with RAF Bovingdon in Hertfordshire, which was then being utilised by the USAAF. No 3 Air Observers Navigation School was formed here on 17 February 1941 but the unit's small fleet of Blackburn Bothas was slow to arrive thanks to bad weather that flooded parts of the airfield, leaving the Bothas at Cosford some miles away. By June a total of nineteen Bothas had arrived and training activities in the area soon became a common sight, although experience with the Botha proved to somewhat troublesome, the aircraft being heavy and under-powered.

The three runways at Halfpenny Green were adequate for most service aircraft but the AONS pilots had use of all the available runways, often swinging the aircraft's tailwheel onto the grass ahead of the threshold in order to squeeze every inch of take-off space from the runway. Needless to say, getting airborne at the other end was a matter of timing and skill, and the Bothas rarely gained little more than a few feet in altitude before lumbering away just above the surrounding fields, which were mercifully free of obstructions. When two accidents (both fatal) occurred on consecutive days, it was sufficient to render the Botha fleet grounded until Avro Ansons could be supplied as replacements; with limited parking space available, the station was hard pressed to accommodate the Ansons as they arrived until the forty-nine stored Bothas could be removed.

The AONS was renamed No 3 Air Observers School on 1 November, Marshall's of Cambridge assuming responsibility for maintenance of the unit's Ansons, and although tentative plans were made to move the unit nearer to the coast, no suitable airfield was available and the move never came. Training activities grew further and the AOS was renamed No 3 (O)AFU on 11 April 1942, but, despite the activity at the airfield, facilities were still surprisingly poor, most of the trainee observers being obliged to live under canvas until later in the year, when Nissen huts were assembled. Although Bellman hangars were constructed, the control tower never progressed beyond a basic watch office type more common on satellite and relief landing grounds.

More Ansons arrived in November 1942 when the School of Flying Control was established here, although the unit (actually based at Bridgnorth) soon returned to its original base at Watchfield. No 1545 BAT Flight arrived from Wheaton Aston on 25 April 1944 and activity at Halfpenny Green grew still further, the airfield often being active both day and night. Accidents were common but few were serious, although an Oxford (HN593) swung off the runway during take-off on 13 December 1944, crashing into five Ansons parked nearby. A very similar accident had already taken place a couple of years previously when an Anson pilot had encountered the same difficulties.

Visiting aircraft added to the variety of types seen on the airfield, various RAF and USAAF types being fairly common, often because of technical difficulties or (in the case of American pilots) confusion as to the identity of the airfield, such was the concentration of active airfields in the UK when compared to the vast expanses of their home country. A Liberator managed to land safely after having become lost in the local area, although a Stirling managed to arrive with rather less grace and, after suffering a double engine failure, made a crash-landing at the base and over-ran into an adjacent field.

The BAT Flight's activities were also a cause for concern, its beam approach system being set up along the main runway 04/22, which ran north-east to south-west. However, with hills at each end of the approach and being located in a depression, the airfield was susceptible to fog and haze, sometimes exacerbated by the industrial output from the adjacent Black Country factories. Visibility restrictions for BAT training were introduced, and for many months the unit was expected to move to a more suitable location, although it was November 1945 before it finally disbanded – still at Halfpenny Green. No 3 (O)AFU disbanded on 11 December of the same year and the station was then transferred to Maintenance Command on 1 January 1946 as a satellite airfield for 25 MU's airfield at Hartlebury. Dakotas were stored and eventually scrapped at the airfield (together with a few other types, including at least one Horsa), but by the early 1960s the airfield was unused and was placed under Care and Maintenance until early in 1953, when the Korean War led to a temporary expansion of training activities. The runways were resurfaced and an Air Navigation School moved in with Ansons until September 1953, when the airfield closed again on the 14th, assigned to RAF Bridgnorth.

Occasional flying did still take place, with light Army types using the airfield for exercises at various times throughout the year. Military flying never fully resumed, however, and when a former Chief Flying Instructor obtained an initial three-month lease on the airfield in order to operate a civilian flying club, Halfpenny Green's future was secured. Since then the airfield has continued to thrive as a site for private flying and limited commercial aviation, although local opposition has persistently quashed various plans to develop it for more ambitious flight operations.

A Terrier pictured at Halfpenny Green in 1965 in front of one of the airfield's wartime T2 hangars, where a DH Rapide is visible. (Rod Simpson collection)

The future for the airfield now seems secure as a home for private flying, now designated as Wolverhampton Halfpenny Green Airport. It has survived in good condition and the three runways are still intact and in use, although the southern threshold of the former main runway now lies across the airport's access road and is disused. The landing thresholds have been moved inwards in typically over-zealous CAA fashion, but the general airfield layout remains unchanged, some of the hangars still remaining while the concrete bases of the others can still be seen. The small entrance to the airfield is a typically nostalgic RAF layout with a roundabout leading off to the technical site and hangars. Military visitors are still fairly common, helicopters from the RAF and Army being familiar sights, together with the fairly frequent overshoots from Hercules transports that make their way through the local low-level areas every day. Even the supersonic Tornado has paid a visit here, temporarily shattering the relative peace that usually prevails at this rural site.

> *Runways:* 166 (1,238yd x 50yd) concrete covered with tarmac, 228 (1,200yd x 50yd) concrete covered with tarmac, 288 (1,150yd x 50yd) concrete covered with tarmac. *Hangars:* Bellman (7), Blister (16). *Hardstandings:* 0. *Accommodation:* RAF: 229 Officers, 524 SNCOs, 832 ORs; WAAF: 6 Officers, 6 SNCOs, 281 ORs.

HARDWICK HALL, Derbyshire

Grid ref SK470636, Lat 53:10:03N (53.16748) Lon 1:17:49W (-1.29692), 190ft asl. 5 miles NW of Mansfield, 1 mile E of M1

Although this site was occupied by aircraft for only a brief period from the end of 1942, it certainly has strong connections with military aviation, being a major base for Airborne Forces training throughout the later stages of the Second World War. Following Winston Churchill's call to establish a corps of parachute troops on 22 June 1940, parachute training commenced at RAF Ringway near Manchester. No 2 Commando, the fledgling parachute unit, was posted to Knutsford in Cheshire. On 31 August 1941 the decision was made to form the 1st Parachute Brigade under Brigadier Richard Gale. This was to be located at Hardwick Camp near Chesterfield in Derbyshire, and thus Hardwick Hall became the new nucleus for parachute training and physical selection for airborne forces. The Hall itself is a magnificent Elizabethan house built between 1591 and 1597 by Elizabeth Countess of Shrewsbury ('Bess of Hardwick'). In 1941 the house and grounds were part of the Duke of Devonshire's Chatsworth estate, and Army Northern Command leased 53 acres of it to establish a camp of red-brick huts with training areas. The camp was located south-west of the Hall with a Parachute Jump Tower on its periphery. Assault courses and trapeze in-flight swing training structures were also next to the camp. When pre-jump training was successfully completed, the recruits that passed out were required to speed march approximately 50 miles to join the parachute course at RAF Ringway. They further marched back to Ringway from the Tatton Park drop zone each time they completed a training descent.

A controlled parachute descent from a training tower at Hardwick Hall, probably in 1941. (Robert Grays)

On 15 December 1941 the 2nd and 3rd Parachute Battalions formed at Hardwick with No 1 Air Troop Royal Engineers and a skeleton Signals Squadron. At the same time the 11th SAS Battalion, which evolved from No 2 Commando, remained stationed at Knutsford. The units at Hardwick selected men from volunteers across the Army through a toughening course allied with pre-jump training. A tethered barrage balloon was installed at Hardwick on 1 November 1941 to provide refresher training for qualified parachutists, and supplementary descents were made from the Jumping Tower.

The 4th Parachute Battalion started to form at Hardwick on 1 January 1942 prior to moving to Keddlestone Park near Derby. This was the last battalion recruited from volunteers across the Army; thereafter battalions were formed by converting nominated infantry battalions to the parachute role. When the 1st Parachute Brigade moved from Hardwick to the Bulford area in Wiltshire, an Airborne Forces Depot was formed at Hardwick from the units left behind. It started as an unofficial establishment, but was created as a properly organised unit, training and holding recruits before they went to the Parachute Training School, as well as rehabilitating those temporarily unfit as a result of their injuries.

The War Office approved a War Establishment for the Depot on 25 December 1942, appointing Lt Col W. Giles MC (Ox & Bucks) as its first Commanding Officer. The Depot was given an extended role and consisted of a Depot Company, a Pre-Parachute Training Company, a Battle School, a Holding Company and an Airfield Detachment, which was stationed at No 1 PTS RAF Ringway. It was during this period that all pre-jump ground training was moved from Hardwick to Ringway. In March 1944 the Battle School closed, the Holding Unit was moved to Clay Cross, and a new preliminary Battle/Tactical School was set up at Dore and Totley (Sheffield). The Selection Company and Depot Administrative Unit remained at Hardwick. In April 1946 the Depot moved to Albany Barracks on the Isle of Wight, and the involvement of Airborne Forces at Hardwick Hall ceased.

Parachute Regiment training is being demonstrated for the media's cameras at Hardwick Hall in October 1944. (Robert Grays)

A site for aircraft here was established in 1942, close to the huge and very impressive country house. Designated No 37 Satellite Landing Ground, the grass field contained a 1,000-yard grass runway and a 16-acre parking area that could accommodate up to sixty-five aircraft. Scheduled to open in May 1941 (but remaining largely dormant until the following year), the first aircraft to arrive were a pair of Defiants, which made the relatively short journey from No 27 MU at Shawbury. More aircraft soon arrived for temporary storage and dispersal, but the use of the site by the Army made operations difficult if not potentially hazardous (a tethered balloon often being present for parachute training), and as the activities of the Airborne Forces increased the RAF became concerned that the use of live ammunition posed a risk to the aircraft and personnel assigned to the airfield. Likewise, the landing strip was always less than ideal, being surrounded by trees. Consequently the RAF abandoned the site on 14 December 1943 and the Army assumed control of the entire site, eventually leaving in April 1946 as mentioned previously. Flying ended in 1943, and when the war ended all traces of the landing field were removed. Today the lush greenery surrounding Hardwick Hall shows no trace of its connections with aviation.

Runways: 0 (grass field); *Hangars:* 0. *Hardstandings:* 0. *Accommodation:* RAF; N/A.

HAVERFORDWEST, Dyfed

Grid ref SM958189, Lat 51:49:55N (51.83193) Lon 4:57:54W (-4.96488), 163ft asl. 2 miles N of Haverfordwest on A40

Known locally as Withybush, RAF Haverfordwest was first established at the station's satellite airfield situated at Templeton, some 13 miles away. This airfield reached completion ahead of Haverfordwest, so, rather oddly, the station HQ was set up there before transferring once Haverfordwest's facilities were completed, officially opening on 10 November 1942. However, airfield construction was still continuing at this stage and progress was slow, with plant machinery often being moved to other new airfield sites such as St David's and Brawdy. The first aircraft to arrive were four Whitleys from No 3 OTU at Cranwell, but after having flown in on 30 November the crews quickly realised that with no hangars and a field largely comprised of mud, the airfield was not fit to accept aircraft, so they returned to Cranwell. Even the local power supply was unfit for the sudden arrival of military activity, and a great deal of work was done to make improvements, much to the benefit of the local community. The OTU from Cranwell had to wait until June 1943 before making a permanent move to Haverfordwest, but within a few weeks the unit was back in business training reconnaissance crews with a fleet of Whitleys, Wellingtons and Ansons. The Whitleys were subsequently replaced by more Wellingtons, at which stage O Flight was formed with Ansons and Wellingtons and detached to the satellite field at Templeton.

By this stage a Ferry Training Unit had also been established at Haverfordwest, and activities continued until December 1943, when the Ansons were reassigned to No 12 Radio School at St Athan. The OTU disbanded on 4 January 1944 and moved to Silloth, its place being taken by No 7 OTU, which brought its Wellingtons from Limavady in Northern Ireland. Although initially assigned to reconnaissance and Air-to-Surface Vessel training, the unit was redesignated as No 4 Refresher Flying Unit on 16 May. It remained active at Haverfordwest until September 1944, at which stage the airfield remained virtually inactive for a few weeks until No 8 OTU arrived from Dyce in January 1945, tasked with the training of Photographic Reconnaissance pilots for Coastal Command. Equipped with Spitfires and Mosquitoes, the unit flew low-level photographic missions both in the local area and beyond, and also maintained long-term work on a photographic aerial survey of the entire United Kingdom, which was undertaken as a secondary task.

With Brawdy now completed as a satellite airfield, aircraft were distributed between this base, Templeton and the main station at Haverfordwest, the multiplicity of airfields in the area sometimes leading to great confusion. One such incident saw an Oxford pilot depart from Haverfordwest en route to St Athan, but thanks to poor weather and navigational errors he found himself at St Eval in Cornwall, at which stage he set off back to St Athan, missed his destination again and landed at Carew Cheriton, at which stage he abandoned his plans and returned to Haverfordwest!

The OTU left for Mount Farm in June 1945 in order to be closer to the RAF's main reconnaissance base at Benson, and by November 1945 Haverfordwest was inactive, closing on the 22nd of that month. It reopened as a civilian airfield in 1952 as a base for Rapide flights to and from Cardiff, operated by Cambrian Air Services, but scheduled flying did not last long as the airfield gradually settled into routine private flying, which continues to this day. As one of only a few active airfields in the area, business, private and commercial aviation takes advantage of Haverfordwest's facilities and the former RAF airfield remains almost exactly as it did seventy years ago, the runways (two still in use), dispersals and even some of the hangars still in existence. The layout of the technical and domestic sites can still be seen, although most of the original buildings have gone, and private flying is now concentrated on the western side of the airfield. However, the airfield survives in good condition, even if the sights and sounds of military aviation are long gone.

> *Runways:* 044 (1,700yd x 50yd) concrete and tarmac, 101 (1,200yd x 50yd) concrete and tarmac, 173 (1,260yd x 50yd) concrete and tarmac. *Hangars:* T2 (2). *Hardstandings:* 125ft concrete (32). *Accommodation:* RAF: 220 Officers, 316 SNCOs, 1,035 ORs; WAAF: 12 Officers, 14 SNCOs, 352 ORs.

HAWARDEN, Cheshire

Grid ref SJ352650, Lat 53:10:41N (53.17816) Lon 2:58:14W (-2.97069), 15ft asl. 1 mile N of Broughton on A5104

Chester Airport is a relatively modest business and commercial aviation site that might seem irrelevant to the history of military flying, but the facility occupies an airfield that has a long and fascinating association with many aspects of aviation. Known as Hawarden, and more recently as Broughton (this name being more applicable to the huge aircraft factory site), the airfield is now the home of BAE's Airbus operations, responsible for the manufacture of the wing structures equipping the countless Airbus airliners that leave their contrails across British skies every day.

Construction of a wartime shadow factory started here in November 1937 for the production of Wellington bombers, and a landing field was created next to the factory as work progressed, although the site was already in use by this stage as a Relief Landing Ground for nearby RAF Sealand. The first of a batch of 750 Wellingtons (L7770) was completed in a Bellman hangar while work on the main factory progressed. The airfield was still in a poor condition at this stage, and after the aircraft made its first flight on 2 August 1939 it was quickly transferred to Brooklands for further testing. However, Wellington production soon got under way and eventually a total of 5,540 had been assembled by the end of 1945, with a secondary production facility established at Cranage. One particular aircraft (R1333) was financed by the employees of the factory and named 'Broughton Wellington'. Sadly, it never saw service, the Luftwaffe ensuring its destruction during a raid on the airfield on 14 November 1940, when the enemy's main attention was the assets of No 48 Maintenance Unit, which had formed at Hawarden on 6 March of that year. With Wellingtons, Lysanders, Bothas, Herefords, Henleys, Magisters and Hurricanes in the MU's care, it was hardly surprising that more than twenty-five aircraft sustained damage, some being written off, although there were no casualties – apart from an unfortunate rat.

No 7 OTU arrived on 15 June 1940 with twenty-five Spitfires, fourteen Hurricanes and thirteen Masters, although the unit subsequently standardised on Spitfires (becoming the only such unit specialising in Spitfire flying); by August the unit had fifty-eight Spitfires together with seventeen Masters and six Battles used for target-towing. A Battle Flight of three Spitfires was maintained at Hawarden; it was manned by instructors and provided a valuable defensive cover for the North West, which was necessary when so many of the RAF's assets were deployed to the South and East. The Flight's first action took place on 14 August 1940 when an He 111 was shot down at Saltney after having bombed nearby Sealand. When the results of the Luftwaffe's raids on Liverpool were reconnoitred by a Ju 88 on 7 September, it was a Hawarden Spitfire pilot who chased the aircraft across Wales, eventually forcing the crew to crash-land in Merionethshire, after which they were taken prisoner. The Flight's last engagement was the interception of a Do 215 off Anglesey on 18 September.

Renumbered as 57 OTU in December, much of the unit's flying was exported to Cranage, Sealand and Speke during the winter, when conditions at Hawarden made flying impossible. With only a single short runway having been laid for Wellington flights, the airfield suffered from flooding; in the spring of 1941 construction of a conventional runway complex began, while numerous aircraft remained stored on the airfield, although many others were removed to newly established satellite fields at Aberffraw, Anglesey and Tatton Park. No 3 Ferry Pilots Pool remained at Hawarden until the ATA was disbanded in November 1945. B Flight of No 4 FPP (later becoming No 9 FPP) was attached to the station from October 1940 until 31 January 1941, tasked with the delivery of various aircraft types to their designated units around the country. Likewise, No 3 Delivery Flight arrived in April 1941 and was responsible for the delivery of fighter aircraft to Nos 9 and 12 Groups, remaining at Hawarden until 10 January 1942.

Meanwhile the OTU remained extremely busy, establishing the all-time OTU monthly record of 5,282 flying hours in June 1942. Such was the intensity of activity that Vickers eventually complained that the flying was interfering with Wellington testing and the OTU was therefore transferred to Eshott in November 1942; just days later, No 41 OTU arrived to take its place, equipped with Mustangs. Hawarden's busy flying schedule was eventually eased when another satellite airfield was established at Poulton in March 1943. Seafires from Nos 808 and 885 Squadrons were temporarily attached to the OTU at the end of 1944 for tactical reconnaissance training, and many other aircraft types visited the airfield, either on weather diversion or to refuel. Thirteen Halifaxes arrived on 9 June 1944, and USAAF aircraft on long flights from the Azores often landed at Hawarden if Valley was closed. More significantly, 1,044 troops were flown to Normandy from here on 16 July 1944 in fifty-nine C-47 transports, a similar operation involving twenty-one aircraft taking place on 7 August.

The OTU became No 58 OTU on 12 March 1945 when the fighter-reconnaissance element moved to Chilbolton and the day-fighter element transferred to Poulton, but by 20 July activity had wound down and the unit disbanded. The airfield was transferred to 41 Group Maintenance Command and the stored aircraft were moved to the airfield boundary so that the surrounding dispersals could be disposed of. Eventually a total of 1,177 aircraft were present on the airfield, most awaiting scrapping; only the immediate runway area was kept clear of aircraft. No 4 Ferry Pool assumed responsibility for ferry flights after the ATA disbanded, and when Atcham closed in April 1946 a detachment of Oxfords and Spitfires from 577 Squadron moved in, together with a Vengeance assigned to target-towing; however, the unit disbanded just two months later.

Factory production had shifted to Lancasters in June 1944, and 235 aircraft were completed at Hawarden before production ended. When de Havilland took over control of the

Inside Hawarden's capacious factory, the first Nimrod fuselage is transported out to Woodford, while HS125 aircraft continue production to the right of the picture. (BAE Systems)

factory in 1948 the production of Mosquitoes, Hornets, civilian Doves and eventually Vampire jets was undertaken here, taking part of the demanding load from the company's main factory at Hatfield. The very last Mosquito to be built was completed here in November 1950, and production of other aircraft continued into the 1950s with types such as the Dove, Vampire, Venom, Heron and Comet all being completed at Hawarden. The last of the many RAF aircraft stored (and eventually scrapped) on the airfield were removed by March 1959, and the RAF station closed on the 31st of that month. By this stage the remaining units were No 47 MU (which had been here for eight years), 48 MU and 173 Squadron, which had been formed out of 4 (H)FU on 7 June 1952, all having disbanded in the months before the RAF vacated the airfield.

After March the only remaining RAF presence was No 631 Gliding School, which remained until May 1963. Aircraft production continued into the 1960s and the hugely successful HS125 (including the RAF's Dominie) was manufactured here before production was eventually transferred to Raytheon in the USA. The last 'military' presence at the airfield was the much-loved Mosquito T2 RR299, which was maintained by BAE for many years and was a highlight of air shows around the country until its tragic loss in 1996.

Today Hawarden is very much a commercial airfield, although some of the Airbus output will undoubtedly be destined for military use in the future as new designs emerge. Although there have been scheduled commercial services to and from Hawarden in past years, there are currently no public scheduled passenger flights to the airport; most flights are chartered, or corporate, but the airport has frequent air freight flights provided by the Airbus Beluga to transport aircraft wings to Toulouse, Hamburg Finkenwerder and Bremen for Airbus. The Beluga also occasionally visits Airbus's second UK site at Filton, Bristol. There are also regular BMI Regional Embraer EMB-145 shuttle flights to Bristol Filton and Toulouse for Airbus workers.

Hawarden's control tower, still in daily use and hardly changed since the Second World War. (Author's collection)

A number of privately owned light aircraft are based at Hawarden, and police aircraft also operate from here. North Wales Military Air Services is also based here, offering maintenance for classic military aircraft such as the Jet Provost, Strikemaster and L-39, with three Strikemasters, one Jet Provost and an Aero L-39 operating from Hawarden for air shows and pilot training. There is much private and general activity at the airport, adding considerably to the number of aircraft movements. Operators include Chester Handling Services, which provides air taxi and charter services, Flintshire Flying School, NWMAS and HeliAdventure Chester, while Cheshire Police base one Islander aircraft at the airfield. The original airfield can still be identified amidst the vast production facilities that now dominate the site, and the main runway (now lengthened) often plays host to the bizarre Airbus Beluga transports; the equally unusual Super Guppies were also once seen here, but have long since been retired. Some of the original hangars survive as does the original Wellington runway, which now forms part of a taxiway. Military aircraft are seen only rarely these days, although the Raytheon support facility created for the RAF's new Sentinel aircraft ensures that Hawarden still retains at least a small link with military flying even to this day.

> *Runways:* 235 (1,576yd x 50yd) concrete and wood chippings, 325 (1,116yd x 50yd) concrete and wood chippings, 195 (1,100yd x 50yd) concrete and wood chippings. *Hangars:* T2 (23-bay) (6), J Type (1), K Type (3), L Type (6). *Hardstandings:* 50ft frying pan (50). *Accommodation:* RAF: 304 Officers, 352 SNCOs, 1,632 ORs.

HELLS MOUTH, Gwynedd

Grid ref SH284265, Lat 52:48:33N (52.80908) Lon 4:32:46W (-4.54604), 95ft asl. 2 miles W of Abersoch, W of Llanengan village

The moving target range at Hells Mouth, the outlines of which can still be seen more than sixty years later. (via John Elliott)

The rather dramatic name of this small airfield contrasts markedly with the relatively uneventful years of RAF presence, which began in February 1937 when a bombing and gunnery range for No 5 Armament Training Camp was established here, although the prevailing weather conditions (mist and fog being very common) rendered the facility less than ideal. However, the same area was subsequently developed into an airfield and became a relief landing ground for the Ansons of No 9 (O)AFU, which were based at nearby Penrhos, as part of Flying Training Command. Although the airfield was not in regular use, it was used fairly continually by the locally based Ansons, and various other aircraft types appeared infrequently, often as a result of weather diversion of mechanical problems. For example, a P-38 landed here on 25 September 1944 having diverted from an intended landing at Atcham. A Wellington is also known to have successfully achieved an emergency landing here and subsequently departed again safely from the small grass field.

The airfield remained open for flying until the spring of 1947, at which stage it was abandoned, the area quickly merging into the surrounding remote countryside. With very few permanent structures to survive, it is hardly surprising that little evidence of the site's connections with the RAF can now be seen, although the small coastal road out of Llanengan uses part of the airfield's former perimeter track, and the concrete base of one of the three Bellman hangars is still evident. A pillbox also survives, as does the general outline of the 200-yard moving target range. Out on the beach the remains of a large concrete arrowhead can still be seen, pointing out to sea where the bombing range was once very active.

Runways: 0 (grass field). *Hangars:* Bellman (3). *Hardstandings:* 0. *Accommodation:* RAF; N/A.

HIGH ERCALL, Shropshire

Grid ref SJ606183, Lat 52:45:42N (52.76159) Lon 2:35:04W (-2.5844), 220ft asl. 1 mile W of Crudgington, off B5062

A fascinating 1945 image of High Ercall, showing a huge number of stored aircraft awaiting disposal. (Author's collection)

U nlike so many airfields created during the early 1940s, High Ercall was fortunate in having been equipped with concrete runways from the very start, and the airfield never fell victim to the flooding and mud problems that hindered operations at so many other sites. No 29 Maintenance Unit was the first user of the airfield, arriving on 1 October 1940 in anticipation of significant deliveries of American aircraft, the first of which were Curtiss Mohawks. However, most of the aircraft handled by the MU were British, and as the temporarily stored aircraft began to swell in numbers they spread out into the extensive hangar complex, which went beyond the main airfield site and out into the surrounding fields. With such good airfield facilities (in stark contrast to the domestic facilities, which were still very poor through 1941), the site was soon selected as a satellite field for the Hurricanes of No 306 Squadron at Ternhill. Lysanders from No 13 Squadron also arrived in February 1941, just a few weeks before the Luftwaffe first took an interest in the airfield on 7 March, when minor bomb damage was caused.

On 10 April 1941 High Ercall became a Sector Station assigned to night-fighters. No 68 Squadron moved in from Catterick with Blenheims, which were quickly replaced by Beaufighters. The unit scored an early victory against the Luftwaffe on 17 June when an He 111 was shot down near Bristol. The squadron moved to Coltishall on 8 March to be replaced by 255 Squadron, which stayed briefly until 6 June, when its Beaufighters moved to Honiley. The next unit to arrive was 257 Squadron with Hurricanes (later replaced by Typhoons), staying until 21 September, by which stage No 1456 Flight had become established with Turbinlite Havocs for just one month (August), and subsequently stood down.

High Ercall then became part of the USAAF's British operations, and when the 31st Fighter Group was formed at Atcham the 309th Fighter Squadron took up residence, equipped with

The 78th Fighter Group on display for the media at High Ercall in March 1943.
(Author's collection)

Another view of the 309th Fighter Squadron Spitfire at High Ercall. (Author's collection)

Spitfires suitably painted in American colours. Leaving for Westhampnett on 4 August, the unit took part in the 8th Air Force's first mission over France. Meanwhile at High Ercall it was replaced by P-38 Lightnings from the 1st Fighter Group. In October 1942 P-39 Airacobras flew in from Burtonwood to form the 92nd Fighter Squadron, but after a period of training the unit swiftly departed and equally swiftly exchanged its rather unsuitable fighters for Spitfires. This was the last resident USAF unit, but many other American aircraft continued to use the airfield either as a temporary diversion or as a suitable emergency landing site if necessary. For example, a war-torn B-17 landed here on 15 September 1943, carrying three wounded crew.

The station was then used as a rear airfield for fighter squadrons resting between operational duties in the south, and various fighter aircraft and units were in residence for short periods from 1943. On 1 May of that year the station acquired full Sector Station responsibility from Atcham (which was handed to the USAAF). A new Operational Training Unit was formed here on 17 May 1942, 60 OTU being equipped with twenty-four Mosquito night-fighters together with two Ansons and an Oxford. The unit merged with No 13 OTU and moved to Finmere in March 1945, after which the airfield was transferred to No 41 Group Maintenance Command. The station's hangars and parking areas soon filled with Halifaxes that were brought in for storage pending reuse or scrapping; a total of 1,527 aircraft were on the airfield by the end of the year, and it was not until 1950 that the last of this huge fleet was finally disposed of, with Spitfires taking their place. Finally came the storage of Prentice trainers, which remained at the airfield until shortly before the MU disbanded in February 1962. In the preceding post-war years no other flying units had operated from High Ercall apart from occasional deployments from the CN&CS at Shawbury and a regular supply of occasional visitors.

Top: *A sub-site No 2 K Type hangar, still in good condition at High Ercall. (Richard E. Flagg)*

Middle: *Sub-site No 3 L Type hangars are still in regular use for storage purposes at High Ercall. (Richard E. Flagg)*

Bottom: *The beautifully maintained warden's office at High Ercall. (Richard E. Flagg)*

Flying ended at the beginning of 1962 and the airfield was soon returned to agricultural use. Today the former technical site where the control tower once stood is long gone and not a trace remains, but in stark contrast all but two of the fifteen hangars have survived, most being in use as storage facilities. The runways have been reduced to narrow tracks, with only a small portion of runway 23's threshold maintaining its former width. A significant amount of the perimeter track can also still be seen, although the dispersals are gone. The main admin site and station entrance can still be seen, many of the original buildings still standing on a typical RAF station layout, completed by the two surviving J Type hangars in this corner of the airfield. Looking out across the fields where the runways can still be traced, it is not difficult to picture the ranks of Halifax bombers, mournfully awaiting their fate.

> *Runways:* 110 (1,612yd x 50yd) concrete, 050 (1,377yd x 50yd) concrete, 170 (1,251yd x 50yd) concrete. *Hangars:* T2 (2), Blister (12), J Type (1), K Type (3), L Type (8). *Hardstandings:* 23. *Accommodation:* RAF: 140 Officers, 80 SNCOs, 1,384 ORs; WAAF: 8 Officers, 32 SNCOs, 351 ORs.

HINSTOCK, Shropshire

Grid ref SJ660262, Lat 52:49:58N (52.83277) Lon 2:30:19W (-2.5054), 265ft asl. 1 mile WNW of Childs Ercall, 1 mile NE of Ollerton, off A442

Situated in the lush Shropshire countryside, Hinstock Airfield was created as part of the Ministry of Aircraft Production's programme of SLGs (Satellite Landing Grounds), which got under way as the Second World War began. A grass landing field was earmarked close to the village of Ollerton (the airfield originally being named after this village, but changed to Hinstock a year later), and RAF personnel were first assigned to the base in October 1941. However, completing the single grass runway to a satisfactory standard took many more months, as did the completion of technical buildings and a complex of sixteen hides, which were planned to accommodate aircraft on behalf of No 37 Maintenance Unit based at Burtonwood. When the airfield did officially open on 20 April 1942 it was allocated to No 27 MU at Shawbury, and aircraft were gradually delivered to the site for temporary storage, including Battles, Magisters and Masters.

However, the Admiralty was already seeking a suitable site from which to conduct instrument flying training, and Ollerton was selected as the most appropriate location. Thus it was transferred to the Navy on 23 July and renamed Hinstock, the station being commissioned as HMS *Goldwit* on 14 June 1943. More construction work commenced, with naval-type Pentad and Mains hangars appearing together with a typical FAA multi-storey control tower. From August 1942 the Naval Advanced Instrument Flying School was based here, and it also acted as a satellite field for RNAS Stretton, with Oxfords and Ansons from No 758 Squadron operating here. The Beam Approach Training Oxford quickly became

A fascinating collection of Fleet Air Arm types undergo routine maintenance at Hinstock. (via Spencer Adcott)

A Tiger Moth from No 758 Naval Air Squadron is pictured at Hinstock in May 1945. (via Spencer Adcott)

a familiar sight in the local area and, with forty aircraft on strength (plus another twenty in reserve), there was certainly plenty of activity to be seen.

No 739 Squadron – the Blind Approach Development Unit – arrived from Lee-on-Solent in February 1943 equipped with Oxfords and Swordfish, but the unit departed again for Worthy Down seven months later. No 758Z Flight was formed at Hinstock towards the end of 1944 as a Calibration & Development unit, working in cooperation with the RAF's Signals Development Unit based at Honiley, and operating a fleet of eight Avro Ansons suitably equipped with ASV radar and calibration gear. On 1 June 1945 No 702 Squadron re-formed here for a brief stay of just two months, with Oxfords and Harvards, and an Engine Handling Squadron operated Whitleys from the base from September 1945 until the following February. No 798 Squadron moved in from Halesworth in January 1946 equipped with Barracudas, Harvards and Fireflies for advanced conversion training, and, when 758 Squadron disbanded in April 1946, No 780 Squadron had already become established at Hinstock, operating a similar fleet of Oxfords and Harvards. Plans to equip the unit with some Lancasters prompted the need for a more substantial runway surface. Hinstock had relied upon the original grass surface, which was eventually covered with metal matting, and in order to accommodate larger and heavier types it was decided that FAA operations would move to Peplow, where concrete runways were laid.

Hinstock's unusual naval-designed control tower still survives, having been converted into a large and rather expensive private residence. Although greatly modified, the tower's original structure can still be determined. (Richard E. Flagg)

Hinstock was vacated in February 1947 and the airfield was abandoned, slowly returning to agricultural use. Today the outline of the airfield is still evident and the original concrete taxiway is still in relatively good condition, as are the hangars, which have survived intact and are now used for storage. The control tower, which lay derelict for decades, has now been rebuilt as private accommodation, and although it has been partially redesigned it still displays the characteristic outline of the typical RNAS facility. The grass runway is virtually obliterated, although from the air its outline can still be determined. With the dispersals mostly overgrown, only the naval hangars give any indication to passers-by that this rural site was once a busy military station.

> *Runway:* 037-217 (1,400yd x 50yd) steel matting. *Hangars:* 185yd x 110ft (2), 91yd x 67ft (5), 60yd x 70ft (1), 60yd x 84ft (2). *Hardstandings:* Bomber (5). *Accommodation:* RN: 130 Officers, 363 ORs; WRNS: 7 Officers, 144 ORs.

HIXON, Staffordshire

Grid ref SJ994266, Lat 52:50:15N (52.83738) Lon 2:00:34W (-2.00938), 267ft asl. Off A51, 2 miles ESE of Weston-upon-Trent

In a snowy scene at Hixon during the winter of 1943, a Tomahawk lands after completing an affiliation sortie with the resident Wellington crews. (via John Elliott)

Built alongside the LNER's Uttoxeter railway line, Hixon airfield began in 1941, with the first RAF personnel arriving in May 1942. The first aircraft to touch down at the site was a Wellington bomber from No 12 OTU from Chipping Warden, although when it arrived on 15 May the airfield was incomplete and the runways were still being laid. A second aircraft followed and the airfield was partially cleared for their arrival, a smoke generator acting as a temporary wind sock. The Wellingtons were used for ground instruction in anticipation of the arrival of another twenty-eight aircraft, which followed at the end of July. The parent station was RAF Lichfield, and when Hixon opened on 13 May 1942 Whitchurch Heath was allocated as its satellite field. No 30 OTU formed on 28 June 1942 as a night-bomber training unit and within a few months aircraft were being sent on missions over Germany, the first being to Essen on 16 September. Four aircraft returned with technical problems, but two aircraft succeeded in reaching the target, one only reaching Tatenhill on its return to the UK.

When 25 OTU disbanded at Finningley in January 1943, ground personnel were sent to Hixon and most were redeployed to a new satellite field at Seighford to maintain twenty-six Wellingtons that had been deployed there. Training operations grew and operational missions also continued, the 'Nickel' raids over France being one major commitment. On 22 June sixteen aircraft flew a mission over Paris, Reims, Orleans and Le Mans, once crew being reported as lost.

Curtiss Tomahawks were deployed to Hixon during 1943 for fighter affiliation, subsequently joined by Masters, Martinets and Hurricanes, all of which flew 'attacks' on the locally based bombers for training purposes. The OTU finally left for Gamston on 2 February 1945 and the Wellingtons made way for thirty-seven Beauforts from No 12 (P)AFU, which transferred to Hixon from Spitalgate on 8 February. Operating from here and the satellite field at Cranage, the Beauforts remained until 21 June, when the unit disbanded and Hixon became a storage site for No 16 MU at Stafford, remaining in this role until 5 November 1957.

This well-known photograph beautifully illustrates No 30 OTU's Wellingtons at Hixon in 1942. (Author's collection)

Flying activity dwindled after the Second World War ended, and although the airfield had played host to significant numbers of RAF bombers (together with countless USAAF transports, bomber and liaison aircraft that visited the station), the final few years of active service saw only occasional delivery flights being made on behalf of the MU. When that unit left in 1957 the site was left disused and was sold off in August 1962. Some occasional private flying was conducted here in subsequent years, but the airfield is now silent, despite being virtually intact. The runways are all still present, even though parts are overgrown, and some of the T2 hangars have also survived, hidden amongst a large industrial estate that covers the former technical site. The control tower is now a private dwelling, and from the adjacent railway line, which still remains, passengers can catch a glimpse of this once busy airfield where countless Wellingtons stood ready to embark upon dark, lonely flights into Germany and occupied France.

The Memorial Hall on Hixon's High Street now contains a memorial plaque that reads: 'R.A.F. Hixon, In Memory Of The Many Airmen Who Gave Their Lives On Active Service Or In Training For The Defence Of This Country While Based At Hixon 1941-1962.'

> *Runways:* 035 (1,650yd x 50yd) concrete and tarmac, 090 (1,400yd x 50yd) concrete and tarmac, 335 (1,200yd x 50yd) concrete and tarmac. *Hangars:* T2 (4), B1 (1). *Hardstandings:* Heavy Bomber (30). *Accommodation:* RAF: 204 Officers, 510 SNCOs, 1,679 ORs; WAAF: 10 Officers, 0 SNCOs, 435 ORs.

HOAR CROSS, Staffordshire

Grid ref SK131221, Lat 52:47:47N (52.79633) Lon 1:48:22W (-1.80601), 130ft asl. Off A515, 1 mile S of Hoar Cross village

One of the least-documented airfields in the Staffordshire area, Hoar Cross was a small grass field that opened on 27 July 1941 as a satellite landing ground for No 51 Maintenance Unit based at nearby Lichfield. The airfield remained in use by the same unit throughout its brief history, which ended in June 1945 when the RAF abandoned the site. Various aircraft types are known to have operated from the airfield, including Whitleys, Hellcats, Typhoons and a variety of USAAF machines, but there were no long-term residents. The airfield was equipped with very few facilities, the grass field eventually being covered with 58,900 square yards of metal mesh track, which enabled it to remain open during periods when the rather dubious weather conditions would have otherwise rendered the site unusable.

A rare photograph of a Royal Air Force Typhoon, believed to have been taken at Hoar Cross, possibly in 1944. (Author's collection)

Situated far from any major centre of population, little is known about the station and it is not known whether any hangars were constructed. Certainly there seems to be no evidence of any today, nor any signs of the former airfield, although a grass strip is still used for gliding and lies across part of the site of the former airfield. A narrow track runs along the site's perimeter, although this is thought to be a more recent construction. The only vague evidence of the site's former military connections is a patch of discoloured farmland adjacent to the current gliding field (known as Cross Hayes), which appears to indicate the position of one of the station's temporary runways. As the gliders drift overhead today, it is difficult to imagine Whitley bombers lumbering over the hedgerows.

Runways: 0 (grass field). *Hangars:* 0. *Hardstandings:* 0. *Accommodation:* RAF; N/A.

HOCKLEY HEATH, West Midlands

Grid ref SP151738, Lat 52:21:46N (52.36273) Lon 1:46:42W (-1.77824), 450ft asl. 1 mile N of Hockley Heath village, adjacent to A3400

Constructed during 1941, Hockley Heath airfield was created as a Relief Landing Ground (RLG) and was first used by aircraft from nearby Church Lawford during late 1941. The site was relatively small with only grass landing strips (each 4,000 feet long) and six Blister hangars (including one pair) together with Nissen huts to provide accommodation for the few personnel who were stationed here. It is also reported that at least one Spitfire was positioned at the station entrance as a gate guard. From 1942 the site was used as a satellite field for No 14 EFTS based at Elmdon, although the unit stayed for only a year, and No 5 GTS arrived in November 1944. The Glider Instructors School stayed at Hockley until February 1945, after which Harvards from No 20 FTS arrived for a brief stay in the summer. After this date the airfield was largely unused, and was abandoned in 1948. As a relatively obscure and undocumented site, the precise location of the former airfield remains unclear, and no traces of the RAF's presence appear to have survived. However, a collection of old huts and concrete tracks off School Lane, which runs west out of Hockley Heath, may well provide a clue as to where the airfield once was.

Runways: SE/NW (1,250yd) grass, E/W (800yd) grass. *Hangars:* Blister (4). *Hardstandings:* Hardcore (1). *Accommodation:* RAF: 0 Officers, 2 SNCOs, 73 ORs.

HODNET, Shropshire

Grid ref SJ614275, Lat 52:50:38N (52.84377) Lon 2:34:23W (-2.5731), 270ft asl. Adjacent to A53, 1 mile S of Hodnet village

The small grass landing field at Hodnet was opened on 12 June 1941 as No 29 Satellite Landing Ground under the control of No 24 Maintenance Unit at Ternhill, transferring to No 37 MU at Burtonwood on 20 April 1942. Burtonwood was subsequently handed over to USAAF control, at which stage the SLG was taken over by 27 MU at Shawbury from 7 July. Although the airfield was expected to be transferred to 51 MU at Lichfield, it remained under the control of Shawbury, mostly being used for the temporary storage of smaller aircraft such as the Martinet and Magister. Metal mesh was laid for the many hardstandings, while the actual landing field remained as grass. At its peak no more than forty aircraft were retained here, and the site was quickly abandoned after the end of the Second World War, closing down in 1945. Little evidence of the site now remains, and with the A442 road having been redesigned and shifted, it is difficult to establish precisely where the small airfield once stood. The area has reverted to agricultural use and there is no longer anything to suggest that the RAF ever maintained a presence here.

Runways: 0 (grass field). *Hangars:* 0. *Hardstandings:* Temporary. *Accommodation:* RAF; N/A.

HONILEY, Warwickshire

Grid ref SP233731, Lat 52:21:22N (52.35621) Lon 1:39:32W (-1.65885), 426ft asl. 1 mile NW of Honiley village on A4177

Honiley's main entrance was graced by the presence of Spitfire M7240 for a few years, resplendent in an overall silver paint scheme. (via Brian Ashley)

Originally constructed as a base for training activities, the first aircraft to use the airfield at Honiley were night-fighters in the shape of Defiants from No 96 Squadron, which arrived in May 1941. No 605 Squadron, based a few miles away at Baginton, first started using Honiley (which was originally known as Ramsey until renamed on 3 August 1941) in late July, and were joined here by the Spitfires of No 457 Squadron for a brief period before they left again for Jurby in August. When 605 Squadron re-equipped with Hurricane IIBs, their Mk IIA airframes were transferred to 135 Squadron at Honiley. As the airfield facilities neared completion it was clear that it would be superior to the parent site at Baginton, and in September both 605 and 135 Squadrons moved their HQs to Honiley, although both units went overseas shortly thereafter.

Some sixteen Hurricanes from 257 Squadron arrived from Coltishall on 7 November, and 257 Squadron changed role from night to daytime air defence. On 24 November No 1456 Flight formed with Turbinlite Havocs, and by January 1942 No 257 Squadron had received Hurricane IICs with which to mount sorties in conjunction with the searchlight-equipped Havocs. Further changes took place in 1942 with B Flight of 285 Squadron moving in to provide AA training for gunners; No 56 Squadron maintained a detachment here for a few weeks with Typhoons, and No 79 Squadron arrived to mount air defence sorties in the area, although the main responsibility remained with 257 Squadron. On 30 May No 255 Squadron arrived with Beaufighters, at which stage 257 Squadron and the Havoc Flight transferred to High Ercall. The resident Beaufighters flew regular missions around the region, but encounters with the Luftwaffe were surprisingly few and no enemy aircraft were brought down.

Top: *A No 56 Squadron Typhoon pictured at rest between sorties at Honiley. (Jim Broadbent)*

Bottom: *No 56 Squadron maintained a detachment of Typhoons at Honiley during 1942, and six of that unit's aircraft are seen here in flight. (Jim Broadbent)*

The numbers of Beaufighters at Honiley climbed still further when A Flight of 96 Squadron arrived on 9 June 1942, and Hurricanes from No 32 Squadron detached here for a brief period in September. No 41 Squadron also operated here for a short period during the year, and after 255 Squadron left for North Africa in November and 135 Squadron went to Gibraltar, the relative lack of enemy intrusions in the area led to the transfer of some of 96 Squadron's crews to Ford in Sussex during April 1943, from where they flew 'Ranger' flights over occupied France during periods of detachments from Honiley. On 20 April Spitfires arrived at Honiley when 91 Squadron was re-formed here with Griffon-engined Mk XII aircraft, although their stay was brief and a month later they left for Wittering.

In May 1943 the Beaufighters returned, this time in USAAF markings courtesy of the 414th Fighter Squadron, deployed here for training prior to moving to Portreath. No 96 Squadron left in July to be replaced by 130 Squadron (with Spitfires), and Harrows from No 234 Squadron arrived with groundcrews from Church Stanton on the 10th. Mitchells from No 98 Squadron then appeared at Honiley in anticipation of a German attack on Portugal, but when this failed to occur the Mitchells left, followed by the Spitfires and Beaufighters, which went to West Malling and Church Fenton respectively. On 17 August 1943 No 63 OTU moved in with Beaufighters, Beauforts, Blenheims, Martinets, Magisters and a single Dominie. Five Wellingtons joined the unit in October, which stayed here until 31 March 1944, when it moved to Cranfield, the unit disbanding on the 21st of that month.

Honiley was now back in operational business, and the Mosquitoes of No 219 Squadron stayed briefly, and the station became responsible for the acceptance of many diverted aircraft during night-time operations. A Typhoon detachment from No 3 TEU was established on 10 May (moving to Acklington in order to free the base for any emergency use during the D-Day period), and the detachment stayed until 14 July, when it moved to Aston Down. Honiley was transferred to bomber operations the next day and the Signals Flying Unit was formed on 20 July with Beaufighters, Wellingtons, Oxfords and Ansons, tasked with development of radio equipment and the calibration of radio aids. The unit's activities ensured that Honiley played host to a variety of interesting aircraft, including Stirlings, Venturas, Hudsons, Spitfires and Mosquitoes.

Stirlings arrived at Honiley in 1944 when the Signals Flying Unit was formed during July of that year. (via John Elliott)

The SFU left for Watton in the summer of 1946 and Reserve Command took control of Honiley on 31 August, at which stage No 605 Squadron was re-formed here with Mosquito night-fighters. The jet age soon arrived, and from July 1948 the Mosquitoes were progressively replaced by Vampires. More jets arrived when No 1833 RNVR Squadron moved in from Bramcote, which was unsuitable for jet operations; the unit quickly exchanged its Sea Vampires for Supermarine Attackers. The eventual decision to revise the role of reserve squadrons (which were ultimately abandoned) led to the disbandment of both units at Honiley on 15 April 1957, by which stage the airfield had been developed into a classic post-war fighter station complete with a concrete ASP (Aircraft Servicing Platform) and Operational Readiness Platforms (ORPs) at each end of the main runway.

However, with the reserve units gone the airfield was redundant and, after having been transferred to the control of RAF Gaydon, it was sold off in July 1961. The site remained abandoned for many years before being purchased by Lucas for vehicle testing. Various companies currently operate from the former airfield, using parts of the old runways for car testing. After being

A very rare picture of post-war activity at Honiley. A Supermarine Attacker is seen taxiing to the runway during August 1954. (AirTeamImages.com)

taken over by LucasVarity for vehicle testing, current non-flying residents include Prodrive, Marcos and TRW. In addition to its existing automotive consultancy business, already based at the site since 2001, in March 2006 motor racing company Prodrive announced its intention to build a £200 million, 200-acre motorsport facility called The Fulcrum.

Prodrive's statement in the planning application for the facility – which could accommodate as many as 1,000 staff – boasted of 'a motorsport complex that could eventually house Prodrive's new British Prodrive F1 team, further cementing Managing Director David Richards's intention to return to F1 in 2008.' As of 3 August 2006, Prodrive had won the support of the Warwick District Council planning committee for development of The Fulcrum. The permission covered a highly advanced engineering research and development campus, a conference facility called the Catalyst Centre, and a new access road, roundabout, infrastructure, parking and landscaping. The plans still have to be presented and agreed by the British Government's Department for Communities & Local Government, and there is local opposition via the Fulcrum Prodrive Action Group (FPAG) to protect the rural nature of the community and the safety of the people that live within it. However, following rule changes banning so-called 'customer' cars from competing in F1, and legal proceedings undertaken by existing F1 manufacturer teams, Prodrive's F1 plans have been shelved indefinitely.

There is no information relating to the effect this may have had on continuing with any part of the site's redevelopment. Prodrive's core motorsport business remains based at its existing Banbury headquarters. Plans have continually been made to develop the site, but local opposition has prevented any progress for some years, and it seems likely that little will change in the foreseeable future. The main runway, complete with its ORPs, is intact, and the northern half of the secondary runway survives (almost all of the third runway is gone). The long ASP is still here, as is the northern taxiway and many of the original technical and domestic site roads, much of the main station complex now being shrouded in trees. Although the aircraft are long gone, the site retains a tenuous connection with aviation thanks to the VOR/DME navigation beacon situated on the south side of the old main runway.

> *Runways:* 057 (2,000yd x 50yd) tarmac, 115 (1,150yd x 50yd) tarmac, 167 (1,400yd x 50yd) tarmac. *Hangars:* Blisters (12), Bellman (3). *Hardstandings:* 0. *Accommodation:* RAF: 96 Officers, 90 SNCOs, 1,397 ORs; WAAF: 13 Officers, 3 SNCOs, 551 ORs.

HOOTON PARK, Cheshire

Grid ref SJ374790, Lat 53:18:16N (53.30447) Lon 2:56:23W (-2.9397), 95ft asl. Off M53, SE of Eastham

Drivers on the busy M53 motorway cannot fail to recognise the vast Vauxhall factories that snuggle on the Mersey, opposite Liverpool Airport. Few observers, however, would be aware that the car production facility stands on a site where Hurricane fighters once roared, and where Meteor jets once thundered into the skies. Before the First World War this same area was the home of Hooton Park's racecourse, but on 4 August 1914 the War Office requisitioned the site for Army training and the 18th Battalion of the Kings Rifles moved in, staying on the site until they left for France and their eventual participation in the Battle of the Somme in 1916.

Development into an airfield then began, and three Belfast hangars were constructed on the site of the former paddock, the original intention being that they would house American-built aircraft that had been shipped to Liverpool for reassembly. The plan never came to fruition, and No 4 Training Depot Station arrived from Ternhill on 19 September 1917 with a fleet of Avro 504s, Sopwith Scouts and Dolphins; by January 1918 there were more than fifty aircraft at the base. When the war ended the TDS ceased operations and its aircraft went to Sealand; the airfield was abandoned in 1919, eventually reverting to farmland.

In 1927 a local businessman and aviation enthusiast, G. A. Dawson, purchased the site in order to develop an airport that could serve the Liverpool and North West area. The Liverpool & District Aero Club was established here and a factory was opened for the production of Comper Swifts, together with a facility for the manufacture of Pobjoy engines. Hooton Park served at Liverpool's airport for three years until Speke was developed, and in 1933 the flying club moved there, Comper went to Heston and Pobjoy became part of Shorts in Belfast. Private flying continued here, however, and No 610 (County of Chester) Squadron RAuxAF arrived on 10 February 1936, flying its Hawker Hinds when it was reorganised as a full fighter unit in 1939. It eventually re-equipped with Hurricanes, although it quickly received Spitfires and moved south.

Regular RAF operations began at Hooton on 9 October 1939 and seven Ansons from A Flight of 206 Squadron arrived the next day. Civil activities ended in that month and the remaining light aircraft were placed in storage, only to be destroyed by fire in July 1940. No 206 Squadron's presence was replaced by 502 Squadron at the end of November, and No 13 Squadron was formed here on 25 May 1940 with eleven Lysanders and one Gladiator, moving to Speke on 17 June. More Ansons arrived when the School of General Reconnaissance's aircraft arrived from Guernsey, before moving again to Squires Gate. No 502 Squadron went to Aldergrove and 48 Squadron's Ansons moved in from Thorney Island on 16 July. Anson patrols continued on a daily basis, and 13 Squadron returned briefly before leaving for Odiham in 1941. No 701 Squadron was accommodated here while stood down, and the Supermarine Walrus became a familiar sight in the local area. The unit soon moved to Arbroath, probably because of the risk of damage caused by stray bombs, which often fell on the airfield during the Luftwaffe's attacks on the Liverpool area. In June 1941 Sealand adopted the airfield as a Relief Landing Ground and 48 Squadron had left for Stornoway by 27 July.

Back in 1935 Martin Hearn had set up a factory at Hooton Park to provide maintenance facilities for the many civil aircraft based there and, with Ministry support, the factory was developed into No 7 Aircraft Assembly Unit, responsible for the acceptance of American aircraft that had been shipped to Liverpool – the role for which the airfield's hangars had first been built. Harvards, Bostons, Canadian Hampdens, Mustangs, Lightnings and Thunderbolts were all reassembled here and sent off to their first units. The factory also handled repair and overhaul work on Ansons, Halifaxes and Mosquitoes, and, although the airfield's boundaries had already been expanded, these larger and heavier aircraft prompted the construction of two concrete runways (one 6,000 feet long) in the summer of 1941, both being completed the following year.

Lysanders from No 116 Squadron operated from Hooton Park at various times on AA calibration tasks and No 1447 Flight arrived on 19 March 1942 with Oxfords, Lysanders and one Battle, to embark on air-to-air gunnery practice off the Welsh coast. The unit left in December when Technical Training Command took over the station, although three Bothas from No 3 Radio School arrived, replacing 1447 Flight, which left for Carew Cheriton. Renumbered as No 11 Radio School, the unit remained at Hooton Park until 3 August 1944, when it disbanded, having previously re-equipped with Ansons. No 100 Sub Storage Site was also established at Hooton Park, and towards the end of the war a large number of RAF aircraft types were ferried here for temporary storage. Meanwhile, Martin Hearn's factory (of which No 7 AAU was a part) remained active, Slingsby gliders being manufactured there after the war; a contract was also eventually secured for the servicing of Canadian F-86 Sabres and T-33 jets.

In June 1946 No 610 Squadron was re-formed here with Spitfires, and soon the unit was operating Meteor jet fighters, joined by No 611 Squadron from Woodvale in March 1951. A third

RAuxAF unit formed here in 1959, No 663 Squadron operating a mixed fleet of Auster 5s and Tiger Moths, which were eventually replaced by Chipmunks. Liverpool University Air Squadron and No 19 RFS also operated here from 1948 until 1951, when they left for Woodvale in order to create space for the Meteor units. When the Royal Auxiliary Air Force was disbanded in 1957, the Meteors at Hooton Park were gradually ferried to Kirkbride for storage or scrapping (some became target drones), and flying at Hooton Park came to an end.

Royal Auxiliary Air Force Meteors operated from Hooton Park until 1957, when the entire RAuxAF was abandoned, rendering Hooton Park redundant. (Author's collection)

A 1950s aerial view of Hooton Park, illustrating the small runway extension that was created in anticipation of the arrival of Meteors. (Hooton Park Trust)

However, the closure of the aerodrome was not the end of the story for Hooton Park, as it became the site of the North's biggest agricultural show (the Cheshire Show) until 1977, and the runways continued to be used by Shell Research for testing cars at high speed. In 1960 the site was purchased by Vauxhall Motors for the construction of a vehicle production plant at Ellesmere Port, the first car to roll off the production line being the ubiquitous Vauxhall Viva. In the summer of 1986 Hooton opened its gates for two days to host the 'Wheels 86 Transport Extravaganza', which was so successful that four other 'Wheels' shows (1988, 1992, 1994 and 1996) were held. More than 80,000 people attended these events, and many thousands of pounds were donated to charities from the proceeds. For the first time since 1957, the runways were used. Harrier jets thrilled the crowd, and for a few precious hours cutting-edge aviation technology paid homage to this pioneering aviation site.

Early in the 1980s the group of four people organising these events successfully approached the local authority to obtain a preservation order on the three historic First World War hangars. English Heritage bestowed on the three hangars Grade II listed building status in 1985 because of their rarity as a group of three double-bay hangars utilising the Belfast truss form of construction. In the late 1980s this group of four formed themselves into an alliance called the Griffin Trust, and Vauxhall Motors granted them a peppercorn lease on two of the hangars. The third hangar continued to be used to service Vauxhall motor cars. After a great deal of work, the buildings were brought into some semblance of order. However, despite many attempts to raise capital for the repair and maintenance of the buildings, the Griffin Trust failed to secure any substantial grant funding.

Inside one of Hooton Park's surviving hangars, illustrating the fascinating and complex structure, all of which is now thankfully being preserved. (Richard E. Flagg)

Looking somewhat forlorn, two of Hooton Park's historic hangars survive, awaiting their fate. (Richard E. Flagg)

On 9 October 2000 the Hooton Park Trust obtained the freehold of the three First World War aircraft hangars, with associated ancillary accommodation and land at Hooton Park. The sale of the freehold concluded twelve months of intensive negotiations between the Trust and Vauxhall Motors, entered into in response to Vauxhall Motor's application in September 1998 to the local planning authority (Ellesmere Port and Neston Borough Council) for Listed Building Consent to demolish the hangars. This created an enormous protest from aircraft enthusiasts and local people, who were determined that the buildings should be saved in recognition of their role in the development of military and civilian aviation. The campaign was also supported by people concerned with the architectural value contained within the site's buildings.

The sad sight of Hooton Park's destruction as the expanding car factory encroaches over the station's abandoned runways. (Hooton Park Trust)

Vauxhall Motors and its parent company General Motors met with representatives of the Hooton Park Trust, who persuaded the car giant of the value of the heritage asset it owned, and as a gesture in recognition of this the freehold was passed to the Trust. The motor giant provided substantial financial support to supplement planned applications for public sector funding as well as support expenses to aid the Trust in the first three years of operation.

In 1988 English Heritage commissioned a thematic review of military aviation sites throughout the United Kingdom, in which Hooton Park was recommended for upgrade to Grade II (two star) listing. Belfast truss hangars were now exceedingly rare, and Hooton Park was in the fortunate position of having three double-bay examples set in context with their original ancillary buildings. In March 2003 the upgraded listing was achieved and a scheme of emergency repairs was devised by consultant engineers working on behalf of the buildings' owners. The Hooton Park Trust has secured initial grants from English Heritage, the Heritage Lottery Fund and WREN (landfill tax credits), and work was due to begin on restoring the hangars and ancillary accommodation in September 2007. Since that date there has been a major roof collapse in one of the hangars, potentially endangering its future. Parts of the site remain open to the public, and the Trust offers guided tours to groups and individuals interested in Hooton Park's rich architectural and aviation history.

In January 2007 the Hooton Park kart circuit opened after twelve months of construction. It is officially licensed by the Motor Sports Association and race meetings are held on the second Sunday of each month, organised by the Cheshire Kart Racing Club. Although Hooton's flying days appear to have ended, the main runway can still be seen, with more than half of it still surviving beyond the factory, used for car storage. The western extremities of the airfield still retain their post-war layout and character, the runway threshold, taxiways and even the aircraft servicing platform are still there, even though the rest of the airfield is long gone.

Runways: 329 (1,500yd x 50yd) tarmac, 042 (1,100yd x 50yd) tarmac. *Hangars:* B1 (1), Bellman (2), Robin (2), Blister (5). *Hardstandings:* 0. *Accommodation:* RAF: 0 Officers, 90 SNCOs, 456 ORs.

HUCKNALL, Nottinghamshire

Grid ref SK525466, Lat 53:00:53N (53.01468) Lon 1:13:04W (-1.21785), 300ft asl. SW of Hucknall on B6009

A historic image of Hucknall, probably taken in the 1930s. (Rolls Royce)

The busy M1 motorway rolls through South Yorkshire and on through Derbyshire and into Nottinghamshire on its long journey south to London. The countryside is relatively featureless and as the traffic flows past signposts pointing to the village of Hucknall, it is perhaps difficult to imagine that one of the country's most significant military aviation sites lies just behind the hedgerows, almost forgotten by all but those who still work there.

The airfield at Hucknall was originally intended to be at nearby Papplewick Moor, but when that field demonstrated its propensity for waterlogging, an alternative site was purchased from the Duke of Portland, eventually emerging as a grass field complete with typical Royal Flying Corps hangars and support buildings and opening as an active airfield in 1916. The first aircraft to use the site were Curtiss Jenny biplanes operated by a Canadian training unit, although various RFC and RNAS aircraft were temporarily based here after returning from France.

When the RAF was formed on 1 April 1918 the station became RAF Hucknall, but with no obvious use for the airfield after the war it was soon declared redundant and offered for sale. Some of the buildings were sold as private dwellings, while the airfield returned to agricultural use. However, the land was repurchased when the Nottingham Aero Club was formed here and a rebuilding programme commenced; then No 504 (County of Nottingham) Squadron arrived, which quickly became an auxiliary bomber squadron equipped with Horsleys and subsequently a fleet of Westland Wallaces, until May 1937 when Hawker Hinds were received. As of October 1938 No 504 Squadron became a fighter unit and moved to Digby in August after re-equipping with Hurricanes. By this stage much of the station's infrastructure had been taken over by Rolls Royce, which moved in during 1934; little more than a year later the company had successfully developed its PV-12 engine here, which later became the world-famous Merlin.

Hawker Hinds became a very common site at Hucknall through the late 1930s, No 98 Squadron residing here during 1936 and No 104 Squadron remaining until May 1938. When the Second World War began, Hucknall was a fighter station, although only Fairey Battles were based here, belonging to 98 Squadron, which left for Scampton in March 1940. The only other unit at Hucknall at this time was No 1 (RAF) Ferry Pilots School as part of Maintenance Command. A Polish training unit briefly began flying here from 14 March, but left for Bramcote in June when Headquarters No 1 Group was established here after evacuating from France, remaining here until July 1941. Throughout this period Rolls Royce was extremely busy, its Experimental Unit operating a varied fleet of aircraft from Hucknall including Spitfires and Hurricanes, which were repaired at the base during the Battle of Britain.

Rare and fascinating images of Hucknall taken in 1919 which illustrate the magnificent hangars and the relatively basic nature of the site. They offer little indication of how extensively the airfield would be developed in later years. (Phil Jarrett collection)

A German prisoner of war attempted to steal one of the aircraft by claiming to be a Dutch pilot who had force-landed. After being driven to Hucknall and even getting into the cockpit of an aircraft, he was subsequently held and returned to captivity.

The Polish pilots returned in January 1941 when No 1 (Polish) FTS was formed with Tiger Moths, Battles and Oxfords. After being renamed No 16 (Polish) SFTS, the unit left for Newton in July, only to be replaced by No 25 (Polish) EFTS, which remained at Hucknall throughout the rest of the war.

When jet engine development got under way, Hucknall's grass field was far from ideal, so Rolls Royce exported test flying to Balderton and eventually Church Broughton. However, the RAF's activities continued at Hucknall and by early 1944 the Polish EFTS was still there, together with No 12 Group Communications Flight; 504 Squadron, which was now equipped with Mosquitoes and Spitfires; Headquarters No 43 Group; Nottingham University Air Squadron; No 54 Maintenance Unit; and 664 Squadron's 1970 Flight with a fleet of Austers. By July 1952 the latter was the only

Spitfires being repaired at Hucknall. (Phil Jarrett collection)

RAF unit remaining at Hucknall, and in 1957 the RAF abandoned its presence here, leaving the airfield and facilities to Rolls Royce.

During the Second World War Hucknall was the location of the first flight of a P-51 Mustang fitted with a Rolls-Royce Merlin engine. The fitting of the Merlin, replacing the existing Allison V-1710 engine, allowed the Mustang airframe to reach its full potential and achieve spectacular high-altitude performance, something the Allison engine could not provide. In the early 1950s the Rolls Royce site at Hucknall developed the world's first vertical-take-off jet aircraft – actually a test rig, officially called the Thrust Measuring Rig, but soon nicknamed the 'Flying Bedstead' because of its shape. The first untethered flight, piloted by Capt Ron Shepherd, took place on 3 August 1954 before a distinguished audience. The rig rose slowly into the air and hovered steadily. It then moved forward, made a circuit of the area and demonstrated sideways and backwards movements before making a successful landing. The flight was a tremendous success and during the next four months a number of free flights were made, up to a height of 50 feet. Hucknall now boasts pubs called 'The Flying Bedstead' and 'The Harrier'.

A 6,000-foot concrete runway was finally laid in the 1950s, enabling jet operations to be conducted on-site, and over subsequent years a wide variety of aircraft types could be seen on the airfield outside the Rolls Royce facility, either as part of the company's trials fleet or as visitors. The aforementioned 'Flying Bedstead' of course led the way for the development of VTOL flying and the legendary Harrier. Likewise, the supersonic Lighting operated here too (overshooting and running off the runway on at least one occasion), as did the Hunter, the Spey-powered Phantom and even the mighty Vulcan bomber. The RB.211 turbofan engine was developed at Hucknall, and a former RAF VC10 was acquired to act as a flying test bed, equipped with one such engine on her port side, but with two standard Conways on the other; the huge airliner provided quite a spectacle for the locals when the various test flights were made. Other trials aircraft included various helicopters (such as the Wessex and Belvedere), which were powered by Rolls Royce's Gazelle turboshaft engine.

An interesting contrast in technologies: the unique 'Flying Bedstead' is pictured at Hucknall in 1955, with evidence of the local coalmining industry visible in the background. (Rolls Royce)

The unique VC10 RB.211 test bed touching down on the western threshold of Hucknall's runway. (Rolls Royce)

The same aircraft is pictured at rest in front of the well-known Rolls Royce flight sheds. (Rolls Royce)

Sadly, flight operations at Hucknall ended in 1971, not long after the airfield had hosted a magnificent air show that included an all-too-rare UK appearance by the US Navy's Blue Angels team, equipped with noisy (and smoky) F-4J Phantoms. From that year the airfield has been far less active and now provides a home for only light aircraft, which buzz around the local area particularly at weekends. Oddly, they all operate from two small grass strips adjacent to Nottingham Golf Club, and the concrete runway is no longer used for flying, thanks to the presence of a large engine test stand that was constructed right in the middle of it. Quite why the test stand couldn't have been built elsewhere on the airfield so that the very substantial runway could continue to be used is a complete mystery.

The original hangars have survived and Rolls Royce remains very much in business at Hucknall, even though flying from this site is undoubtedly a thing of the past. So many developments in aerospace technology have relied upon Hucknall's input that the site could arguably claim to be one of the most important in the whole country. Certainly, without the Merlin engine and the concept of fitting it to the American Mustang, the outcome of the Second World War might have been very different. It is perhaps a shame that the only aircraft engines heard over Hucknall these days are the tiny American power plants fitted to the private planes that soar over the runway from where the mighty Lightning once roared skywards.

Runways: ENE/WSW (1,200yd) grass, W/E (1,200yd) grass. *Hangars:* Bellman (7), Blister (5). *Hardstandings:* 0. *Accommodation:* RAF: 137 Officers, 118 SNCOs, 1,509 ORs; WAAF: 13 Officers, 0 SNCOs, 215 ORs.

LANGAR, Nottinghamshire

Grid ref SK743330, Lat 52:53:24N (52.89011) Lon 0:53:48W (-0.89667), 106ft asl. 6 miles E of A46, 1 mile SE of Langar village

Situated some 12 miles south-east of the busy centre of Nottingham, this airfield was built largely inside the parish of Langar-cum-Barnstone during 1941-42. The flying field spanned the Nottinghamshire and Leicestershire county border and in the early days it was often referred to as Harby, after a village situated to the south of the site. Built to Class A standard, the runways were laid in a standard bomber-type pattern at 2,000 yards and 1,400 yards for each of the two secondary runways, although shorter lengths were stated on the original specifications. There was a total of thirty-six pan dispersals, together with one T2 hangar on the technical site and another to the south. Domestic accommodation provided for 2,007 males and 246 females was dispersed in farmland to the north-west around Langar village, with the bomb stores located on the east side of the airfield. Additionally, a large hangar workshop complex was built on the west side of the Langar-Harby road with access tracks across the road to the airfield. An Avro unit was also established for major repair and modification of Lancasters, and came into operation when the airfield opened in September 1942. A major part of the construction work was by George Wimpey & Co Ltd.

In September 1942 the Lancasters of No 207 Squadron moved in from Bottesford, flying raids from the airfield for just over a year. During this period two more T2 hangars were erected for winter storage of Horsa gliders, thirty-two of which were placed on the airfield during the summer of 1943. In August of that year Langar was one of fifteen airfields in the Grantham area allocated to the USAAF to receive a troop carrier division. To meet this future use, some fourteen loop hardstandings were added along the perimeter track, and additional domestic sites were constructed to provide total accommodation for 2,253 people. Soon after this, No 207 Squadron moved out in October, having lost twenty-nine Lancasters on operations while in residence, and the first US service units arrived.

In November 1943 the 435th Troop Carrier Group flew in from the United States with C-47s and a few C-53s, remaining until late April 1944 when it moved out to Merryfield. Langar then became a glider modification station where Waco CG4As were to be seen in large numbers. The 441st TCG arrived with ninety C-47s in September 1944 to participate in the Operation 'Market' mission to Holland, after which Langar was returned to the RAF.

In October No 1669 Heavy Conversion Unit arrived with some thirty Lancasters. This organisation remained until March 1945, when a surplus of trained crews allowed No 7 Group to disband the unit. The airfield continued to be used by Avro for the reception and despatch of Lancasters to its works, as had also happened during the American occupation. In fact, practically all the flying activity at Langar during the rest of 1945 until the airfield closed in December 1946 was connected with the Avro operation, and even after this date the company retained its workshop complex.

After five years of inactivity Langar was selected as a base for the Canadian contribution to NATO, and extensive construction work took place to provide better accommodation and other facilities, the main runway being extended to

No 207 Squadron groundcrews prepare a Lancaster for a mission to Germany in 1943. (via John Elliott)

6,000 feet. The RCAF made Langar its primary supply base in Europe and its link between Canada and its fighter airfields in Britain and on the continent. It remained at Langar for some 11 years, and a variety of air transports visited during that period, including Bristol Freighters, North Stars, Expeditors and the ubiquitous Dakotas. When the Canadians departed in 1963, Avro was again using the airfield for flying before the company left in 1968.

Although the aircraft type was certainly familiar at Langar, the colour scheme wasn't. Canadian Air Force Lancasters are seen on the airfield in 1957. (via John Elliott)

Still in remarkably good condition, a Nissen hut survives at Langar and is still in use. (Richard E. Flagg)

Although modified substantially, Langar's watch office retains its original Second World War structure and remains in regular use. (Richard E. Flagg)

The buildings were then soon acquired by various commercial outlets and the former Avro complex by the international farm machinery manufacturer John Deere. Today the airfield remains in reasonable order and has been used by the British Parachute School for many years, its offices being in the old control tower. Light aircraft and a gliding club also use Langar on a regular basis and the skies over the airfield are generally occupied either by flying machines of parachutists almost every day. The airfield has survived in good condition, the runways, dispersals and hangars all still present. All that is perhaps missing is the roar of the Shackletons that once frequented the Avro works here.

Runways: 194 (2,000yd x 50yd) concrete and tarmac, 252 (1,400yd x 50yd) concrete and tarmac, 315 (1,400yd x 50yd) concrete and tarmac. *Hangars:* T2 (2), Glider (2). *Hardstandings:* Heavy Bomber (50). *Accommodation:* RAF: 163 Officers, 342 SNCOs, 1,689 ORs; WAAF: 3 Officers, 9 SNCOs, 88 ORs.

LAWRENNY FERRY, Dyfed

Grid ref SN018067, Lat 51:43:27N (51.72405) Lon 4:52:16W (-4.87106), 40ft asl. Off A4075, 4 miles NE of Pembroke

Although a relatively unknown station, Lawrenny Ferry hosted some interesting aircraft, including the Vought-Sikorsky Kingfisher. (Author's collection)

Situated in a remote and picturesque part of Dyfed, little evidence of military aviation is visible among the lush trees and fields surrounding the lazy banks of the river at Lawrenny. But back in May 1941 these shores provided a home to No 764 Squadron when the unit moved from Pembroke Dock just a few miles further out towards the coast. As the Seaplane Training Squadron, the unit was equipped with Supermarine Walrus amphibians, although it also operated a small fleet of Sikorsky-Vought Kingfishers, and both types were regularly seen in the area until 7 November 1943 when the unit disbanded, leaving the small base under the care of Lee-on-Solent until it was disposed of shortly afterwards. As an RNAS seaplane base there was never any airfield to survive, and few technical or domestic facilities were constructed. Today all that remains is the concrete slipway, which now provides easy launch and recovery for sailing boats. Few of the recreational sailors are aware that seventy years ago the same slipway accommodated the magnificent Walrus.

Runways: 0 (sea surface). *Hangars:* 0. *Hardstandings:* 0 (slipway). *Accommodation:* RN; N/A.

LICHFIELD, Staffordshire

Grid ref SK148125, Lat 52:42:37N (52.71019) Lon 1:46:51W (-1.7809), 220ft asl. 3 miles NE of Lichfield off A38

Probably best known for its participation in the 'Thousand Bomber' raid on Cologne on 30 May 1942, RAF Lichfield was once one of the RAF's busiest airfields, some 113,800 movements taking place in the period from January 1943 to June 1945. Many factors contributed towards the station's popularity, such as its role as the control airfield for Birmingham's balloon barrage network, its geographical position (aircraft flying through between the Pennines and Birmingham often used it to refuel or divert), and its proximity to the main LMS railway line, which enabled personnel on leave to make good connecting journeys to London and beyond.

The airfield was first opened on 1 August 1940 as an Aircraft Storage Unit controlled by No 51 Maintenance Unit under No 41 Group. Among the first aircraft to be stored here were Hurricanes, Ansons and Oxfords, and satellite fields at Blidworth and Hoar Cross were soon brought into use, creating plenty of space for the arrival of No 27 Operational Training Unit, which was formed at Lichfield on 23 April 1941. Ansons and Wellingtons quickly became familiar sights around the airfield, and by July the unit was flying missions over France, dropping leaflets. Another satellite field was opened at Tatenhill on 2 November 1941 but, with insufficient runway length for Wellingtons, the SLG was soon abandoned in favour of Church Broughton.

As the sun set on the evening of 30 May 1942 a total of twenty-one Wellingtons climbed away from Lichfield en route to Cologne, each carrying a 500lb bomb and 360 incendiaries. Three aircraft were forced to return, but eighteen Wellingtons successfully delivered their loads to Cologne and returned safely. The next night a second mission was launched and Lichfield provided another nineteen Wellingtons, this time targeted against Essen. Again, three aircraft were forced back to base while the remainder reached the target and returned safely, although some aircraft were in less than top condition by the time they came home. No 27 OTU flew a further seven operations before the end of 1942, including missions to Emden and Bremen (25 June), Dusseldorf (31 August) and Bremen (13 September). The Wellingtons were far from ideal for the task, being relatively aged and much-used before being allocated to the training unit; by the end of 1942 they were clearly beyond being used for such dangerous missions, and no further raids were embarked upon until more capable Wellington Mk III and Mk X aircraft became available, at which stage the unit resumed their missions to Germany and France.

By this stage the condition of the airfield at Lichfield had deteriorated quite significantly, the regular pounding of the runways, which had been built rather hastily, leading to a decision to inspect them and the taxiways at regular intervals – up to six times every day – in order to ensure that the surfaces were fit to handle aircraft. Flight operations often had to be temporarily suspended while works teams drove out onto the airfield to make rapid repairs. In 1943 a complete resurfacing programme was completed in less than six months without any major disruption to flying training.

Aside from the OTU's activities and the comings and goings of aircraft handled by the MU, Lichfield also saw a wide variety of visiting aircraft types that diverted to the station because of mechanical or weather problems. On 5 August 1944 no fewer than eight Lancasters and eight Halifaxes arrived, and nine USAAF B-17 Fortresses flew in on 16 November. A more regular sight was a C-47 used by the US Postal Service for two months; it flew mail delivery service to and from Prestwick, taking mail from the Midlands onwards to the USA and vice versa.

Although normally associated with RAF bomber aircraft, Lichfield also saw many other aircraft types at various times. This Lockheed Neptune was one of many such aircraft operated by RAF maritime reconnaissance squadrons prior to the arrival of Shackletons. One of Lichfield's many hangars is visible in the distance. (AirTeamImages.com)

Rolls Royce established its Development Flight at Lichfield in April 1944, and 27 OTU (which had been manned by Australian personnel) began to take in Canadian personnel from Gamston, before disbanding on 8 July 1945 after having trained more that 1,000 crews for Bomber Command. Activity at Lichfield was then confined to the MU, which had been largely committed to the preparation of Typhoons, Fortresses and Liberators for the RAF and, from 4 April 1941, had been joined by 82 MU, which prepared a significant number of Spitfires and Hurricanes for Russia. No 82 MU disbanded on 31 October 1945.

As the war ended, Lichfield became the home to huge numbers of aircraft awaiting disposal or scrapping, and by September 1945 it housed 900 Typhoons, 500 Liberators, 150 Fortresses and countless other types, all parked among the station's dispersals, while others crept out into surrounding fields and yet more remained hidden inside the many hangars scattered around the site. When most of the aircraft had gone, No 6 Air Navigation School arrived in February 1952, and No 99 MU was established for three years. However, after the latter unit disbanded on 1 March 1957, RAF Lichfield was closed in April 1958 before being sold off for £240,000 in May 1962.

One of many surviving hangars at Lichfield, still in daily use as a storage facility. (Richard E. Flagg)

These Vickers Vallettas are from No 6 Air Navigation School, one of Lichfield's last resident units. (via Tom Greenaway)

The Lucas company now owns the site and other businesses have gradually appeared, taking advantage of existing buildings or (in most cases) setting up in new-built facilities. Despite the gradual appearance of more and more of these buildings, the original RAF station is still very recognisable and all of the scattered hangars remain intact, most being used for storage. Out on the airfield most of the runway surfaces have gone, although the north-western half of one runway survives and is usually covered in stored cars. Parts of the perimeter track can also still be seen, and a new area of housing has been constructed in the north-eastern corner of the airfield, next to the A38 road. Worthington Road, which winds through the estate, is built directly on top of an old perimeter track, part of which still extends out into an adjacent field. No doubt few of the local residents pause to consider that their houses are built on top of Lichfield's dispersals where Wellingtons once stood, waiting to take their crews to Germany.

Despite major construction work that has destroyed much of the airfield layout, most of Lichfield's hangars have survived. (Richard E. Flagg)

Runways: 170 (1,100yd x 50yd) tarmac, 216 (1,100yd x 50yd) tarmac, 260 (1,600yd x 50yd) tarmac. *Hangars:* J Type (3), T2 (2), B1 (1), K Type (4), L Type (8). *Hardstandings:* Heavy Bomber (25). *Accommodation:* RAF: 166 Officers, 542 SNCOs, 2,536 ORs; WAAF: 8 Officers, 14 SNCOs, 595 ORs.

LITTLE SUTTON, Cheshire

Grid ref SJ360762, Lat 53:16:45N (53.2792) Lon 2:57:38W (-2.96069), 240ft asl. Off A550, on W outskirts of Little Sutton, 5 miles W of Ellesmere Port

All traces of Little Sutton's airfield are gone, but a solitary Blister hangar remains, hidden in a farmyard. (Richard E. Flagg)

With the rather better-known RAF presence at Hooton Park just a couple of miles away, the small airfield at Little Sutton might easily be overlooked. Opened early in 1941, the site was set up as a Relief Landing Ground for Sealand and was used initially by aircraft from No 5 SFTS, and also by units from Hooton Park when required. Tiger Moths frequented the airfield, where two grass strips were created, one 3,000 feet long and the other just over 2,000 feet. When Sealand was temporarily closed in order to have a runway laid, Little Sutton took responsibility for No 24 EFTS's flight operations for many months.

Although a short-lived airfield which was certainly never over-populated, Tiger Moths were relatively common sights at Little Sutton. (via Dean Ashley)

Over the course of the airfield's short existence, two Moths were involved in accidents; one swung into a tree on take-off on 16 November 1941, and another stalled on approach on 9 January 1946. The only other accident known to have happened here took place on 20 February 1945 when an Anson from No 1 Ferry Unit at Pershore overshot the airfield and came to rest on an adjacent road.

Martin Berner recalls his short stay at the station:

'I see from my Log Book that I first flew with the RAF on 3 July 1944 and flew solo on 19 July 1944. It took me 11 hours instruction to solo, which wasn't bad going. I managed a total of about 11 hours actual flying at this unit (after deducting taxiing time) and our flying took place from a grass field called Little Sutton, of which I recall little except the farmhouse at the edge of the field which we had to descend over in order to land. Luckily we all managed to miss it!'

Little Sutton closed to flying in May 1946 and the site was sold off shortly afterwards, quickly returning to agricultural use. Today there is little evidence of what was a small and rather rudimentary facility. The B5463 road out of Little Sutton passes endless rows of housing before suddenly emerging into open countryside, and at this point, out in the adjacent fields, stands a Blister hangar, a couple of overgrown concrete huts and traces of a long concrete track, providing evidence of the RAF's brief presence at this site so many years ago.

Runways: WSW/ENE (1,100yd) grass, WNW/ESE (700yd) grass. *Hangars:* Blister (3). *Hardstandings:* 0. *Accommodation:* RAF; N/A.

LLANBEDR, Gwynedd

Grid ref SH575260, Lat 52:48:46N (52.81272) Lon 4:06:54W (-4.11507), 18ft asl. Off A496, 2 miles SW of Llanbedr village

Few airfields could claim such a remote location as Llanbedr, perched on the Welsh coastline to the west of Snowdonia's mountains. The airfield here was first opened on 15 June 1941 under the control of RAF Valley, as a forward airfield for daytime air defence operations mostly conducted out over the Irish Sea. However, the first aircraft to fly here were the six Ansons from No 6 AONS, which arrived from Staverton for six months from 24 August. Spitfires finally followed in October when 74 Squadron began flying convoy patrols from the base, and on 26 November the first intercept (of three Ju 88s) was conducted over Cardigan Bay; although one Luftwaffe aircraft was destroyed, one of the Spitfires was also lost.

The squadron moved to Northern Ireland the following January to be replaced by 131 Squadron from Atcham, which stayed until March 1942. No 232 Squadron then took over from May until August, although a deployment was made to Merston in order to participate in a raid on Dieppe. It was at this point that eight P-38s from the USAAF's 48th Fighter Squadron came to Llanbedr for a period of air-to-air firing training, and all of the unit's pilots rotated through here over the next few weeks, before returning to Atcham. No 41 Squadron then arrived, leaving again for High Ercall in February 1943. No 306 Squadron then made a short stay (and returned again some months later), as did Czech unit No 312 Squadron, in December 1944.

By this stage the airfield was mostly used as an Armament Practice Camp, and as a result a wide variety of units visited the base for varying periods, in order to train in the area. The USAAF's 2025th Gunnery Flight arrived early in 1943 with a fleet of Lysanders, and many different American aircraft types could often be seen at the airfield, among them a B-24, which landed here on 11 March 1944 after flying from Marrakesh and failing to locate its intended destination at Valley. No 129 Squadron converted from Spitfires to Mustangs here in March 1944, and the following month the Typhoons of 195 Squadron arrived, joining Spitfires from 302 Squadron that had already deployed here.

When the war ended No 631 Squadron was at Llanbedr; it was renumbered as No 20 Squadron on 7 February 1949 before disbanding in October 1951. The jet age arrived shortly afterwards when No 5 CAACU moved in with Mosquitoes, Beaufighters and subsequently Vampires and Meteors. No 12 Fighter Gunnery School had been present from 1943, and its use of towed targets provided a taste of what would eventually become Llanbedr's longer-term future, namely the provision of manned and unmanned aerial targets.

The RAF's presence had virtually ended by 1957, and it was the Ministry of Defence (Procurement Executive) that then presided over the airfield, which was renamed RAE Llanbedr. The two existing runways, which had been laid when the station opened, were of conventional design, but a third, longer runway was constructed, both approaches being positioned to run out into Cardigan Bay. This was in anticipation of the development of unmanned 'drone' aircraft, which would be under the control of ground-based operators, and the runway's position would ensure that these unpredictable aircraft would remain safely over the sea until shortly before landing.

The first drone aircraft to appear at Llanbedr were Fairey Fireflies, the first unmanned sortie taking place here in February 1954. Over subsequent years countless Firefly drones operated from the airfield, some acting as targets, others as tugs for towed targets. They were supplemented and later replaced by the Meteor, which became a long-term resident at Llanbedr until the last was withdrawn shortly before the airfield closed in 2004. The most common sight, however, was the brightly-painted Jindivik target drone, a small straight-winged aircraft powered by a Viper jet engine, of which countless examples were stored and maintained in one of Llanbedr's hangars. With no cockpit and no undercarriage, the Jindivik had to be towed to the runway and launched from a trolley, and most flights were accompanied by a Meteor, manned by a safety pilot.

Although Llanbedr was one of the RAF's wartime bases, it is better known as the main base for unmanned target facilities flying. Countless Meteor drones operated from this site for more than thirty years. (Author's collection)

Although the unmanned Meteor drones were far more reliable than their predecessors, not all launches and recoveries from Llanbedr were successful, as illustrated by WK783, losing a wheel during what appears to be a heavy landing. (via Don Green)

As the fleet of Meteor drones dwindled, Sea Vixens were expected to arrive, but the conversion programme for these aircraft was cancelled and only two reached Llanbedr; one became the very last active Sea Vixen, and still flies to this day in civilian hands, repainted in more familiar FAA colours. Other aircraft types occasionally visited the airfield through the 1960s and beyond, particularly Vulcans, as it was designated as one of the V-Force's dispersal sites; a two-aircraft Operational Readiness Platform was constructed for these bombers at the northern threshold of the main runway.

However, most day-to-day activity comprised the occasional unmanned target flight, together with other trials work conducted by the RAE from here, using a pair of Canberra target tugs. These were eventually repainted in the RAE's eye-catching 'raspberry ripple' paint scheme, and with their black and yellow target tug undersides they were undoubtedly the most colourful Canberras ever to wear British military markings. Shortly before the RAE left Llanbedr an even more unusual aircraft had arrived in the shape of an Alpha Jet, a batch of these Franco-German aircraft having been purchased for the RAE when the availability of British Hawks became a concern. At least one Alpha Jet was normally visible at Llanbedr, replacing the brightly coloured Hawk based here for many years for use as a 'shepherd' aircraft for the Jindiviks, which eventually flew more than 7,000 flights from the airfield.

As the RAF's training requirements changed (and synthetic training began to be introduced) the need for unmanned targets quickly diminished and the Jindivik was finally redundant. Support for the Aberporth range also slowed to almost zero, and by 2004 the RAE (which became DERA) left Llanbedr and the airfield closed. Since then the area has fallen silent, the runways have been deserted and only a solitary Jindivik remains on display to remind local passers-by of the station's unusual history. However, the future may be brighter as a business proposal has been put forward by the operators of Kemble airfield to set up a flight operation from Llanbedr, catering for private, recreation and business flying and possibly the operation of UAV's (Unmanned Aerial Vehicles), which are being developed and will certainly require a base from where they can be safely tested.

The local population and local government are in favour of the airfield's reopening, but the plan has been consistently blocked by members of the Snowdonia Society, who seem to feel that their interest in hill-walking should take priority over the needs and wishes of the local community. A taste of the controversy surrounding Llanbedr's future can be found in the following BBC report:

'Deputy First Minister Ieuan Wyn Jones said after careful environmental and legal considerations the sale to Kemble Air Services could go ahead. Kemble director David Young said he was "very happy" but was not "popping the champagne corks yet" as the planning process still lay ahead. Conservationists have been battling to stop the development. Ieuan Wyn Jones said he was satisfied the disposal of Llanbedr airfield to Kemble would "maximise the economic benefits". Mr Jones said he believed the new airfield would bring jobs to the area: "Llanbedr airfield lies within the Snowdonia National Park and has until very recently been a busy military facility," he said. "I am content that this new facility fully complies with our duty to have due regard for the purposes for which the National Park was designated, and that this less intensive use will not have an adverse effect on the conservation of the area."

The sale had been delayed because the Snowdonia Society claimed that the Assembly Government had broken the law by arranging a 125-year lease. Snowdonia Society director Alun Pugh said that, as a result of the Society's actions, the Assembly Government "accepts that their original decision-making process was flawed". He said there were environmental and legal issues that had yet to be resolved: "It is our view that these matters could best be resolved in an open and transparent way by making a formal application for planning permission for their intended future uses," he added. Mr Pugh said the decision to open Britain's newest civilian airfield in Snowdonia "doesn't sit well with its legal obligations to protect the special qualities of the area, including its natural beauty and wildlife." The Snowdonia National Park Authority said it welcomed the decision by the Assembly as it had been made with regard to the National Park purposes. A spokeswoman added that it would be inappropriate to comment on the development until it was clear what Kemble Air Services planned at the site. Mr Young said the company was very happy that the Assembly Government had decided to agree the 125-year lease: "We hope that matters proceed smoothly now," he said. "Any further delays would lead to further degradation of the buildings on the site. It would be a tragedy if there were any more big delays." Mr Young said there was support from the local community, and his company was appreciative of that. He said the company's planning officer would be visiting the airfield in the first week of January to finalise the planning application to the Snowdonia Park Authority. If everything proceeded quickly, he hoped that some operations and flying would return to Llanbedr in the spring or summer of 2009, he added.'

A year later, the skies over Llanbedr are still silent. Hopefully the selfish countryside fanatics will eventually be silenced and Llanbedr will once again become the home to flying machines – either with or without pilots!

> *Runways:* 058 (1,540yd x 50yd) concrete, 160 (1,440yd x 50yd) concrete. *Hangars:* T2 (2), Blister (4). *Hardstandings:* 6. *Accommodation:* RAF: 85 Officers, 84 SNCOs, 762 ORs; WAAF: 4 Officers, 13 SNCOs, 182 ORs.

LLANDOW, Glamorgan

Grid ref SS959719, Lat 51:26:12N (51.43659) Lon 3:29:54W (-3.4982), 290ft asl. On B4270, 1 mile W of Sigingston

Originally opening as a grass field site for No 614 Squadron, operating Hawker Hinds and Hectors at that time, Llandow fell silent again in September 1939 when the unit moved to Pengam Moors. It reopened on 1 April 1940 as part of No 38 Maintenance Unit, three Lysanders moving in just days later. Tiger Moths and a Fairey Battle followed shortly afterwards, together with three Blenheims that came directly from the manufacturer (produced at Woodford). The main types stored here were Spitfires and Whitleys, the first of which began to arrive in August, although at this stage the runways were still being constructed and only one was able to handle aircraft movements until the autumn.

No fewer than eleven Super Robin hangars were built, and the original L Type hangar was supplemented by six more, followed by two K Type, one J Type, two T2 Type, one A1 Type and twelve Blister hangars, giving the station an impressive storage capability. More aircraft gradually arrived, including Albemarles, Bostons (in 1943) and Mustangs, followed by Lancasters. By May 1945 more than 500 aircraft were on the station either in external or external storage, and the total had reached 856 by November, the surrounding fields filling with Lancasters, which were all eventually cut up as scrap.

From 1 July 1941 the Spitfires and Masters of No 1 OTU had arrived at Llandow for single-seat fighter training and countless Spitfire crews were trained here until the unit moved to Kirton-in-Lindsey on 9 May 1943. On 1 July No 3 Overseas Aircraft Preparation Unit was established here, tasked with the preparation of Beaufighters, Wellingtons, Warwicks and Venturas destined for overseas theatres. The unit moved to Dunkeswell in August 1945, and thereafter the airfield was relatively quiet; indeed, the station had enjoyed a quiet war, thanks to its role as a training and storage base.

The most serious encounter with the Luftwaffe took place on 6 August 1940 when a Ju 88 deposited four bombs on the station, damaging one hangar but not causing any injuries. Rather less serious was the escape of German prisoners of war from a camp at Bridgend on 10 March 1945, many of the escapees being tracked down around the airfield's perimeter.

No 614 Squadron was formed here as an auxiliary fighter unit on 26 August 1947, originally equipped with Spitfires but converting to Vampire jets in the summer of 1950; the unit remained here until disbandment on 10 March 1957, together with 1952 Flight of No 663 Squadron, with Auster AOP6 aircraft that provided spotting aircraft for local Territorial Army units. The only other unit to be based here in this period was No 4 CAACU from 1 August 1951 until 1 July 1954, flying Mosquitoes and Spitfires, and providing target facilities for Army units in the area.

Sadly, the airfield's most famous occurrence was not a fortunate one. On 12 March 1950 Avro Tudor G-AKBY returned here from Dublin carrying local rugby supporters, but on final approach to Llandow it appeared to lose control, rearing upwards, stalling and crashing, killing all but three of the eighty-three occupants – it was at that time the world's worst air disaster.

The tragic remains of Avro Tudor G-AKBY at Llandow. (Author's collection)

Llandow closed in 1957 after the Vampires left and, after a period of abandonment, the site was sold off and many buildings were acquired for business use, including the control tower, which survives to this day. Not surprisingly the many hangars have been used for storage for many years, and although much of the original admin, technical and domestic sites is gone, the station is still littered with buildings and still certainly looks like an airfield. The runways have also survived, even though they are slowly crumbling. On the south side of the airfield a go-kart racing track (operated by the Llandow Cart Club) now occupies part of the old main runway, and the B4270 road now cuts straight across the airfield, passing the threshold of the secondary runways and neatly bisecting the remains of the main runway. Traces of the perimeter track and access tracks to the countless dispersals can still be found in the surrounding fields.

> *Runways:* 280 (1,600yd x 50yd) tarmac, 240 (1,000yd x 50yd) tarmac, 330 (1,000yd x 50yd) tarmac. *Hangars:* Various (38). *Hardstandings:* Frying pan (40), Loop (5). *Accommodation:* RAF: 95 Officers, 320 SNCOs, 1,208 ORs; WAAF: 18 Officers, 29 SNCOs, 262 ORs.

LLANDWROG, Gwynedd

Grid ref SH444583, Lat 53:05:59N (53.09985) Lon 4:19:29W (-4.32484), 10ft asl. 4 miles SW of Caernarfon, 5 miles W of A487

Caernarfon Airport is perhaps a misleading title, suggesting a facility that is rather more ambitious than the one that actually lies adjacent to the beaches of Foryd Bay. But even though the airport is in fact a relatively small centre for private and recreational flying, it boasts a large and surprisingly complete airfield that was first constructed in 1941, opening as RAF Llandwrog at the end of January.

As part of Bomber Command the station first received Whitleys and Ansons from No 9 Air Gunnery School, which quickly suffered from the attentions of the Luftwaffe, a solitary Ju 88 sweeping over the airfield at low level just two days after the unit had commenced flight operations at the base. Some of the parked aircraft were machine-gunned and one Whitley (P5024) was damaged. Llandwrog's Whitleys reciprocated when three aircraft were deployed to Driffield in order to take part in the 'Thousand Bomber' raid on Cologne, these being N1345, N1428 and T4155, one of which was reported as missing after the raid. During the summer of 1941 a fleet of Oxfords from No 11 SFTS arrived at Llandwrog to catch up on a delayed night-flying programme.

When No 9 AGS disbanded on 13 June 1942 the station became a satellite field for No 9(O)AFU at Penrhos, a strange situation in that the satellite field had three concrete runways whereas the parent station was a grass field. Likewise, more personnel were based at Llandwrog, and all night-flying for the unit was conducted here. The illogical situation was rectified on 11 February 1942 when the HQ moved to Llandwrog. The AFU continued to operate here until 14 June 1945, at which stage flying activities ended and the station was used by No 2 ACHU.

Aircraft returned to the airfield again when the site was reactivated for private aircraft visiting Caernarfon Castle for the Prince of Wales's Investiture in 1969. Once reopened, the airfield began to be used infrequently for private and recreational flying, and eventually the site became established as Caernarfon Airport, and is now active on a daily basis with light aircraft taking advantage of two of the former bomber runways, which have survived in good condition. The entire airfield remains virtually unchanged since the days of the Second World War, with all of the taxiways still in situ, although only the concrete bases now remain where the Bellman, T1 and Blister hangars once stood. The small technical site has been demolished but a gaggle of small airport buildings now occupy the area adjacent to the control tower.

Although Llandwrog's wartime activities were relatively uneventful, it is certainly worth noting that the RAF Mountain Rescue Service was created here in January 1944, as outlined by the MoD:

> 'In 1942 Flight Lieutenant G. V. Graham, a medical officer at RAF Llandwrog in North Wales, was appalled at the number of aircrew lost when aeroplanes were lost in the mountains. He took it upon himself to gather a group of service personnel to form a rescue

party. From here, more funding was received in due course, and the Mountain Rescue Service was formally established. Today the primary remit of the MRS has not changed despite the use of helicopters. Accidents have a tendency to happen during the worst weather conditions and helicopters cannot work in these conditions. The role of the Service has been increased to include the rescue of service personnel while on exercise or Adventure Training and to assist civilian mountaineers, the latter category being the bulk of their work. There are now four teams providing rescue cover for the UK: RAF Valley (N & S Wales & Peak), Leeming (N England), Leuchars (S Scotland) and Kinloss (N Scotland). Each unit has been chosen to host a MRT because of its location and its ability to sustain a viable working team of Service volunteers. All four teams are 36-man teams. Each team has permanent staff of eight volunteers; however, the bulk of the teams are made up from all ranks and trades within the Service, each person giving up their free time to train.'

The airfield also played host to a staggering 71,000 bombs containing the nerve agent Tabun, which were stored here after being seized in Germany, and they were finally scuttled in ships off Ireland in the mid 1950s as part of Operation 'Sandcastle'. Thankfully, these horrific artefacts are long gone and now a holiday caravan site sits next to the runway approach, and a small aviation museum is open to the public at the airport, complete with a twin-seat Hunter, which sits outside the airport buildings, painted in a ghastly bogus paint scheme. However, inside the museum a fascinating collection of exhibits is on show, including another Hunter, this being a rather more unusual F Mk 1 variant, which shares the display space with a Vampire and Sea Hawk.

> *Runways:* 226 (1,100yd x 50yd) tarmac, 335 (1,000yd x 50yd) tarmac, 277 (1,000yd x 50yd) tarmac. *Hangars:* T2 (2), Bellman (1), Blister (7). *Hardstandings:* 0. *Accommodation:* RAF: 134 Officers, 298 SNCOs, 713 ORs; WAAF: 4 Officers, 5 SNCOs, 159 ORs.

LONG MARSTON, Warwickshire

Grid ref : SP 1708 4883, Lat 52.138(52:08:17N) Lon -1.753 (1:45:12W), 145ft asl. 6 miles N of Chipping Campden, adjacent to B4632

Constructed during 1941, Long Marston began to receive its first aircraft towards the end of that year, when the station was briefly used by a Ferry Training Unit. In March 1942 (as part of No 91 Group) it became a satellite field for No 24 Operational Training Unit, its Gunnery Flight (equipped with Wellingtons) being established here and remaining active until November. Conversion flying on Wellingtons became a familiar presence at the airfield until July 1945, aircraft from No 23 OTU also being present at various times. On 8 March 1944 No 1681 Bomber Defence Training Flight arrived from Pershore with four Tomahawks, these being replaced by Hurricanes just a few days later. As the Second World War drew to a close, Wellington operations wound down and the Operational Training Units (together with the flight of Hurricanes) eventually abandoned their presence at Long Marston, and by the end of 1945 flying activities had ended.

No 8 Maintenance Unit took over the station as a sub-storage site and the airfield was then placed under Care and Maintenance until Oxfords from No 10 Advanced Flying Training School began to use it as a satellite field, under the control of their home base at Pershore. When they left, the station was finally closed down in 1954, the site being returned to the ownership of the Hodges family, from whom it had been purchased prior to construction. Little flying activity took place in subsequent years, although a small number of light aircraft have continued to use part of the airfield for recreational flying at various periods.

A small museum was established on the airfield, which has been the home of a small collection of aircraft for many years, these being located in a compound on one of the three concrete runways, all of which continue to survive in good condition. Sadly, the aircraft have not fared so well and many of the exhibits lay virtually abandoned for many years. Thankfully, some have now been moved elsewhere (some to East Midlands) and it is to be hoped that the remaining examples receive some attention before they succumb to the ravages of the weather and the attention of vandals. The airfield is also used for a variety of recreational purposes, including microlight flying and even drag racing, but flying activities are now restricted to only sporadic appearances by light aircraft. The hangars are gone, but the control tower can still be seen, and it has recently been treated to some renovation work, which must suggest that its future is now secured.

Although Long Marston was a very active field during the wartime years, most of the station's flying activities were connected with training, and the station had little involvement with operational flying. Indeed, Long Marston's most dubious claim to fame is that it was once used as the filming location for the long-running *Crossroads* soap opera!

> *Runways:* 050 (1,500yd x 50yd) tarmac, 121 (1,100yd x 50yd) tarmac, 173 (1,100yd x 50yd) tarmac. *Hangars:* T2 (2), B1(1). *Hardstandings:* Heavy Bomber (27). *Accommodation:* RAF: 142 Officers, 165 SNCOs, 612 ORs; WAAF: 2 Officers, 0 SNCOs, 105 ORs.

LOUGHBOROUGH, Leicestershire

Grid ref SK526210, Lat 52:47:06N (52.78491) Lon 1:13:17W (-1.22137), 170ft asl. Near town centre off A6 on Bishop Meadow Road

There are in fact two separate sites at Loughborough that have connections with military aviation. The first was a private field at Loughborough Meadows, established next to the Brush Electrical Engineering Company's factory complex for test-flying aircraft manufactured there. Activity began in 1915 and various types of aircraft emerged from the factory, including eighty-seven Farman Longhorns, 350 Avro 504s, twenty Shorts 827 seaplanes, 142 Shorts 184 seaplanes, and a Henri Farman Astral bomber. With the exception of the seaplanes (which were shipped out by rail in crates), all of these aircraft were test-flown from the small grass airfield, which was abandoned by mid-1919. Today there is no trace of the airfield and Loughborough Meadows are indeed now nothing more than empty fields.

During the Second World War the Brush factory resumed aircraft production and another airfield was created, this time north-west of the town and equipped with a longer 2,000-foot grass strip and a couple of flight sheds. Brush Coachworks used the site for test-flying the DH 89 Dominie, and more than 330 examples were built here between March 1943 and March 1946. Airwork also set up a base here and refurbished many RAF types including Lancasters, Hampdens, Albemarles and Douglas Bostons. The largest and heaviest aircraft to use the airstrip was probably a Halifax, which was delivered here for Loughborough University (a site that still houses a few aircraft including a Jaguar, Jet Provost and the ACA demonstrator); it over-ran the grass strip by some distance. The Luftwaffe obviously recognised the strategic importance of the factory and airfield, and many of its maps show the site's location, although no raids were ever recorded here.

A 1944 image of Loughborough, showing the landing field and the single runway. (via John Elliott)

The Brush factory at Loughborough was responsible for the production of de Havilland Rapides and Dominies, manufactured for civilian customers and the Royal Air Force. (Author's collection)

Loughborough College used the airfield for occasional flights, and some glider flying also took place here, but although the site was originally intended to become the basis for a local airport, the site was never used as such and was abandoned after the Second World War when Brush ceased aircraft production. The grass strip is now long gone, mostly hidden under sprawling industrial development. However, the original flight test shed does survive, being the basic internal structure of the 3M building on Derby Road. The adjacent roundabout was once the site of another hangar, but all that now remains is a patch of concrete next to a sports field on Derby Road. It is difficult to imagine that Lancasters once taxied over this same spot.

Runways: 0 (grass field). *Hangars:* Various (civil). *Hardstandings:* 0. *Accommodation:* Civil; N/A.

LYNEHAM, Wiltshire

Grid ref SU021791, Lat 51:30:41N (51.51131) Lon 1:58:15W (-1.97084), 440ft asl. On A3102, 1 mile S of Bradenstoke

The scattered storage hangars at Lyneham were first constructed in 1939 in anticipation of the arrival of No 33 Maintenance Unit, which was established here on 18 May 1940.

The station opened with no great ceremony; indeed, very few people witnessed the event. Records state that the station strength on the first day was just four officers, one other rank and fifteen civilians. There were just nine vehicles, comprising one staff car, two tenders, one van, two tractors, a mobile crane and an ambulance, together with a Crossley fire engine – a modest collection when compared to the huge transport facility that now occupies the site. To refuel aircraft there was a 450-gallon tanker with two petrol trailers, and – rather oddly – two bicycles! By contrast there were no aircraft, but by the end of the month the first two examples had arrived, these being a Tiger Moth and an Albacore.

Over the next few months the strength of the unit built up rapidly, and by the end of the year there was a total of 422 civilians, eighteen officers (including the first two WAAFs), and 181 other ranks. Construction was still going on, and activity had been disrupted on 19 September when a Luftwaffe aircraft approached from the south-west at speed and at low level, before dropping one incendiary and two high-explosive bombs and making a strafing run. Five civilian workmen were killed, and the eastern end of the hangar that they were building was destroyed. Despite this setback, construction continued and the MU's storage activities continued to expand.

The airfield quickly acquired a variety of aircraft types, most of which were stored in the hangars for varying periods. In August 1941 the station transferred to 23 Group Training Command, and No 14 SFTS arrived from Cranfield with a fleet of Oxfords, departing again in February 1942. By now Lyneham had been provided with hard-surfaced runways, two being built during 1940 and 1941, at 4,375 feet and 3,542 feet long. During the following years these were both extended, and in 1943 the 6,000-foot-long north-south runway was opened.

Ferry Command assumed control of the station as of 14 February 1942 and a Ferry Training Unit was established a month later with No 1 Flight operating Beauforts, Hudsons, Marylands and

Wellingtons, while No 2 Flight trained crews to fly the aircraft out to the Middle East. No 3 Flight trained test pilots for No 41 Group, and left for Filton in June. In April No 1425 Flight brought in four Liberators from Honeybourne and was joined by 1444 Flight with Hudsons and 1445 Flight with more Liberators. The well-known Liberator AL504 'Commando', complete with VIP interior, was assigned to 1425 Flight, and many distinguished personnel were transported, including Winston Churchill, while Liberator AM922 brought General de Gaulle to the station in September. The Flight's aircraft were eventually absorbed into No 511 Squadron, which continued the transport role with Liberators and a handful of Albemarles, flying routes across the globe including regular sorties to Gibraltar and Africa.

Training operations were restructured in November 1942 when No 301 FTU was established at Lyneham with Blenheims, Beauforts, Hudsons and Liberators, in addition to aircraft scheduled for overseas delivery, training crews to ferry aircraft out to the Middle East via Portreath.

In March 1943 British Overseas Airways Corporation took over a hangar at Lyneham for its fleet of Liberators. Normally based at Bristol Whitchurch airfield, there was insufficient hangarage for them there, and Bristol's runway was also rather short for safe operations. They remained at Lyneham until 1945, flying scheduled and special routes to non-occupied areas of Europe and to the Mediterranean area.

By this stage No 33 MU was handling mostly Spitfires, with more than 250 aircraft at the station at one stage. Towards the end of 1943 the unit started assembly of Hamilcar gliders, and responsibility for maintenance of the Hamilcar fleet (including powered versions) rested with the MU throughout the type's career. After the war the MU handled jets, the Meteor being the most numerous type. The MU subsequently became responsible for the storage and overhaul of Lightning interceptors, and the unit's most famous incident occurred on 22 July 1966 when Wing Commander 'Taffy' Holden inadvertently got airborne in Lightning XM135 while attempting a series of investigatory ground runs. With no significant flying experience and no live ejection seat, he successfully flew the mighty beast around Lyneham's airfield circuit and safely landed again; the aircraft now resides on public display as part of the IWM Duxford collection.

In 1944 No 301 FTU moved to Pershore, and Lyneham moved to Transport Command on 24 July as the UK's main passenger hub. No 525 Squadron arrived in February equipped with Warwicks, and from the end of July until the unit's departure in July 1945 the squadron flew Dakotas. The first Dakotas at Lyneham arrived in October 1943 when four aircraft were assigned to 511 Squadron, and its first Avro York (MW100) arrived on 22 November. More VIP-equipped Yorks arrived, together with standard transport versions, and on 21 July 1944 the first scheduled York flights to the Far East began, with Liberators taking over the Middle East flights from the Dakotas from August. Many of the station's operations were run in association with BOAC, and a variety of types operated by that airline were seen at Lyneham through this period.

For many years Lyneham was host to countless Avro Yorks engaged on transport duties across the UK, Europe and beyond. (Author's collection)

The station was kept busy, with more than 300 daily movements taking place in 1944, and the airfield circuit was constantly occupied by Dakotas, Yorks, Liberators and even Stirlings. Early in 1945 a Halifax Development Flight was set up here to look at the type's potential as a transport.

When the Second World War drew to a close, RAF Lyneham's activity grew still further with countless aircraft heading out to Europe and beyond before the major task of bringing home the nation's personnel began. In October 1945 No 1409 Flight was assigned to Lyneham with Mosquitoes, tasked with weather reconnaissance along the various transport routes, ensuring that the least turbulent routes could be identified for the VIP transports, which – being unpressurised – could fly at only relatively low altitudes.

On 1 December 1945 No 1389 Flight was formed with Lancastrians, operating fast courier flights for VIPs prior to moving to Bassingbourn in February 1946. A year later, major restructuring took place at Lyneham and Nos 99 and 206 Squadrons were re-formed, both flying Yorks. No 242 Squadron arrived in mid-June 1949, and in October Nos 99, 242 and 511 Squadrons re-equipped with Hastings transports. No 206 Squadron kept its Yorks until 20 February 1950, when the unit disbanded.

The gradual reduction in transport requirements led to the disbandment of 242 Squadron on 1 May 1950, and from November 1950 No 24 Squadron was assigned to route flying with a fleet of Hastings, until 9 February 1951, when No 53 Squadron took over until January 1957. In 1955 No 216 Squadron arrived back in the UK at Lyneham and a year later it became the world's first military jet transport squadron when the first Comets were delivered; by May 1957 the unit was fully operational on the type. No 99 Squadron began to re-equip with Britannias in 1959, and 511 Squadron followed later in the year; Lyneham continued to operate Britannias until June 1970, when they left for Brize Norton.

The graceful de Havilland Comet entered RAF service at Lyneham during 1956, the last examples of the type being retired (also at Lyneham) in 1975. (Author's collection)

From February 1960 No 216 Squadron's Comet 2s were supplemented by new Comet 4s, which could handle almost twice as many passengers (ninety-four in all), but by 1966 the Comets were gradually withdrawn, the last C2 leaving service in March 1957. The Comet C4s continued in service at Lyneham until 30 June 1975, when the squadron disbanded and the Comet was retired.

RAF Lyneham's fire section, and the airfield control tower, illustrating the post-war 'greenhouse', which remains in use. (Richard E. Flagg)

The station's worldwide transport commitments were reflected in the construction of a new terminal building, opened on 5 April 1967. For a brief period the new VC10s of No 10 Squadron operated from Lyneham, while awaiting construction of facilities at Brize Norton. No 33 MU finally left Lyneham at the end of 1967, and on 1 August of that year the first Hercules arrived, marking the beginning of a gradual shift from strategic to tactical transport operations. Eventually a six-squadron wing of Hercules aircraft was established here and the station became the RAF's centre for tactical transport and the sole operator of the Hercules.

A K Type hangar at Lyneham, currently used for deep servicing of Hercules transports. (Richard E. Flagg)

Lyneham is inevitably associated with the ubiquitous Lockheed Hercules. The type is destined to remain in RAF service for decades to come, although all Hercules operations shifted to Brize Norton in 2011. (BAE Systems)

No 36 Squadron disbanded in 1975 (as a result of defence cuts) and 48 Squadron followed in 1976, but the remaining four squadrons (24, 30, 47 and 70) remain active at Lyneham to this day. The Hercules fleet has been a vital asset to the RAF, used exhaustively during the 1982 Falklands conflict and again during both Gulf Wars. With commitments in Afghanistan and elsewhere, the Lyneham Transport Wing (LTW) is as busy as ever, although many of the first-generation Hercules aircraft have now gone, replaced by new-build Hercules that will doubtless remain in service for another thirty years at least. Sadly, plans were made over recent years to rationalise the RAF's transport operations and the Hercules fleet was transferred to Brize Norton in 2011, in order to establish a single tactical and strategic transport base there. This inevitably meant the abandonment of Lyneham but the Hercules fleet remained unaffected for some years while new facilities were constructed at Brize Norton. During 2010 and 2011 the Hercules fleet was still busy at Lyneham and the base remained fully active as a functioning RAF station, hosting visits from many RAF and other aircraft from foreign nations. Perhaps the most unusual (and certainly one of the most publicised) use of the airfield in recent years was civilian-owned Vulcan XH558 which was based here for some time both for winter servicing and as an operating base for the summer show season. Its impressive (and noisy) presence attracted visitors from across the country and its eventual departure for a new home in 2011 at Finningley (which was of course its original home) was met by a great deal of sadness in the South West region.

An unusual view of Lyneham's runway 36, showing the marks of countless transport aircraft that have pounded its surface. (Richard E. Flagg)

Rather more darkly, Lyneham also became well-known as the arrival point for repatriation flights when bodies of the war dead were brought back from Afghanistan. Flight operations were suspended when each of the C-17 flights was expected and each flight was met by full ceremonial proceedings, with countless locals lining the local road to pay respects to each funeral cortege as it made its way from Lyneham, through Royal Wootton Bassett and beyond. It was sad that this function was amongst the last of Lyneham's major responsibilities but it undoubtedly emphasised the very real nature of the RAF's modern role and that Lyneham remained a vitally important RAF asset.

With commitments in Afghanistan and elsewhere, the Lyneham Transport Wing (LTW) remained as busy as ever, although the first-generation Hercules aircraft have now gone, replaced by new-build Hercules that will doubtless remain in service for another thirty years at least.

But although the RAF's Hercules fleet is set to remain active for decades to come, Lyneham's future is much less secure. Hercules operations at Lyneham slowly wound-down during the summer of 2011 and by September the Lyneham Transport Wing had effectively relocated to Brize Norton. Even the occasional repatriation flights from Afghanistan were shifted to Brize and Lyneham's aircraft movements dwindled to almost zero by the end of 2011, in preparation for the station's complete closure in 2012. Despite being one of the RAF's most significant, historical and active flying stations, Lyneham has quietly joined an ever-growing list of abandoned airfields. The station may well be retained by the MoD (possibly for use by the Army) but whether flying activity ever returns to the airfield remains to be seen.

Runways: 252 (2,000yd x 50yd) concrete covered with tarmac, 135 (1,600yd x 50yd) concrete covered with tarmac, 066 (2,000yd x 50yd) concrete covered with tarmac. *Hangars:* J Type (4), K Type (2), L Type (8), Blister (30). *Hardstandings:* Frying pan (32), Diamond (1), Concrete apron (1). *Accommodation:* RAF: 290 Officers, 263 SNCOs, 2,196 ORs; WAAF: 11 Officers, 6 SNCOs, 286 ORs.

MADLEY, Worcestershire

Grid ref SO419375, Lat 52:02:00N (52.03327) Lon 2:50:50W (-2.84726), 265ft asl. Off B4352, 2 miles S of Madley village

A relatively small airfield with a short history, Madley was created as a school for wireless operators, opening somewhat prematurely on 27 August 1941, at which stage the supporting domestic and technical infrastructure had yet to be completed, and the first personnel assigned to the station had to be accommodated at RAF Hereford. No 4 Signals School was tasked with training up to 2,800 ground and 1,200 aircrew wireless operators, equipped with a fleet of sixty Proctors and eighteen Dominies. The airfield comprised a grass landing field, which was eventually covered with metal tracking; late in 1943 three concrete runways and supporting perimeter tracks were laid. Unusually, the hangar complex included three Hinaidi-type structures of pre-war design, as well as two Callender-Hamilton hangars and thirteen smaller Blister hangars.

A detachment from No 8 AACU arrived in July 1941 with a small collection of Lysanders, responsible for the training of local Army personnel, although the unit's operations continually shifted between Madley and Shobdon. A variety of aircraft visited the station in association with Army Cooperation exercises, Tomahawks, Hurricanes and Mustangs being seen here regularly. Some notable VIPs visited too, General George S. Patton Jnr among them, as well as Hitler's former deputy Rudolph Hess, who was flown out of Madley in one of the station's Dominies to stand trial in Nuremburg in 1946.

The station enjoyed a fairly uneventful history and avoided the attentions of the Luftwaffe throughout the war. The most notable occurrence recorded here was the crash of a Liberator on 25 December 1944. Station personnel embarked on a thorough but fruitless search for survivors; it was later established that the crew had successfully bailed out over Belgium and the aircraft had managed to reach Madley purely by chance, without a pilot.

Madley survived into the 1950s until the Radio School disbanded, many of the Proctors being sold to civilian buyers. The airfield was then abandoned and gradually returned to agriculture. Today a significant proportion of it remains, although the runways are crumbling and some sections have been dug up completely, while other areas now provide the base for farm buildings. The B4532 road runs straight through the very centre of the former airfield and the station's remains are visible on both sides. Virtually all of the perimeter track is still visible, as are some of the hangars, now used for storage. The north-eastern corner of the airfield is now the site of a BT communications centre, and large dish aerials dominate the locality, providing an interesting link with Madley's wartime role as a radio communications training base.

> *Runways:* 160 (1,100yd x 100yd) concrete (partial) and tarmac, 250 (1,100yd x 70yd) concrete (partial) and tarmac, 290 (1,400yd x 380yd) concrete (partial) and tarmac. *Hangars:* Hinaidi (2), Callender (3), Blister (13). *Hardstandings:* Sommerfield track (4). *Accommodation:* RAF: 116 Officers, 195 SNCOs, 5,982 ORs; WAAF: 15 Officers, 16 SNCOs, 670 ORs.

MANORBIER, Dyfed

Grid ref SS071973, Lat 51:38:30N (51.64167) Lon 4:47:19W (-4.78867), 194ft asl. Off A4139, 1 mile SE of Manorbier village

One of the most unusual military sites in Wales, not least because it is still in use, Manorbier opened in the late 1930s as a base for target-towing aircraft and radio-controlled drone operations in support of Army gunnery units in the area. B Flight of No 1 AACU was established here by the summer of 1937 and the unit was absorbed into the Pilotless Aircraft Unit during 1939. The small grass field was enlarged slightly during 1940, but relatively little land was required by the diminutive Queen Bee drones operated here. However, the poor condition of the airfield (which was often waterlogged) led to the refit of the Queen Bees with floats; instead of relying on the grass strip, the aircraft were launched from a catapult constructed on a cliff face adjacent to the airfield. A salvage vessel was brought in to tow the aircraft back to Tenby Harbour after each flight, after which they would be towed back to base by road.

Unfortunately, the Queen Bee operations rarely proceeded smoothly, most launches being troublesome; on many occasions the aircraft would leave the catapult only to descend into the sea or turn back into the cliff face. Sometimes they would drift off uncontrolled out to sea, and even if a sortie was completed successfully, the remote-controlled landing was no less challenging. A trailing wire was designed to set up the aircraft to land automatically once it made contact with the water, but many landings ended in disaster and the local AA gunners arguably got little training value from the quirky drones.

Given that Manorbier's own aircraft were more than capable of creating havoc, it was probably fortunate that the Luftwaffe paid little attention to the site, although on 17 January 1941 one German aircraft did get close enough to be engaged by the local gunners. This led to the construction of a retractable pillbox on the airfield boundary, although there is no evidence of this unusual creation there today.

Apart from the Queen Bees, few other aircraft have ever used the site, the only exceptions being occasional visits by Army communications aircraft, including Austers and Beavers, which continued to appear after the war when the Pilotless Aircraft Unit closed down and the airfield was absorbed into the wider array of ranges set up there. Today the site is known as Air Defence Range Manorbier (ADRM) and drone aircraft are still very much present, although they are now even smaller than the Queen Bee, in the shape of the tiny Banshee.

The bizarre pop-up helicopter target pictured during a training exercise at Manorbier. (QinetiQ)

A Banshee aerial target is seen at the moment of launch from Manorbier. (QinetiQ)

The old airfield is still there amongst the Army facilities, and one of the sheds currently on the site may well be built around the old Bellman hangar, constructed when the site first opened. Fixed-wing aircraft are seldom seen, although helicopters still visit the site, and the co-located Air Warfare Centre occasionally hosts exercises that attract various RAF types (including Typhoons, Nimrods and others), which can be seen off the coast, sometimes launching defensive flares. The range area is naturally difficult to see (being inaccessible for obvious reasons), but thankfully there is no longer any risk of an uncontrolled biplane frequenting the area!

Runways: NE/SW (750yd) grass, NW/SE (500yd) grass, E/W (800yd) grass. *Hangars:* Bellman (1). *Hardstandings:* 0. *Accommodation:* RAF: 8 Officers, 20 SNCOs, 160 ORs.

MEIR, Staffordshire

Grid ref SJ942407, Lat 52:57:52N (52.96451) Lon 2:05:13W (-2.08708), 164ft asl. On B5029, 2 miles SE of Longton

Opened on 18 May 1934 as Staffordshire's first municipal airport (and known as the 'City Airport'), the small grass airfield near Longton was initially used by the DH 86s belonging to Railway Air Services, together with a variety of private aircraft and eventually those operated by the North Staffordshire Aero Club, which was set up here. However, the site became the home of No 28 Elementary & Reserve Flying School from 1 August 1938, and its Tiger Moths and Hawker Harts were maintained and operated by Reid & Sigrist under contract to the Air Ministry. The airport was used as a turning point for the 1937 King's Cup Air Race, and famous test pilot Alex Henshaw landed his Mew Gull here after retiring from the event.

No 1 Flying Practice Unit, the first and only unit of its kind, was established at Meir on 12 February 1940, tasked with the maintenance of flying currency for 120 Acting Pilot Officers and 120 Sergeant Pilots who had completed their FTS courses. Initially flying Hectors, Hinds were quickly brought in as replacements. These crews were Finnish, and the plan was to train them up to the same standards as the equivalent Polish pilots, but the hostilities in Finland naturally led to the eventual abandonment of the whole concept.

As the Second World War broke out, defensive plans were put into place at Meir, dispersal exercises being conducted whereby the resident aircraft were scattered around the airfield perimeter, and the grass field was suitably camouflaged; adjacent roads were continued across the airfield courtesy of suitable paintwork, which rendered the site almost indistinguishable from its surroundings when seen from the air. The airfield never did attract the attention of the Luftwaffe, although a few stray bombs did fall on it during attacks on the Potteries.

The FPU disbanded on 16 June 1940 and the base was allocated to No 5 EFTS, its base at Hanworth in Middlesex being judged as in a vulnerable area. The unit's Magister aircraft became a familiar sight in the local area, and some 134 pilots were successfully trained and sent on to the SFTS by the end of 1940. Visiting aircraft were few, although a Blenheim (L1218) landed on 5 December (skidding into a perimeter hedge in the process), and a Harrow attempted to land on 23 December although the local AA defences opened fire on it (mistaking it for an enemy aircraft) and the crew landed in an adjacent field. The EFTS closed down on 31 December 1941 (demand for pilots having diminished) and No 16 FTS then used the airfield as a Relief Landing Ground for its Magister aircraft based at Burnaston.

The Rootes shadow factory at nearby Blythe Bridge produced Blenheims and Beaufighters during the war. Upon completion they were towed to Meir for test-flying, and for this purpose a small concrete runway was laid together with a connecting track to the factory. Production ended in September 1945, after which the airfield returned to private flying, mostly the activities of the Staffordshire Light Plane Group, the Staffordshire Gliding Club, and the Dove operated by Staffordshire Potteries. The airfield site was never ideal, being situated close to local housing, close to a hillside, built on sloping ground and prone to haze, and it was therefore inevitable that the site would eventually close. The last known flight here (made by a home-built aircraft) took place in 1973.

Blenheims were test-flown from Meir after completion at the nearby Blythe Bridge factory. (via Doug Pollard)

Although the landing field and runway are gone and most of the airport buildings have been demolished, some of the original hangars have survived and are now part of the industrial complex that dominates the site. Parts of the old track that linked the shadow factory to the airfield are still to be seen on the former airfield's eastern boundary.

> *Runways:* 0 (grass field). *Hangars:* Various (civil). *Hardstandings:* 0. *Accommodation:* RAF; N/A.

MONA, Anglesey

Grid ref SH423760, Lat 53:15:28N (53.25782) Lon 4:21:51W (-4.36423), 185ft asl. On A5, 2 miles SE of Gwalchmai

Originally known as Heneglwys, the futile efforts of English pronunciation quickly led to the substitution of the name Mona for this RAF station, which opened in December 1942 as part of No 25 (Armament) Group. Built on the former site of a First World War airship base (Llangefni),

RAF Mona's control tower, somewhat modified (with distinctly unorthodox windows) but still largely unchanged from seventy years ago. (Paul Francis)

One of Mona's original Nissen huts, still intact and still in regular use by the Royal Air Force, seventy years on. (Paul Francis)

three concrete runways were laid together with three T1 hangars and an array of seventeen Blister hangars, all of which were necessary to protect aircraft from the harsh weather conditions that frequently battered this exposed airfield. Completed in 1942, the station was allocated to No 6 AGS, but the unit was never fully established here (moving to Castle Kennedy instead), and its Bothas and Ansons soon disappeared.

In March 1943 a detachment of Masters from No 5 (P)AFU came here from Ternhill, tasked with the training of Turkish officers; weather conditions delayed the unit's departure until 16 March. No 8 (O)AFU was formed here on 15 November, equipped with Ansons, and stayed until 14 June 1945, joined briefly by a detachment of Martinets from Bodorgan during January 1944. Although a relatively inactive airfield, many aircraft paid occasional visits, many of these landings being unintentional, as the Americans using the nearby airfield at Valley often had difficulty in distinguishing the two sites, being situated so closely together. A B-24 arrived here on 14 March 1944, three C-47s flew in a month later, and even a C-54 landed here on 11 April.

The station was placed under Care and Maintenance in 1945, but in 1951 the site was allocated to No 202 AFS as a Relief Landing Ground, the unit's Vampire jets eventually being replaced by the diminutive Gnats of No 4 FTS, which were much in evidence at nearby Valley. The main runway was extended to 6,000 feet in order to safely accommodate jet operations, and the two secondary runways were abandoned.

Since the 1950s the airfield has remained active as an RLG for Valley, and RAF Mona is now regularly used by the black-painted Hawk jets that come and go from Valley. A handful of private light aircraft operate here too, although the airfield is almost always busy with Hawk operations. On 20 April 2007 a Hawk pilot ejected from his aircraft during a weather reconnaissance flight from Valley, and the jet crashed onto Mona airfield, breaking into two sections upon impact. Routine operations are far less spectacular, and Mona remains relatively peaceful for most of the time when the Hawks are not active.

One hangar survives, as does the control tower (which has been extensively modified), and the remains of the airship base can still be found to the east of the main runway. Still very much in use, the main runway and connecting taxiway are in excellent condition, although the disused runways and dispersals are slowly crumbling.

> *Runways:* 230 (1,800yd x 50yd) concrete, 104 (1,100yd x 50yd) concrete, 315 (1,100yd x 50yd) concrete. *Hangars:* T1 (1), Blister (17). *Hardstandings:* 900yd x 100ft Sommerfield track. *Accommodation:* RAF: 110 Officers, 220 SNCOs, 1,048 ORs; WAAF: 2 Officers, 1 SNCO, 60 ORs.

MONTFORD BRIDGE, Shropshire

Grid ref SJ435170, Lat 52:44:54N (52.74835) Lon 2:50:14W (-2.83722), 265ft asl. Off A5, 1 mile N of Montford Bridge village

Constructed in 1941, RAF Montford Bridge opened in April 1942 with three standard concrete runways, connecting perimeter track and twenty-five small hardstandings together with just four Blister and seven Bessoneau hangars. As a satellite field for No 61 OTU, Spitfires were the most common sight here, the rudimentary accommodation and appalling winter conditions making the station a less than popular posting for the crews who were sent here to train. Few units used the airfield, and apart from the OTU a detachment of Piper Cubs from the US Army's 83rd Artillery Division was here in May 1944, a detachment of Oxfords from No 11 (P)AFU in July 1942 (Shawbury using the airfield as a Relief Landing Ground until Condover was completed), and a flight of Oxfords from No 6 AACU (which became 577 Squadron) from May 1943 until mid-1944. When 61 OTU moved to Keevil in June 1945, the airfield was assigned to No 34 Maintenance Unit as a storage site for Masters and Hotspurs, most of which came from No 5 GTS at Shobdon. Virtually all of these aircraft were broken up at Montford Bridge, and when this work was done towards the end of 1945 the airfield was left unused. It was abandoned in 1946, quickly returning to agricultural use.

A Spitfire from No 61 Operational Training Unit at Montford Bridge. (Author's collection)

Today the basic outlines of the airfield are still present, and the three crumbling runways are still intact, although a line of trees now occupies the south-western portion of one. The control tower is still standing (albeit in relatively poor condition) and a few of the dispersals can still be seen on the airfield's western perimeter. A handful of the old (and distinctly temporary) OTU buildings have survived, but Mountford Bridge lies silent, a classic example of a site that held great potential, but one that was ultimately forgotten.

Still defiantly standing, Montford Bridge's watch office sits stranded amidst the farmland. (Richard E. Flagg)

This crumbling concrete block at Montford Bridge, once used by No 61 Operational Training Unit, is now abandoned, and is doubtless destined for demolition. (Paul Francis)

Runways: 250 (1,470yd x 50yd) tarmac and rubber chippings, 020 (1,300yd x 50yd) tarmac and rubber chippings, 330 (1,000yd x 50yd) tarmac and rubber chippings. *Hangars:* Blister (4), Bessoneau (2). *Hardstandings:* 27. *Accommodation:* RAF: 24 Officers, 60 SNCOs, 616 ORs; WAAF: 2 Officers, 1 SNCO, 60 ORs.

NEWTON, Nottinghamshire

Grid ref SK685414, Lat 52:57:58N (52.96622) Lon 0:58:49W (-0.98019), 150ft asl. Off A46, 1 mile NW of Bingham

Established in 1936 and eventually becoming operational in July 1940, RAF Newton was first assigned to No 1 Group, and Nos 103 and 150 Squadrons operated Fairey Battles here until Wellingtons were received in October 1940. These were subsequently used to participate in raids over Germany and on a raid against the *Gneisenau* in Brest Harbour. As of July 1941 the station transferred to Flying Training Command and No 16 (Polish) SFTS arrived from Hucknall, the Poles establishing strong ties with the station, which were incorporated into the design of its official badge. The unit operated Battles, Oxfords, Moths and Masters, with Magisters and Ansons arriving in April 1943. Unusually, despite the construction of five huge C Type hangars, the airfield was never equipped with concrete runways and the grass field was often unusable when waterlogged. Sutton Bridge was eventually established as a satellite field in order to ease the training burden on Newton. In addition to the resident SFTS, No 1524 BAT Flight was established here and eventually both Orston and Tollerton were assigned to RLG (Relief Landing Ground) status for use by both this unit and the SFTS.

This heavily damaged Wellington from No 103 Squadron is pictured shortly after making a crash landing at Newton. (via Ken Billingham)

An atmospheric image of one of Newton's massive C Type hangars, shrouded in fog. (Richard E. Flagg)

Inside one of Newton's capacious C Type hangars. Unused since the last Bulldog trainers left the station, the future of these magnificent structures remains unclear. (Richard E. Flagg)

Wellingtons from the Central Gunnery School (based at Sutton Bridge) operated at various times from Newton. (via John Elliott)

Activities continued until October 1946 when the SFTS disbanded and Newton was transferred to Fighter Command as No 12 Group's headquarters, flying activities being confined to the Group's Communications Flight and the Nottingham University Air Squadron (later renamed East Midlands UAS) with its Chipmunk trainers. In August 1958 the station was transferred to Technical Training Command, and No 9 School of Technical Training was moved here, combining courses formerly undertaken at Yatesbury and Melksham.

Although the airfield was now largely unused (apart from the activities of the UAS), a few aircraft did occasionally visit and a handful of aircraft were delivered to the SoTT by air, including – incredibly – a Vulcan bomber. Eventually the various training courses were transferred to Halton and in 1970 No 9 SoTT stood down, its place being taken by the RAF School of Education, the Royal Air Force Police School, the Management Training Squadron and the Air Cadet Training Centre, all of which were non-flying units.

No 644 Gliding School arrived in 1975 (although operating from Syerston), and was joined by the Air Cadet Central Gliding School, which came from Swanton Morley in August 1977. The UAS Chipmunks were eventually exchanged for Bulldogs and these were joined by Slingsby Fireflies from Cranwell prior to the end of flying activities in 2000, when the RAF vacated the station.

The ubiquitous de Havilland Chipmunk was a familiar sight at countless RAF airfields. RAF Newton hosted a considerable number of 'Chippies' until the arrival of the Scottish Aviation Bulldog. (Author's collection)

Newton's control tower was a relatively uncomplicated structure, and it remains intact on the disused airfield, awaiting a decision on its future. (Richard E. Flagg)

Newton's station headquarters building stands empty and available for purchase. (Richard E. Flagg)

Since then the site has been abandoned and the large grass field is unused, the huge hangars stand empty and the control tower stands alone and unused. The domestic and technical sites are all intact, as are the concrete dispersals where many aircraft once stood (the last of these being a Hunter, which is now at Caernarfon Airport), but since the rowdy buzz of the Bulldogs disappeared, Newton's associations with aviation appear to have ended for good.

Runways: NW/SE (1,010yd) grass, N/S (1,030yd) grass, NE/SW (1,300yd) grass. *Hangars:* C Type (5), Blister (14). *Hardstandings:* Circular (35). *Accommodation:* RAF: 153 Officers, 172 SNCOs, 1,448 ORs; WAAF: 0 Officers, 16 SNCOs, 288 ORs.

NORTHLEACH, Gloucestershire

Grid ref SP111152, Lat 51:50:10N (51.83615) Lon 1:50:21W (-1.83927), 682ft asl. Adjacent to A429 and A40 roads, 1 mile NW of Northleach village

Created as an Emergency Landing Ground during 1941, RAF Northleach opened early in 1942 and during July of that year was transferred to the control of No 3 Glider Training School based at nearby Stoke Orchard. Tasked with the training of pilots for the Glider Pilot Regiment, the unit first deployed a flight of Hotspur gliders and Miles Master GTII aircraft to the airfield on 2 November, and Northleach was designated at a Relief Landing Ground for Stoke Orchard. Also based here briefly were personnel assigned to the RAF Regiment, and some training was conducted until the detachment moved to Mythe Camp. During the winter of 1942 the grass airfield's condition deteriorated rapidly and became so waterlogged that flying from the site became impossible. The 3 GTS detachment was therefore forced to return to Stoke Orchard until February 1943. Flying then resumed, but in a matter of weeks the airfield's condition worsened again and eventually a second detachment was set up at RAF Wanborough in order to maintain training commitments.

In May 1944 Northleach was upgraded to Satellite Landing Ground status, but the proposal to equip the airfield with hangars and possibly runways was never pursued, and it continued to suffer at the mercy of the prevailing weather conditions. Problems arose again during the winter of 1944 and another detachment was established at RAF Zeals in Wiltshire on 21 October. When the aircraft moved from Northleach, it was the last time that any flying was conducted at this site. No 3 GTS moved to Exeter on 11 January 1945 and Northleach was placed under Care and Maintenance, but in May 1946 the entire site was sold off and agriculture quickly returned to the area. No evidence of the airfield remains, although historians indicate that the site was close to the junction of the A429 and A40. However, a little further along the A40 to the west a small concrete track survives in an adjacent field, and suggests that this may well once have been part of the airfield.

Northleach from the air.

The diminutive Hotspur glider was, for some years, a familiar sight at Northleach, often being towed into the air by (as illustrated) Tiger Moth tugs. (via David Greenstreet)

Runways: NE/SW (750yd) grass, E/W (1,050yd) grass. *Hangars:* Blister (2). *Hardstandings:* 0. *Accommodation:* RAF: 14 Officers, 23 SNCOs, 66 ORs.

NUNEATON, Warwickshire

Grid ref SP376961, Lat 52:33:42N (52.56153) Lon 1:26:48W (-1.44676), 378ft asl. N of Nuneaton on A5, adjacent to Higham-on-the-Hill village

Created as a satellite field for nearby Bramcote, work on the airfield at Nuneaton began in 1942. Three standard concrete runways were laid together with a total of twenty-seven dispersals, which were built towards the western side of the airfield because of rising ground and an adjacent railway line towards the east. Only one T2 hangar was assembled and a fairly small complex of technical and domestic buildings, which could accommodate 1,400 personnel. Opened on 7 February 1943, the station came under the control of Bramcote's No 18 (Polish) Operational Training Unit, and its Wellington bombers gradually moved in over successive weeks. However,

RAF Nuneaton in 1945. Numerous Wellingtons and at least one Dakota are visible on the airfield's dispersals. (ATC)

shortly after flying began here a change in official policy led to a decision to move the OTU to Finningley and the Wellingtons quickly departed again. Both Nuneaton and Bramcote were then transferred to No 44 Group Transport Command during April, and No 105 Operational Training Unit took over Nuneaton as a satellite field, although it was not until 25 June that the first of the unit's Wellington aircraft arrived here.

Early in 1945 Dakotas began to replace the Wellingtons, and during August the unit was renamed as No 1381 Transport Conversion Unit until 21 November 1945, when it left for Desborough. The Transport Command Examining Unit then moved to Bramcote with Dakotas and Oxfords, Nuneaton continuing to operate as a satellite field until August 1946, when the unit disbanded and flying ended at Nuneaton. The airfield was placed under Care and Maintenance and eventually sold off during the 1950s. Today it is a testing ground for the Motor Industries Research Association, and although various test tracks have been laid across the airfield, the three runways still remain, as do parts of the original perimeter track and some of the dispersals. The hangar remains in use on the site and the control tower is still used for its intended purpose, although only cars are now scrutinised from here, rather than Wellingtons. Most of the site is fenced off, but the former airfield can be seen from many vantage points and one group of dispersals lies crumbling outside the test site's perimeter.

Runways: 130 (1,400yd x 50yd) concrete, 240 (2,000yd x 50yd) concrete, 180 (1,400yd x 50yd) concrete. *Hangars:* T2 (1). *Hardstandings:* Spectacle (27). *Accommodation:* RAF: 87 Officers, 286 SNCOs, 928 ORs; WAAF: 2 Officers, 18 SNCOs, 140 ORs.

ORSTON, Nottinghamshire

Grid ref SK779412, Lat 52:57:47N (52.96311) Lon 0:50:25W (-0.8402), 100ft asl. On Spa Lane heading out of Orston village, N of A52

Opened in 1941 as part of No 21 Group, Orston's small grass field was designated as a satellite field for No 16 (Polish) SFTS based at Newton. The unit's Oxfords and Masters were detached to Orston when necessary although the airfield's condition was poor and after any heavy rain was rendered unsuitable for flying for some time. A number of Blister hangars were constructed, although they were rarely used to house aircraft (the Polish personnel being reluctant to provide guards for the airfield at night, when the site was deserted), and they were eventually used for storage by the Army, which had a Royal Army Service Corps base a few fields away. Flying from the site ended during 1945 and the RAF abandoned the site during the same year. No evidence of the airfield survives apart from the remains of what once might have been a dispersal or the concrete base of a hangar.

Runways: N/S (1,000yd) grass, E/W (1,200yd) grass, NW/SE (1,000yd) grass. *Hangars:* Blister (9). *Hardstandings:* 0. *Accommodation:* RAF: 2 Officers, 4 SNCOs, 120 ORs.

OSSINGTON, Nottinghamshire

Grid ref SK756649, Lat 53:10:35N (53.17631) Lon 0:52:10W (-0.86938), 211ft asl. On Main Street, 1 mile W of Ossington village, 5 miles E of Kneesall

A small road leading off the A616 at Kneesall runs across open countryside to Ossington, emerging from trees just a couple of miles from the village, at which stage the road takes a curious turn northwards before twisting back south. There seems to be little reason for this small diversion unless one has the advantage of an aerial view, but from the air it can clearly be seen that the road follows the path of two former bomber runways that were once laid here.

Oxfords were the first aircraft to operate from Ossington when the station opened in 1942. (Author's collection)

*Halifax HR782 was
severely damaged on
30 August 1943 whilst
returning to Ossington
from a raid on
Monchengladbach.
(Author's collection)*

RAF Ossington opened in January 1942 after three standard runways had been constructed during 1941 in a clearing between two large areas of woodland to the north and south of the site. Originally allocated to No 5 Group with a decoy airfield at Upton, the station was actually assigned to training, and Flying Training Command and No 14 (P)AFU arrived on 19 January 1942 with a fleet of Oxfords. When the unit moved to Banff in May 1943 the station finally returned to the control of Bomber Command as had been planned from the outset, and this time the bombers actually arrived when No 82 Operational Training Unit's fifty-four Wellingtons flew in during June. Five Martinets were also acquired for target-towing, and nearby Gamston was selected as a satellite field.

By June 1944 the unit was still very much in business at Ossington, although some Hurricanes were also being used by this stage and No 1685 (B)DTF was also flying Tomahawks from the airfield. From 9 January 1945 (by which stage the RAF's training requirements had started to dwindle), Ossington was transferred to Transport Command and the Wellingtons left, to be replaced by the Lancasters of No 6 LFS, a joint Transport Command and BOAC unit tasked with the training of aircrew to fly Lancastrians on the long New Zealand route that had been set up. Renamed as No 1384 Heavy Transport Conversion Unit on 1 November, the unit's first Avro Yorks were received during that month, many being painted in BOAC livery.

*Looking out across the remains of
Ossington's runway 14/32.
(Richard E. Flagg)*

*Buried among the undergrowth at
Ossington, an air raid shelter
survives intact. (Richard E. Flagg)*

The HCU's activities ended in May 1946 and in August of that year RAF Ossington closed down and lay abandoned for many years until the entire airfield site was slowly broken up for re-sale as hardcore. Today virtually nothing of this once huge bomber base remains. A few crumbling technical site buildings can still be seen but the runways, most of the taxiways and almost all of the dispersals have gone, and from the ground it is difficult to picture how an airfield of any great substance could ever have existed here. But the road that now crosses the site follows the path of two of the former runways, and provides at least a hint of how very different things used to be seventy years ago.

Runways: 240 (2,000yd x 50yd) concrete, 268 (1,400yd x 50yd) concrete, 318 (1,400yd x 50yd) concrete. *Hangars:* T2 (4). *Hardstandings:* Heavy Bomber (30). *Accommodation:* RAF: 205 Officers, 456 SNCOs, 1,461 ORs; WAAF: 9 Officers, 5 SNCOs, 327 ORs.

PAPPLEWICK MOOR, Nottinghamshire

Grid ref SK554508, Lat 53:03:08N (53.05223) Lon 1:10:28W (-1.17442), 220ft asl. On B6011 on SE side of Papplewick village

Once examined as a possible site for what eventually became RAF Hucknall, Papplewick Moor's history was short and uneventful. First established in 1918 as an RLG (Relief Landing Ground) for No 15 Training Depot Station at Hucknall, the station's activity lasted for just one year, after which the site was largely abandoned, although local residents report that aircraft still occasionally used it. On 4 June 1947 an Avro Anson landed here while flying a navigation sortie from RAF Manston. After encountering bad weather, the pilot elected to land at the nearest available airfield, which he assumed to be Hucknall, but in bad visibility (and a heavy thunderstorm) it transpired that the Anson had landed heavily on Papplewick Moor, on the site of the former airfield.

The site came back into use during the Second World War under the control of No 21 Group as a Relief Landing Ground for No 25 EFTS based at Hucknall, but it is believed that few aircraft actually landed here, as local housing had started to encroach upon the site's approaches, and most flying was confined to circuits and overshoots. Never a particularly active site, Papplewick Moor was redundant by the end of the war and was not used for flying again after 1945. No evidence of the airfield is now visible; indeed, there is some doubt as to where the field actually was, with different locations being identified by different historians. However, it seems most likely that it was somewhere south of the B6011, west of the B683, but there is now no obvious evidence of the airfield's brief existence.

Runways: 0 (grass field). *Hangars:* 0. *Hardstandings:* 0. *Accommodation:* RAF; N/A

PEMBREY, Dyfed

Grid ref SN402037, Lat 51:42:33N (51.70927) Lon 4:18:49W (-4.31359), 17ft asl. Off A484, 7 miles NW of Llanelli

Although the airfield at Pembrey first became operational in 1939, the site's association with military aviation began in 1936 when a training facility for anti-aircraft gunners was established here and No 280 Ground Defence Squadron arrived. When No 2 Armament School formed here in 1939 the airfield was still being completed, but as the station's facilities were developed (including the construction of three runways in a typical triangular layout) the first fighter squadrons arrived, the Spitfires of No 92 Squadron flying in during June 1940. Although the unit was officially 'resting' at Pembrey, the Luftwaffe was still engaged occasionally and a bomber was shot down over Wiltshire on 4 July, followed by the destruction of a Ju 88 on the 24th near Porthcawl.

When the squadron left for Biggin Hill in September at the height of the Battle of Britain, No 79 Squadron arrived with Hurricanes and flew convoy and sector patrols from Pembrey for nearly a year. The unit intercepted a formation of He 111s off St David's Head during one sortie and on 20 November it claimed the destruction of a Ju 88 that had been photographing the results of the

Luftwaffe's raid on Coventry. No 32 Squadron (also flying Hurricanes) move to Pembrey during April 1941 and both stayed active until June, at which stage they left. No 316 'City of Warsaw' Squadron was formed here on 15 February 1941 and became operational ten days later, its Hurricanes being assigned to patrols around the Bristol Channel; this unit also vacated Pembrey in June. The last fighters to operate here at this stage were Tomahawks from 26 Squadron, a detachment having been sent during June to participate in exercises with the School of Artillery at Sennybridge.

With the fighters gone, the station was occupied by No 1 Air Gunnery School from 15 June, Blenheims and Lysanders gradually becoming a familiar site on the airfield, although thirty-four of the Blenheims were flown to Upwood in May 1942 for possible use on the 'Thousand Bomber' raid being planned for Cologne. Ultimately they were not needed, which is probably just as well, considering that the aircraft were already well used and somewhat weary, and after returning to Pembrey they were soon replaced by Ansons.

The airfield's location (and proximity to many other military units) attracted a variety of visiting aircraft, including the temporary accommodation of a Fairey Albacore during December 1941, for trials of an anti-submarine bomb, followed by trials with a Whitley bomber during 1942, towing illuminated targets for night-firing training use (the concept wasn't adopted). In April 1944 the Vickers Warwick was flown on trials here on behalf of the Ministry of Aircraft Production, but the most famous visitor of all was certainly a Luftwaffe Fw 190, which landed at Pembrey on 23 June 1942. The aircraft's pilot had been engaged in a dogfight with RAF units from Exeter and Portreath and, having become disorientated, he headed for what he thought to be occupied France, flying victory rolls with some flair upon arrival at what he assumed to be his home base. After landing he quickly realised that he was at Pembrey, but before he had a chance to destroy the aircraft he was captured by RAF personnel and the Fw 190 was saved for close scrutiny and evaluation – an invaluable gift to the RAF.

A poor-quality image that shows the once busy flight line at Pembrey during the 1950s, with the Operational Conversion Unit's Hunters accompanied by a handful of Vampires in the background. (Author's collection)

The incongruous sight of a Focke-Wulf 190 pictured at Pembrey after its surprise arrival in 1942. (IWM)

Rather less exotic visitors included Halifax DT551 on 9 December (one engine disabled), Liberator 41-23817 in January 1943 (followed by more Liberators in April, en route to Valley from Marrakesh) and a number of C-47s evacuating casualties from Normandy. Also based here for varying periods were some Beaufighters from 238 and 248 Squadrons, as well as Defiants from 256 and 307 Squadrons. No 1 AGS continued to operate from Pembrey, its Ansons being replaced by Wellingtons late in 1944, followed by Spitfires to replace the Martinets (for fighter affiliation duties) and the unit finally disbanded on 14 June 1945. No 3 ACHU moved in after this date, but for some time the airfield was virtually deserted. It was not until November 1946 that significant flying activity resumed, with No 595 Squadron having moved in from Fairwood Common during the previous month with Spitfires and Martinets, to continue working with the School of AA at nearby Manorbier. The unit's Spitfires were gradually supplemented by and eventually replaced by Vampire jets and the unit was renumbered as No 5 Squadron on 11 February 1949.

The airfield's main runway was extended in anticipation of further jet operations, and on 1 September 1952 No 233 Operational Conversion Unit was formed at Pembrey, operating Tempests, Vampires, Meteors and eventually Hunters. The OCU became extremely busy with a huge demand for suitably qualified Hunter pilots, and it remained in business at Pembrey until 1 September 1957, at which stage the Hunter training had become established across the Bristol Channel at Chivenor in Devon.

At first glance this photograph could well have been taken at Chivenor, but it is in fact Pembrey during the OCU's stay, while operating Hunters. (Ted Gauntlett)

The magnificent Hunter, pictured at Pembrey while serving with the OCU. Note the Vampires in the background. (Ted Gauntlett)

The RAF vacated Pembrey in 1957 and the airfield remained largely abandoned for more than thirty years with only parts being used for various exercises and other tasks. However, the RAF maintained a close connection with the base, as a bombing range is situated close by and the airfield provided a useful navigation fix for crews using the range.

In 1997 the airfield was finally established as a civil airport facility and is now active again with private, recreational and commercial aircraft operating here. Unfortunately, more than half of the airfield has been used for many years as a racing circuit, and the airport uses only the northern third of the old main runway. It seems quite absurd that a large airfield lies virtually unused while a thriving airport facility is obliged to use only a small portion of the site. It is to be hoped that the wisdom of local planners will eventually see the racing exported to a less important site, enabling the airport to reach its full potential. But for now the runways still remain (although the central portion of the main runway has been partially removed), the old OCU aircraft servicing platform survives, and even a couple of hangers still stand. Virtually all of the RAF technical and domestic site is gone, but the airfield is remarkably intact and as the occasional Cessna drifts over the adjacent coast and down to Pembrey, it isn't difficult to picture the OCU Hunters screaming home after another sortie on the nearby ranges.

Although the RAF has long since abandoned Pembrey airfield, the adjacent range is still very much in business, as illustrated by this Hercules from Lyneham, operating from the beach. (Jason Holloway)

Pembrey range attracts a variety of military users, including helicopters from Odiham. Two Chinooks are pictured here, approaching over the range tower. (Jason Holloway)

An aerial view of Pembrey in 1987. The airfield has survived remarkably well although most of the station's technical and domestic site has now gone. (D. J. Akerman via Richard E. Flagg)

Runways: 220 (1,740yd x 50yd) concrete covered with tarmac and wood chippings, 270 (1,340yd x 50yd) concrete covered with tarmac and wood chippings, 340 (1,180yd x 50yd) concrete covered with tarmac and wood chippings. *Hangars:* VR1 (3), Cranwell type (2), F Type (4), Blister (13). *Hardstandings:* Circular (27), Fighter pens (3), Apron (1). *Accommodation:* RAF: 85 Officers, 180 SNCOs, 1,263 ORs; WAAF: 5 Officers, 4 SNCOs, 234 ORs.

PEMBROKE DOCK, Dyfed

Grid ref SM962034, Lat 51:41:33N (51.69262) Lon 4:57:00W (-4.94994), 30ft asl. At W end of A4139, 4 miles SE of Milford Haven

One of the best-known and significant former RAF bases in Wales, Pembroke Dock never commanded acres of grass or concrete, but the base became home for countless flying boats and will be forever associated with the magnificent Sunderland, which flew from Milford Haven's waters.

As an extremely important and historical dockyard, the first military presence can be traced back to 1845 when Royal Marines from the Portsmouth Division were based here in order to provide a defensive capability for the area, Martello towers being assembled at each end of the dockyard. The military presence at this garrison continued until the dockyard closed in 1926, but in 1930 the RAF arrived and RAF Pembroke Dock opened on 1 January. The first aircraft to be based here were Supermarine Southamptons from Nos 210 and 230 Squadrons, the latter being formed here on 1 December 1934, although it was not until September 1935 that the first hangar was completed and all servicing work had to be conducted in the open air from a floating dock for many months.

When the Second World War began it was Nos 201 and 228 Squadrons that were based at Pembroke Dock (or 'PD' as it was referred to by the crews based here), both units equipped with Sunderlands. They were tasked with the patrol and protection of the local shipping lanes, and the wider expanses of the Irish Sea, the English Channel and the South Western Approaches. U-boat patrols became a routine part of the squadron's daily operations, and before September 1939 was out No 228 Squadron had already scored two victories against the German marauders. Unfortunately, the action was not all one way and during May 1941 Pembroke Dock was hit by bombs that had been directed at the nearby town, one airman being killed, although damage to the station and aircraft was not significant.

After the fall of France, many of the Sunderlands ventured out to the Bay of Biscay so that the U-boats could be intercepted as they left their pens in Brest, Lorient and St Nazaire, destined for the Atlantic where they would relieve the Wolf Pack crews, which posed such a huge danger to allied convoys. No 210 Squadron re-equipped with Catalinas, and on 30 May 1943 one of its aircraft (FP264) was badly damaged by gunfire, one of the crew being killed. The aircraft recovered to Milford Haven and the

An excellent aerial view of Pembroke Dock in its heyday, with Sunderlands and Catalinas spread around the site. (via Doug Pollard)

The mighty Sunderland, in this case ML824, was the very last of a long line of Sunderlands to leave the historic station. (Phil Jarrett collection)

crew managed to escape before it beneath the surface. Other sorties could sometimes be no less formidable, and on 2 June a Sunderland crew from No 461 Squadron engaged no fewer than eight Ju 88s off the Bay of Biscay. With the Sunderland's port outer engine disabled and the rear turret's hydraulics shot through, the crew battled on and successfully destroyed three of the Ju 88s, prompting the remaining aircraft to head back to base. The hapless Sunderland limped back as far as Cornwall and was ultimately beached at Praa Sands.

The US Navy eventually joined the RAF at Pembroke Dock, a detachment from VP-63 arriving on 20 June 1943 with Catalinas. However, when anti-submarine policy shifted to land-based aircraft, the unit left Pembroke Dock again on 15 December, most of the unit's personnel going to Fleet Air Wing 7 at Dunkeswell to fly Liberators. By the end of October 1943 the station had three resident squadrons, a satellite field at Angle a few miles away, and a new T2 hangar erected for No 78 Maintenance Unit, tasked with Sunderland repairs.

The magnificent Shorts Sunderland, heading out into Milford Haven for take-off. (Author's collection)

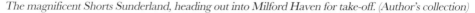

At the end of the war Nos 201 and 230 Squadrons remained active at Pembroke Dock until 1957, when the mighty Sunderland was finally retired from RAF service. Maritime reconnaissance and anti-submarine warfare duties were now the responsibility of land-based units flying the Shackleton and, with no flying boats to support, Pembroke Dock was redundant. On 31 March 1957 the station was placed under Care and Maintenance before being handed back to the Admiralty.

A well-preserved barrack block still stands inside the former RAF Pembroke Dock site. (Paul Francis)

For some years a single Sunderland aircraft was kept here on display in tribute to the countless crews who were stationed here during the wartime years. However, in 1976 the aircraft (ML824) was transported to the RAF Museum at Hendon where it now resides in the rather more benevolent climate of a display hangar. More than fifty years have passed since the RAF vacated Pembroke Dock, but some of the original RAF buildings survive to this day, the former Sergeants' Mess now being a hotel. The original station entrance survives, as do the C Type and T2 hangars that once housed Sunderlands and Catalinas. Sadly, the slipway from which so many flying boats were launched was removed many years ago to make way for new port facilities, but the evidence of the RAF's presence remains and out over the adjacent waters of Milford Haven little has changed since the Second World War, and it isn't difficult to imagine the hundreds of Sunderlands that were once moored here when Pembroke Dock was the world's largest operational flying boat base.

A B Type aeroplane shed among the growing weeds at Pembroke Dock. (Paul Francis)

Another B Type aeroplane shed, still standing but abandoned at Pembroke Dock. (Paul Francis)

Runways: 0 (sea surface). *Hangars:* Various. *Hardstandings:* 0 (slipway). *Accommodation:* RAF; N/A.

PENGAM MOORS, Glamorgan

Grid ref ST216769, Lat 51:29:09N (51.48579) Lon 3:07:45W (-3.12926), 180ft asl. On Rover Way off A469, Cardiff

Opened in September 1931 as Cardiff Municipal Airport, the site was first known as Splott airfield (in recognition of a nearby suburb), but this rather unflattering name was dropped by 1936. From the outset the site was never ideal for flying, being close to the city of Cardiff and perilously close to the coast, and a sea wall was erected in order to prevent continual flooding. In 1932 the site was frequented by Fox Moths, Fokker Spiders and de Havilland Dragons, the ubiquitous Rapide beginning to appear by the end of the 1930s.

An aerial view of Pengham Moors, illustrating the hangar and technical complex and the short concrete runway. (via Doug Pollard)

Commercial operations naturally came to an end at the outbreak of the Second World War and, although a large number of civilian aircraft were assembled here as part of plans to form a National Air Communications pool, they were removed during 1940 and Pengam was taken over by the RAF, No 614 Squadron having arrived from Llandow with Hinds and Hectors during 1939. The unit stayed only briefly and in February 1940 Pengam became the home of No 43 Maintenance Unit, tasked with packing aircraft for shipment overseas. The first aircraft to arrive were Vickers Vildebeestes followed by Tiger Moths from Brize Norton, and subsequently Hurricanes, Lysanders, Harts and Gladiators – even a Northrop Nomad staged through the MU. Confusion with No 43 Group led to the MU being renumbered as No 52 Maintenance Unit on 13 March 1941, at which stage no fewer than seventy-eight Hinds were being prepared for a journey to South Africa. On 4 May some twenty-one Magisters flew in, together with two Walrus amphibians and a Vega Gull.

No 2 Ferry Pilots Pool from Whitchurch set up a detachment at Pengam in order to tackle the heavy workload and the station was renamed as RAF Cardiff. Further aircraft staged through the MU, including Fairey Sea Foxes, Albacores and more Nomads. In order to camouflage what had become a strategically important target, the airport apron and surrounding roads were painted, buildings were camouflaged and netting was used to cover packing areas, while more barrage balloons were erected in order to protect both the airfield and nearby city. This failed to dissuade the Luftwaffe from visiting, however, and on 27 February 1941 Cardiff was attacked, one bomb straying onto the airfield, damaging a hangar. Oddly enough, the only victim of the barrage balloons was a visiting Harvard, which severed a cable with its wing but managed to land safely at Pengam.

During the winter of 1941 Sommerfield track was laid across the grass airfield until a small concrete runway could be constructed during the following summer. During 1942 more Hurricanes staged through (173 in July, for example) together with some Spitfires and Harvards, with at least 150 aircraft of various types being processed during most months. No 8 AACU arrived in November 1940 with a mix of civil aircraft and a few Blenheims and Lysanders, tasked with Army cooperation for the 9th Anti-Aircraft Division based in South Wales. From May 1941 the unit had a uniquely equipped Dominie, which had lights fitted to its undersides, illuminating the wings in such a way as to represent an enemy aircraft caught in a searchlight beam. The equipment was subsequently fitted to other Dominies and Dragonflies flown by the unit, but abandoned when the unit re-equipped with Oxfords and Masters, which remained in use until the unit disbanded in December 1943.

During 1944 even more varied aircraft types appeared at Pengam, including Avengers, Hampdens, Marauders and Thunderbolts, and in August the MU handled a staggering 898 aircraft. A detachment from No 587 Squadron, with Martinets, stayed briefly until September. During November a number of USAAF C-47s arrived to collect stores, and a whole squadron of Piper Cubs was assembled here before being sent to Europe. The number of aircraft being handled started to diminish (Seafires being the most common by this stage) and the RAF took over deliveries from the ATA in July until the MU disbanded on 31 October 1945.

This view of Pengham Moors in the mid-1950s shows the airfield's almost perilous proximity to the coastline. (via Doug Pollard)

After the war the airfield was used by Ansons and Tiger Moths from No 3 Reserve Flying School, and civil flying returned courtesy of BEA, Western Airways and Cambrian Air Services. However, the airfield's small runway was inadequate for even the Dakota and, with larger and heavier aircraft having become more common, a new airport site was established at Rhoose. On 1 April 1954 flying ended at Pengam and the site was taken over by the Ministry of Transport and the CAA's fire-fighting school. When one of the RAF's last Lancasters was burned here as part of a training exercise in 1956 a significant protest was mounted, but to no effect. One can only imagine what would happen if any authority tried to burn a Lancaster fifty years later!

Industrial development slowly covered the airfield site at Pengam and now nothing remains, apart from the appropriately named roads (such as Avro Close and Runway Road) that surround the former airfield site. The runway is gone, buried under the buildings that sprawl across the area. However, the empty fields behind Hind Close include a small concrete track, which may well be a surviving portion of the old runway – all that is left from what was once a small but incredibly busy part of the RAF's wartime activities.

Runways: 0 (grass field). *Hangars:* Various (civil). *Hardstandings:* 0. *Accommodation:* Civil; N/A.

PENKRIDGE, Staffordshire

Grid ref SJ935122, Lat 52:42:30N (52.7083) Lon 2:05:47W (-2.09641), 340ft asl. Between B5012 and M6, SE of Penkridge

Drivers on the busy M6 motorway heading south out of Penkridge might easy fail to notice that among the relatively featureless fields to the east a small centre of private and recreational flying thrives, on the site of a former RAF facility where countless RAF pilots learned the basics of airmanship. Originally known as Pillerton and subsequently Otherton, the site opened on 17 June 1942 as a Relief Landing Ground for No 28 EFTS based at Wolverhampton. Initially the airfield was tasked with the unit's night-flying schedule, as the home base at Wolverhampton was surrounded by barrage balloon defences and operating aircraft near these lethal defences at night would be suicidal. The grass airfield was also used for daytime flying, and was often busy with Tiger Moths flying circuits and practice landings. Few other aircraft types frequented the airfield although a Hurricane diverted here on at least one occasion, and an Anson (DJ634) from No 9 (O)AFU landed here in August 1944 after suffering an engine failure.

The RLG closed in 1945 when flying activities dwindled rapidly and the area quickly reverted to agricultural use, although occasional private flying continued here sporadically. Today the airfield (now known as Otherton again) is home to the Staffordshire Aero Club, although the grass field utilises only a portion of the original airfield. The old RLG buildings have mostly survived (including some of the Robin hangars) and these can be seen in the adjacent (private) farm, but on the small airfield a series of three grass strips is maintained in perfect condition, together with a small clubhouse and small shelters for some of the many microlight aircraft that fly from here. Although all of the flying here is now civil-orientated, one frequent user of the site is a Tiger Moth, reminding locals of the wartime years when the skies around this site were full of these fine old machines.

Runways: E/W (950yd) grass. *Hangars:* Double Standard (1), Blister (1). *Hardstandings:* 0. *Accommodation:* RAF: 2 Officers, 4 SNCOs, 120 ORs.

PENRHOS, Gwynedd

Grid ref SH343336, Lat 52:52:31N (52.87514) Lon 4:27:48W (-4.46337), 40ft asl. Off A499, 1 mile NE of Llanbedrog

This small RAF station opened on 1 February 1937 after a troubled development period hampered by Welsh nationalists who opposed the creation of airfields both at this site and nearby Hells Mouth. Although the local community welcomed the jobs and improvements to its economy, a group of nationalists set fire to the airfield contractor's offices and a subsequent trial was held at the Old Bailey – an odd decision as it immediately drew Germany's attention to the perceived importance of the two airfields and associated ranges that were being developed.

No 5 Armament Training camp was established at Penrhos with six Westland Wallaces together with five range patrol boats based in nearby Pwllheli. On 3 April 1937 no fewer than thirty-four Gloster Gauntlets flew in from Ternhill and aircraft from various Flying Training Schools deployed to the airfield for training, together with aircraft from many operational Squadrons (including Nos 4, 13 and 600), which visited rather more briefly to refuel or lunch-stop during navigational sorties.

By May 1938 the initial opposition to the station appears to have disappeared as an Empire Air Day event was held on the 28th and attracted more than 11,000 spectators. No 9 Air Observers School moved in on 9 September 1939 with Harrows and Battles, and was renamed No 9 Bombing School two months later. Germany finally expressed her interest in the airfield on 8 July 1940 when a Luftwaffe bomber destroyed two Henleys from No 1 AACU, wrecked three blocks of accommodation and damaged a hangar, causing the death of two airmen. Steps were quickly taken to camouflage the airfield, and the surrounding fields were replicated on the airfield through the judicious use of paint, which – at least from a distance – rendered the site almost indistinguishable from the surrounding farmland. However, this was a mixed blessing, as it also caused difficulties for British aircrew who were unfamiliar with the area. Despite the camouflage the Luftwaffe returned on subsequent occasions, but no further damage was sustained.

Hawker Henleys were commonly seen at Penrhos during the early 1940s. (via John Elliott)

In order to provide local air defence a flight of six Spitfires from No 611 Squadron at Ternhill was deployed to Penrhos, later replaced by Hurricanes from 312 Squadron at Speke. The Czech squadron moved en masse to Valley in April 1941 after having spent six months at Penrhos without any sign of further visits from the Luftwaffe. When Llandwrog airfield was completed, No 9 Air Gunnery School was established there and the Penrhos unit became No 9 (O)AFU in February 1942; when No 9 AGS was disbanded, Llandwrog was designated as a satellite field for Penrhos as of 13 June 1942. By this stage No 9 (O)AFU was equipped with Ansons, one of which was damaged by a Halifax that force-landed here, rolling over the edge of the small hillside that skirts the airfield perimeter. The local terrain was a problem for quite a few aircraft, a US Navy Catalina suffering similar indignities on 6 November 1942 when it landed at Penrhos with engine difficulties, struck a hangar and slid off the airfield 'plateau' into an adjacent field. By comparison, Llandwrog had a full compliment of concrete runways, and eventually the AFU headquarters was established there, and Penrhos was designated as the satellite field.

A rare image of an Avro Anson from No 9 (O)AFU, at Penrhos. (via Doug Pollard)

No 9 (O)AFU disbanded on 16 June 1945 and No 21 ACHU occupied the station until 31 March 1946, when it closed, the land being sold off shortly afterwards. Some private aircraft did continue to use the airfield sporadically for many years but today the site is better knows as the home of a caravan park, most of which occupies the main technical area where the Bellman hangars once stood. Some old airfield buildings have survived in various states of disrepair and part of the old perimeter track is still visible, together with a couple of dispersals. Walking through the caravan site it is possible to trace all of the roads that once weaved through the technical and domestic buildings, and although the aircraft are long gone the site still maintains the very obvious atmosphere of a former RAF station.

Runways: NE/SW (860yd) grass, NW/SE (700yd) grass, E/W (700yd) grass. *Hangars:* Bellman (3), F Type (1), Blister (9). *Hardstandings:* Apron, 300yd x 100ft. *Accommodation:* RAF: 106 Officers, 226 SNCOs, 663 ORs.

PEPLOW, Shropshire

Grid ref SJ654235, Lat 52:48:29N (52.80805) Lon 2:30:48W (-2.51329), 230ft asl. Off A442, 1 mile NE of Eaton-upon-Tern

When an airfield first opened for flying at this site, it was known as Childs Ercall aerodrome, in recognition of a nearby village. As a small grass field it was designated as a Relief Landing Ground for Ternhill's Miles Masters, with No 11 SFTS (based at Shawbury) also occasionally flying its Oxfords from the site when necessary, from October 1941. However, the Oxford pilots soon regarded the airfield as too small for safe and regular usage and, with another satellite field available just a mile away at Ollerton, it was decided to develop Childs Ercall into a fully equipped station capable of accommodating a bomber Operational Training Unit, and work on the construction of concrete runways began during 1942. By July 1943 the first crews for No 83 Operational Training Unit were ready to begin training, but the airfield was still being constructed, so crews went to Finningley, Hixon and Lichfield prior to arriving

A T2 hangar at Peplow, surviving in excellent condition. (Richard E. Flagg)

at Childs Ercall later in the year. By this time the runways had been laid and the station had been renamed Peplow (on 20 August) in order to avoid confusion with High Ercall.

Some forty Wellingtons moved in together with four Masters and an Oxford, but with no designated satellite field the unit's full strength was reduced by 25% in order to ease the workload on the station. Regular training quickly got under way both by day and night and some longer cross-country flights were conducted, including missions to France as part of the on-going 'Nickel' exercises. The unit also occasionally conducted reconnaissance sorties, flying Air to Surface Radar searches when required, one such mission taking the crew on a long flight over the North Sea on a fruitless search for missing USAAF crews. More routine flying involved circuit handling and continual landings, overshoots, take-offs and 'rollers', and as a training unit is was hardly surprising that there were many incidents that often looked more catastrophic than they actually were; despite a number of Wellingtons being severely damaged or even written off during training, there were surprisingly few injuries. Even the 'Nickel' operations over France proceeded without any losses and the OTU's activities gradually increased in response to the growing need for qualified crews. The Wellingtons were often marshalled on the grass in order to expedite training efficiency and also in an effort to avoid using the concrete perimeter track, which was in poor condition and was eventually resurfaced.

A moody night image of Wellingtons heading out on a training sortie. Peplow was home to countless Wellington bombers and their crews during the Second World War. (via Ken Billingham)

On 20 July 1944 the unit's gunnery flight was disbanded, to be replaced by a Bomber Defence Training Flight equipped with Hurricanes, used for fighter affiliation. Visiting aircraft were few (the airfield was generally busy with its own traffic), but aircraft did occasionally divert to Peplow, one notable date being 8 August when twenty-five Halifaxes flew in. Following the loss of many glider crews at Arnhem, the OTU was closed and replaced by No 23 Heavy Glider Conversion Unit as of 28 October 1944, and the Wellingtons slowly departed, Albemarles and Horsas taking their place. Most of the unit's glider landings were performed at Seighford, a station that had been allocated as Peplow's satellite field and which had the advantage of being away from the congested skies around Peplow and nearby Hinstock.

The HGCU disbanded on 31 December and No 21 (P)AFU arrived with a fleet of Oxfords, using Peplow as a satellite field until February 1945. No 1515 BAT Flight came to Peplow on 30 January 1945, but training activities were hampered by difficulties caused by the proximity of Hinstock's airfield circuit, the approach beams for the two airfields being almost parallel. The situation was resolved a few weeks later when the BAT Flight moved to Coleby Grange. Peplow was then transferred to the Admiralty as a satellite field for Hinstock. A detachment of Oxfords from 758 Squadron operated here for a short period, then No 780 Squadron was formed at the station in February 1946 with Oxfords, Harvards, Fireflies and even a few Lancasters.

Runway 12/30 at Peplow, still intact and recognisable. (Richard E. Flagg)

Peplow's watch office has suffered a rather drastic 'makeover' and retains very little of its original structure, which begs the question as to why it was even retained by its new owners. (Richard E. Flagg)

Flying continued until the end of 1949, at which stage the station was closed and sold off a few years later. Sixty years on, most of the runway surfaces have been removed, although the farming of the surrounding fields has left most of the airfield layout easily visible, especially from the air. The south-western parts of the main and secondary runways have survived, although top soil and trees make them almost indistinguishable from any distance. Most of the dispersals have gone and, although they too can still be recognised from the air, they can barely be seen from ground level. The control tower is effectively gone, but surprisingly the hangars have survived and continue to function as useful shelters for farming stores and equipment. Although virtually all of the airfield buildings have gone and much of the runway and taxiway surfaces have long since disappeared, the site is still recognisable as an airfield and now a small road runs off Eaton Road, directly across the old main runway, affording an excellent view of the former airfield in all directions. Some private flying takes place from the former eastern perimeter tracks, but the runways are silent and the roar of the Wellington bombers is no more than a distant memory.

> *Runways:* 183 (1,400yd x 50yd) concrete and wood chippings, 223 (2,000yd x 50yd) concrete and wood chippings, 300 (1,400yd x 50yd) concrete and wood chippings. *Hangars:* T2 (4), B1 (1). *Hardstandings:* Heavy Bomber (30). *Accommodation:* RAF: 222 Officers, 590 SNCOs, 879 ORs; WAAF: 6 Officers, 4 SNCOs, 344 ORs.

PERSHORE, Worcestershire

Grid ref SO972495, Lat 52:08:39N (52.14423) Lon 2:02:31W (-2.042), 120ft asl. 4 miles NE of Pershore off A44

The history of this airfield can be traced back to June 1934 when the Worcestershire Flying Club began operations from a grass landing field near Tilesford House. A small flight shed was assembled and among the resident aircraft (which included a couple of Tiger Moths) a pair of Supermarine Walrus amphibians paid a visit during 1938. As the Second World War approached, the site was identified as being suitable for development into a larger airfield, and in February 1941 RAF Pershore opened (the site was briefly known as Throckmorton). However, as with many airfields constructed at this time, the runways and other airfield facilities were still incomplete. To add to the contractor's problems, the Luftwaffe dropped sixteen bombs on the airfield on 16 March, causing damage before any aircraft had even arrived. The newly laid runways caught the attention of another enemy bomber crew on 10 April, by which stage six aircraft had arrived at Pershore, one of which (a Wellington) suffering damage. The Luftwaffe made a third visit on 10 May but, after attracting ground fire, the He 111 flew off.

No 23 Operational Training Unit formed at Pershore on 1 April 1941, responsible for the training of Canadian crews for the RAF's Commonwealth squadrons. Wellingtons quickly filled the airfield and a few Ansons and a Tiger Month also moved in. The airfield dispersal and taxiways were still incomplete at this stage and training activities were also hampered by the lack of a suitable satellite field until Defford became available in September. The first 'Nickel' leaflet-dropping raid over France took place on 20 July, one Wellington being damaged by a barrage balloon cable while passing Weybridge on the return flight, although the crew returned safely to Pershore.

Visiting aircraft were few, although a Hampden from 144 Squadron is known to have diverted here on 28 May, and Stirling N6087 from No 15 Squadron landed here after the crew became disorientated after raiding Cologne on 27 September. More notable was the arrival of twelve Wellingtons from No 103 Squadron on 27 March 1942, deployed to Pershore as a starting point for a bombing raid over Germany, although only two aircraft returned here, the rest flying on to other bases. When Defford was withdrawn as a satellite field on 18 May the Operational Training Unit had to conduct all of the unit's activities directly from Pershore, a difficult task made worse by the need to assign aircraft and crews to bombing raids on Essen and Cologne.

On 30 July thirty-seven of the unit's Wellingtons attacked Dusseldorf, one aircraft (X9917) being reported as missing. In September sorties were flown against targets in Dusseldorf, Essen and Bremen, three aircraft failing to return from the raid on Essen. One aircraft (X3751) disappeared without trace during a sortie on 1 October 1942, and on 2 October the following year a similar fate befell X3470. As a training unit, accidents were common, although injuries and fatalities were rather less so, but many aircrew lost their lives during the unit's stay at Pershore.

On 16 November 1942 RAF Stafford was designated as a new satellite landing field and A Flight was deployed there with immediate effect, easing the situation at the home base. Visiting aircraft during this period included eight Wellingtons on 1 March (returning from a raid on St Nazaire) and sixteen Lancasters (which had attacked the same target) on 23 March. The Operational Training Unit's last mission took place on 30 August 1943 when six aircraft attacked a target in France. By November the unit's strength had been reduced to forty aircraft, together with four Martinets for target-towing and Tomahawks for fighter affiliation.

The unit finally disbanded on 15 March 1944, after which Pershore passed to Ferry Command and No 1 Ferry Unit was formed here the next day, tasked with the ferrying of aircraft from many overseas bases. Types handled included Mosquitoes, Beaufighters, Halifaxes, Venturas, Wellingtons and Warwicks, as well as sixteen Beaufighters that were delivered to the Portuguese Navy in March 1945. The unit disbanded early in 1948, after which No 10 Advanced Flying School arrived with Oxfords, staying here until 1953. The RAF's presence at Pershore effectively ended at this stage, although the airfield continued to play host to a variety of RAF aircraft as the station passed to the control of the Royal Radar Establishment, which moved here from Defford in September 1957.

A post-war aerial image of Pershore, illustrating the west-east road that crosses the main runway, and the V-Bomber ORP to the south-west of the runway. (QinetiQ)

In anticipation of the arrival of jet aircraft (particularly new jet bombers), Pershore's main runway was extended across Long Lane, which linked two small villages. Rather than divert the road, traffic lights were installed and a runway crossing was manned by local policemen. From this unique vantage point a strange and fascinating collection of unusual aircraft could be seen over successive years, although the sensitive nature of the RRE was always hidden from public scrutiny and security patrols discouraged any members of the public from gazing upon Pershore's facilities for too long. Hastings, Varsity and Canberra aircraft became common sights on the airfield, together with many other test aircraft and RAF types that either visited or were assigned to the RRE for trials. Additionally, a V-Bomber ORP (Operational Readiness Platform) was constructed just off the main runway's southern threshold and Vulcans, Victors and Valiants were deployed here at frequent intervals to practise dispersal techniques. The familiar radar-nosed Canberras were joined by a Viscount, Meteor and even a Buccaneer, but as radar trials and development slowed down, the RRE (later named RS&RE) aircraft were merged into RAE Bedford's test fleet and Pershore was closed to flying in 1978.

Pershore's runway 04/22 is still visible, but long withdrawn from flight operations. (Richard E. Flagg)

Looking across Pershore's main runway to the old RS&RE flight line, where Canberras, Hastings, Buccaneers and Viscounts once stood. (Richard E. Flagg)

Thirty years later, Pershore remains almost untouched from the days when flying ended. The runways are somewhat overgrown and the hangars are largely deserted, but with most of the site still under MoD control little has changed, and the airfield is unused, apart from occasional training exercises conducted by Police, Army and Special Forces units. Parts of the airfield were used to burn and bury 100,000 cattle during the 2001 foot and mouth disease epidemic, and other plans have included a prison, an eco-estate and an immigrant centre, but each successive plan has been subsequently dropped and Pershore remains unused, awaiting an uncertain future. The airfield's runways, hangars and other facilities can be easily observed from many locations, including Long Lane, which still crosses the main runway, but traffic lights no longer stop the local vehicles or pedestrians, and the mighty V-Bombers no longer thunder past.

Runways: 217 (2,000yd x 50yd) concrete and asphalt, 275 (1,500yd x 50yd) concrete and asphalt, 336 (1,400yd x 50yd) concrete and asphalt. *Hangars:* J Type (1), T2 (4). *Hardstandings:* Pans (31). *Accommodation:* RAF: 214 Officers, 448 SNCOs, 1,275 ORs; WAAF: 10 Officers, 6 SNCOs, 396 ORs.

PERTON, West Midlands

Grid ref SO862999, Lat 52:35:49N (52.597) Lon 2:12:18W (-2.2049), 400ft asl. Off A454 in centre of Perton

Sitting inside the Pear & Partridge pub, looking out across the endless houses and shops, it is impossible to imagine a Boeing B-17 roaring past the window. But seventy years ago, from the very same vantage point, such a view was almost commonplace, and the sprawling housing developments that make up this modern suburb of Wolverhampton were no more than a distant dream. Back in 1941 this same area of land was an open field, first used as a landing site during the First World War for No 38 (Home Defence) Squadron RFC, which was based here during 1916 and 1917. The field was abandoned after the war, but brought back into use on 2 August 1941; at this stage that was no clear role for the station but the construction of earth-banked dispersals suggests that fighter operations must have been the most likely preference. However, the airfield remained unused and the Princess Wilhelmina Brigade of the Royal Netherlands Army moved into the station's living quarters towards the end of the year. The only aircraft to use the site at this stage was a Magister (N7626), which made a force-landing on 11 November 1941, damaging its tail wheel on the unfinished runway surface in the process.

The Parachute Training School inspected the site as a possible base for training operations, but, being close to densely populated Wolverhampton, it was accepted that the airfield was no more suitable than the unit's current base at Ringway. By this stage three runways had been laid, and Shawbury adopted Perton as a Relief Landing Ground. The first Oxfords from No 11 SFTS arrived on 26 January 1942 and, with a heavy training schedule being handled back at Shawbury, the detachment became virtually independent from its home base. A single T2 hangar was built at Perton to enable servicing to be conducted there, and both instructors and students were accommodated on-base.

When No 21 (P)AFU was formed at Wheaton Aston, Perton became a satellite field for that station, although the airfield was also used by Helliwells Ltd, a company contracted to overhaul Douglas Boston and Havoc aircraft, and these were flight-tested at Perton after having been repaired at the company's Walsall factory. The company eventually took on the larger B-17 Fortress, and although Perton was more than capable of handling aircraft of this size, a pronounced dip in the middle of the airfield made take-offs and landings slightly unnerving, even if they were still safe.

The airfield was declared redundant when Helliwells ended its work and the requirement for a satellite field lapsed, and by the end of 1945 the RAF's presence here had ended. After this year the only flying at Perton was the occasional light aircraft, and some model aircraft flown by local enthusiasts. The fields were slowly encroached upon by nearby Wolverhampton and eventually the entire airfield site was engulfed by housing. Today Perton is a busy town that shows no trace of any links with the RAF, apart from a memorial erected near the local Sainsburys supermarket. Every inch of the runways and perimeter tracks is gone, and the development of so many houses and shops has obliterated the former airfield. All that remains is a crumbling concrete hut off Wrottesley Park Road, and the names of the roads that have been built on top of the former airfield, such as Browning Grove and Shawbury Grove. The co-located Shackleton Drive seems slightly inappropriate, as there is no record of this post-war aircraft having ever visited the airfield. A more subtle reminder of the airfield's former existence is just behind the shops, where a lake fills the once notorious dip that used to sit in the middle of the main runway.

Runways: 220 (1,400yd x 50yd) tarmac, 160 (1,100yd x 50yd) tarmac, 280 (1,100yd x 50yd) tarmac. *Hangars:* T2 (1). *Hardstandings:* Loop (3). *Accommodation:* RAF: 39 Officers, 78 SNCOs, 600 ORs; WAAF: 6 Officers, 7 SNCOs, 202 ORs.

POULTON, Cheshire

Grid ref SJ401593, Lat 53:07:39N (53.12751) Lon 2:53:45W (-2.89576), 50ft asl. 2 miles W of Aldford off B5130

Constructed as a projected satellite for Hawarden, 4 miles away to the west, Poulton was opened on 1 March 1943 when No 3 Squadron of No 41 Operational Training Unit arrived with Hurricanes and Mustangs. This move, together with that of No 57 OTU to Eshott, eased the burden on Hawarden, which was extremely busy at this time. Built by George Wimpey & Co on the edge of the Eaton Hall estate, few buildings were ever erected here, although fourteen Blister hangars were eventually constructed, together with a canvas Bessoneau hangar for the Oxfords of No 1515 BAT Flight, eight of which were deployed here, staying until 30 June 1945 when the unit moved to Peplow. Most of the unit's flying was conducted either at night or in poor visibility conditions. The Standard Beam Approach equipment obviously did not rely upon good weather or daylight, and this ensured that the BAT Flight's activities rarely interfered with the routine Mustang and Hurricane operations.

However, another lodger unit arrived in February 1944 when the Woodvale (or 'W') Detachment of No 12 (P)AFU was set up at Poulton with a fleet of Blenheims. The unit's home base at Grantham was suffering from waterlogging and, in order to maintain its training programme (producing pilots for the Beaufighter squadrons), a detachment was set up at Woodvale. However, when that base was tasked with the temporary accommodation of some fighter units, the Blenheims had to move to Poulton, to a station that was already busy and hardly over-equipped with facilities. Thankfully the detachment lasted for only a few weeks.

At the end of 1943 the training system was reappraised and, because of a surplus of trained crews, a holding unit (No 3 Tactical Exercise Unit) was set up at Hawarden, and the Operational Training Unit was divided into three squadrons, the Mustangs going back to Hawarden and the Hurricanes being based at Poulton together with a small fleet of Harvards. Training then continued until March 1945 when No 41 OTU moved to Chilbolton while the day-fighter wing (which was by then at Poulton) was renumbered and established back at Hawarden as No 58 Operational Training Unit. This was also divided into three squadrons, one of which was allocated to Poulton. Crews ended their course with advanced training here, flying bombing sorties over the Fenns Moss range near Whitchurch, and conducting air-to-ground sorties on the Prestatyn ranges. No 58 OTU's activities ended on 20 July 1945, and Poulton was placed under Care and Maintenance.

The RAF never returned and the airfield was soon sold off, although occasional appearances by private aircraft continued, including a visit by the Duke of Westminster in his Grumman Turbo Goose. Other aircraft landed here after mistaking the airfield for Hawarden, but today all flying activity has long since ended and the entire site is once more a peaceful part of the Cheshire countryside. The buildings (including the hangars and control tower) are all gone, but the runways are still intact, the main runway running across Pulford Approach Road. However, with trees having been planted on a major section of the southern secondary runway, it is difficult to see the airfield until the runway is actually crossed. Behind the trees the airfield is still there, complete with dispersals, some of which are now buried in the trees beside Pulford Approach Road. Built on a private estate, access to the airfield is not easy, but virtually all of the site can be seen from the adjacent roads. Despite the removal of all the buildings, there is still a virtually complete airfield layout here to be seen.

> *Runways:* 020 (2,000yd x 50yd) concrete with wood chippings, 065 (1,400yd x 50yd) concrete with wood chippings, 140 (1,400yd x 50yd) concrete with wood chippings. *Hangars:* Blister (8), Bessoneau (1). *Hardstandings:* 100ft frying pan (24). *Accommodation:* RAF: 79 Officers, 178 SNCOs, 720 ORs; WAAF: 2 Officers, 8 SNCOs, 90 ORs.

RATCLIFFE, Leicestershire

Grid ref SK635159, Lat 52:44:15N (52.73759) Lon 1:03:38W (-1.06044), 115ft asl. On A46, 2 miles W of Thrussington

A small and relatively unknown site, Ratcliffe was constructed during 1930 by Sir Lindsay Everard, who operated a small number of light aircraft from the grass airfield. Opened with a blaze of publicity, an air display was held here on 6 September, the star of the show not being an aircraft, but the famous aviator Amy Johnson. More than 100 aircraft took part in the show, one crashing on take-off after the show, although only one person suffered injuries as a result. Many other public events were staged here and the airfield became a very popular and well-used site with a well-appointed clubhouse and other facilities, which even included a pool! Possibly the most significant event to occur here was on 3 May 1939 when the first flight of the Taylorcraft Model Plus C (G-AFWN), the forerunner of the famous Auster, took place.

The site's military connections began in 1939 when the airfield was requisitioned by the War Office. No 6 Ferry Pilots Pool of the Air Transport Auxiliary operated from here until mid-1945; the unit then abandoned the airfield and it was returned to civil use. Many RAF aircraft came to Radcliffe, including Spitfires from Castle Bromwich, Ansons, Hurricanes, Typhoons, Lancasters and Halifaxes, together with many Tiger Moths, which were overhauled at the site. When the ATA left, a farewell show was staged on 6 October, which included a display by Alex Henshaw in a Spitfire and Sir Geoffrey de Havilland flying a Vampire jet.

XR271 was one of numerous Austers operated by the Army Air Corps. Pictured at Ratcliffe, the aircraft wears standard Army camouflage, plus high-visibility orange patches. (Author's collection)

This undated photograph of Ratcliffe evidently illustrates one of the air displays held at this site. (via John Deansmith)

A fascinating glimpse of Ratcliffe aerodrome, with a Lancaster, Stirling, Halifax, Dakota and Rapide among the aircraft visible – quite a selection for a small site. (via John Deansmith)

After the war the Leicester Aero Club moved here, but in May 1949 Sir Lindsay died and his prized aerodrome was sold, a final sixteen-aircraft flight taking place on 25 March 1950. Having been returned to agricultural use since this date, all traces of the airfield are now gone, including the remains of a Harrow that once languished on the airfield perimeter. But just off the busy A46 a track leads to some farm buildings and a large patch of concrete. This was the original aerodrome headquarters and most of the buildings are survivors from those days. Even the pool survives – just!

Ratcliffe's famous pool, a luxury for visiting crews that still survives, albeit in a derelict condition. (via John Deansmith)

Runways: 0 (grass field). *Hangars:* Civil (1). *Hardstandings:* Concrete apron (1). *Accommodation:* Civil; N/A.

REARSBY, Leicestershire

Grid ref SK652141, Lat 52:43:16N (52.72106) Lon 1:02:10W (-1.03598), 105ft asl. On A607, SE of Rearsby village

Another small grass airfield, Rearsby opened just before the outbreak of the Second World War as a base for private flying, and the Leicestershire County Flying Club became the main resident with a fleet of varied types. During 1938 Taylorcraft Aeroplanes established a factory here and embarked upon the production of aircraft, the company's first machine having made its first flight at nearby Ratcliffe on 3 May 1939. By September some twenty-three aircraft had been manufactured. Private flying came to an end as the war began, but Taylorcraft took on subcontract work for the major aircraft companies, and twenty-two of the completed aircraft were impounded, re-engined and delivered to the RAF. Taylorcraft had already loaned some aircraft to the RAF so that the type could be evaluated as a potential artillery observation aircraft, and the Model Plus D eventually saw service in France and participated in the Dunkirk evacuation. A further 100 aircraft were ordered and these became the famous Auster Mk 1 aircraft. Taylorcraft then assumed the task of repairing Tiger Moths and progressed to Hurricanes, four hangars being assembled for this purpose and the airfield extended in order to provide a larger landing space.

A Taylorcraft Auster III performs a commendably short take-off for the cameraman at Rearsby in September 1943. (Author's collection)

This is Rearsby from the air, illustrating the small size of the site and an interesting line-up of Austers, awaiting delivery. (Author's collection)

Production of the ubiquitous Auster continued throughout the war, and on 8 March 1946 the company name was changed to Auster Aircraft Ltd, with Rearsby as the headquarters and main production facility. However, by 1947 production dipped, sales of civilian aircraft being slow and the surplus of military aircraft making demand fall even further. By 1959 the company was attempting to venture into helicopter production (without success) and was finally taken over by British Executive & General Aircraft Ltd (Beagle), Rearsby becoming the Beagle-Auster division. Production continued here until 1964, the last aircraft to emerge being Beagle Husky G-ASNC, certified on 23 April of that year. In 1968 the company was sold to Hants & Sussex Aviation and the Rearsby factory closed in 1969. No further flying was conducted from the site thereafter and the landing field was resold for agricultural use. The factory site became an industrial unit, which still stands adjacent to the B674 road, but, with no obvious airfield buildings to identify the site, there is nothing to remind visitors of Rearsby's small but important role in the development of British military aviation.

Although associated with the Auster family of aircraft, the Beagle Basset was also manufactured at Rearsby. The RAF ordered the Basset as a VIP transport aircraft which enjoyed a relatively short and uneventful service career. (Phil Jarrett collection)

An excellent aerial view of the small manufacturing site at Rearsby. Austers are visible to the left of the image and a pair of Bassets can be seen in the foreground. (Phil Jarrett collection)

An Auster T7 at Rearsby in 1959 (Rod Simpson)

Runways: 0 (grass field). *Hangars:* Civil flight shed (1). *Hardstandings:* 0.
Accommodation: Civil; N/A.

REDNAL, Shropshire

Grid ref SJ371275, Lat 52:50:31N (52.84208) Lon 2:56:06W (-2.93489), 275ft asl. 2 miles E of B5009, 1.5 miles SE of Rednal village

Opening during April 1942, Rednal became the home of No 61 Operational Training Unit, whose Spitfires became long-term residents at the airfield. Indeed, the unit was the station's only user, apart from a detachment of Masters from No 6 AACU that operated here briefly. With a satellite field at Montford Bridge, the OTU moved in from Heston, in order to keep its training activities well away from the busy (and dangerous) operational areas to the south.

Situated in a rural area of Shropshire, the station's isolation led to the creation of a special railway service to Shrewsbury, enabling personnel to connect with the main Birkenhead-London route. The unit had a shadow designation as No 561 Squadron, but this designation was only taken up on one occasion on 27 June 1943 when eight Spitfires were scrambled to intercept a Ju 88 over the Irish Sea. No contact was made and this was the unit's only engagement with the enemy.

A Spitfire lands at Rednal in 1942. (Author's collection)

Use of a firing range near Llanbedr became a regular part of training, but a target was also set up on the airfield at Rednal so that dive-bombing techniques could be practised more locally. The target was removed after two Spitfires collided over the airfield. As a training unit equipped with relatively aged and well-used Spitfires (many being Battle of Britain veterans), accidents were common.

Rednal became home to a military hospital in 1944, in anticipation of many casualties after D-Day. The first (flown in by C-47) arrived from Normandy on 3 July and seventy-seven C-47s delivered more to Rednal during August, some 1,750 men arriving here directly from the battle zones.

Douglas C-47 transports pictured at Rednal from the watch tower roof. (Author's collection)

Visiting aircraft were few, although a Liberator diverted here on 24 April 1944 (en route from Cairo to Prestwick), and a Lockheed Electra (LA621) and Baltimore AG698 are both known to have been seen on the airfield. On 8 January 1945 a flight of five Mustangs arrived from No 55 Operational Training Unit to supplement the Spitfires, and more aircraft were subsequently delivered; they were joined by Harvards, which eventually replaced the Masters for dual-control instructional flying.

Perhaps the most unusual event to have taken place at Rednal was the discovery of a German prisoner of war on 18 February 1945, sitting in the cockpit of a Mustang on one of the airfield's remote dispersals, armed with a knife and a bag of pepper. Having escaped from a camp at Oswestry, he had planned to escape in the Mustang, but without any flying experience he gave himself up to the authorities without a struggle.

The Operational Training Unit left for Keevil on 16 June 1945 and, although the unit's personnel had initially been unimpressed by Rednal's remote location, its facilities were far better than Keevil's and it was with some reluctance that the last aircraft departed, prior to the airfield being placed under Care and Maintenance before being sold off in 1962.

Fifty years on, the eight Blister and three Bellman hangars are gone, although their concrete bases are still visible. The technical and domestic site buildings have also mostly disappeared and a scattering of agricultural and industrial buildings now occupies the site, together with the remains of the control tower. The runways are intact and in surprisingly good condition (except for the south-eastern thresholds, which are now occupied by small farm buildings), indeed part of the NE/SW runway is still used by light aircraft. A stretch of trees has been planted along a portion of the southern runway, flanking a road that now links Haughton village with the Rednal Industrial Estate, which sits on the former station complex. The road winds through the southern and western runways, affording an excellent view of the entire airfield. Most of the dispersals can also be seen, the most interesting being far away on the eastern perimeter of the airfield, tucked away in woodland. Hidden among the trees, it is tempting to picture a solitary Spitfire roaring into life before emerging into the daylight.

Rednal's control tower has been abandoned for decades but appears to be finally receiving some attention, suggesting that its future might be secured. (Richard E. Flagg)

A concrete building in Rednal's former technical site, long since allocated to agricultural use. (Richard E. Flagg)

Runways: 280 (1,600yd x 50yd) tarmac, 130 (1,100yd x 50yd) tarmac, 160 (1,100yd x 50yd) tarmac. *Hangars:* Bellman (3), Blister (8). *Hardstandings:* 50. *Accommodation:* RAF: 98 Officers, 130 SNCOs, 1,126 ORs; WAAF: 22 Officers, 20 SNCOs, 252 ORs.

RENDCOMBE, Gloucestershire

Grid ref SP029092, Lat 51:46:54N (51.78173) Lon 1:57:30W (-1.95823), 210ft asl. On White Way, off A435, 1 mile ESE of Rendcombe village

Just to the north of Chedworth, the remains of Rendcombe aerodrome are easy to locate, the lush countryside disrupted by some small stretches of concrete just off the White Way road, and a scattering of buildings that, although modern, are laid out as if to describe the proportions of a small airfield – which is precisely what they do. The site is certainly an historic one, the Royal Flying Corps having been the first occupants back in 1916 when No 48 Squadron moved here from Netheravon with a fleet of BE12 biplanes. These were replaced by Bristol F2As during February 1917 just before the squadron left for France.

During August 1916 No 21 Wing had been established at Cirencester, and No 38 Reserve Squadron was formed at Rendcombe on the 1st with Bristol Fighters. The unit was renamed No 38 Training Squadron in May 1917, and on 17 July No 62 Squadron moved here and converted to Bristol Fighters before departing for St Omer on 29 January 1918. No 110 Squadron was formed at the station on 1 November 1917 with BE2c and BE2d aircraft, leaving again on the 12th. No 38 Training Squadron was absorbed into No 45 Training Depot Station, the new name for Rendcombe from the middle of 1918.

Other units known to have been based at Rendcombe (albeit briefly) include No 48 Reserve Squadron with DH6 elementary trainers (located here probably in 1916 before moving to Waddington) and No 59 Training Squadron with DH6 and F2B aircraft from February 1918. Detachments from Nos 45 and 46 Squadrons came to Rendcombe in February 1919, disbanding again later in the year. The site was then abandoned, and although the War Office did consider repurchasing the field in 1936 the plan was dropped and the airfield remained unused for decades until private flying was established here some years ago.

Today the grass airfield is active again, famous as the home of Aerosuperbatics with its Team Guinot wing-walking Stearman display team. Sadly the hangar is gone, but the former Officers' Mess (now a private residence) can still be seen. The RFC is long gone, but the modern Royal Air Force has certainly returned here on occasions, the world-famous Red Arrows having displayed here in 2008. One can only imagine what the RFC pilots in their flimsy biplanes from eighty years ago would have thought!

Runways: 0 (grass field). *Hangars:* Temporary. *Hardstandings:* 0. *Accommodation:* RAF; N/A.

RHOOSE, Glamorgan

Grid ref ST069672, Lat 51:23:48N (51.39653) Lon 3:20:23W (-3.33959), 200ft asl. W of Barry on B4265

An early aerial photograph of Rhoose, illustrating the unusual runway layout and the simplicity of the site. (via John Elliott)

Construction of an airfield here began in 1941 as a prospective satellite field for nearby Llandow. Rhoose was first occupied by Spitfire K9933 from No 53 Operational Training Unit, which flew in on 8 October 1941, long before the airfield's runways and facilities had been completed. However, the arrival was unplanned, engine failure forcing the pilot to force-land here, and the hapless Spitfire was deposited on its belly on rough ground between the new runways. The Spitfire's parent unit moved to Rhoose on 7 April 1942, but Spitfires were already using the site by this date, one having overshot the airfield boundary on landing a few days previously. As a training unit, accidents were common, but the unfinished state of the airfield did nothing to make things any less dangerous.

The OTU's Spitfires and Masters stayed here until May 1943, when they moved to Kirton-in-Lindsey and Rhoose was left inactive for some time until No 7 Air Gunnery School arrived on 8 February 1944, using the station as a satellite field while construction work was completed at its home base back at Stormy Down. The unit's twenty-three Ansons, twenty Martinets and fifty pilots were based at Rhoose until 2 August. Operations were difficult, the marshalling areas being small, so that airmen were obliged to walk at the aircraft's wing tips while manoeuvring on the ground. The lack of hangar space (only four Over Blister hangars were built here) made the unit's stay even more troublesome.

When the AGS left, the airfield was placed under Care and Maintenance until 1 November 1944, when No 40 Group Maintenance Command took over and it became a sub-site for No 214 Maintenance Unit based at Newport. Little flying was conducted at Rhoose, but a significant number of aircraft were stored here until the MU's activities wound down.

However, in 1953 the airfield was identified as a suitable site for a new airport, the rather cramped conditions of the existing airport at Pengam Moors being regarded as unsuitable for expansion. Although Rhoose was some 14 miles from Cardiff (Pengam Moors being just minutes away), it was decided that Rhoose would be the site for a new Cardiff Airport and flying was transferred here on 1 April 1954, although Aer Lingus had already started using the site in 1952 for a Dublin-Cardiff link flow by Dakotas. New airport facilities were built and in April 1965 the site's overall control was handed to Glamorgan County Council, which renamed it Glamorgan (Rhoose) Airport. Oddly, the name was changed again in 1978 to Cardiff (Wales) Airport, sadly abandoning the link with the site's RAF connections.

Rhoose is now a major airport, although the outlines of the original airfield (particularly the runways) can still be seen among the modern developments. (Richard E. Flagg)

The unusual runway layout (two runways laid in a cruciform pattern) is still visible here, although the main runway was extended in 1970 to enable jet airliners to operate from the base. Concordes made occasional visits, although only lightly loaded and without many passengers, but the runway was extended still further in 1986. In addition to scheduled and charter flights, together with private flying, the airport is now the home of a huge maintenance facility run by British Airways, its huge hangar dominating the surroundings. Parts of the original RAF site can still be seen on the airport's south-east and south-west perimeters, but to the north a sprawling and modern airport complex now engulfs what was once only a relatively small RAF airfield

Runways: 216 (1,475yd x 50yd) tarmac, 126 (1,066yd x 50yd) tarmac. *Hangars:* Blister (4). *Hardstandings:* 40ft circular (25). *Accommodation:* RAF: 24 Officers, 64 SNCOs, 450 ORs; WAAF: 2 Officers, 5 SNCOs, 105 ORs.

RUDBAXTON, Dyfed

Grid ref SM959202, Lat 51:50:38N (51.84378) Lon 4:57:47W (-4.96299), 100ft asl. Off A40, 3 miles NE of Haverfordwest, S of Rudbaxton village

Opened in April 1941, this small grass field was operated by No 38 Maintenance Unit based at Llandow. Very little activity occurred here because the site was quickly identified as being unsuitable for the MU's use as low cloud over the Welsh hills often shrouded the area, making the immediate delivery of aircraft to operational units impossible on occasions. The proximity of Haverfordwest aerodrome just a mile away made matters worse, and when the latter site was completed one of the runway approaches was directly over Rudbaxton; the possibility of Haverfordwest being bombed meant that the smaller field just to the north would doubtless suffer too, so it was hardly suitable for the storage of valuable aircraft.

Only occasional periods of activity were recorded here until 25 September 1942, when the MU released the site to the Ministry of Aircraft Production and the airfield was sold off on 1 July 1943. No traces remain today and few people are even aware that the site even existed, often being overlooked by the much larger airfield at Haverfordwest, literally just a couple of fields away.

Runways: 0 (grass field). *Hangars:* Temporary. *Hardstandings:* 0. *Accommodation:* RAF; N/A.

ST ATHAN, Glamorgan

Grid ref ST005687, Lat 51:24:34N (51.40943) Lon 3:25:51W (-3.43082), 50ft asl. On B4265, 7 miles W of Barry

Although the RAF was once blessed with a large number of airfields assigned primarily to aircraft storage and maintenance, the modern Royal Air Force now has just one, and it is, appropriately, the station that was most suitably equipped for the role right from the very beginnings of its history. Opening in February 1939, St Athan was the home of No 4 School of Technical Training, but just one month later No 19 Maintenance Unit was established here and the storage of numerous aircraft types began almost immediately. By the beginning of 1940 more than 280 aircraft were held at the station, comprising mainly Hurricanes and Battles, but by the summer these had been joined by many Blenheims, Lysanders, Defiants and Beaufighters.

The airfield was certainly well suited to the MU's tasks, with a staggering array of hangar facilities. In addition to the main D Type (of which there were two), E Type (six examples) and C Type (four examples) hangars, four more workshop hangars (of a non-standard, unspecified design) were assembled, together with twenty Bellman-type and twenty Robin-type hangars, scattered around the sprawling site.

A C Type hangar still in use at St Athan. (Richard E. Flagg)

The School of Air Navigation came to St Athan for approximately a year, flying a fleet of Ansons in an area that was safely distant from the unit's home base at Manston, but in September 1940 the unit left for the even safer skies of Canada. Of course, even St Athan was not immune from the attentions of the Luftwaffe, and in August 1940 the airfield was bombed (probably by chance), although no damage was caused. However, on 29 April 1941 a dozen enemy aircraft (rumoured to have been Ju 87 Stukas) deposited high-explosive bombs and incendiaries on the station's hangars, more than a dozen aircraft being damaged, and some destroyed completely. The Luftwaffe returned on 11 May and caused more damage, together with three fatalities. Rather less serious had been a surprise appearance of a solitary Luftwaffe bomber on 15 July 1940. The aircraft was intercepted while bombing Barry Docks by a pilot who was test-flying a Hurricane for the MU at the time. Without any ammunition he was unable to shoot down the aircraft, but a series of dummy attacks was sufficient to persuade the Luftwaffe crew to head for home.

The risk of attack eventually prompted the creation of Satellite Landing Grounds at St Brides and Chepstow, which opened in April and May 1941 respectively, enabling significant numbers of MU aircraft to be moved away from St Athan. No 32 Maintenance Unit moved to St Athan during August 1939, initially tasked with the fitment of aircraft systems such as Airborne Intercept radar or IFF

(Identification Friend or Foe) gear (mostly in Catalinas), although by 1941 the unit was repairing war-damaged Whitleys and undertaking strengthening work on Wellingtons following a series of in-flight structural failures. One unusual job was the dismantling and subsequent reassembly of a Heinkel He 111 for a public exhibition (part of Weapons Week) in Caernarfon during November 1940.

No 12 Radio School was formed at St Athan on 1 September 1943 and received Ansons from No 7 Operational Training Unit in December. Oxfords and additional Ansons were eventually acquired and the training of wireless operators was conducted until 31 May 1944 when, rather perversely, the unit disbanded again. On 3 February of the same year a major fire in the station's Picketston site E Type hangar caused a huge amount of damage, ten Beaufighters and a Mustang being totally destroyed. Ironically, it was more damage than the Luftwaffe had ever managed to cause.

An E Type hangar on St Athan's Picketston sub-site. (Richard E. Flagg)

By this stage Beaufighters and Mustangs were the main types being handled by No 19 MU, and No 32 MU also prepared sixty Mustangs for the Normandy invasion, subsequently preparing Lancasters for the Tiger Force. The arrival of the larger Lancaster led to one runway being extended, two concrete runways having been laid in an unusual cruciform pattern shortly after the MU's arrived. With a suitably modified runway and a major complex of storage hangars, it was not surprising that St Athan's MUs stayed in business after the Second World War when many other similar units were disbanded.

After the war airmen in the airframe and engine trades continued to train at St Athan, but in 1955 this training was dispersed to RAF Kirkham and RAF Weeton. No 4 SoTT then became a Boy Entrant School, with new recruits being trained in engine and airframe mechanics, armament, and electrical and instrument mechanics. Following the demise of the Boy Entrant scheme in 1965, airman training returned to St Athan for vehicle and general (non-aircraft) maintenance trades. During the 1970s a driving school was established here, with a fleet of Morris Minors. The driving tests were normally taken in Cardiff and, once students had passed, they were allowed to train in night and motorway driving, and practise on a skid-pan. St Athan also became the RAF's main maintenance base, handling Vulcan, Victor, Buccaneer, Phantom, Harrier, Tornado, Jaguar, Hawk and VC10 aircraft, originally under direct RAF control, but latterly under the auspices of the Defence Aviation Repair Agency (DARA). Highly specialised major servicing of the Battle of Britain Memorial Flight's Avro Lancaster bomber was also conducted at St Athan.

In March 2003 it was confirmed that a new hi-tech maintenance centre would be built, Project Red Dragon replacing RAF St Athan's existing repair centre and creating a new state-of-the-art

An unusual view of St Athan taken from a Meteor T7 during an aerobatic display.
(Author's collection)

St Athan's huge 'superhangar', which was designed to accommodate the VC10.
(Richard E. Flagg)

St Athan's control tower has been extensively modified since the Second World War, the modern 'glasshouse' being the obvious addition. (Richard E. Flagg)

facility. In March 2004, however, DARA announced the loss of 550 jobs at St Athan as part of streamlining to make the Agency more efficient and better able to compete with the private sector for lucrative aircraft repair contracts (it had also lost a bid for a contract to upgrade the RAF's Harrier fleet). The MoD later decided to close DARA's fast jet and engine facilities while retaining the large aircraft division, and on 14 April 2005 the Project Red Dragon 'superhangar' opened and DARA moved its VC10 operations into the new facility.

In 2006 the Special Forces Support Group was established at St Athan and the station was renamed MoD St Athan. A large swathe of land was acquired by the Welsh Assembly Government and commercial aircraft companies such as ATC Lasham started to operate from former RAF buildings, including the former VC10 hangars. DARA steadily drew down its operations, but the large aircraft facility remains, as part of the Defence Support Group (DSG). In 2009 building work is due to commence on a new Defence Training Academy, which is due to accept its first intakes in 2012 and will be fully operational in 2017, unless plans change – which is by no means unlikely.

In addition to the resident University of Wales Air Squadron and No 634 Volunteer Gliding Squadron, military aircraft are still handled by the DSG, and the new Training Academy may well see more aircraft coming to St Athan, but although the station remains busy flying operations are a mere shadow of the wartime years. The station retains most of its original layout and most of the original buildings are intact and in use, including most of the hangars. But although St Athan is a very active military site and a fascinating example of airfield and station design, the skies above it are surprisingly quiet.

Runways: 260 (1,200yd x 50yd) tarmac, concrete and Sommerfield track, 350 (1,100yd x 50yd) tarmac, concrete and Sommerfield track, 330 (1,000yd x 50yd) tarmac, concrete and Sommerfield track. *Hangars:* Bellman (20), D Type (2), C Type (4), E Type (6), Workshop type (4). *Hardstandings:* Sommerfield track (1). *Accommodation:* RAF: 359 Officers, 775 SNCOs, 11,460 ORs; WAAF: 36 Officers, 41 SNCOs, 1,299 ORs.

ST BRIDES, Glamorgan

Grid ref SS899738, Lat 51:27:12N (51.45333) Lon 3:35:05W (-3.58485), 80ft asl. On B4265, SE of St Brides Major

Beauforts were among the first aircraft to be based at St Brides when the airfield opened for flying in 1941. (Author's collection)

Established as No 6 Satellite Landing Ground for No 19 Maintenance Unit at St Athan, the airfield at St Brides was used as a storage facility for many aircraft that were swiftly moved from St Athan when it became a recognised target for the Luftwaffe. Officially opened late in 1940, the site was not used until the following April, when the first Hurricanes were delivered here, followed by Beaufighters and Beauforts. Aside from the MU's activities, very little other activity occurred here apart from the unscheduled arrival of a Spitfire from No 53 Operational Training Unit, which crash-landed on 10 June 1942. Ironically, the MU had just established that the small grass field was unsuitable for Spitfire operations and the incident served to confirm the wisdom of that decision.

Accommodation for both airmen and aircraft was distinctly basic, and only one Robin hangar was erected together with a small number of concrete support buildings. By the middle of 1945 the airfield was largely disused and the site was retained until September of that year, by which stage the remaining Henleys and Beaufighters had been broken up as scrap. Closing on 26 September 1945, the site was sold off and quickly merged into the surrounding agricultural land. Today there is little to indicate the RAF's wartime presence here, although a small cluster of farm buildings on the site of the former station contains one structure that may well be the original Robin hangar. All traces of the airfield, though, have gone.

Runways: 0 (grass field). *Hangars:* Robin (1). *Hardstandings:* 0. *Accommodation:* RAF; N/A.

ST DAVID'S, Dyfed

Grid ref SM781258, Lat 51:53:12N (51.88666) Lon 5:13:28W (-5.22451), 250ft asl. 1 mile NW of Solva off A487

First opened in September 1943, St David's was originally constructed as a projected base for US Navy Liberators, but the plan was subsequently changed and these aircraft went to Dunkeswell in Devon, and RAF Coastal Command aircraft were assigned to the base instead. The first to arrive were Fortresses from Nos 206 and 220 Squadrons, which moved from Thorney Island. It was not until December 1943 that the first long-term residents arrived, when Nos 58 and 502 Squadrons began a gradual move to the airfield, beginning their operational anti-submarine patrol sorties from their existing base at Holmsley, but recovering to their new base at St David's. Their first engagement with enemy U-boats came during the following January when nine of a fleet of ten were attacked. One of the Halifax crews was attacked and destroyed by a Ju 88 over St Brides Bay while returning from a sortie in February; a second Halifax made a fuel-starved landing at St David's, but the Ju 88 crew showed no interest in this aircraft and headed back to base.

Brawdy was opened as a satellite field in February 1944 and 517 Squadron (which had not been at St David's for long) immediately moved there in order to ease congestion. Oddly, Brawdy's runways were rather longer than those of the parent airfield and were also better positioned into the prevailing wind. When crosswinds prevented operations for fully loaded aircraft at St David's, they were routinely ferried over to Brawdy, fuelled up and sent off on their patrols.

Engagement with the enemy continued on a sporadic basis, one incident taking place in the early hours of 26 April when a radar target was picked up and flares were dropped, illuminating a U-boat and a small ship that fired off a brutal defensive barrage against the Halifax crew. Four anti-submarine bombs were dropped and the U-boat appeared to have been broken in two, albeit at the expense of a 2-foot hole in the Halifax's wing.

St David's participated in the D-Day operations, three aircraft flying a patrol off St Nazaire and Brest. On 22 June a U-boat was attacked in Alderney harbour, and on 20 August three U-boats were sighted off the French coast. Sadly, the Halifax flown by 58 Squadron's Commander was hit by defensive fire and two crew were killed, the rest being picked up from their dinghies the next day. Just a week later No 58 Squadron moved to Stornoway, followed by the departure of No 502 Squadron. In the other direction came a detachment from No 220 Squadron on a two-month conversion course, followed by the arrival of No 53 Squadron with a fleet of Liberators, which remained at St David's until the unit moved to Merryfield on 17 September 1945.

A reconnaissance image of St David's airfield, taken in 1950. Although disused, the airfield has changed little over the past sixty years. (via Neil Jedrzejewski)

Little activity of any note took place after this date, apart from an emergency arrival of a Mosquito from No 8 Operational Training Unit, which had lots its airspeed indicator. A second Mosquito accompanied the aircraft into St David's, only after having been delayed by a Halifax (with brake pressure failure), which was blocking the runway. The station HQ moved to Brawdy on 1 November 1945 and the airfield was placed under Care and Maintenance, before being transferred to the Royal Navy on 1 January 1946. It then became a Relief Landing Ground for Brawdy (neatly reversing the roles for which the airfields had originally been constructed). In 1955, while Brawdy's runways were rebuilt and extended, a Fleet Requirements Unit detachment was established here, operated by Airwork and equipped with Mosquito T3 and Sea Hornet NF21 aircraft. When the Navy finally left Brawdy, St David's was returned to RAF control and the airfield remained in use as a Relief Landing Ground for Brawdy's Tactical Weapons Unit until Brawdy finally closed. Although Hunter and Hawk aircraft used St David's for circuit flying occasionally, the TWU's Meteor F8 and T7 aircraft did operate directly from St David's when necessary, in order to ease the burden on Brawdy's busy airfield; banner-towing sorties were often mounted from the satellite field rather than the home base.

With the closure of Brawdy, St David's also fell silent and today the airfield is abandoned. Some of the (few) station buildings are still here but the three hangars are gone; the base of one T2-type is still prominent together with the base of another (fourth) T2-type that was never erected. The tower is gone but the runways and dispersals are intact, and as part of the Pembrokeshire Coast National Park it is possible to walk or even drive around most of the site, the main runway being accessible and disturbed only by a hedgerow that cuts across the centre. The thirty diamond-shaped dispersals have all survived and from the vantage point of the small track that leads north out of Whitchurch it is possible to look along the main runway and picture the mighty Halifax bombers, thundering away, off out to sea.

> *Runways:* 094 (2,000yd x 50yd) concrete and wood chippings, 049 (1,400yd x 50yd) concrete and wood chippings, 140 (1,200yd x 50yd) concrete and wood chippings. *Hangars:* T2 (3). *Hardstandings:* Spectacle (30). *Accommodation:* RAF: 195 Officers, 385 SNCOs, 1,670 ORs; WAAF: 10 Officers, 5 SNCOs, 270 ORs.

SEALAND, Clwyd

Grid ref SJ342702, Lat 53:13:30N (53.225) Lon 2:59:10W (-2.98614), 15ft asl. On A494, 1 mile NE of Queensferry

The origins of this airfield are rather unusual in that it was a result of the combination of two separate airfields, separated by a railway line. To the south was Queensferry, which was still being completed as the First World War ended. Intended to become an Acceptance Unit for American aircraft shipped to the UK, when hostilities ceased the site's development slowed down and eventually stopped. Meanwhile, to the north was Shotwick, a site that had first been used for flying in 1917 when a local businessman set up a flying school on a field rented from the adjacent John Summers steelworks. Shortly after being established it was sequestered by the Royal Flying Corps, and Nos 95 and 96 Squadrons moved here in October 1917 with a mixed fleet of Sopwith Pups and Camels, Dolphins, Salamanders, Martinsydes and Avro 504s. No 90 Squadron arrived from Shawbury a month later. When these units moved to France the airfield was expected to shift to training tasks, and on 1 April 1918 (coincidentally the day on which the Royal Air Force was formed) No 61 Squadron arrived with more Camels, Pups and 504s. No 90 Squadron eventually moved to Brockworth and Nos 95 and 96 Squadrons disbanded, replaced by No 55 Squadron, which was joined by No 67 TS to form No 51 Training Depot Station on 15 July 1918.

After the war the RAF's training requirements dwindled and No 51 TDS became No 5 Flying Training School with a fleet of Avro 504s. In 1924 the combined sites at Queensferry and Shotwick were combined as RAF Sealand, the name having been chosen in order to avoid the confusion of Shotwick with the similarly named RAF Scopwick in Lincolnshire. The name change was also welcomed by locals, who resented the fact that an airfield in Wales had originally been named after a village that was across the border in England.

The RAF Packing Depot arrived here from Ascot on 23 May 1929, tasked with the crating of aircraft destined for shipment to overseas theatres. A wide variety of aircraft types came to Sealand for this purpose, but routine flying here was rarely interrupted by any unusual incidents. Perhaps the most notable event was on 17 June 1926 when Pilot Officer Eric Pentland got into difficulties while spinning his Avro 504 over the Wirral. Successfully bailing out from the aircraft, he earned himself the distinction of becoming the first RAF pilot to escape from an aircraft by parachute. Another notable event was the arrival of two Americans in a Lockheed Vega on 24 January 1931, stopping at Sealand during their nine-day flight around the world. Five years later the legendary

Charles Lindberg landed here in fog and was entertained in the Officers' Mess for five days until the weather improved and he could continue his epic journey.

Training activities eventually saw the arrival of Avro Tutors followed by Hart, Fury and Audax aircraft. The RAF's Expansion Scheme saw the Packing Depot joined by No 3 Aircraft Storage Unit on 2 December 1935. Both the north and south sites were developed, and nine Belfast hangars on the South Camp were joined by two C Types and two L Types, while a third C Type was constructed on the North Camp. Additionally, eighteen Blister hangars were scattered around the airfield perimeter. Oxfords were added to the FTS line-up, although the main type by 1940 was the Miles Master, and a few of these were of the armed six-gun variety. No 5 FTS maintained some of these aircraft at readiness, as fighter defences for the region were almost non-existent while the Battle of Britain was under way to the south. Unfortunately, when the Masters were first needed on 14 August they were unable to get airborne before the Spitfire Battle Flight from nearby Hawarden took over, intercepting a Heinkel He 111 that had made a surprise attack on Sealand, killing several airmen. The bomber crashed in a nearby field and the crew set fire to the wreck before surrendering themselves to the local Home Guard.

A rare pilot's-eye view of RAF Sealand illustrating just part of the huge site. The presence of the very obvious hedgerow may be a remnant of the site's former agricultural status although it may have been retained as part of attempts to camouflage the site. (Phil Jarrett collection)

No 30 MU formed at Sealand on 28 July 1939 and 5FTS moved to Ternhill in December 1940, enabling more space to be allocated to the MU, which became responsible for the fitting of AI radar to Beaufighters and the installation of floodlights in Havocs. The Packing Depot, which had become No 36 MU, then became No 47 MU, eventually processing countless aircraft, some 700 being handled in February 1941 (including 329 Fairey Battles destined for Canada). Flying training resumed on 21 January 1941 when No 19 EFTS arrived with Tiger Moths, conducting intensive training here until 31 December, when the unit left. No 6 AACU established a detachment at Sealand from March 1941 with Lysanders, Leopard Moths, Dragons and Dominies, and No 24 EFTS arrived from Luton in February 1942, tasked with the teaching of Royal Navy pilots.

By this stage the much-worn grass field was equipped with a single concrete runway, necessary for the larger and heavier aircraft being handled by No 30 MU, which included the Mosquito, Wellington and Lancaster. The airfield (or two airfields, to be precise) was certainly busy, with countless aircraft stored around the airfield perimeter and the hangars filled to capacity. When the Royal Navy requested the use of Sealand for disembarking squadrons for aircraft carriers, its request was refused, and Stretton was acquired as a result.

The AACU disbanded on 1 December 1943, forming No 577 Squadron at Castle Bromwich, but a detachment remained at Sealand until 19 November 1944 with Oxfords and Hurricanes. No 24 EFTS transferred to the training of RAF pilots and left for Rochester in March 1945, and the MU's activities slowed down until only the packing unit remained. When this finally closed, Sealand's flying activities virtually ended.

The USAF used many of the hangars for storage and the RAF developed the site for a variety of ground units, mostly associated with the repair of avionics equipment. The airfield was left inactive until No 631 Gliding School arrived in March 1963, maintaining a presence here until 2006. The last notable event in Sealand's aviation history was when Gnat XR536 force-landed here in 1963 after a flame-out, taking advantage of the small runway, which was removed just a couple of years later.

Areas of the sprawling base at Sealand are now easily accessible, including these historic hangars, currently awaiting a buyer. (Paul Francis)

Other areas at Sealand are still distinctly inaccessible, as illustrated by this long shot of two C Type hangars. (Paul Francis)

The RAF's presence here ended in 2006, and the Defence Support Group occupies much of the original RAF site. The busy A560 cuts through the site, and although the Blister hangars are gone, the magnificent Belfast and C Type hangars can still be seen among the many former RAF buildings, some of which were built to unusual design standards unique to Sealand. The North Camp is now swamped by industrial buildings and the runway's traces are all gone, but the C Type hangar is still there. The grass field on the South Camp also survives and is still occasionally used for private aircraft and helicopters, but flying activity is now rare.

> *Runways:* North site: 310 (1,270yd x 50yd) grass and tarmac, NE/SW (1,300yd x 50yd) grass and tarmac, E/W (1,100yd x 50yd) grass and tarmac. South site: N/S (1,330yd x 50yd) grass and tarmac, E/W (1,030yd x 50yd) grass and tarmac. *Hangars:* Blister (18), Bellman (4), C Type (3), Sheds (6), A1 Type (1), L Type (2). *Hardstandings:* 0. *Accommodation:* RAF: 124 Officers, 438 SNCOs, 2,600 ORs; WAAF: 15 Officers, 19 SNCOs, 885 ORs.

SEIGHFORD, Staffordshire

Grid ref SJ868255, Lat 52:49:39N (52.82745) Lon 2:11:47W (-2.19641), 310ft asl. On B5405, 2 miles SW of Great Bridgeford

Having opened during January 1943, Seighford was designated as a satellite airfield for Hixon, occupied by the Wellingtons of No 30 Operational Training Unit, some twenty-six aircraft being based here while construction work on the site was still being completed. Operations were unhindered by this work (and 'Nickel' sorties over France were sometimes flown), but on 26 August a Wellington (BK359) swung off the runway during take-off and headed towards workmen nearby. The pilot attempted to get airborne in order to avoid them, but the aircraft's wing hit a truck and the aircraft came to rest in a crumpled heap, thankfully without injury to crew or contractors.

The completed main runway was longer than Hixon's and all emergency landings were therefore made at Seighford, diversions here becoming fairly commonplace. On 16 November 1944 some thirty-five B-17 Fortresses landed here after returning from a mission over Aachen, and the airfield's perimeter was jammed with aircraft, mixed with the resident Albemarles of No 23 Heavy Glider Conversion Unit, which utilised the airfield for Horsa mass-landing practices. Shortly after the last of the Fortresses departed the next day, the fog returned and another twenty-five aircraft landed, the last becoming bogged down in the grass after steering off the runway.

The Wellington OTU left Seighford on 28 October 1943 in order to shift the airfield to the control of the HGCU based at nearby Peplow. Some of the mass landings performed here by the gliders were quite eventful, especially when they were performed at night, the unlit and silent aircraft occasionally colliding with other Horsas, all of which had to be repaired on base. The HGCU left during January 1944 and Oxfords from No 21 (P)AFU moved in from Wheaton Aston on the 26th. Other aircraft were still seen at Seighford, however, not least American types that occasionally diverted from the American replacement depot at Stone. B-17s and even Marauders were sometimes seen, together with Libertors and some Curtiss C-46 Commando transports.

Countless Allied prisoners of war were flown back to Seighford, which was used as a reception point. The first major ferry operation took place on 10 May when forty-one Lancasters arrived with 917 personnel. The AFU's activities slowly wound down and when the unit left for Moreton-in-Marsh in December 1946 the airfield was scheduled to be abandoned in 1947. However, Wolverhampton's Boulton-Paul Aircraft was actively seeking a suitable site from which to conduct flight-testing, and the company assumed control of the airfield, lengthening the main runway to 6,000 feet in 1959, while other parts were fenced off and resold for agricultural use. With Boulton-Paul acting as a sub-contractor, aircraft were overhauled here and countless Canberras were processed on behalf of English Electric; one aircraft was used for low radar visibility trials, the sinister black-painted panels occasionally being seen on the aircraft out on the largely deserted airfield. The unique Tay-engined Viscount also operated here for a while, and Lightning interceptors were modified, the ear-splitting roar of the aircraft's engines undoubtedly being far more of a disturbance to the local community than anything that had occurred during the war.

Seighford's control tower is still standing, although it is in poor condition and gradually deteriorating. (Paul Francis)

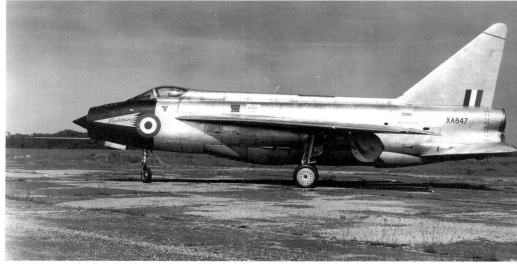

Boulton-Paul conducted a considerable amount of work on Lightnings at Seighford. While a great deal of the airfield was effectively abandoned, the runway and some parking areas were retained for company use. (BAE Systems)

This rather battered Nissen hut at Seighford is now used for agricultural storage. (Paul Francis)

The impressive concrete admin block at Seighford is unused but still largely intact. (Paul Francis)

When the ill-fated TSR2 programme was ended, English Electric (now part of BAC) was short of work for its Warton and Samlesbury factories, so Boulton-Paul was no longer needed as a sub-contractor. Consequently, work promptly disappeared and Seighford became redundant, closing in January 1966. The local council refused permission for the airfield to be used for commercial flying, and since the 1960s it has remained largely unused, save for the occasional unlicensed private visitor. However, the Staffordshire Gliding Club has now established itself at the airfield, occupying a small flight shed adjacent to the B5405 road, opposite the old Boulton-Paul hangars, which are still standing. The runways are mostly gone apart from a portion of the main runway's eastern end and the threshold of one of the secondary runways, and the gliders operate from a grass strip from where part of the original perimeter track is still visible. Seven 'frying pan' dispersals can still be seen, slowly crumbling away, but miraculously the old control tower is still standing, even though it is little more than a shell. The adjacent huts in which so many prisoners of war were processed upon their return to England are still here, but with the roar of Lightnings long gone, most of the flying at Seighford is now of the silent variety again, as it was late in 1944 when the resident gliders were undoubtedly somewhat bigger.

> *Runways:* 192 (1,400yd x 50yd) concrete, 282 (1,400yd x 50yd) concrete, 237 (2,000yd x 50yd) concrete. *Hangars:* T2 (2), B1 (1). *Hardstandings:* Heavy Bomber (27). *Accommodation:* RAF: 72 Officers, 279 SNCOs, 926 ORs; WAAF: 4 Officers, 0 SNCOs, 135 ORs.

SHAWBURY, Shropshire

Grid ref SJ554220, Lat 52:47:40N (52.79456) Lon 2:39:42W (-2.66178), 245ft asl. On B5063, 6 miles NE of Shrewsbury

One of a slowly dwindling number of historic Royal Air Force bases, and one that is still very much in business, Shawbury's history dates back to 1917 when No 29 (Training) Wing was established here on 1 September, comprising three squadrons, Nos 10, 29 and 67, and three others based at nearby Ternhill. The combined units relied on the use of a varied fleet, so much so that maintenance of so many different aircraft became a logistical nightmare for the personnel at both stations. From 1 March 1918 two of Shawbury's squadrons combined to be come No 9 TDS and the other squadron moved to Gloucestershire. Training continued on this more rationalised basis until May 1920, by which stage the RAF's training requirements had reduced.

An early aerial view of Shawbury during construction with the runway layout already clearly visible. (Peter Broom collection)

By now the grass landing field had become well established and the station boasted technical and domestic buildings and hangars, most of which were demolished during the 1920s. However, the War Office renewed its interest in the site in 1935 and Shawbury was selected as a suitable site on which a larger and more permanent station could be built, to house both a Flying Training School and a Maintenance Unit. In order to accommodate the needs of the MU, the airfield layout included six dispersed sites each with a pair of Lamella L Type hangars, together with two larger D Type and four standard C Type on the main site adjacent to the technical and admin buildings.

No 27 MU was formed here on 1 February 1938, while the station was still being constructed, but aircraft slowly began to be transferred here and a varied mix of types was soon in residence, including Blenheims, Whitleys, Hurricanes and Battles; by the end of 1939 more than 350 aircraft were being held at the station. No 11 SFTS arrived from Wittering on 14 May 1938 with a mix of Audax, Gauntlet, Fury and Tutor aircraft, with Blenheims and Oxfords being introduced for multi-engine training. Surprisingly, no runways had been laid and the grass field was often unsuitable for use. Bridleway Gate and Bratton were introduced as Relief Landing Grounds when necessary, but they too were only grass fields and generally suffered from the same problems as Shawbury. Eventually, airfields as distant as Chipping Norton, Llandwrog and even Lindholme were used to maintain the heavy training schedule.

Shawbury was also a potential target for the Luftwaffe and decoy flare paths were set up in an attempt to distract the attention of enemy crews heading for Merseyside. These efforts had some success, but on 27 April 1941 the airfield (which was illuminated for night-flying) was bombed quite severely, although no significant damage was caused. No 27 MU remained active throughout this period and construction of permanent runways was finally started in September 1941, completion being achieved during the following summer. The FTS was renamed No 11 (P)AFU on 1 April 1942, reflecting its expanded role of retraining overseas pilots who were returning to operations in the UK.

No 1532 BAT Flight moved to Shawbury on 16 January 1943 and No 6 AACU set up a detachment here with Lysanders and Masters, eventually becoming part of No 7 AACU in 1941, although the unit did return briefly in 1942. On 31 January 1944 the AFU transferred its Ansons, Tutors and Oxfords to Calveley, making way for the Central Navigation School. This unit boasted a range of aircraft types including Wellingtons, Stirlings, Lancasters, Hudsons and smaller aircraft such as the Proctor and Magister. The CNS specialised in the training of navigators and the development of navigational techniques, one of its aircraft (Lancaster PD328 'Aires') becoming the first British aircraft to fly around the world. The CNS eventually became the Empire Air Navigation School before merging with the School of Air Traffic Control from Watchfield; it became the Central Navigation & Control School from 10 February 1950.

The MU remained at Shawbury, processing hundreds of redundant aircraft as the Second World War ended, and remained in business right up until 1972 when defence spending cuts finally forced its disbandment. By this stage the MU had handled many post-war types including countless Vampires, Provosts and Javelins. The CN&CS continued to maintain a varied fleet of aircraft with more Lancasters and eventually Lincolns being taken on strength, but standardisation finally arrived in the form of the ubiquitous Varsity from 1953.

The final line-up of CATCS Vampires shortly before their retirement. The same apron now accommodates Griffin and Squirrel helicopters. (Author's collection)

The Ground Controlled Approach School moved to Shawbury in 1953 and a flight of Vampire jets was set up with which to provide realistic training for the ground-based controllers, supplementing the piston-engine Provosts that were also assigned to this role. The sound of Vampires winding their way around the airfield circuit quickly became a familiar sound almost every day, continuing in the same role when the CN&CS was transferred to Manby in 1963, and Shawbury became the home of the Central Air Traffic Control School. The CATCS Provosts and

Vampires were finally replaced by Jet Provosts, and these remained busy training air traffic controllers until July 1989, when synthetic training replaced them, and the fleet was retired.

Fixed-wing activity then diminished quite markedly, apart from the Chipmunks operated by Birmingham University Air Squadron, which had moved here from Castle Bromwich in March 1958. However, from 1976 Shawbury had begun to forge links with helicopter flying when No 2 Flying Training School moved here from Ternhill with a fleet of Whirlwinds and Gazelles. Helicopter training became the station's main task from this date and the Gazelles and Whirlwinds (the latter type replaced by the Wessex) became a familiar part of the local area, operating both in and around the airfield perimeter, and also at the satellite fields at Ternhill and Chetwynd. The FTS disbanded on 1 April 1997 to be replaced by the Defence Helicopter Flying School, a larger unit responsible for the training of helicopter pilots for all three services, flying a fleet of Squirrels and Griffins.

RAF Shawbury remains active as a busy helicopter training base and, having being continually active since 1938, the airfield has naturally survived in excellent condition. Most of the original buildings and the airfield layout are unchanged, although the main runway was extended to the south (in anticipation of jet operations) and a V-Bomber Operational Readiness Platform was constructed immediately to the north-west of the main runway's threshold. All of the MU's dispersed sites are still here together with the Lamella hangars, many of which still store aircraft for eventual reuse, resale or scrapping. In recent years these hangars have boasted a varied collection of types including numerous Tucanos and Sea Harriers. Visiting aircraft are fairly common, one of the most notable being the RAF's last Victor bomber, which made its final flight to Shawbury before being dismantled for transportation to Cosford. Just to the north of the airfield on the A49 at Preston Brockhurst, a solitary Robin hangar appears to be the only surviving evidence of the original First World War airfield.

An aerial view of Shawbury in the 1990s, illustrating the wartime hangars and adjacent runways, together with the V-Bomber ORP in the background. (RAF Shawbury)

Where Vampires once stood, helicopters now dominate the airfield at Shawbury, as illustrated by this Griffin from No 60 Squadron. (Author)

A rare example of a surviving Robin hangar, still standing in a former sub-site area at Shawbury. (Richard E. Flagg)

Shawbury's storage hangars are still in good condition, many of them housing aircraft awaiting reuse or disposal. Recent residents include Tucanos and Sea Harriers. (Richard E. Flagg)

Runways: 192 (1,400yd x 50yd) tarmac, 237 (1,500yd x 50yd) tarmac. *Hangars:* C Type (1), D Type (2), L Type (4), AR (1), Lamella (6), T2 (2), Bellman (2), Blister (16). *Hardstandings:* Oblong (70), Apron 1,200yd x 100ft (1). *Accommodation:* RAF: 244 Officers, 298 SNCOs, 848 ORs; WAAF: 11 Officers, 7 SNCOs, 491 ORs.

SHOBDON, Worcestershire

Grid ref SO397607, Lat 52:14:29N (52.24131) Lon 2:53:01W (-2.88365), 300ft asl. 2 miles S of Shobdon off B4362

First established in 1940 as Pembridge Landing Ground, the grass airfield was allocated to No 8 AACU with a small fleet of Lysanders and Battles, used in support of Army units in the area. When it was decided to develop the site into a fully equipped airfield, the aircraft were temporarily deployed to Madley, but came back to the airfield in full force when it reopened as RAF Shobdon on 28 May 1942. The airfield layout when completed was unusual, in that only one concrete runway was laid; it was 6,000 feet long but somewhat wider than standard (being developed in cooperation with the USAAS as a potential distribution facility for two hospitals), and although a concrete perimeter track was built around the airfield, the pair of secondary runways were left as grass surfaces. It is believed that the poor condition of the ground was incapable of supporting additional runways and the resulting layout was certainly unique, with a concrete track running across the grass runways to link two separate hangar complexes on each side of the airfield.

No 5 Glider Training School arrived here on 30 July 1942 from Kidlington and the skies around Shobdon village were soon busy with Miles Masters towing Hotspur gliders into the air, all of which normally recovered to the single concrete runway, the additional width being ideal for glider operations, with aircraft manoeuvred to one side while others could recover on the other. Tractors were in short supply and cart-horses were often used to pull the Hotspurs around the airfield.

Visiting aircraft were quite common at Shobdon, the first being a Grumman Martlet, which force-landed en route from Yeovilton on 28 May 1942. Other types included a B-17 recovering with almost no fuel after flying a mission over France, a P-47 Thunderbolt flown by a pilot who had become lost, and a pair of Canadian Spitfires, their pilots having become similarly disorientated in this (to them) foreign land. A detachment of Bostons from 88 Squadron was based here in July 1943 for smoke-laying demonstrations, but no other detachments are recorded as having taken place.

Hockley Heath was established as a Relief Landing Ground from 22 May 1944 although it had already been used by 5 GTS when Shobdon's runway was resurfaced and the grass strips were waterlogged. Sommerfield tracking was eventually laid on the grass strips and intensive training took place here in order to replace crews that had been lost at Arnhem, but by the spring of 1945 the unit's role was diminishing and twenty-three Hotspurs (and twenty-three Masters) were flown to Montford Bridge during November for scrapping, the GTS disbanding at the end of that month.

A total of 1,335 glider pilots, 291 gliding instructors and 280 tug pilots had been trained here, mostly without any serious incidents, although one Master was written off on 25 February 1944 when it suffered engine failure while towing a Hotspur, and another tug-glider combination crashed on 12 October 1944 after having been struck by lightning, one of the crew being killed. Otherwise Shobdon had been a relatively quiet and uneventful place during the war, and with the GTS flying at an end, the airfield became a detached site for No 25 Maintenance Unit based at Hartlebury, although no significant aircraft movements developed as a result and the entire site was sold off to Herefordshire County Council.

It remained unused for many years but private flying swiftly developed here and today the airfield is fully active again as the home of the Herefordshire Aero Club and a variety of other privately owned aircraft. Only a small portion of the once large runway is used for flying, but most of the original strip is still there, apart from the extreme eastern end, which has long since disappeared. The perimeter tracks are still in evidence and almost all of the original hangars are still standing, most used for storage or agricultural use. The western hangar complex has been developed into a larger group of industrial buildings, and the oddly designed chain of Blister hangars has gone, the concrete bases now underneath private residences, but a great deal remains of the airfield's unusual layout. Even more bizarre is the presence of a small lake right in the middle of it – little wonder that the site was so prone to soggy ground!

> *Runway:* 275 (2,000yd x 100yd) concrete and tarmac. *Hangars:* T2 (6), Blister (6). *Hardstandings:* Circular. *Accommodation:* RAF: 91 Officers, 395 SNCOs, 864 ORs; WAAF: 6 Officers, 12 SNCOs, 198 ORs.

SLEAP, Shropshire

Grid ref SJ482260, Lat 52:49:58N (52.83264) Lon 2:46:12W (-2.7701), 272ft asl. 2 miles N of Harmerhill, off B5476

This aerial image of Sleap appears to have been taken during the early stages of the airfield's construction as the basic runway layout is already in situ. (Peter Broom collection)

Sleap airfield is something of a contradiction. Having enjoyed a quiet and uneventful history, its size seems almost out of proportion, but like so many built during the war it never realised its potential. Constructed as a satellite field for Whitchurch Heath (Tilstock), it opened behind schedule on 15 January 1943 as part of No 93 Group Bomber Command. It was not until the following April that the site was declared ready for flight operations and C Flight of No 81 Operational Training Unit arrived with a number of Whitleys. A couple of Lancasters had already landed here, however, having diverted in fog on the 5th of that month, and another weather diversion arrived in September in the shape of a B-17 Fortress, carrying nineteen ferry pilots. Further unplanned arrivals came on 16 November 1944, when no fewer than thirty-one Fortresses landed here, their home bases at Molesworth, Grafton Underwood and Great Ashfield being fogged in.

One of Sleap's most eventful nights was on 26 August 1943, when a Whitley swung off the runway on landing, crashing into the control tower, killing both the pilot and air bomber and injuring many others. Sadly, a similar accident happened again just two weeks later, but this time the pilot attempted to climb away, resulting in the loss of the aircraft and the death of all but one crew member, and the deaths of three personnel in the control tower. After being repaired, the tower survives to this day, showing no trace of the two terrible accidents that befell it.

On 1 January 1944 the station was transferred to No 38 Group (Airborne Forces) and, with a Heavy Conversion Unit having moved into Tilstock, it was decided to concentrate all of 81 OTU's flying at Sleap. Thus the sight of Whitleys tugging Horsas into the air soon became familiar to the station personnel and the few people who lived near this remote site. Training culminated in an eighteen-aircraft combination flying a mass launch exercise in April. The OTU re-equipped with Wellingtons in December and, once reorganised into three flights, C Flight moved back to Tilstock while A and B Flights remained at Sleap with Wellingtons until 28 December 1945, when the station was closed down.

The picket post on Sleap's No 2 sub-site. (Richard E. Flagg)

Sleap's control tower, the wartime structure still visible under the post-war private aviation developments. (Richard E. Flagg)

Placed under Care and Maintenance, the site reopened in 1958 as a satellite field for Shawbury, the Central Navigation & Control School using the airfield for air traffic control training. Provosts and Vampires regularly proceeded around Sleap's airfield circuit, a ground control caravan being brought in for this task. Training continued until 1964, at which stage the air traffic training was consolidated at Shawbury, and Sleap was finally closed, being sold off shortly afterwards. After a spell of inactivity (during which most of the airfield buildings were demolished), the Shropshire Aero Club moved in, sharing the airfield with a vehicle testing firm.

In a wintry scene at Sleap in November 1944, a 303rd Bomb Group B-17 Fortress receives some attention after making an emergency diversion to the airfield. (via John Elliott)

Today there is an enclave of private aircraft in a southern corner of the airfield on an old dispersal, where one Blister hangar survives (and still accommodates aircraft). The Shropshire Aero Club and a popular cafe occupy the ill-fated control tower further to the north, and the whole complex still survives with two of the three runways still active.

> *Runways:* 192 (1,400yd x 50yd) concrete, 282 (1,400yd x 50yd) concrete, 237 (2,000yd x 50yd) concrete. *Hangars:* T2 (2), B1 (1). *Hardstandings:* Heavy Bomber (27). *Accommodation:* RAF: 66 Officers, 148 SNCOs, 840 ORs; WAAF: 2 Officers, 8 SNCOs, 135 ORs.

SNITTERFIELD, Warwickshire

Grid ref SP196596, Lat 52:14:05N (52.23463) Lon 1:42:48W (-1.71327), 375ft asl. 1 mile SE of Bearley, off A46

Snitterfield was used intensively for Oxford flying from 1943 when the airfield first opened. (via Doug Pollard)

Like Sleap airfield described earlier, Snitterfield was another example of a relatively ambitious construction programme creating an airfield that was never put to any significant use. Constructed as a bomber Operational Training Base, the station opened early in 1943 not for bomber operations but as a satellite for No 18 (P)AFU based at Church Lawford. It was used for intensive flying training, Oxfords being present in the airfield circuit both day and night. The RAF (Belgian) Initial Training School was based here from January 1944 until October, training many personnel who would become part of Belgium's post-war air force. The AFU disbanded on 29 May 1945, but on 3 April No 20 Flying Training School had been established here, and it was this unit that continued to use the airfield as a Relief Landing Ground until 1946, when it was closed.

Sadly, this was the only activity to take place here, despite the airfield being equipped with three concrete runways, twelve circular dispersals and hangars. Oddly, the main runway was extended across the Snitterfield to Bearley road, presumably in anticipation of heavy bombers that never arrived. Abandoned since 1946, the airfield is still recognisable although most of the site is slowly disappearing. Virtually all of the runways have been dug up, although the thresholds of each can still be seen, apart from that of the main runway, the northern extension having disappeared under a golf course. The public road is back in its original place cutting straight across the runway, and the hangars are gone. The tower is also gone and only a handful of buildings remain, scattered around the airfield perimeter. The main dispersal complex was situated to the north-east next to the bomb storage area, but the dispersals are long gone, obliterated by the golf course. However, deep in the adjacent trees, the traces of the bomb dump can still be found. Some of the southern dispersals can still be recognised but they are slowly decaying and soon there will be little evidence of the RAF's presence here. But despite this, the airfield is now active again, the Stratford-upon-Avon Gliding Club operating from a grass strip adjacent to the old main runway. The gliders' silent flight is probably appropriate, given the uneventful history of this large but underused site.

> *Runways:* 040 (2,000yd x 50yd) concrete covered with tarmac, 340 (1,350yd x 50yd) concrete covered with tarmac, 270 (1,250yd x 50yd) concrete covered with tarmac. *Hangars:* T2 (4). *Hardstandings:* Circular (30). *Accommodation:* RAF: 175 Officers, 243 SNCOs, 1,004 ORs; WAAF: 10 Officers, 10 SNCOs, 410 ORs.

SOUTH CERNEY, Gloucestershire

Grid ref SU054984, Lat 51:41:06N (51.6849) Lon 1:55:20W (-1.92226), 350ft asl. On A419, 3 miles SE of Cirencester

Constructed in 1936, the RAF station at South Cerney was built for No 3 SFTS, which, being based at Grantham, was in an area of operational activity, so a safer area to the south and west was needed for the unit to continue its training activities. Such was the relative urgency for the move that the first personnel arrived on 16 August 1937, long before the station was complete; as only one hangar was able to accept the unit's Hawker Audax trainers, many aircraft were kept outside for some time. Eventually the station's facilities were completed, but not before the unit's personnel had enjoyed a summer in the most basic of circumstances. The Audax biplanes were slowly replaced by Oxfords from 17 June 1938, and by the autumn the unit was fully equipped with the new twin-engined aircraft, with at least 150 aircraft being on strength occasionally.

On 8 September 1939 the Wellington bombers of No 37 Squadron arrived for two weeks as part of a dispersal exercise, and in June 1940 part of No 15 SFTS moved here from Middle Wallop for two months. During a night-flying exercise one summer evening, the unit's training was interrupted by the appearance of a Luftwaffe bomber, which successfully reached the airfield and deposited a full bomb load shortly before midnight, but causing little damage and no casualties. On 29 June the Luftwaffe returned, but this time the bombs were dropped in open countryside nearer to Down Ampney. On 25 July the enemy bombers were more successful and two Heinkel He 111s dropped bombs on the airfield; however, as they all fell onto the grass field no significant damage was caused, only the inconvenience of some fairly serious relandscaping!

Training continued throughout this period and, although the set-up of the unit changed, the SFTS remained very active, eventually becoming No 3 (Pilots) Advanced Flying School as of 14 March 1942. No 1539 BAT Flight arrived on 15 April 1943, moving to Bibury (which had been South Cerney's Relief Landing Ground for some time) on 13 July. A second BAT Flight (No 1532) came to South Cerney from mid-1943 and a third (1547) was separated from No 3 (P)AFU on 4 December 1945 when the AFU disbanded. It became No 3 Flying Training School four months later and moved to Feltwell. Meanwhile, South Cerney abandoned Bibury as a Relief Landing Ground in November 1944 and shifted to Aston Down, while Charmy Down was adopted as a satellite field, albeit on a Care and Maintenance basis.

Post-war changes began on 24 May 1946 when Flying Training Command's Instructors School moved to South Cerney from Wittering, equipped with a variety of types, but by February the unit's tasks had been assumed by the Central Flying School. The CFS (Basic) Squadron began operations at South Cerney in May 1952, absorbing the duties of 2FTS, which had arrived here in March 1948 equipped with Harvards, Prentices and Provosts. Also arriving here was the Central Link Trainer School, the Aircrew Transit Unit and the Aircrew Allocation Unit. The CFS (Helicopter) Detachment moved from Middle Wallop and combined with the CFS here, flying a mixed fleet of Dragonflies, Whirlwinds and

A Central Flying School trio comprising a Magister, Master and Oxford, pictured on a sortie from South Cerney. (Author's collection)

An Oxford from No 3 (P)AFU at South Cerney. (via John Elliott)

Sycamores. The Provosts moved to Little Rissington in May 1957 and the Aircrew Officers Training School arrived from Kirton-in-Lindsey (flying Chipmunks and Ansons) on 22 June 1957.

Helicopter flying continued here until 10 August 1961, when the CFS unit left for Ternhill, and fixed-wing flying ended when the Primary Flying School (which had been formed here with Chipmunks in July 1965) moved to Church Fenton. After the Aircrew Officers Training School completed its last course on 22 December 1967 the unit also left for Church Fenton a few weeks later, and South Cerney's flying operations were over. However, the RAF retained control of the station and, after being used as an accommodation site for Brize Norton and Fairford, it was transferred to Army control on 1 July 1971. No 635 Gliding School was the last of the RAF's flying units to be based here, leaving South Cerney for Hullavington in July 1992.

South Cerney in 2006. The airfield and buildings are maintained in good condition, under MoD ownership. (Richard E. Flagg)

Today the station is still controlled by the Army, although the RAF maintains a presence and combined exercises are often conducted. Flying activity is much less than in the heyday of the CFS presence, but aircraft do still use the site, and liaison types can sometimes be seen here as well as larger aircraft used to dropping parachutists. Even more impressive are the regular appearances by RAF Hercules aircraft, which make practice stores drops over the airfield. As an active military site, the station has been maintained in excellent condition and remains virtually unaltered from the days when it was first opened. The hangars and control tower are still present and the grass strip (with a concrete perimeter track) looks as flat and serviceable as it did seventy years ago.

Runways: 190 (975yd) steel matting, 270 (1,075yd) steel matting. *Hangars:* C Type (3), ARS (1), Bellman (2), Blister (11). *Hardstandings:* 0. *Accommodation:* RAF: 212 Officers, 112 SNCOs, 1,640 ORs; WAAF: 13 Officers, 8 SNCOs, 382 ORs.

SOUTH MARSTON, Wiltshire

Grid ref SU188876, Lat 51:35:16N (51.58768) Lon 1:43:45W (-1.72906), 410ft asl. On A419, NE of Swindon

An aerial image of South Marston, pictured before the main runway was extended to accommodate jet aircraft. (via Neil Jedrzejewski)

Driving along the busy A419 road, it is difficult to imagine, as one passes between the sprawling industrial complexes, that a significant airfield was once active here and that a huge number of famous aircraft emerged from it. It was in 1938 that South Marston was chosen as the site for a factory that would act as a 'shadow works' to the Phillips & Powis factory at Woodley, and by 1940 the new factory was busy completing Miles Magister trainers for the RAF. In the spring of 1941 the first Master rolled off the production line and by the end of the year more than eighty aircraft were being produced every month. The factory's grass landing field was quickly occupied by numerous Magisters and Masters awaiting delivery.

South Marston produced countless Magister trainers for the Royal Air Force in 1940. (via Adrian Groves)

Meanwhile, the Shorts factory at Rochester had suffered terribly at the hands of the Luftwaffe and it was decided that a new production facility would be set up at Stratton St Margaret, where the company already had facilities. Stirling bombers were subsequently built in the local area (fuselages at Blunsdon and other components at the GWR works in Swindon) for final assembly at South Marston. In order to accommodate the bulky and heavy Stirling, two runways were laid, one 6,000 feet in length and the other shorter at just under 4,000 feet. Both were immediately painted in camouflage, and wood chips were scattered over them when not in use so as to render them even less visible from the air.

Plans were made for the production of Lancasters here, but demand for Spitfires led to the creation of an assembly line for this aircraft type, and the factory was taken over by Supermarine as a shadow factory to the famous Castle Bromwich facility further north. Initially, the factory conducted repair work on existing airframes, but eventually the production of the Mk 22 and 24 was completed here, followed by countless Seafires of varying marks. Walrus and Sea Otter amphibians were also overhauled here at the same time.

After the war the factory became part of the Vickers-Armstrong empire, as the Supermarine Division, and production of the jet-powered Attacker was based here, followed by the Swift fighter and the elegant Scimitar – Supermarine's last aircraft. When the last aircraft was completed and flown out of South Marston in January 1961 for service with the Royal Navy, aircraft production ended at the site and Supermarine eventually merged with Vickers-Armstrong at Weybridge, but only after having drawn up what would eventually become the ill-fated TSR2 strike aircraft. Had aircraft production continued at South Marston, it is quite possible that TSR2's first flight might have taken place here, instead of Boscombe Down.

The factory continued in business as an engineering concern for many years, and although test-flying had long since ended, aircraft still occasionally visited the site, but by the 1980s the airfield was unused and eventually the entire site was bought by Honda as a car manufacturing centre. Today the South Marston site is dominated by Honda's massive facility, which has engulfed virtually all of the original factory and airfield. The secondary runway has disappeared beneath

Supermarine Swifts await delivery to the RAF at South Marston. No 4 Shop is visible in the background. (via Adrian Groves)

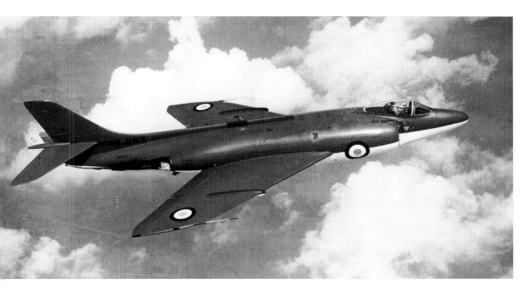

Despite being a relatively unknown airfield site, South Marston was associated with the production of many Supermarine aircraft including the elegant Scimitar strike fighter. (Author's collection)

Aircraft awaiting delivery from South Marston, pictured during production of the Supermarine Attacker for the Fleet Air Arm. A Dominie is also visible in the distance. (via Adrian Groves)

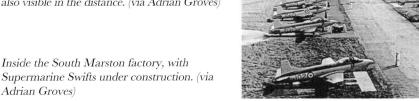

Inside the South Marston factory, with Supermarine Swifts under construction. (via Adrian Groves)

A 1965-vintage image of a Blanik glider at South Marston. Gliders were the last remnants of flying activity at the site prior to its abandonment. (Rod Simpson collection)

Honda's new facilities but the old main runway is still there, running alongside the factory and now used as a car test track. A small patch of grass still remains where the eastern portion of the airfield once was, and a lonely hangar still stands in a small patch of trees on the south-eastern corner of the site. Where the mighty Stirling once stood and the sleek Scimitar roared into the skies, Honda cars now race back and forth along South Marston's historic runway.

> *Runways:* 0 (grass field). *Hangars:* Civil (Flight sheds). *Hardstandings:* 0. *Accommodation:* Civil; N/A.

STOKE ORCHARD, Gloucestershire

Grid ref SO923273, Lat 51:56:42N (51.945) Lon 2:06:44W (-2.11229), 100ft asl. E of M5, 1 mile SE of Stoke Orchard village

An aerial photograph of Stoke Orchard taken in 1950, showing the single grass runway. (via Neil Jedrzejewski)

Situated in the glorious Gloucestershire countryside, Stoke Orchard was a small airfield with a correspondingly modest admin and technical site, completed late in 1941. The grass landing field (which was suitably camouflaged to replicate the surrounding farmland) was given a concrete perimeter track and four designated runways, and four Bellman hangars were constructed, together with a scattering of Blister hangars placed around the airfield, some standard, some double-size and some even triple-size. The first aircraft to arrive here were the Tiger Moths of No 10 EFTS, which moved in on 23 September 1941, and more than fifty examples were based here by the end of that month. On the opposite side of the airfield, the Gloster Aircraft Company established a Shadow factory as an outpost to its Brockworth facility just a few miles away. Various aircraft were assembled here over subsequent years, Hurricanes being one of the most common types, and for the first months of the station's existence the Gloster factory shared the airfield with the resident EFTS.

Training was intensive but largely uneventful, apart from one unfortunate incident where a Tiger Moth (N9492) flew into high-tension cables near Boxham Ferry. The aircraft crashed into the Severn but the crew survived. The Tiger Moths stayed at Stoke Orchard until 21 July 1942, when the unit disbanded, and the station's future was re-evaluated. Glider pilot training had become an important requirement and selecting suitable bases for the task was far from simple. Naturally, it would be difficult to merge glider operations with routine fixed-wing flying, and it required air space that was not used by operational or training aircraft. Stoke Orchard appeared to be a potentially useful site, and on 10 March a Hector and Hotspur were deployed to the airfield to conduct suitability trials, which were completed favourably.

The magnificent de Havilland Tiger Moth, once a familiar shape in the air above Stoke Orchard. (Author's collection)

Following the departure of the EFTS, No 3 Glider Training School was formed here on 21 July 1942 and a considerable number of Hotspurs quickly began to appear on the airfield, together with a small fleet of Miles Masters equipped as glider tugs. Training activities quickly built up and, despite the proximity of Cleeve Hill (which was considered a potential hazard), the unit did not suffer from any serious accidents. The most troublesome aspect of its stay at Stoke Orchard was the variable quality of the landing field, which soon suffered from the heavy use it had to endure. Eventually some of the GTS training was exported to Northleach, Aldermaston and Wanborough in order to ease the pressure on Stoke Orchard's airfield. The unit remained active here until January 1945 when the gliders and tugs moved to Exeter, leaving only the Gloster facility in residence.

Hangars at Stoke Orchard, illustrating how one of this pair has been reclad and substantially rebuilt, destroying much of its original architecture, but ensuring its survival. (Richard E. Flagg)

The RAF abandoned its presence here in 1945, although Gloster remained for a few years, but, when the remaining aircraft had been ferried over to Hucclecote, Gloster also moved out and the site was sold off. Today the airfield is still very much in evidence but no flying activity has taken place here for fifty years, and the grass field is now farmland. The four Bellman hangars are still in use and although three have been refurbished, one retains much of its original style (and condition). The tower was demolished during the 1960s and the Blister hangars are gone, but traces of the perimeter track can still be seen, and over on the north side of the field a tree-lined lane leads off to the former Gloster factory, parts of which are still recognisable among the industrial buildings that now occupy the area. From the vantage point of nearby Cleeve Hill the airfield looks almost as if the Tiger Moths might return at any moment.

Runways: NW/SE (1,200yd) grass, N/S (1,100yd) grass. *Hangars:* Bellman (4), Double 69ft (7), Triple 69ft (1). *Hardstandings:* 0. *Accommodation:* RAF: 46 Officers, 116 SNCOs, 483 ORs; WAAF: 4 Officers, 8 SNCOs, 189 ORs.

STORMY DOWN, Glamorgan

Grid ref SS848799, Lat 51:30:23N (51.50631) Lon 3:39:40W (-3.66102), 350ft asl. Off A48, 1 mile NW of Tythegston

A rather poor-quality but nonetheless interesting image of Stormy Down, illustrating the station's technical and admin site. (via Brian Aldis)

The rather romantic name might suggest a site far more ambitious than that which occupies an area of land just off the busy A48, a few miles from Porthcawl. Constructed in 1938, Porthcawl aerodrome became No 9 Armament Training Station, renamed No 7 Air Observers School on 1 September 1939. It was renamed again (as No 7 Bombing & Gunnery School) just two months later, and the station name was changed to Stormy Down in 1940. Ansons and Martinets were the most common aircraft types here, the gunners (in the Ansons) training their sights on targets trailed by the Martinets. Thus the sound of gunfire became familiar to everyone living along the South Wales coast, sometimes relieved by displays during 'Wings for Victory' weeks, which showed goodwill to the countless locals who were obliged to endure the daily disturbances. On one occasion in April 1943 the residents of Mountain Ash were treated to a formation display from nine Lysanders, and a team of four Martinets displayed over the Rhondda a few days later.

When No 7 B&GS acquired Whitleys, one was despatched to Fairwood Common to give local air cadets some air experience flying. However, some of Stormy Down's flying was of a much more serious nature and, with no fighter cover during the early days of the Second World War, the attentions of the Luftwaffe went largely unopposed, but Stormy Down's pilots did what they could to defend the area. On one occasion the Flying Wing's OC, in a Hawker Henley, chased a marauding Ju 88 out past Mumbles Head. Armed only with a Very pistol, the Henley pilot managed to persuade the Luftwaffe crew to head off for cover. Thankfully, no attacks were mounted on the station, the only incursion recorded being a partly deflated barrage balloon that broke free from its moorings in Port Talbot and landed on the airfield. The closest that the station came to a full-scale engagement with Germany was on 30 May 1943 when a U-boat was sighted and an Anson crew was sent out to search for it. Nothing was seen, but with an armament of only two .303 machine guns available to them, it was probably just as well.

Training activities continued at considerable pace and in November 1943 a flight of Martinets was assigned to cine-gun use, enabling crews to practise curve-of-pursuit attacks on the target aircraft, thereby enhancing their skills still further. With a mixed fleet of aircraft that now included Ansons, Martinets, Henleys and Whitleys, the airfield was often very busy, and a runway caravan was introduced in 1944 to improve control of the many aircraft using it. Built on an uneven and convex surface, visibility of the entire field was difficult from some locations and observers in both the caravan and watch tower were needed (using radio communication) to maintain control of the whole site.

Visiting aircraft were few, although two Piper Cubs were based here late in 1943 for overhaul, these belonging to a US Infantry Brigade at nearby Porthcawl. A pair of Wellingtons also arrived in January 1944 in order to evaluate the type as a possible replacement for the Anson. The trial was inconclusive as the landing field's condition worsened and the aircraft were despatched to Llandow (together with a flight of Martinets) to continue the trials from an airfield equipped with a concrete runway. This led to plans for the construction of a paved runway at Stormy Down, but eventually the proposal was abandoned in favour of less ambitious improvements to the grass surface, and the laying of PSP strips, together with the construction of new hardstandings. In the meantime, some of the station's training was exported to Rhoose, which was designated as a satellite field. With twenty-three Ansons and twenty Martinets deployed to Rhoose, only essential flying was conducted from Stormy Down while the airfield was improved, although a Cessna Crane (43-31816) and a Beaufighter both made crash-landings here in 1944.

On 2 August the aircraft were ferried back from Rhoose, but on the 21st No 7 B&GS disbanded, as the RAF now had a surplus of trained gunners. The station accommodation was reoccupied by No 40 Initial Training Wing, which moved from Newton on 1 September but disbanded on 27 November. By the end of the year flying activity here had ended. The station closed in the summer of 1945 and was quickly sold off.

Since then the site has been restored to farmland, although many of the airfield buildings survived for many years. Some civilian gliding has taken place on the old airfield. Today the main landing ground has been returned to agriculture but the remains of the main site are still here and a large 'VR' hangar is still standing, although development of the site has been under way for some time and only this hangar is likely to remain, many other surviving remnants of the station having been bulldozed. There are tentative plans to build a wind farm on the former airfield. If this plan goes ahead, the area will soon be changed – some would say ruined – perhaps forever.

Runways: N/W (980yd) grass, N/S (1,010yd) grass, NE/SW (1,000yd) grass, SE/NW (1,000yd) grass, E/W (880yd) grass. *Hangars:* Bellman (4), SP (1), F Type (1), Bessoneau (1), Blister (5). *Hardstandings:* Apron 200yd x 100ft (1), 600yd x 90ft (1). *Accommodation:* RAF: 65 Officers, 204 SNCOs, 1,375 ORs; WAAF: 6 Officers, 30 SNCOs, 497 ORs.

SWINDERBY, Lincolnshire

Grid ref SK880619, Lat 53:08:50N (53.14718) Lon 0:41:07W (-0.68527), 53ft asl. Off A46, 2 miles SE of Swinderby village

Television viewers will no doubt recognise Swinderby as the home for numerous antique fairs that are held on the site of the former RAF station. It is perhaps ironic that the airfield itself is something of an antique, having been carved out of a large swathe of fields and woodland back in 1939 when the nation was concerned with matters far more urgent and serious than collectors' fairs. Although Lincolnshire is notorious as a flat and relatively featureless landscape, the chosen site for this RAF station was rather less so, and the construction process proceeded far from smoothly, not least when the contractors discovered that the site they were clearing lay on top of an underground river. Despite the difficulties, the station opened on 17 August 1940, although it was far from complete by this stage, and work continued based on pre-war plans that included some distinctly non-essential designs, such as a fountain and fish pond for the front of the Officers' Mess. It was, in fact, the last station to be built to these specifications.

Swinderby's second control tower, a typical post-war design complete with a standard 'glasshouse' observation facility. (Richard E. Flagg)

Swinderby's hangars, now abandoned but still in good condition, await a decision on their future. (Richard E. Flagg)

When the station opened, the nearby bomb dump that had previously been referred to by the same name, was redesignated Norton Disney, and the first aircraft arrived on the 22 August, these being Fairey Battles from No 300 Squadron. On 28 August No 301 Squadron arrived with more Battles (and a solitary Anson, as had happened with 300 Squadron previously), and the Polish airmen assigned to these units soon became familiar within the local community, so much so that many of the personnel stayed in the area after the war ended.

The first action came on 14 September when three crews from each squadron bombed Boulogne Harbour, this being the first Polish operational bomber raid and the first of many similar missions flown against the invasion shipping gathering in the French ports. The Poles certainly had a fighting spirit, and in a dark reflection of the brutal attacks that had been made on their homeland by Luftwaffe Ju 87s, some of the squadron's Battles had sirens fitted to recreate the terror that the Germans had inflicted on their homes. Of course, the attacks on the French harbours inevitably incurred retaliation and Swinderby was struck on 13 October, some buildings being hit (forcing telephone communications to be shifted to the village Post Office) and a couple of Battles being damaged. Further raids followed, but no significant damage was ever caused. Eventually a decoy airfield was created at Bassingham, although it was used only briefly. One of the worst nights for the station was the result not of Luftwaffe action but poor weather, when two Battles crashed near Blidworth on 14 October, after returning from a mission.

Later in October the squadrons began converting to Wellingtons, and by the end of the year the transition was complete. Operations were suspended while the conversion took place, but by this stage they had already delivered 45 tons of bombs to occupied France. The first operational mission with Wellingtons took place on 22 December when six aircraft attacked a refinery at Antwerp, and a repeat mission was flown on the 28, but when the aircraft returned to Swinderby one crashed into a tree in freezing fog, killing two crew members.

More missions followed in January 1941 but heavy rain caused the airfield to become unusable and many aircraft were transferred to the station's satellite airfield at Winthorpe, just a few miles to the south. As the situation worsened, aircraft were despatched to other airfields in the area so that operations could continue. By March the airfield was active again, and more missions were mounted including attacks on Berlin, Brest, Keil and Bremen. On 21 June a Wellington from No 300 Squadron crashed near Southwell after a propeller broke away. Too low to enable the crew to bail out, a landing was attempted but the aircraft struck trees and burst into flames, killing one of the crew.

When the threat of invasion passed, the two Polish squadrons moved to Hemswell on 19 July and Swinderby became part of No 5 Group. Nos 50 and 455 (RAAF) Squadrons arrived with Hampdens, although their first aircraft did not arrive until a month after their official arrival on 6 June. The station was still being completed at this time, work having been hampered by labour shortages and foul weather that was bad enough to cause one Hampden pilot to land on the A46 Fosse Way one night during November; to make matters worse the aircraft then ran into a ditch. On 26 November No 50 Squadron moved to Skellingthorpe so that a more concentrated effort could be made to construct permanent runways. At the beginning of 1942 Skellingthorpe and Wigsley were designated as satellite fields and in February No 455 Squadron moved out to Wigsley. No 50 Squadron returned to Swinderby on 20 June after having re-equipped with Manchesters, but its stay was brief and on 14 October the unit's last operational mission was flown from Swinderby and the unit returned to Skellingthorpe. That same month saw the creation of No 1660 Heavy Conversion Unit at Swinderby, equipped with a mixed fleet of Manchesters, Lancasters and Halifax aircraft.

A fascinating panoramic view of Swinderby, illustrating a typical wartime day on the airfield with Lancasters scattered across the site. (via John Elliott)

From 14 November 1942 Swinderby was no longer assigned to operational duties and became a training base. However, life at the station was no less precarious, and on 2 January 1943 a Manchester (L7482) was abandoned near Metheringham, suffering from icing problems; the crew escaped safely. Training at Swinderby intensified (the base being redesignated as No 51 base, tasked with the coordination of Lancaster crew training for No 5 Group), and by November the station was re-equipping with Stirling bombers. As D-Day approached activity intensified still further, and the station was both extremely busy and seriously overcrowded both in terms of equipment and personnel. During July it was transferred to No 7 Group, Bomber Command, and the resident Stirlings were progressively replaced by Lancasters.

Inside one of Swinderby's hangars. Now empty, the Lancasters, Halifaxes, Varsities and Chipmunks that were once housed here are only memories. (Richard E. Flagg)

This well-known photograph shows a Swinderby-based Stirling being bombed up for a mission over Germany. (Author's collection)

By the middle of 1945 activity at Swinderby had slowed considerably, and on 15 September the station held an 'At Home' day, the first of many similar events that took place here in subsequent years. No 1660 HCU gradually wound down but continued to train crews at a reduced level until 23 November 1946, when it moved to Lindholme. Meanwhile, on 20 September 1945 No 13 Aircraft Modification Unit was formed here, tasked with the conversion of Lancasters for the Tiger Force, but when the aircraft were no longer needed the unit disbanded again on 1 August 1946.

On 21 December 1946 the station was transferred to No 91 Group. No 17 Operational Training Unit arrived during November with a fleet of Wellingtons, and the station shifted to Flying Training Command during May 1947. The OTU then became No 201 Advanced Flying School and remained active at Swinderby, eventually being joined by No 204 AFS with Mosquitoes in June 1950. This unit then moved to Bassingbourn on 20 February 1952, by which stage No 201 AFS was gradually replacing its aged Wellingtons with new Varsities and the unit was redesignated as No 11 Flying Training School on 1 June 1954, moving to Thorney Island in the process. No 8 FTS then arrived from Driffield on 4 July and Swinderby entered the jet age, the airfield now becoming home to a fleet of Vampire and Meteor trainers together with a flight of Provosts, which was subsequently disbanded on 2 October 1956.

In order to accommodate jet operations the taxiways and parking areas were improved and a large area of woodland was cleared. A new control tower was constructed and airfield lighting was upgraded. At this time the East Midlands Gliding Club also moved here, remaining until 1976. Training continued with surprisingly few incidents, although the crew of a Vampire were forced to eject from their aircraft after becoming unable to escape from an inverted spin. No 8 FTS remained in business until March 1964, and on the 20th of that month Swinderby was transferred to Technical Training Command, and No 7 School of Recruit Training was established here. Flying activities ended at this stage, although aircraft still occasionally visited the airfield and passing out parades attracted some spectacular flypasts.

Graduation parades at Swinderby usually involved a ceremonial flypast, and these became increasingly adventurous over successive years. This picture shows Joe L'Estrange livening up a parade in typical flamboyant style. (Joe L'Estrange)

No 7 SRT became the RAF School of Recruit Training in July 1970 and, much to the surprise of the local community, flying returned in the late 1970s when Chipmunks were brought in for flying selection purposes, remaining in use until shortly before the SRT moved to Halton in 1993. Swinderby then closed down and the site was sold off in 1996. For some years it remained abandoned, but by 2004 most of the domestic and technical site had been bulldozed and the new village of Witham St Hughes was built on the site.

Surprisingly, Swinderby had two control towers, the original watch office having been left abandoned but intact when a new post-war building was constructed. (Richard E. Flagg)

The former Station Headquarters building at Swinderby, abandoned and facing an uncertain future. (Richard E. Flagg)

Thankfully the airfield has survived and today three of the original hangars are still in place together with the control tower and a few support buildings, although their future clearly depends on the airfield, which, at least for the time being, appears to have been left in good condition. The three runways are all intact together with the many dispersal pans around the perimeter, including those that reach across the busy A46 and re-emerge on the far side. Hopefully the progressive destruction of this once busy station has now largely ended and the site will perhaps survive in recognisable form for many years to come.

Runways: 246 (2,000yd x 50yd) concrete, 201 (1,400yd x 50yd) concrete, 294 (1,400yd x 50yd) concrete. *Hangars:* J Type (3), T2 (3). *Hardstandings:* Heavy Bomber (36). *Accommodation:* RAF: 194 Officers, 612 SNCOs, 1,321 ORs; WAAF: 11 Officers, 16 SNCOs, 322 ORs.

SYERSTON, Nottinghamshire

Grid ref SK736476, Lat 53:01:16N (53.02118) Lon 0:54:13W (-0.90363), 211ft asl. On A46, 1 mile W of Syerston village

First opened on 1 December 1940, Syerston occupies a stretch of land sandwiched between the busy A46 road an the River Trent. As a bomber airfield within No 1 Group, the station received two Polish units in the days after the station opened, these being Nos 304 and 305 Squadrons, both equipped with Wellingtons. Once settled in after their move from Bramcote, the units flew their first operational mission on 25 April 1941, five aircraft attacking targets in Rotterdam. Many more missions followed before both squadrons moved to Lindholme in July. In the opposite direction came No 408 (Goose) Squadron RCAF, flying Hampdens. On 11 August the unit completed its first bombing mission (to Rotterdam) and continued to mount strikes against the enemy until 8 December, when it moved to Syerston's satellite airfield at Balderton. A decoy airfield was also set up at Kneeton, although Syerston managed to escape the attention of the Luftwaffe and ultimately emerged from the war unscathed.

The station temporarily closed at the end of 1941 while three concrete runways were laid and permanent accommodation was built, reopening in May 1942. The first unit to use the completed airfield was No 61 Squadron, which came from Woolfox Lodge with Lancasters. It was followed by No 61 Conversion Flight, which moved from North Luffenham on 5 May with a mix of Manchesters and Lancasters. These units were briefly joined by No 408 Conversion Flight, which operated for only a few weeks before disbanding again. No 106 Squadron moved to Syerston from Coningsby in September, also equipped with Lancasters, and the two resident bomber squadrons increased their efforts to mount bombing missions, some of which were flown by the legendary Guy Gibson, who was with 106 Squadron during this period. Both he and his equally famous dog Nigger became familiar faces at Syerston, Nigger often frequenting the Sergeants' Mess in search of food, while his master was far away over Germany.

In a typical wartime scene at Syerston, a Lancaster is bombed up for a mission to Germany. An Avro Manchester is visible in the background. (Author's collection)

Crews from No 61 Squadron at Syerston walk out to their Lancasters in preparation for a bombing mission. (Author's collection)

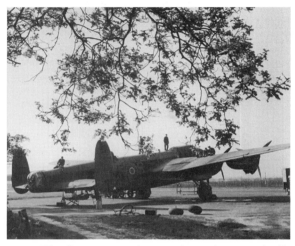

A Lancaster from No 106 Squadron is seen at Syerston in May 1943. (via John Elliott)

The Syerston squadrons took part in many significant bombing missions, targets including Le Creusot, Hamburg, Dusseldorf and Peenemunde. Perhaps the most notable event during this perilous period was a raid on Dusseldorf mounted on the night of 3 November. One aircraft was attacked by an Me 110 while crossing the Dutch coast but, despite a shattered windscreen, it pressed on, even though the pilot (Flt Lt Reid) had head, shoulder and hand injuries. With control difficulties and a damaged radio, the hapless Lancaster was again attacked, this time by an Fw 190, resulting in the death of both the navigator and wireless operator. Reid was also injured again, but he continued to the target and successfully delivered a bomb load before heading back to Syerston, relying on the moon, the Pole Star, the engineer and the bomb-aimer to get the aircraft back home safely. For his efforts Reid received the Victoria Cross.

Both units left Syerston in November 1943, 61 Squadron going to Skellingthorpe and 106 to Metheringham. With operational activities at an end, No 1485 Bombing & Gunnery Flight arrived by December, equipped with Martinets and Wellingtons. They were joined by No 1668 Heavy Conversion Unit and its eighteen Lancasters, the unit being renamed as No 5 Lancaster Finishing School on 15 January 1944. In February No 1690 Bomber Defence Training Flight was formed, and in March the Bombing & Gunnery Flight disbanded again, No 1690 BDTF moving to Scampton in July. The latter unit returned on 1 October with its Spitfires and Hurricanes, and on 31 March 1945 No 5 LFS disbanded and its Lancasters slowly departed, only to be replaced by more Lancasters, this time from the Bomber Command Film Unit Flight, which remained at Syerston until October.

Meanwhile, No 49 Squadron had moved in from Fulbeck on 22 April, and Syerston was once again (albeit briefly) an operational bomber station. The squadron's Lancasters taking part in an attack on Berchtesgaden on 25 April, but this was the last bombing mission conducted from Syerston and 49 Squadron began training for Tiger Force operations before leaving for Mepal in September. When No 1690 BTDF left in July, No 382 Maintenance Unit arrived and stayed at Syerston until October. On the 20th of that month the station was transferred to Transport

A variety of well-known and familiar aircraft types operated from Syerston at various stages in the station's history. Amongst these was the Miles Master, as illustrated. (Author's collection)

Command, Winthorpe being designated as a Satellite Landing Ground. No 1333 TSCU duly arrived from Melton Mowbray with a fleet of Dakotas and Horsa gliders, being renamed as the Transport Support Training Unit before departing for North Luffenham in July 1947.

No 1331 HCU moved from Dishforth with Halifax bombers on 14 December 1946 before becoming part of No 240 Operational Conversion Unit on 5 January 1948. Mosquitoes arrived on 10 May when No 504 Squadron was reformed here, remaining until November 1947, at which stage the station transferred to Flying Training Command. On 7 January 1948 No 22 Flying Training School began operating from Syerston, equipped with Tiger Moth and Prentice aircraft for the training of Royal Navy personnel, and from the end of 1949 until 1955 Tollerton was used by this unit as a satellite field.

In May 1955 No 2 FTS was replaced by No 1 FTS, only to change back to No 2 FTS in November 1957. Equipped with piston-engined Provosts, the first Jet Provost trainers arrived early in 1960 and Syerston earned the distinction of becoming the first military station anywhere in the world to train its students with jet-powered aircraft. Sadly, it also became infamous as the site of a tragedy when Vulcan prototype VX770 broke up over the airfield during a demonstration at the station's Battle of Britain Air Show on 20 September 1958. The aircraft's safe structural limits were exceeded in a high-speed turn, and it crashed onto the runway close to the A46, killing the crew and personnel in the runway caravan.

The tragic loss of VX770 over Syerston in September 1958. (Author's collection)

An aerial view of Syerston's runway 25, illustrating the main impact debris from VX770 (Author's collection)

A magnificent picture of a Jet Provost from No 2 FTS pictured on a sortie from Syerston, resplendent in a typical 1960s silver and dayglow orange paint scheme. (Author's collection)

No 2 FTS finally left Syerston in 1971 and, with the Jet Provosts gone, the airfield fell silent. Placed under Care and Maintenance, it was not until 1975 that flying resumed when No 644 Volunteer Gliding Squadron moved in, followed eventually by both the Royal Air Force Central Gliding School and No 643 VGS. Air Cadet gliding activities have continued at Syerston since the 1970s and, although the airfield is largely unused, it is at least active while the glider units (and a handful of private civilian aircraft) remain. The station is maintained in good condition, the runways and taxiways all still in use, the control tower and two hangars still very much in business, and all of the original dispersals still in place. Oddly, a couple of Jaguar aircraft are visible on the airfield, although their flying days are long gone; they are used for ground exercises by officer cadets from Cranwell. Most of the station's original technical and admin site has been demolished, but Syerston survives. Hopefully the gradual improvements to the adjacent A46 road will not intrude on the airfield's boundaries any further.

Syerston's former Officers' Mess in 2009, last used as an immigrant accommodation centre and now abandoned. (Richard E. Flagg)

Runways: 073 (1,950yd x 50yd) concrete, 120 (1,400yd x 50yd) concrete, 163 (1,400yd x 50yd) concrete. *Hangars:* J Type (2), T2 (3), Glider T2 (3), B1 (1). *Hardstandings:* Heavy Bomber (36). *Accommodation:* RAF: 190 Officers, 380 SNCOs, 2,026 ORs; WAAF: 10 Officers, 27 SNCOs, 377 ORs.

TALBENNY, Dyfed

Grid ref SM835111, Lat 51:45:26N (51.75711) Lon 5:08:13W (-5.13705), 230ft asl. Off B4237, 4 miles NW of Milford Haven

Just a few miles from the crumbling remains of RNAS Dale, the remnants of another former airfield can be seen, perched on the Pembrokeshire coast high above St Brides Bay. Talbenny opened on 1 May 1942 as part of No 19 Group, Coastal Command, with nearby Dale designated as a satellite field. No 311 (Czech) Squadron arrived here with Wellingtons on 12 June and during the same month the satellite field was occupied by No 304 (Polish) Squadron. The primary task assigned to these units was the patrol of the Bay of Biscay, and on 6 August their first U-boat was sighted and an attack was mounted, although the results are unknown. Another significant mission took place on 25 August when an Altmark-type tanker was attacked in La Pallice Harbour, all available aircraft from both squadrons being involved; they all returned safely to base. The same outcome almost eluded a 311 Squadron aircraft in September when it was attacked by two Arado 196 floatplanes, but managed to struggle back to Talbenny with significant damage and an injured tail gunner.

Talbenny is seen here from a reconnaissance aircraft in about 1945, the 'frying pan' dispersals clearly visible. (via Dan Hale)

In order to protect the Wellingtons, detachments from Nos 235 and 248 Squadrons were despatched to the station and their Beaufighters were attached to most missions, escorting the Wellingtons to and from their targets. Operations continued (including a shipping strike off the Gironde Estuary in November) until March 1943 when the Wellington squadrons departed from both Talbenny and Dale, to be replaced by No 303 Ferry Training Unit. The FTU brought another fleet of Wellingtons down from Stornoway, and these were subsequently joined by Warwicks and Venturas, as part of preparations to send many aircraft overseas.

Wellington W5711 at Talbenny. This aircraft completed fifty combat missions before being attacked by two Luftwaffe Bf 110s in February 1942. (via Dan Hale)

Resplendant in typical Coastal Command colours, a Wellington gets airborne from Talbenny. (via Dan Hale)

On 11 October 1943 Talbenny was transferred to Transport Command, although No 4 Armament Practice Camp remained in situ as a lodger unit, controlled by No 19 Group and tasked with anti-submarine bombing and air-to-air and air-to-sea firing training. This unit provided facilities for many visiting squadrons, and in addition to RAF Hudson and Halifax aircraft, US Navy Liberators from Fleet Air Wing 7 came to the APC from their base at Dunkeswell in Devon. Many other aircraft came to Talbenny when weather conditions forced diversions from their intended routes or destinations, the station being designated as a weather diversion field that was often capable of remaining open when other airfields were closed, thanks to its geographical position far out on the Welsh peninsula. Many USAAF Liberators were seen here, together with C-47s, B-17 Fortresses and many other types.

No 303 FTU handled more than 100 Wellingtons during March 1944, all being ferried overseas, and the unit was joined by No 3 OAPU (which became No 11 Ferry Unit) from Hurn on 26 July. This unit's primary task was the collection of replacement components from various locations, and preparation of the equipment for transportation overseas. Wellingtons and Warwicks were still the most numerous types being processed through Talbenny at this stage, although Ansons and Spitfires became more numerous as the months went by.

In August 1945 No 11 FU moved to Dunkeswell, and Talbenny was placed under Care and Maintenance, controlled by RAF Pembroke Dock. No further activity took place here and the site was sold off on 23 December 1946. Now part of the Pembrokeshire Coast National Park, Talbenny's three concrete runways are still evident, although only the southern portions remain intact. The eastern and northern halves of two runways have been removed and only part of the third runway remains, suggesting that it may not survive much longer. Of the original thirty-six 'frying pan' hardstandings, only seven have survived, together with most of the perimeter track's southern portion. Virtually all of the airfield and station buildings are gone, including the two T2 hangars that once stood here, and from the surrounding roads there is little evidence of the RAF's once significant presence here.

> *Runways:* 034 (1,600yd x 50yd) concrete and tarmac, 272 (1,100yd x 50yd) concrete and tarmac, 350 (1,100yd x 50yd) concrete and tarmac. *Hangars:* T2 (2). *Hardstandings:* Frying pan (36), Apron (1). *Accommodation:* RAF: 145 Officers, 491 SNCOs, 1,820 ORs; WAAF: 8 Officers, 8 SNCOs, 300 ORs.

TATENHILL, Staffordshire

Grid ref SK166238, Lat 52:48:42N (52.81179) Lon 1:45:19W (-1.75515), 450ft asl. 2 miles NW of Rangemore on B5234

Constructed during 1940, Tatenhill was created as a satellite airfield for No 27 Operational Training Unit, which was operating Wellingtons from Lichfield. When the station opened on 2 November 1941, the unit's Wellingtons quickly arrived and one Flight was established here, tasked with night-bomber training. Aircraft from No 16 EFTS also used Tatenhill briefly as a Relief Landing Ground for their home base at Burnaston, but as the airfield was still being constructed at this time no significant deployments were made here by that unit. Three concrete runways were laid in a standard layout together with 'frying pan' dispersals and hangars, but the site was considered less than ideal for Wellington operations and, when the larger airfield at Church Broughton was completed, the Wellingtons immediately shifted to that site and Tatenhill was placed under Care and Maintenance.

Flying activities resumed on 7 November 1942 when No 15 (P)AFU deployed a number of Oxford aircraft here, its home base at Leconfield having been assigned to more urgent tasks, forcing the unit to export its Oxfords to a variety of satellite fields around the country. The unit eventually moved to Grove in Berkshire, only to be replaced by a fleet of Miles Masters from No 5 (P)AFU from Ternhill, this move being completed by May 1943. No 5 (P)AFU's E Flight was established at Tatenhill, tasked with navigation and night-flying training. On 28 January 1944 the station shifted full circle and No 21 (P)AFU moved in, bringing Oxfords back to the station.

Miles Masters arrived at Tatenhill in May 1943.
(Author's collection)

Training activities continued with few significant incidents, although on 17 August a student pilot flying Oxford EB731 failed to notice a second Oxford flying below him on approach, and after a Very light was fired by the runway controller he quickly turned to starboard, losing control in the process. The aircraft crashed but the crew escaped with only minor injuries. Rather more spectacular was a huge explosion that shook the airfield on 22 November 1944 when the bomb store at No 21 Maintenance Unit's site at Fauld (just 3 miles away) accidentally exploded, creating what is reputed to have been the biggest explosion ever experienced in the United Kingdom. The devastating accident (which resulted in numerous fatalities) completely destroyed the MU's facilities, and No 21 MU was re-established at Tatenhill, No 21 (P)AFU moving to Seighford on 26 January 1945 in order to vacate the station's facilities for this transfer. Apart from the arrival of the School of Explosives in October 1945, no further changes were made at Tatenhill until that unit disbanded in January 1947 and the airfield was closed shortly thereafter.

Situated just a few miles from Burton-upon-Trent, it was perhaps not surprising that a variety of private aircraft used Tatenhill after the war for occasional communications flights associated with the brewing industry, and Allied Breweries eventually purchased the site for this purpose. In 1987 the airfield was taken over by a new company called Tatenhill Aviation and, after being licensed during the 1990s, it has now developed into a thriving centre for private and recreational flying, combined with aircraft maintenance and overhaul services. The wartime hangars and control tower are gone but a surprising number of the original airfield buildings are still here, mostly abandoned and slowly crumbling away. The three runways are still intact, two still being used for flight operations even to this day. The many dispersals are also still present around the perimeter track, although some are now overgrown and difficult to locate. However, the rather unusual loop of dispersals to the north of the B5234 road are still visible, close to the current private aviation cluster at the eastern end of the airfield. It is somewhat ironic that even though Tatenhill was largely unused and unwanted through the wartime years, it has survived intact and remains in business when many contemporary sites have long since disappeared.

Runways: 090 (1,600yd x 50yd) Concrete and wood chippings, 040 (1,000yd x 50yd) concrete and wood chippings, 180 (1,100yd x 50yd) concrete and wood chippings. *Hangars:* T2 (1), Blister (2). *Hardstandings:* Circular (19). *Accommodation:* RAF: 62 Officers, 236 SNCOs, 726 ORs; WAAF: 4 Officers, 3 SNCOs, 128 ORs.

TEDDESLEY PARK, Staffordshire

Grid ref SJ948164, Lat 52:44:45N (52.74593) Lon 2:04:41W (-2.07818), 310ft asl. 2 miles NE of Penkridge off A34, N of Teddesley Hay village

One of the more obscure and undocumented sites in the Staffordshire region, Teddesley Park aerodrome was established in July 1941, a relatively small area of land having been requisitioned from the owners of the adjacent stately home. Two grass runways were laid, both 800 yards long and positioned in a clearing between woodland. Compensation was paid to the land-owners for the tree-felling, but the work was kept to a minimum in order to keep the airfield camouflaged as much as possible. As No 48 Satellite Landing Ground, it became part of No 29 Maintenance Unit based at High

Ercall, and many aircraft handled by that unit were despatched to Teddesely Park for storage. Venturas, Hudsons and Avengers were among the types seen here, including Venturas AE736 and AE699. Even a rare Brewster Bermuda (FF580) was noted here during 1944. Hotspur gliders were among the last of the types accommodated at the site, and although some were offered for sale it is thought that most (if not all) were broken up before the aerodrome was abandoned in 1945.

No permanent structures were ever constructed here, so it is not surprising that no remnants of the aerodrome have survived. Steel matting was eventually laid on the grass runways, however, and some of this material can still be found among the hedgerows of the surrounding fields. A brick wall skirts what was once the southern boundary of the landing field, but the site has long since merged back into the lush countryside that stretched in all directions. However, from the small road that runs north-west from Teddesley Hay, the proportions of the airfield can still be seen, particularly the wedge-shaped gap between the tress where one of the two runways was once laid.

Runways: 0 (grass field). Hangars: 0. Hardstandings: 0. Accommodation: RAF; N/A.

TEMPLETON, Dyfed

Grid ref SN101107, Lat 51:45:47N (51.76295) Lon 4:45:11W (-4.75296), 350ft asl. Off A4115, 1 mile SW of Templeton village

Established as a satellite field for Haverfordwest, Templeton aerodrome was constructed during 1942, opening on 7 January 1943 when No 306 Ferry Training Unit was formed here. Tasked with the training of Beaufort crews for long-distance ferry flights, its first aircraft did not arrive until 24 February, and it was not until March that the unit's first new-build aircraft began to arrive from No 2 Overseas Aircraft Preparation Unit at Filton. The first crews to set off on a ferry flight were despatched to Portreath on 13 April. However, when the unit finally settled into an established training routine, it was transferred to Maghaberry in Northern Ireland, from 15 June.

The next unit to arrive at Templeton was O Flight of No 3 Operational Training Unit, based at Haverfordwest. Equipped with Ansons, the unit also operated Wellingtons and Whitleys (being a Coastal Command training unit), but these types rarely visited Templeton and it was mostly Ansons that occupied the airfield circuit. The OTU left for St Athan on 8 December 1943 after having been assigned to No 12 Radio School, and at the end of the year No 3 OTU disbanded, being absorbed into No 6 OTU based at Silloth.

A wartime image of Templeton, illustrating the typical triangular runway layout and associated 'frying pan' dispersals. (via Dan Hale)

Templeton was temporarily abandoned until August 1944, when No 595 Squadron (based at Aberporth) established a detachment here. Martinets were used to tow a variety of new winged aerial targets, but the tug aircraft were found to be unsuitable and Spitfires were subsequently allocated to the task, being faster and more powerful. The target-towing procedure was complicated and far from risk-free. Talked down by a pilot who stood next to the runway with a radio link, the Spitfire tug brought the glider target back over the runway at 115 knots and, when it was at about 10 feet above the runway, the tug pilot would enter a steep climb, releasing the target to settle onto the runway. These rather precarious approaches became a common sight over Templeton until 1945, when the airfield became rather busier due to the arrival of A Flight of No 8 Operational Training Unit in January of that year. Equipped with Spitfires and Mosquitoes, the unit stayed only until 27 February, at which stage the larger and well-equipped airfield at Brawdy opened.

Templeton today, still in remarkably good condition despite the slow encroachment of woodland and scrubland. (via Richard E. Flagg)

From March 1945 onwards Templeton remained largely unused, with just an engineering section occupying the hangars, repairing aircraft for No 8 OTU until June, when the unit moved from Haverfordwest to Benson. By the end of 1945 the airfield had been abandoned and no further flying activity took place here. Surprisingly, the site has survived in good condition and, although the hangars are gone, many of the original buildings are still here, scattered around the site. The runways are still intact, although some storage activity now occupies the south-eastern portion of the airfield. The perimeter tracks still wind around the airfield among the growing tress and shrubs, and the 'frying pan' dispersals can still be found. Also of interest are the remains of the main runway's instrument landing system, which can be seen half a mile or so to the west beside the road that skirts the airfield's southern boundary. The site is occasionally used for military exercises and it is believed that RAF Hercules aircraft have landed here in support of these activities.

> *Runways:* 246 (1,600yd x 50yd) concrete and wood chippings, 304 (1,100yd x 50yd) concrete and wood chippings, 176 (1,100yd x 50yd) concrete and wood chippings. *Hangars:* T2 (1). *Hardstandings:* 125ft circular (25). *Accommodation:* RAF: 66 Officers, 140 SNCOs, 630 ORs; WAAF: 2 Officers, 0 SNCOs, 132 ORs.

TERNHILL, Shropshire

Grid ref SJ644306, Lat 52:52:20N (52.87219) Lon 2:31:44W (-2.529), 280ft asl. On A41, 1 mile NW of Stoke Heath

While undoubtedly one of the RAF's most picturesque stations, Ternhill is also one of the oldest and most significant, having been created on a site that traces its associations with aviation back to 1916, when Major Atcherley force-landed in a hot air balloon here, and subsequently informed the War Office of the site's potential as an aerodrome. It was agreed that construction should commence, and by the end of 1916 the first training activities began here with a mix of Avro 504 and Sopwith Camel aircraft. By the end of the First World War, Ternhill had become No 13 Training Depot Station but, although it was proposed that the station be retained, no use could be found for it and it was eventually sold off in 1922 and became a racehorse stable.

A rare image from a damaged glass negative shows Ternhill from the air, probably in about 1919. (Phil Jarrett collection)

A fascinating image of a hangar being constructed at Ternhill during 1916. As can be seen, the construction techniques were surprisingly simple and the collapsed structure in the background suggests that some sort of accident occurred during assembly. (Phil Jarrett collection)

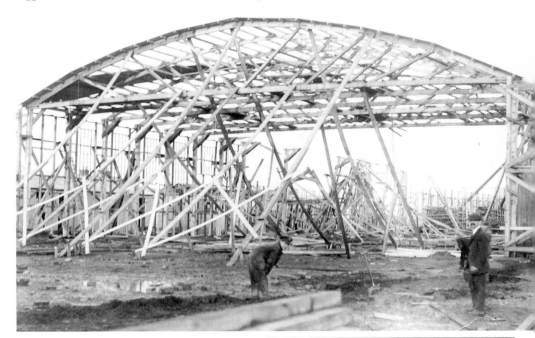

A rare picture of the aftermath of a hangar fire which occurred early in 1919. The ashes of the hangar structure contain the mortal remains of numerous aircraft. (Phil Jarrett collection)

A historic First World War-era image of a BE2c at Ternhill. (via Doug Pollard)

However, the Expansion plans of 1934 necessitated the re-examination of many former airfield sites for development into new stations, and Ternhill was quickly recognised as a good candidate, situated in an obstruction-free area of land and owned by just one person, making purchase relatively simple. The former landing field was swiftly levelled, drained and repaired, and on 1 January 1936 the station reopened as a base for No 10 Flying Training School. Equipped with Audax, Hart and Tutor aircraft, the FTS was tasked with the advanced training of newly qualified pilots, and when training began on 3 February it marked the start of the station's long and continuous association with training activities that lasted for another forty years.

Ternhill witnessed more than a few accidents, particularly during the first years after the station opened in 1916. Thankfully, most of these incidents were casualty-free. (via Doug Pollard)

Some of the early accidents at Ternhill were quite spectacular. Although the aircraft were short on performance, they could often be notoriously difficult to handle. (via Doug Pollard)

In addition to training, Ternhill was designed to accommodate a Maintenance Unit, and the airfield was divided into five distinct sections: one large site was positioned to the south (equipped with two D Type hangars and one C Type); the main site was to the north; and three dispersal sites each boasted two Lamella hangars. No 4 ASU was established here on 1 June 1937, long before construction was completed (personnel were forced to sleep in the hangars for some time), and the storage of Wellingtons, Lysanders and Swordfish began almost immediately. By 1939 the ASU had become No 24 MU, and more than 350 aircraft were in storage at Ternhill, comprising some twenty-six different types. Even this figure was exceeded when Whitleys from Nos 10 and 78 Squadrons were deployed here as part of the RAF's Scatter scheme.

No 10 FTS re-equipped with Harvards and Oxfords and many of these aircraft were destroyed when a Luftwaffe Ju 88 attacked the station on 16 October 1940, dropping bombs and incendiaries that destroyed a Blenheim and twenty trainer types. One C Type hangar was damaged so badly that it had to be dismantled, and a smaller Bellman hangar was constructed alongside as a replacement.

Ternhill became a No 9 Group Sector Station in August 1940, and No 29 Squadron deployed Blenheims here from Digby for night defence, while Spitfires from No 611 Squadron took responsibility for daytime operations. Their first success came on 18 August when a Heinkel He 111 was intercepted near Chester and a Blenheim crew pursued the aircraft for some 2 hours, eventually shooting it down over the North Sea off Spurn Head. On 11 November two Do17s were shot down, and patrols continued until 611 Squadron was replaced by aircraft from No 306 Squadron based at Church Fenton.

In November 1940 No 10 FTS and was replaced by No 5 FTS, which brought its Miles Masters from Sealand, but poor weather made the grass airfield unusable for long periods and the FTS had to deploy aircraft to stations with concrete runways. It was not until October 1941 that construction of two relatively modest concrete runways was started at Ternhill, and detachments from many different squadrons continued to come here to provide fighter defences for the Sector, mostly equipped with Spitfires, although No 403 Squadron was also detached here with Tomahawks. The last unit to operate fighter patrols here was No 131 Squadron, which returned to Atcham in September 1941. No 5 FTS became No 5 (P)AFU and received Hurricanes to supplement its fleet of Masters, and by the middle of 1943 the huge fleet of 145 Masters (divided into ten Flights and deployed to satellite fields at Condover, Tatenhill, Bratton, Calveley and Chetwynd) had gone.

No 24 MU became part of No 43 Group in April 1942 and assumed responsibility for the repair of Spitfires and Lancasters. Spitfire work was reassigned to other units by the middle of 1944, enabling the MU to concentrate on Lancasters, although Wellingtons began to appear from November 1945. No 5 (P)AFU was now operating Harvards, Oxfords and Hurricanes, but in June 1945 the unit disbanded, its number being reapplied to No 9 (P)AFU, which moved in from Errol. This unit remained at Ternhill until April 1946, when it disbanded and No 6 SFTS arrived from Little Rissington with Harvards and Tiger Moths. No 24 MU was joined by No 30 MU from Sealand, amalgamating to become No 30 MU before moving back to Sealand on 1 February 1959.

No 6 SFTS (now 6 FTS) remained as Ternhill's sole occupant, using nearby Chetwynd as a satellite field, but on 4 August 1961 the unit moved to Acklington, Ternhill's runways being too short for the safe operation of the jet trainers that were now being introduced. With the fixed-wing aircraft gone, the Central Flying School's helicopter element moved in from South Cerney, and Sycamores, Skeeters, Sioux and Whirlwind aircraft became familiar sights and sounds on the airfield; Gazelles appeared shortly before the CFS moved to Shawbury in September 1976. The only resident flying unit at the station after this date was No 632 VGS, with a small fleet of gliders, but Ternhill remained in use as a satellite for RAF Shawbury and helicopter operations have continued here until the present day.

The main station site was transferred to Army control and is now known as Clive Barracks. Still very much under MoD control, the entire station remains in excellent condition, although much of the domestic site has now been sold off for private housing. The runways are still in regular use (mostly for helicopter landings) and the hangar complexes are still here, including those on the south side of the airfield, which, being so separate from the main site, became known as RAF Stoke Heath during the 1960s. The dispersed sites are still here too, including the most easterly outpost, which lies far beyond the airfield, across the A41 in the former domestic site where one hangar still stands. Ternhill's unique layout is certainly of interest, the short concrete runways confined by the A41, which cuts through the site, with dispersed hangar complexes visible far beyond the airfield boundaries. Flying activity is certainly far less than in the days of the Second World War, but few sites can boast so many interesting features in such good condition.

> *Runways:* 094 (2,000yd x 50yd) concrete and wood chippings, 049 (1,400yd x 50yd) concrete and wood chippings, 140 (1,200yd x 50yd) concrete and wood chippings. *Hangars:* T2 (3). *Hardstandings:* Spectacle (30). *Accommodation:* RAF: 197 Officers, 255 SNCOs, 1,418 ORs; WAAF: 24 Officers, 10 SNCOs, 376 ORs.

TILSTOCK, Shropshire

Grid ref SJ556377, Lat 52:56:07N (52.93514) Lon 2:39:42W (-2.6617), 307ft asl. On A41, 3 miles S of Whitchurch

Originally known as Whitchurch Heath, an airfield was constructed here in 1942, opening on 1 August. The first aircraft arrived during September, these being the Wellingtons of No 81 Operational Training Unit, which moved in from Ashbourne, joined by a further fifty-two Whitleys in February 1943. On 1 June the station's name was switched to Tilstock in order to avoid confusion with Whitchurch Airport near Bristol.

From 1 January 1944 the station came under the control of No 38 (Airborne Forces) Group, and the task of training pilots for glider-towing began. No 1665 Conversion Unit arrived from Woolfox Lodge on 22 January and at this stage some of the training operations were exported to the station's satellite airfield at Sleap, although the unit's presence here was brief, thanks to Sleap's poor condition and a series of accidents that cast an atmosphere of gloom over the personnel stationed there. By the middle of March training was again concentrated at Tilstock, where 1665 HCU was now busy operating Stirlings. The huge bombers, standing on astonishingly tall undercarriage legs (the fuselage was some 22 feet above the ground), operated largely without incident from Tilstock, although one night, when the HCU was busy with flying activities, a Stirling pilot overshot the runway and proceeded to plough through fencing and taxi back along the adjacent A46 road before trampling yet more fencing in order to rejoin the perimeter track. Such was the size and sturdiness of the mighty Stirling that no aircraft showed any signs of damage and no crew admitted responsibility.

The mighty Stirling, once a common sight at Tilstock, demonstrating its weapons load and crew for the media. (Author's collection)

Tilstock occasionally hosted American visitors, two US Army hospitals having been established nearby in anticipation of heavy casualties following D-Day. When the numbers of wounded were eventually found to be much lower than anticipated, the expectation of casualty evacuation flights into Tilstock receded and only a few C-47 transports actually arrived. Other American types seen here included many Thunderbolts and Harvards from nearby Atcham and a formation of four Piper Cubs, which diverted here due to fuel shortage. Even an A-26 Invader was seen, having landed with engine failure. More significant were diversions of Liberators from the 44th Bomb Group at Bungay when fog prevented the crews from returning to their home base after completing missions over Europe. On one occasion thirty-one aircraft diverted to Tilstock, and on another thirty-four arrived.

The HCU deployed Stirlings to Fairford and Keevil to participate in the supply drops over Arnhem during September 1944, and two aircraft were damaged by enemy fire during these operations. More routine HCU activities continued without incident, although take-off accidents did occasionally occur, the Stirling being particularly prone to uncontrolled swing and subsequent undercarriage collapse on take-off. The only truly serious incident, however, was when a Halifax was shot down by a Luftwaffe intruder near Peterborough on 20 March 1945.

The HCU moved to Saltby on 26 March and No 42 Operational Training Unit moved in from Ashbourne. Equipped with Albemarles, the unit merged with No 81 OTU and worked up on Wellingtons, increasing the fleet to a total of fifty-one aircraft. On 10 August 1945 the unit changed its role to transport conversion training and became No 1380 Transport Support Conversion Unit, retaining the same aircraft, together with a few Ansons. Much of the initial flying was performed at Sleap, while Tilstock's runways were resurfaced. Training slowly wound down, however, and the unit disbanded on 21 January 1946. The Wellingtons, Ansons and Spitfires (which had been used for fighter affiliation until gunnery training was abandoned) were disposed of, and Tilstock was reduced to Care and Maintenance under the control of Ternhill. It remained thus for many years and was occasionally activated for Territorial Army exercises, which sometimes involved deployments of aircraft (including a Royal Navy Avenger, which crashed on the airfield), but by the 1960s it was abandoned and finally sold off.

*Tilstock's tower still stands, but, with doors and windows filled in, its future looks bleak.
(Richard E. Flagg)*

One of Tilstock's surviving hangars, partially rebuilt but still retaining much of its original structure. (Richard E. Flagg)

Block No 43, as the numerals indicate above the door, has long since been abandoned, and looks likely to remain in a similar condition for years to come. (Richard E. Flagg)

Sadly, most of the airfield has been progressively destroyed and only a handful of buildings remain, although the hangars are still standing and remain in use for storage. The crumbling control tower is still present, but the runways are almost gone, having been broken up and littered with concrete, rubble, trees and assorted vegetation in an effort to prevent them from being used for motorbike racing (without much success). Only a small portion of one of the secondary runways has survived, and is still used for occasional flights by the light aircraft operated by a small parachute centre. Most significantly, the A41 now cuts straight through the centre of the airfield, but the general layout is still recognisable and the perimeter track can still be seen, together with seven of the thirty-one 'frying pan' dispersals that once surrounded the site. But from a distance it is difficult to see any evidence of the RAF's presence now, and the days when Wellingtons and Stirlings rumbled around the local skies are just memories.

Runways: 030 (2,000yd x 50yd) concrete, 072 (1,400yd x 50yd) concrete, 154 (1,400yd x 50yd) concrete. *Hangars:* T2 (4). *Hardstandings:* Frying pan (30). *Accommodation:* RAF: 150 Officers, 442 SNCOs, 1,359 ORs; WAAF: 10 Officers, 27 SNCOs, 385 ORs.

TOLLERTON, Nottinghamshire

Grid ref SK617361, Lat 52:55:09N (52.9191) Lon 1:05:01W (-1.08353), 127ft asl. Off A52, 2 miles NE of Tollerton

This historic site was first established in 1930 when an area of land was developed as a landing field and opened for flying on 19 June, the ceremony being performed by Sir Sefton Branker, the Minister for Aviation, who was subsequently killed in the R101 airship crash. Nottingham Corporation secured a licence for the airfield and it was leased to National Flying Services, which commissioned the construction of a clubhouse and hangar, although the aerodrome's first few months of activity were overseen by an engineer who was housed in a tent on the field's perimeter. Nottingham Flying Club moved to Tollerton in September 1931 from its previous home at Hucknall and the aerodrome became an active and popular pre-war site for private recreational flying.

In 1937 the dark days of the Second World War were looming and the Civil Air Guard formed a unit here, its school comprising of some fifty pupils. This was followed by No 27 E&RFTS, a Royal Air Force Volunteer Reserve Training School, established on 24 June 1938 equipped with Miles Magisters, Ansons and some Hawker Harts. The Training School expanded quite rapidly and in addition to support facilities (such as a map room, a cinema for the showing of training films, a parachute section and a canteen) a Bellman hangar was erected. Simultaneously, a larger flight shed was built by Field Aircraft Services from Croydon, which created a repair and maintenance facility on the western side of the airfield.

When war began the civilian flying club was closed down and the Civil Air Guard unit was also withdrawn. No 27 E&RFTS moved to Burnaston and Tollerton was temporarily silent while the Air Ministry decided on its potential use as a Royal Air Force base. It was quickly brought into use as a scatter field, housing Hampdens from Nos 44 and 50 Squadrons from nearby Waddington. The airfield was then designated as a satellite for RAF Newton, while Field Aircraft Services developed its maintenance facility as a lodger unit.

Tucked away behind Tollerton's control tower, a pillbox still survives, dedicated as a memorial to No 50 Squadron. (Richard E. Flagg)

Three concrete runways were laid during 1941 and a large R Type hangar was constructed on the northern perimeter, while a second Bellman hangar was erected on the main apron and a variety of support buildings slowly appeared. These included crew rooms and dispersal huts, together with a communal site on the western side of the main Tollerton road. No 16 (Polish) SFTS began using the airfield from July 1941, many of its aircraft deploying from their home base at Newton over the following years, up until 1946. Likewise, Field Aircraft Services took on a large amount of war work, overhauling Dakotas, Halifaxes, Hampdens, Lancasters, Manchesters, Liberators and Bostons, some of which were brought in by Queen Mary Trailer, although most were flown in by Air Transport Auxiliary pilots. As Field's commitments increased, the company eventually took over all of the airfield's hangars and became the most active user of the aerodrome.

A very unusual transport conversion of an Avro Lincoln, pictured at Tollerton. Intended for freight duties between Paraguay and Peru, the aircraft was never delivered and it was broken-up at Tollerton in 1959. (Rod Simpson collection)

When the war ended the civilian flying club was reopened and both Blue Line and Trent Valley Airlines started scheduled and charter operations. Field Aircraft Services, which had handled more than 1,700 aircraft for the MAP, now began to receive large numbers of Lancasters from No 5 Group. These were stored all around the airfield, often jammed nose-to-tail, while the breakers began their sad and exhausting task of dismantling each airframe for removal as scrap. The small airline companies ended their operations in 1949 and the flying club also closed down when the Ministry of Aviation abandoned its tenure of the site, leaving only individual private owners occupying the empty hangars.

This is Tollerton's unusual flight shed, from where so many RAF bombers emerged after overhaul during the Second World War. Today the structure is still housing aircraft, albeit far smaller and less warlike types. (Richard E. Flagg)

An unusual surface air raid shelter, still intact at Tollerton. (Richard E. Flagg)

The RAF began to use the airfield again late in 1949 when No 22 FTS at Syerston adopted Tollerton as a satellite field and continued operating here until 1956 when the Air Ministry withdrew. A year later Field Aircraft Services moved to Wymeswold and the Sherwood Flying Club was established as the new occupant of the airfield. In 1963 Truman Aviation took a lease on the site and began developing Tollerton as a long-term home for private and recreational flying. An air taxi service was soon created and helicopters also became a common sight; civil flying has continued at Tollerton since then until the present day.

Plans to develop the site into a full-scale regional airport were never seriously pursued, the airfield being too small to accommodate anything significantly larger than light aircraft, but Tollerton remains active, and most of the airfield's layout remains much the same as when it was first constructed, although most of its architecture is gone. The runways are still intact, two still being used for private flying, and most of the perimeter track is still there, apart from a section along the northern perimeter that is long gone and replaced by farmland. Some of the old dispersals can still be seen even though they are mostly overgrown, and the old Field Aircraft Services shed is still there, although the RAF bombers that used to occupy it have long since been replaced by Cessnas. From Tollerton Lane it is possible to watch the little aircraft come and go, and picture the scene from seventy years ago when Lancasters used to claw their way into the air from Tollerton's modest runways.

> *Runways:* 040 (1,119yd x 50yd) concrete and wood chippings, 100 (1,146yd x 50yd) concrete and wood chippings, 160 (1,035yd x 50yd) concrete and wood chippings. *Hangars:* Bellman (1), Blister (4). *Hardstandings:* Circular (20), Sommerfield track (33). *Accommodation:* RAF: 4 Officers, 6 SNCOs, 132 ORs.

TOWYN, Gwynedd

Grid ref SH586009, Lat 52:35:17N (52.58793) Lon 4:05:16W (-4.08764), 10ft asl. N of A493, 1 mile NW of central Tywyn

This small airfield was constructed as a support facility for the Royal Artillery's AA Practice Camp at Tonfanau. Army cooperation flights were to be the main role for the station and U Flight of No 1 AACU moved here during the autumn of 1940 with a fleet of Queen Bee target drone aircraft, joined by C Flight from the same unit, which transferred its Hawker Henleys from Penrhos. However, the first aircraft to arrive here landed some weeks previously when a Miles Magister flew in from Penrhos to warn of an invasion alert. The station's personnel (who were still in the process of setting up the station) immediately arranged to destroy vital documents, but thankfully the alert soon passed, like so many others. Other unusual visitors were quite common, as Towyn was the only airfield in the area for some time, and on 11 November a Beaufort from No 217 Squadron landed with engine difficulties while flying from St Eval in Cornwall.

The resident C Flight became No 1605 Flight from 1 October 1942 and merged with 1628 Flight to become No 631 Squadron on 1 December 1943. At this stage the unit was still flying Hawker Henleys for target tug duties, even though most units had already replaced this type with Martinets, and it was not until February 1945 that the last Henley was withdrawn. No 1 AACU was based here from 1940 until 1942, when it was replaced by No 6 AACU, which remained until September of that year. More emergency diversions came on 16 December 1942 when twelve P-38 Lightnings from the USAAF's 97th Fighter Squadron force-landed here, one of them skidding off the grass runway into a gun post and remaining at Towyn for some time awaiting repair, while the other eleven flew on to St Eval two days later, en route to their destination in North Africa.

Towyn's landing field was prone to waterlogging and the site was often unusable during the winter months, aircraft being exported to Llanbedr when necessary, in order to take advantage of that airfield's concrete runways. Undoubtedly the best-known emergency diversion that came here was B-17 Fortress 42-31321 from the 309th Bomb Group, which force-landed at Towyn on 8 July 1944. The crew had become disorientated upon arriving in the UK from North Africa and, after flying along the Welsh coast with rapidly dwindling fuel, Towyn was the first available landing field that they saw. Hardly big enough to accommodate the mighty Fortress, the aircraft landed safely but continued to roll across the adjacent railway line and finally hit an air raid shelter, causing a fire in the aircraft's wing root in the process. The crew managed to escape without injury.

In May 1945 No 631 Squadron made the move to Llanbedr permanent, and Towyn was transferred to No 22 Group Technical Command, but the station was closed down on 25 July 1945. The site was then transferred to the Army, which used it for accommodation and an outward bound school, the landing field mostly being used for sports. However, Army communications aircraft

Fortress 42-31321 at Towyn after making its unscheduled arrival in July 1944. (PRO)

(particularly Beavers) continued to appear here from time to time, but today the airfield is abandoned and little remains of the station, apart from a cluster of crumbling accommodation and admin blocks, together with the concrete apron. The wartime hangars (two Bellmans, two Blisters and two canvas Bessoneau) that stood here are also long gone, but traces of this station are certainly still visible, as is the former grass landing field from where the precarious flights of the diminutive Queen Bees used to begin and (sometimes) terminate.

> *Runways:* E/W (700yd) grass, NE/SW (1,100yd) grass, NW/SE (1,200yd) grass.
> *Hangars:* Bellman (2), Blister (2), Bessoneau (2). *Hardstandings:* 0. *Accommodation:*
> RAF: 13 Officers, 29 SNCOs, 393 ORs; WAAF: 2 Officers, 8 SNCOs, 92 ORs.

VALLEY, Anglesey

Grid ref SH309757, Lat 53:15:07N (53.25186) Lon 4:32:09W (-4.53581), 25ft asl. 2 miles NW of Rhosneigr, off A5

Visitors to Wales might be forgiven for thinking that the Royal Air Force has somehow abandoned the western portions of the United Kingdom in favour of the South and East. But out on the island of Anglesey, the RAF maintains what is undoubtedly one of its most important and busiest stations, which looks set to remain part of the modern RAF for many years to come.

RAF Valley first opened on 1 February 1941 as a Fighter Sector Station under the control of No 9 Group, tasked with the provision of fighter cover for the North West region. Like so many stations that opened at this time, it was poorly equipped, and its location on the exposed coastline made the lives of the station's personnel all the more miserable. Originally named Rhosneigr (in recognition of the nearby village), it came as no surprise that it was changed to Valley by 5 April, by which stage the first aircraft had arrived in the shape of Hurricanes from No 312 Squadron, based at Speke. These were replaced by aircraft from No 615 Squadron on 18 April when the former unit moved to Jurby.

No 615 Squadron became engaged in no fewer than four combats while conducting convoy patrols from Valley, intercepting a Ju 88 on 4 May, another just three days later over Snowdonia, another on 27 June, and yet another on 26 August, which force-landed in Ireland after having suffered major damage over Cardigan Bay. Night-fighters were also assigned to Valley, No 219 Squadron deploying Beaufighters here from their home base at High Ercall.

On 30 June No 456 Squadron was formed here, a Royal Australian Air Force squadron equipped with Defiants, although most of the initial aircrew were British, this shortage preventing the unit from becoming operational until 5 September. In October 1941 No 275 Squadron was established at Valley in response to the growing number of accidents in the region. Tasked with air-sea rescue, the unit initially operated Lysanders, but subsequently received Walrus amphibians, Ansons and Defiants. In addition to the resident aircraft, No 68 Squadron also used Valley as a forward base for numerous night patrols, and during November one of the unit's pilots shot down a Heinkel He 111 near Gwalchmai.

Despite the bleak conditions at Valley, the overall weather record was good, at least in terms of visibility and flying conditions, as exemplified by the events of 11 January 1942, when all of No 9 Group's airfields were closed due to fog apart from Valley, from where a Beaufighter successfully got airborne and intercepted a Do 217, shooting it down near Nuneaton. This good-weather factor, combined with the airfield's location adjacent to the Irish Sea, made it ideal as a potential transatlantic ferry base, and plans were made to extend the main runway and improve the hardstandings and dispersals, this work eventually being completed in 1943.

No 242 Squadron left for the Far East in December 1941, and No 350 Squadron was formed on 13 November with Spitfires, being drawn from No 131 Squadron at Llanbedr; that unit also subsequently moved to Valley, only to return to Llanbedr in April 1942 after having suffered serviceability problems, mostly caused by the ever-present sand that blew in from the beach and caused endless difficulties for engineers. This left No 456 Squadron at Valley, and from May the unit conducted regular daytime patrols with Beaufighters off Carnsore Point in Ireland. Its efforts were rewarded on 18 May when a Ju 88 was intercepted and shot down. On 30 July a Heinkel was shot down at night on Pwllheli beach, but this was to be the last of the unit's encounters and, after converting to Mosquitoes, it departed in March 1943.

Combat continued, however, and on 23 August 1942 a Ju 88 was intercepted by a pilot from a 315 Squadron detachment, and although the enemy aircraft force-landed, one of the Spitfire pilots was wounded and later died. Thankfully, this event marked the end of such encounters. From the end of 1942 attention shifted towards ferry operations and, although Valley remained under the control of No 9 Group, it would subsequently be used by Ferry Command, which would take up residence as a lodger unit.

With a longer runway, new hardstandings and an American-managed radio range for instrument let-down, the airfield soon began to play host to many transient aircraft, among the first being six Lancasters that diverted here on 22 March after completing a raid over Germany. The USAAF's 414th Night Fighter Squadron then arrived for a few months to work up alongside No 406 Squadron, before leaving for Exeter in November. From 19 June 1943 the USAAF's Ferry Terminal became operational and the first aircraft (a B-17) arrived on 28 July. Liberators (eleven aircraft) arrived on 17 August, and two B-25s arrived from Stornoway in company with three C-47s on 12 September, moving on to St Mawgan the next day.

Despite the availability of radio aids, the resident Beaufighters were sometimes called upon to shepherd aircraft towards the airfield (particularly those that had suffered damage at the hands of enemy aircraft), and a wide variety of aircraft types could be seen on the airfield. On 19 December, for example, no fewer than thirty-eight aircraft were present, including four P-38 Lightnings, an Airacobra, a C-54, a Hudson, and six P-47 Thunderbolts. The increase in ferry traffic (together with more runway improvements) eventually saw the closure of the Fighter Sector Station and operations moved to Woodvale on 1 November.

When No 125 Squadron's Mosquitoes left on 21 January 1944, Valley's main role became the receipt of aircraft from the USA, which arrived here prior to being flown on to bases in East Anglia and elsewhere, with USAAF and RAF aircraft being handled by their respective authorities under a joint operational procedure. During the winter of 1943-44 the ferry route was switched to the Azores in order to avoid the harsh Atlantic weather, and on 18 February some sixty-two C-47 aircraft flew in, although B-17 Fortresses, B-24 Liberators and B-26 Marauders were the most common visitors. Perhaps the most notable transient aircraft was a UC-64 Norseman, which arrived on 30 June 1944. After landing it was revealed that the aircraft had been stolen from Warton by an American serviceman who was attempting to fly to France. Another equally notable day was 17 September, when a staggering ninety-nine B-17 Fortresses and B-24 Liberators flew in from Ireland.

Among all this ferry activity, No 1528 BAT Flight came to Valley on 1 November 1944 with a fleet of Oxfords. The unit stayed until 17 December 1945, by which stage it had been renamed No 1528 Radio Aids (Range) Training Flight, responsible for the teaching of American let-down techniques to RAF Transport Command pilots.

As the Second World War came to an end, the station's ferry tasks were reversed and more than 2,600 USAAF bombers staged through Valley en route to the USA. By September 1945 Valley's activity had dwindled to little more than the hosting of temporary detachments for night-flying training. In June 1947 the station was placed under Care and Maintenance, although the airfield remained available for emergency diversions, and works were completed on the station's facilities in preparation for the base's reopening.

In March 1951 No 202 AFS was formed here with Vampire jets, and Valley began its long association with flying training. In 1958 No 7 Flying Training School began advanced training at Valley and the unit was subsequently renumbered as No 4 FTS on 15 August 1960. In addition to Vampires, the new FTS also acquired Varsities, these being used for the training of Coastal Command pilots, although this task was shifted to Oakington in March 1962, by which stage the first Gnat trainers were beginning to replace the Vampires, this transition being completed the following year. In 1964 No 4 FTS formed a five-aircraft display team, the 'Yellowjacks', their diminutive Gnats being painted yellow in recognition of the team's name; their formation displays provided the basis for the formation of the world-famous Red Arrows team, which began training towards the end of the same year.

Although the diminutive Folland Gnat trainer became a famous and integral part of the RAF's training system for many years, the type was operated only from two main sites. A small number of aircraft were operated by the Central Flying School at Little Rissington (their Red Arrows detachment being based at Fairford and Kemble) but the main Gnat fleet was maintained at Valley. (Author's collection)

Hunters were delivered to No 4 FTS in 1967, supplementing the Gnats for advanced training of foreign students and also providing a more suitable aircraft for longer-legged RAF students who simply couldn't fit into the tiny Gnat's cockpit. The last Gnats and Hunters were retired in November 1979, and since that year No 4 FTS has operated the Hawk trainer, operations currently being divided between two component units, Nos 19(R) and 208(R) Squadrons.

An excellent vertical image of RAF Valley taken in the 1980s. Numerous Hawks are visible on the flight lines (plus one on the runway) and Lightnings are parked on the south-west flight line, on Missile Practice Camp. (RAF Valley)

No 4 FTS Gnat XR544 crashed on final approach to Valley during April 1978. (Author's collection)

Three Hawks break right into the airfield circuit at Valley, with more Hawks visible on the northern flight line below. (RAF Valley)

A pair of Valley-based Hawks streak skywards over the Menai Bridge where Catalina flying boats once roamed. (RAF Valley)

For many years RAF Valley also played host to Missile Practice Camps, with operational squadrons deploying to the base to fly live firing sorties over the nearby Aberporth range against unmanned targets. Through the 1960s and into the 1990s the southern apron was regularly occupied by detachments of Lightnings, Phantoms and Tornado fighters, but the gradual shift towards synthetic training has seen such deployments dwindle in recent years, and are now rare.

Helicopter operations came to Valley in the 1960s when the CFS Helicopter element first moved here. Today the RAF's Search & Rescue headquarters is based here, and the familiar all-yellow Sea Kings are a common sight in the local area. The Defence Helicopter Flying School operates both the Squirrel and Griffin from Valley within the SARTU (Search And Rescue Training Unit) and the intensive helicopter operations are likely to continue here for a few more years until the task is contracted out to civilian operation. Hawk operations look set to continue for many years into the future, with new-build Hawks slowly entering service, ensuring that any visitor to the area will inevitably find plenty to see.

The airfield remains largely unchanged from the wartime era, all of the hangars, runways and hardstandings still in use, although a great deal of the technical, admin and domestic sites has been rebuilt. A viewing area provides an excellent vantage point from which to watch the daily comings and goings, but from a small road leading past the western approach to the main runway an even closer look at the black-painted Hawks is possible, as they streak over at head-top height ... sometimes even lower!

> *Runways:* 188 (1,785yd x 50yd) tarmac, 251 (1,400yd x 50yd) tarmac, 132 (2,000yd x 50yd) tarmac. *Hangars:* T2 (3), Bellman (3). *Hardstandings:* Various (51). *Accommodation:* RAF: 98 Officers, 84 SNCOs, 1,302 ORs; WAAF: 16 Officers, 8 SNCOs, 580 ORs.

WARWICK, Warwickshire

Grid ref SP270631, Lat 52:15:59N (52.26627) Lon 1:36:16W (-1.60435), 160ft asl. 1 mile SW of Warwick between A429 and A46, S of A4189

Opened in December 1941, RAF Warwick was a small site created as a Relief Landing Ground for Church Lawford. It was first used in January 1942 as part of No 23 Group, Oxfords and Tutors being based here for instructor training. From October 1942 Church Lawford's training operations had developed and the Tutors were gradually withdrawn. No 18 (P)AFU eventually operated a fleet of Oxfords and Ansons, both types being common visitors to Warwick. The very basic grass landing field was blessed with few support buildings, and only four Blister hangars were assembled here, two close to the station's entrance and two on the south-west perimeter of the field. A small cluster of eight huts provided all of the necessary admin accommodation and most of these buildings were eventually demolished after the station closed in May 1945.

Placed under Care and Maintenance, no flying was conducted here from that date and the entire site was eventually sold off. Not surprisingly, few traces of the airfield's existence have survived, but the landing field is still here, now used by the Riding for the Disabled Association. Sports pitches occupy part of the former airfield and a couple of concrete huts remain, adjacent to the A429 road. But with Warwick's housing slowly encroaching from the north and west, the RAF station's remnants will doubtless disappear completely before too long.

> *Runways:* NE/SW (1,050yd) grass, N/S (1,050yd) grass. *Hangars:* Blister (4). *Hardstandings:* 0. *Accommodation:* RAF: 2 Officers, 4 SNCOs, 88 ORs.

WATCHFIELD, Wiltshire

Grid ref SU257903, Lat 51:36:42N (51.61173) Lon 1:37:44W (-1.62889), 330ft asl. 6 miles N of Swindon on A420, N of Watchfield village

An aerial image of Watchfield taken shortly after the station opened, with a small number of aircraft visible near the hangar complex. (via Neil Jedrzejewski)

The first aircraft to appear at this site were Tiger Moths from No 3 EFTS, which arrived from Hamble (being forced north by the attentions of the Luftwaffe) on 20 July 1940. Simultaneously, Ansons from No 11 AONS were also arriving from Hamble, together with more Ansons from No 4 AONS at Ansty. Despite being a relatively small grass field with view support buildings, Watchfield was immediately very busy. Even more aircraft were due to arrive with plans for No 1 Blind Approach School to move in on 2 August, but without suitable equipment its arrival was delayed until 28 October, by which stage its first six Ansons had duly arrived. Two of the Ansons (R9828 and R9830) had arrived on the 20th from the Wireless Intelligence Development Unit, and R989 and R9837 arrived a day later (two more were held in reserve).

The combined activities of the Blind Approach School and the EFTS made Watchfield a difficult place from which to operate, and a careful control of flying was maintained by a BAS instructor in the airfield control tower, from where a red light would be displayed whenever a BAS aircraft was on approach at 100 feet. All other aircraft would then be required to remain stationary until the approach had been completed. Despite the potentially hazardous nature of such intensive flying, accidents were few, the most significant damage at Watchfield being created by the Luftwaffe, which was responsible for the delivery of high-explosive bombs and incendiaries that struck the south-east section of the airfield on 27 February 1941.

Busy times at Watchfield, with Oxfords from the resident Blind Approach School scattered across the field. (via Spencer Adcott)

A Tiger Moth from No 3 EFTS pictured on a sortie from Watchfield. (via Spencer Adcott)

By the middle of that year blind approach equipment had been installed at many other airfields and this prompted the creation of the Blind Approach Calibration Flight in May, equipped with three Oxfords. However, by July the airfield was clearly far too busy and No 11 AONS ended operations on the 19th, followed by No 4 AONS on 4 August. Training activities increased, and the station's complement of Ansons grew temporarily, until it was decided that blind approach training would become a part of the SFTS syllabus, for which Oxfords would be used. Consequently the BAS re-equipped with Oxfords, the first three (V4051, V4052 and V5054) arriving on 17 September 1941.

Airspeed's ubiquitous Oxford was a long-term resident at Watchfield, often present on the airfield in substantial numbers. (via Ken Billingham)

Night approach training also began that month, and during October the unit was redesignated as No 1 Beam Approach School. The Regional Control School (Bomber Command) moved in from Brasenose College on 15 December, becoming the School of Flying Control in the process and utilising facilities that had been vacated by No 3 EFTS, which moved to Shellingford on the 18th. It was not until February 1942 that the first significant accident occurred, when Anson AT775 stalled on approach in extremely poor weather conditions; although the incident was not catastrophic, it broke what had been a surprisingly long record of accident-free flying, the only other notable event having been a forced landing caused by the inadvertent selection of cockpit switches.

On 9 February four Dominies were despatched to Watchfield in order to give flying experience to the SFC students. An increase in training requirements led to the creation of a second BAT Flight, and three Dominies were delivered during April, followed by Oxfords from Docking's BAT Flight, combining to create a new Flight at Watchfield. The Calibration Flight Oxfords left in July (in order to ease the pressure on Watchfield's circuit) and a Satellite Landing Ground was adopted at Kelmscot from 17 October. By this stage a great deal of beam approach training had been exported to other airfields, including Boscombe Down, Abingdon, Little Rissington and Harwell. Kelmscot was usually only used for approach training and aircraft were not normally accommodated there, although on 6 January 1943 poor weather at Watchfield forced a student to land at Kelmscot, the overnight stay requiring security guards to be sent from Watchfield.

The satellite field also proved to be useful in subsequent months when weather conditions prevented flying at the home base (and while lighting was being installed). A second RLG was established at Wanborough in July 1943 and this site became extremely busy with up to 110 airfield controllers being trained there at any one time. Throughout this period the combined training operations proceeded without serious incident, and the only serious accident to occur was one that involved an aircraft unconnected with Watchfield. On 10 June a Lancaster from Lindholme crashed just a mile from Watchfield's north-west boundary, killing everyone on board. Rather less serious was the damage sustained by some of the resident Oxfords on 22 October when a tornado swept through the airfield, lifting one Oxford off the ground and stripping sheet metal from a hangar roof.

The Beam Approach Technical Training School moved to Cranwell at the end of 1943, and airfield controller training was temporarily moved in from Wanborough, enabling No 3 GTS to deploy a Flight to that airfield while its home base (Stoke Orchard) was temporarily out of use. By early 1944 the area around Watchfield was congested, with many gliders and transport aircraft participating in exercises on a daily basis. Master flying control for the whole area was set up at South Cerney and, although Kelmscot remained in use as Watchfield's satellite until 1947, it became a much-used site for paratroop drop exercises in 1944 and the BAS was unable to use it again until after D-Day.

Training then continued, with many BAT Flights deploying to Watchfield either to use the facilities or to work up prior to moving elsewhere. No 1 BAS finally disbanded on 1 January 1947, its Oxfords departing together with a few Harvards that had been acquired, some 8,500 pupils having been successfully trained. The School of Air Traffic Control was created from the School of Flying Control in 1946 and this remained at Watchfield until January 1950. From that date the station no longer hosted any resident units, but the airfield remained in use for occasional stores-dropping exercises performed by RAF transport crews.

The grass landing field eventually returned to agricultural use and the RAF station was subsequently closed down and bulldozed. Today virtually nothing remains of this once-busy site and the only trace of Watchfield's hangars and support buildings consist of no more than the small patches of concrete that can be found close to the A420. From 2008 a wind turbine farm was constructed on the centre of the old airfield and now the skies above this former airfield are currently scarred by the presence of five large, and rather ugly, windmills.

Runways: NW/SE (1,400yd) grass, NNW/SSE (1,700yd) grass, N/S (900yd) grass. *Hangars:* Bellman (50), Blister (5). *Hardstandings:* 0. *Accommodation:* RAF: 130 Officers, 168 SNCOs, 391 ORs.

WESTON PARK, Shropshire

Grid ref SJ812086, Lat 52:40:32N (52.67568) Lon 2:16:44W (-2.27883), 210ft asl. On Offoxley Road, 1 mile E of Tong Norton, off A41

Opened as No 33 Satellite Landing Ground, this small site required a great deal of preparation before it was declared fit for use in June 1941. Spitfires from No 9 Maintenance Unit were despatched to the site from their main site at Cosford from that date, and although this aircraft type was the most common sight at this station a Wellington bomber also made a successful test landing here, in anticipation of possible allocations to this airfield, although there appears to be no record of any Wellingtons having been stored here. By the end of July some thirty-five Spitfires were already being accommodated at Weston Park, most of these being positioned in the surrounding woodlands, which form the backdrop to the huge estate on which the airfield was built.

No 27 Maintenance Unit at Shawbury was also afforded the use of Weston Park from October 1942, but there is no record of any of that unit's aircraft being stored here. No 29 Maintenance Unit at High Ercall did use the site in late 1943 and 1944 as a temporary dispersal site for some of its aircraft, at a time when almost 700 machines were under its control. From early 1944 the airfield became a satellite for a second airfield, this being RNAS Hinstock (HMS *Goldwit*), and the Oxfords of No 780 Squadron became regular users of the site until it was finally closed in the summer of 1945.

Only a handful of buildings had been constructed to support the airfield and these were eventually demolished. Now only the former watch tower remains, rebuilt as a private dwelling. The airfield, long since abandoned, is now part of the lush countryside and the trees where Spitfires once hid are occupied only by woodland animals. Flying activities are still common to the area and various air displays and fetes are held at Weston Park, many of which attract a variety of aircraft types, although all are held towards the main estate to the north, and the former RAF field is no longer host to any such activity.

Runways: 0 (grass field). *Hangars:* 0. *Hardstandings:* 0. *Accommodation:* RAF; N/A.

WHEATON ASTON, Staffordshire

Grid ref SJ835155, Lat 52:44:14N (52.73712) Lon 2:14:41W (-2.24464), 350ft asl, 2 mile N of Wheaton Aston village

Constructed in 1941 as a proposed satellite for a bomber Operational Training Unit to be formed at Hixon, Wheaton Aston was transferred to the control of RAF Shawbury on 5 December as a

Satellite Landing Ground. Construction of runways at Shawbury necessitated the transfer of flying training from that base, and No 11 SFTS exported its activities to a number of bases while work progressed. As soon as Wheaton Aston became available, it became a useful and relatively local diversionary field, and the SFTS Oxfords soon became permanent residents here. The unit was renamed No 11 (P)AFU on 1 April 1942 and, with a large influx of students arriving directly from basic training in the USA, the task of re-educating pilots for the very different conditions prevailing in the UK ensured that Wheaton Aston was kept very busy, especially when night-flying was introduced.

By 1943 the unit had expanded to include three Flights back at Shawbury together with a Flight at Condover, Perton and Wheaton Aston, and aircraft were generally based on a permanent basis at each site, returning to Shawbury only for servicing. The Flight structure was rationalised on 1 August 1943 and the Wheaton Aston element became No 21 (P)AFU, with 120 students being posted from Shawbury over the next few weeks. Equipped with seventy-one Oxfords, two Ansons and one Magister, training was conducted both here and at Perton, and included a week's training with No 1511 BAT Flight, which moved in on 28 September.

Visiting aircraft were comparatively rare, although a Fortress from the 95th Bomb Group at Horham landed here short of fuel after completing a mission over France on 16 August, and a P-47 Thunderbolt pilot attempted to land here on 4 July 1944 after losing engine power at 3,000 feet above the airfield. Unfortunately the pilot misjudged his approach and crashed into the canal that skirts the airfield, but escaped without injury.

No 1545 BAT Flight was formed here on 14 February 1944, affiliated to No 21 (P)AFU and No 3 (O)AFU at Halfpenny Green, but by 25 April the unit had moved to Halfpenny Green in order to ease pressure on Wheaton Aston's already very busy airfield circuit. Meanwhile, the busy activity had prompted the adoption of a second satellite field, at Tatenhill, which came into use from 1 February by which stage almost 150 Oxfords were in use. The disbandment of No 19 (P)AFU saw more Oxfords arrive at Wheaton Aston, and by May 1944 a monthly total of 10,837 flying hours was achieved – impressive by any standards.

The station remained busy into 1945, but as the end of the war approached the training commitments began to slow and the fleet of 120 Oxfords was gradually reduced until August 1946, by which stage only seventy-one aircraft remained available. The AFU moved to Moreton-in-Marsh on 1 December 1946 and flying activities ended, the station closing down on 31 July 1947. Some of the accommodation was used into the 1950s and the site was not relinquished until September 1953, when control was passed to the Ministry of Agriculture & Fisheries, which subsequently sold it off for agricultural use.

Today the former station is crumbling, many of the buildings already gone, and those that remain are slowly decaying. The old control tower still stands, occupied only by sheep, but a few concrete huts still provide evidence of the RAF's presence. The runways and perimeter track are also still present but overgrown to such an extent that the concrete surfaces can hardly be recognised, and the south-western portions of two runways are now occupied by poultry sheds and lines of trees. To the south-east a couple of dispersals are still very evident, and to the north the canal still runs past the threshold of the main runway, where the hapless P-47 pilot made his unscheduled arrival nearly seventy years ago.

Wheaton Aston's watch office, slowly crumbling in the encroaching vegetation. (Richard E. Flagg)

Part of Wheaton Aston's maintenance site, still intact and used for agricultural storage. (Richard E. Flagg)

The remains of Wheaton Aston's communal site, abandoned and partially boarded up. (Richard E. Flagg)

Runways: 220 (1,310yd x 50yd) concrete covered with tarmac, 280 (1,100yd x 50yd) concrete covered with tarmac, 340 (1,100yd x 50yd) concrete covered with tarmac. *Hangars:* T1 (3), Blister (8). *Hardstandings:* Circular (4), Fighter pen (1). *Accommodation:* RAF: 143 Officers, 338 SNCOs, 975 ORs; WAAF: 20 Officers, 42 SNCOs, 378 ORs.

WIGSLEY, Nottinghamshire

Grid ref SK861696, Lat 53:13:03N (53.21739) Lon 0:42:41W (-0.71128), 33ft asl. W of Lincoln of A1133, 1 mile E of Spalford

Opening in February 1942 as a satellite for Swinderby in No 5 Group, RAF Wigsley was literally carved out of the countryside, sprawling across the old Wigsley road and cutting into the adjacent woodlands. It was not one of the best-known wartime stations, perhaps a symptom of its location, which is actually in Nottinghamshire but only just over seven miles west of Lincoln – not quite in Lincolnshire and only just in Nottinghamshire. The wartime code (and call sign) for the base was 'UGS', but it was colloquially often referred to as 'the cemetery with lights', a phrase that said a great deal about the station's popularity with its personnel.

The first unit to be based here was No 455 Squadron, Royal Australian Air Force, which arrived on 8 February with Hampden bombers, tasked primarily with mine-laying sorties and

An aerial view of Wigsley taken in 1942 and showing the standard triangular runway layout and 'frying pan' dispersals. (via John Elliott)

occasional 'Nickel' leaflet drops over occupied France. However, when the squadron had barely settled in at the new base, a move to Leuchars was dictated by a change in role to torpedo strike duties within Coastal Command, and the Hampdens duly left for Scotland from 19 April.

In May the first Lancaster Conversion Unit was formed here, eight Lancasters and eight Manchesters forming No 1654 Heavy Conversion Unit with aircraft brought over from Swinderby in June. The unit was tasked with transitional training from the twin-engine Manchester to the four-engine Lancaster, producing qualified crews for No 5 Group. On 15 March 1943 Swinderby was designated as No 51 Base, with Wigsley allocated as a sub-station; however, despite the construction of runways and hardstandings, the station's facilities remained primitive. As an HCU equipped with often tired aircraft, assigned to the demanding task of training, there were many crashes. The Manchesters (which preceded the unit's Lancasters) in particular suffered heavy losses, although this was not unusual for Manchesters because of their troublesome Rolls Royce Vulture engines.

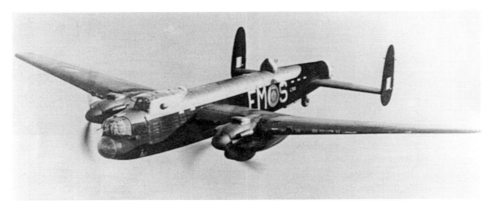

RAF Wigsley was one of only a handful of RAF stations from where the short-lived Avro Manchester operated. (Author's collection)

However, it was a crash involving a Lancaster for which RAF Wigsley is often remembered. This occurred on 11 June 1943 and involved Lancaster No ED833, from RAF Wigsley, which was on a training flight practising three-engined flying over Lincoln when it banked to the south towards open country. Unfortunately, a wing tip hit a telegraph pole, causing the aircraft to hit Nos 22 and 24 Highfield Avenue in Lincoln. The aircraft then turned in mid-air to crash into Nos 25 and 27 on the other side of the road. Five civilians died as a result, including three children, and all but the rear gunner in the crew of seven were also killed.

This was not the only fatal crash associated with RAF Wigsley – a number of aircraft came down in the area, but without causing civilian loss of life. A Hampden of 455 Squadron hit electric cables near Eagle and came down behind Sutton's Farm on Friday 13 February 1942. On 5 July of that same year a Manchester of 61 Squadron crashed and was burned out at Wigsley. Another Manchester,

Groundcrew at Wigsley examine a Lancaster's impressive bomb load prior to a mission. (via Brian Silcott)

L7457, this time of 'home' unit 1654 HCU, crashed on the west bank at Saxilby on 24 January 1942, and two days later Manchester R5772 of 49 Squadron crashed near Wigsley. Another close one was on 2 March 1943 when a Manchester, L7277 of 1654 HCU, crashed on North Scarle.

During November 1943 the unit exchanged its aircraft for Halifaxes so that its Lancasters could be redistributed to operational units, and on 3 November Wigsley was designated as No 75 Base within No 7 Group. When the war ended No 1654 HCU moved to Woolfox Lodge, and on 20 September No 28 Aircrew Holding Unit was formed at Wigsley, although it disbanded again during the following year. However, the airfield remained in use as a satellite for Swinderby until 1 July 1958, when it was abandoned as a Relief Landing Ground and flight operations ended.

Wigsley's watch office, still standing but long abandoned and undoubtedly doomed. (Richard E. Flagg)

No 1654 HCU operated Stirlings at Wiglsey from December 1943 until January 1945. (via Brian Silcott)

The station was quickly decommissioned and sold off shortly afterwards. Apart from the attempts to fly a home-built aircraft here during 1969, no further flying activity took place and the entire site has long since reverted to its former agricultural status. Some of the original buildings survive, not least the crumbling remains of the control tower and a few remnants of the communal site. The runways have long since been removed and it is only the presence of vegetation that indicates their original positions, although small stretches of concrete are still to be found among the fields. Most of the perimeter track is gone and the dispersals have disappeared, but among the pig shelters the airfield's layout is still discernable. The old Wigsley road has resumed its pre-war route and now happily snakes through the middle of the former airfield.

> *Runways:* 207 (1,400yd x 50yd) concrete, 268 (2,000yd x 50yd) concrete, 325 (1,400yd x 50yd) concrete. *Hangars:* T2 (2), B1 (1). *Hardstandings:* Heavy Bomber (36). *Accommodation:* RAF: 55 Officers, 488 SNCOs, 1,201 ORs; WAAF: 2 Officers, 8 SNCOs, 340 ORs.

WINTHORPE, Nottinghamshire

Grid ref SK833558, Lat 53:05:36N (53.0934) Lon 0:45:23W (-0.75651), 55ft asl. Off A46, 1 mile NE of Newark

Just north of Newark, the RAF's presence at Winthorpe began in September 1940 when the airfield was first opened as a satellite for Swinderby, which is situated just a few miles further north. It was not until October that the first units moved in, these being Nos 300 and 301 Squadrons, Polish units equipped with Fairey Battles. Operations proceeded from both the parent and satellite field with three aircraft from each squadron normally dispersed to Winthorpe. One aircraft (L5356) crashed while flying near Sutton-on-Trent.

The less-than-successful Fairey Battle was one of a variety of types that operated from Winthorpe during the Second World War. (Author's collection)

Towards the end of October 1940 the first Wellingtons were delivered and operations over Germany were suspended while the new aircraft type was brought into service, although by 18 October the two squadrons had flown some eighty-five sorties over enemy territory. In return, the Luftwaffe turned its attention towards Winthorpe on 14 November when a land mine was dropped on the airfield, creating a 20-foot-deep crater, although no aircraft were damaged and nobody was injured. By the beginning of January 1942 operations had resumed and on the 2nd the returning Wellington crews were faced with poor visibility and heavy snow. The first aircraft (R1006) crashed on landing (without any casualties) and the remaining Wellingtons diverted to nearby airfields; two crashed at Waddington and only one crew member survived.

Training operations continued in support of Swinderby, particularly when heavy rain occasionally prevented operations at the main base. On 27 November 1941 Winthorpe was transferred to the control of Ossington, and on 7 February 1942 it became a satellite field for Syerston and No 455 Squadron became a regular user of the airfield with its fleet of Hampdens. When that unit departed early in 1942 construction of concrete runways at Winthorpe was initiated, and a standard bomber airfield layout was adopted. Oddly, the main runway was aligned with a local roller-bearing factory and, with this facility assigned to vital war work, it was agreed that Winthorpe would be used as little as possible, as the risk of a fully laden bomber crashing into the factory was considered to be very real. Why this potential predicament had not been identified before the runways were constructed remains a mystery.

On 15 October 1942 the station was returned to the control of Swinderby and No 1661 Heavy Conversion Unit moved here from Skellingthorpe with eight Manchesters and ten Lancasters. Training activities were often eventful and accidents were common, at least one Manchester being written off and eight Lancasters being lost during the unit's stay here. In September 1943 the first of sixteen Halifaxes were delivered to the HCU, but in November these were replaced by Stirlings and most of the Lancasters were reassigned to operational squadrons in January 1944. At this time Winthorpe ceased to be a satellite field and became an independent station while the HCU continued its activities.

The first Stirling accident occurred on 26 May when LJ558 swung off the runway on take-off and crashed into the station workshops, fortunately without injury to crew or ground personnel. Less fortunate was the crew of LK616, which crashed near Hawton on 27 August and only the air gunner survived.

Looking across Winthorpe's airfield, eight Lancasters from No 1661 HCU are visible. (via John Elliott)

The crew of No 1661 HCU pose under the massive undercarriage of their Stirling bomber at Winthorpe. (via John Elliott)

A Lancaster from No 1661 HCU is seen high above Lincolnshire on a sortie from Winthorpe. (via John Elliott)

Later in 1944 significant numbers of Horsa and Hamilcar gliders were stored at Winthorpe in preparation for Operation 'Market Garden', and on 3 November the station was transferred from No 5 Group to No 7 Group. At the end of the year Lancasters started to return to the HCU and the final Stirling training sortie was completed on 4 February 1945. By March the HCU was busy training automatic gun laying procedures; this required fighter affiliation, for which a number of Spitfires and Hurricanes were attached to the station. Accidents continued to occur and three more Lancasters crashed on 24 March (at Langford), 16 April (Oxton) and at Winthorpe on 25 May.

When the war ended the HCU's tasks were quickly wound down and flight operations ended on 8 August 1945, the unit disbanding on 10 September. Ten days later the station was transferred to Transport Command and reduced to Care and Maintenance status as a satellite to Swinderby once more. No 1333 Transport Support Training Unit used Winthorpe occasionally as a drop zone, its Halifaxes, Dakotas, Oxfords and Horsas being based some miles away at Syerston. Their use of the airfield ended in 1947, by which stage most of Winthorpe's accommodation was being used by Royal Army Service Corps personnel. No 1331 HCU (also based at Syerston) used Winthorpe briefly during 1947, and the familiar shape of the mighty Halifax returned to the local area, albeit for only a few months. After this the airfield was rarely used for flying activities, although the station remained active as a home to the Central Servicing Development Establishment until January 1958. The station was then transferred to Home Command and allocated to the USAF as a potential hospital site, but the plan never reached fruition and the MoD resumed control on 30 June 1958. Swinderby then resumed control of the site until July 1959, when Winthorpe finally closed.

After languishing in an abandoned state for some time, the former airfield came back to life as the East of England Showground, and the old runways occasionally attracted a few light aircraft in connection with various events held there. Virtually all of the station's buildings were eventually demolished and the A17 and A46 roads were redeveloped and rerouted, removing major chunks of the RAF site in the process, while a smaller road to the north of the airfield was re-established to resume its original path straight across the old north-south runway.

Vulcan XM594 lands for the last time after a short hop from nearby Waddington to Winthorpe's runway 09/27, ready to join the Newark Air Museum's collection. (NAM)

This road now leads to the Newark Air Museum, which was first established here in the 1970s on a couple of the old bomber dispersals. With only a handful of aircraft and few resources, the fledgling museum looked unlikely to prosper, but over subsequent years it continued to grow and some of its aircraft were able to be delivered directly to the site, courtesy of the old east-west runway that remained in useable condition. The successful arrival of a Varsity from Finningley in 1976 was followed by the equally impressive sight of a Hastings from Scampton, this Halifax derivative reminding local onlookers of the many Halifaxes that had used the same runway more than thirty years previously. However, the best-known arrival was the museum's magnificent Vulcan, which literally 'hopped' down from Waddington and landed safely before being moved to the museum complex where it remains on show to this day. Sadly, more recent arrivals have been delivered by road, the old runway having been declared unsafe, although gliding took place from the airfield alongside the runway until 2006. Today, the Newark Air Museum is still expanding (it is now one of the country's largest and most significant collections) and Winthorpe is certainly high on the list of places to visit for any aviation enthusiast.

> *Runways:* 042 (2,000yd x 50yd) concrete, 093 (1,400yd x 50yd) concrete, 151 (1,400yd x 50yd) concrete. *Hangars:* T2 (2), B1 (1). *Hardstandings:* Heavy Bomber (36). *Accommodation:* RAF: 137 Officers, 653 SNCOs, 872 ORs; WAAF: 4 Officers, 14 SNCOs, 252 ORs.

WOLVERHAMPTON, West Midlands

Grid ref SJ893031, Lat 52:37:35N (52.62629) Lon 2:09:32W (-2.15894), 340ft asl. Off A449, E of Codsall, NW of Wolverhampton

Boulton-Paul first opened an aircraft factory at Pendeford in 1936 and a landing field was soon established adjacent to the factory, linked by a concrete taxi track. Famous as the site where some 1,060 Defiant fighters were constructed, the first of these aircraft made its maiden flight here on 11 August 1937. Blackburn Rocs and Barracudas were also built here under licence, and the grass field became an obvious choice for development into a local airport. By 1938 a small terminal building had been constructed and the airport opened for business on 24 June, marked by a flying display that included three Gloster Gauntlets, a Whitley bomber, a Blenheim and a Battle, and Amy Johnson flying a Kirby Kite.

Shiny new Defiants emerging from the Pendeford factory to await delivery to the RAF. (Boulton-Paul)

In 1941 the RAF arrived when No 28 EFTS was formed here on 1 September under the control of No 51 Group. Initially equipped with thirty Tiger Moths, more aircraft followed until some 108 aircraft were present, divided into six Flights. Battlestead Hill and Penkridge were adopted as satellite stations in order to spread the flying as much as possible, including night-flying, which got under way at Pendeford in October. Operating so many aircraft presented many problems, not least the coordination of large numbers of aircraft at specific times, most notably during lunch breaks, when controllers (without the use of radio equipment) were obliged to maintain safety by the judicious use of Very pistols.

Training continued at some pace during the wartime years, and it was not until 1945 that the unit had reduced its activities to encompass refresher flying or the training of foreign students. The latter task was not new to the unit as neutral Turkish Air Force officers had been trained here during 1942. On 26 June 1947 the EFTS became No 25 RFS, operated under contract by Air Schools Ltd with the instructing staff now comprising only civilians again. By this stage the huge fleet of Moths had dwindled to just twelve, accompanied by one Anson.

Civil flying was quickly re-established at Pendeford and the Wolverhampton Flying Club was set up with a fleet of former RAF Magisters. Air displays were regularly staged and at one event a rare Grumman Duck (NC5506M) appeared, operated by Goodyear. When the RAF decided to abandon its Reserve Flying Schools in 1953, No 25 RFS was among the first to go, disbanding on 31 March. Pendeford's association with military flying ended at this stage although Boulton-Paul maintained a presence at the adjacent factory site and production of aircraft for the RAF and Navy continued, as described by the Boulton Paul Association:

'The first aircraft built at Pendeford was the Hawker Demon two-seat fighter. A total of 106 were produced; the first one flew on 21 August 1926. The factory was extended in 1937, eventually covering three times the area of the original Pendeford works. The number of employees also increased, reaching a wartime peak of 4,800. In March of the same year the company received an order for eighty-seven Defiants. The Defiant fighter was Boulton-Paul's first aircraft incorporating an all-metal stressed skin. The first flight took place on 11 August 1937 and flight trials continued during the following year. The first production aircraft flew on 30 July 1939. Initially 363 Defiants were built, followed by orders for another 113. The Royal Navy put out tenders for a turret-equipped fighter. The contract went to Blackburn for its Roc aircraft. Blackburn had a lot of orders at the time for other aircraft, so Boulton-Paul was subcontracted to manufacture the aircraft, which were basically Blackburn Skua dive-bombers fitted with Boulton-Paul Type A turrets. Boulton-Paul did all of the redesign work, and the first aircraft flew on 23 December 1938.

After the outbreak of the Second World War the factory was camouflaged, and in 1940 a dummy factory, complete with dummy aircraft, was built a mile along the canal. In April 1940 two important visitors were received at the factory, King George VI and Queen Elizabeth. They saw an aerobatic display and toured the works. The factory, however, never became a target during the many German bombing raids. The Defiant was followed by the Fairey Barracuda. Orders for 1,688 were received in 1941, so Fairey subcontracted Boulton-Paul to produce 300 of the aircraft.

After the war 270 Wellington bombers were converted to T10 navigation trainers and the Balliol T1 and T2 advanced trainers were built for the RAF. Initial flying trials were quickly completed at Wolverhampton, Boscombe and Farnborough, well before the second prototype had been completed. The aircraft was also redesigned as the Sea Balliol for use as a Royal Navy deck landing trainer with a strengthened undercarriage, folding wings and an arrester hook. A total of thirty were ordered, the first ones being delivered on 7 December 1954. The company carried out a lot of modification work on the English Electric Canberras. It was the main Canberra contractor and continued this work for fourteen years. The company became a world leader in the production of aircraft power control units and fly-by-wire systems. The electronics department designed and built a computer called "The Brain" in the early 1950s.

A lot of work was carried out on Vampires for de Havilland, and Boulton-Paul became a subcontractor for Beagle Aircraft. The company built the wings and undertook structural testing of the fuselage. The last two Boulton-Paul aircraft to fly were the P.111 and P.120 delta wing jets. The P.111 used a Rolls Royce Nene jet engine, and had a top speed of 650mph at 35,000 feet. It first flew on 6 October 1950 and was developed into the P.120. In 1961 Boulton-Paul joined the Dowty Group to become solely an aircraft component manufacturer. Today it is a part of the even larger TI Group.'

When the jet-powered BP.111 was produced, an airfield more suitable for jet operations was eagerly sought and Boulton-Paul's activities were soon transferred to Seighford. By 1956 all of the company's flight testing had moved here and Pendeford was finally bereft of all military

This is Pendeford airfield in the 1950s, illustrating the modest size of the site and the proximity to local housing, which increased dramatically in subsequent years. (via John Rowe)

Above: *Balliol trainers under construction in the Pendeford factory in 1952. (Boulton-Paul)*

Below: *Balliol T Mk 1 prototype WL892 at Pendeford in June 1948. (Boulton-Paul)*

Bottom: *Balliol WL892 is seen again on the airfield at Pendeford, with part of the Boulton-Paul factory visible in the background. (Boulton-Paul)*

connections. Sadly, its association with civil flying was also soon to end as the airfield's limited facilities, grass landing field, and growing urban development meant that it was rapidly becoming a less than ideal airport site. When a Dove aircraft stalled on approach on 9 April 1970, killing the occupants and a victim on the ground, it was the final straw, and growing opposition to the airport's presence led to the site's closure.

The remnants of Wolverhampton Airport as the site is slowly demolished. (Neil Jedrzejewski)

Unlicensed use of the airfield continued on a sporadic basis, but all flying came to an end during the 1970s and the landing field, together with the airport buildings and hangars, was bulldozed. Today the former Boulton-Paul factory survives, but every trace of the airport and the landing field is gone, trampled by the progress of industrial complexes and urban development. All that remains is a simple memorial, lost amid the ever-expanding housing complexes.

Runways: E/W (1,050yd) grass. *Hangars:* Bellman (4), Civil (1), Blister (7). *Hardstandings:* 0. *Accommodation:* RAF: 55 Officers, 121 SNCOs, 630 ORs.

WORCESTER, Worcestershire

Grid ref SO860571, Lat 52:12:45N (52.21239) Lon 2:12:19W (-2.20529), 100ft asl. NE of Worcester on B4482

Known locally as Perdiswell, a landing field was established here during the 1930s as a site for civilian flying, although its first association with aviation can be traced right back to 1914, when the same area of land (which was then a park) was used for a small flying display. Plans to develop the field into a more substantial local airport were eventually dropped when it was accepted that the development of local housing would make airline operations here impossible, and the aerodrome was confined to the operation of only light aircraft.

However, in 1938 some rather larger aircraft arrived in the shape of Fairey Battles, which were manufactured by Austin at the nearby Longbridge factory. With only a small landing strip available at the factory, it became standard procedure to fly out each completed aircraft to Perdiswell for flight testing, prior to delivering the aircraft to the RAF; more than 200 aircraft eventually completed their flight testing at Perdiswell over a period of four years.

Nearby Perdiswell Hall became the headquarters of No 81 Group Fighter Command and its Communications Flight was based at the airfield. On 2 June 1942 No 6 Flying Instructors School was deployed here from Staverton and Tiger Moths arrived, although the unit eventually reacquired its previous incarnation as No 2 EFTS prior to leaving Perdiswell in 1945. The unit employed Perdiswell as a satellite field, particularly while a runway was laid at the main base, but the unit continued to use the site long after Staverton's airfield had been relaid. Operations from the relatively small station meant that the unit could be divided into only two Flights, each with no more than thirty Moths at any given time.

The grass runways were short, the longest being only 800 yards in length, and facilities were basic, with only a handful of small hangars (including four Blister examples) and accommodation that consisted of huts and tents. Aside from the resident Moths, little other activity took place here, although some Defiants are known to have been deployed occasionally in order to mount patrols in the area, and a few emergency diversions saw larger aircraft on the airfield on rare occasions, including Lancasters, Wellingtons, Whitleys, Halifaxes and a B-17. The best-known emergency diversion was a C-47, which suffered engine failure after taking off from Pershore on 2 September 1942. After making a forced landing at Perdiswell, it slid along the wet grass, ran across the perimeter road and deposited itself in the local rubbish tip. On board was Hollywood actor Clark Gable, who had recently re-enlisted in the USAAF.

The geographical position of Perdiswell's airfield made it a useful site for emergency diversions and a variety of aircraft made un-planned arrivals here during the station's otherwise unremarkable years of operation. Undoubtedly the biggest and heaviest aircraft to successfully recover here was a USAAC B-17 Flying Fortress. (Author's collection)

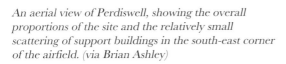
An aerial view of Perdiswell, showing the overall proportions of the site and the relatively small scattering of support buildings in the south-east corner of the airfield. (via Brian Ashley)

In 1944 Ansons began to appear more frequently here, operating a regular service to Normandy for the recovery of American servicemen who were destined for various hospitals around the Worcester area. However, when the EFTS moved to Yatesbury in August 1945, flying ended at Perdiswell and the site was returned to Worcester City Council. Perdiswell Hall was abandoned and eventually demolished in 1956, and the various hangars and airfield buildings suffered a similar fate. For many years the local ATC squadron maintained a Spitfire 'gate guard' adjacent to its headquarters here; this was replaced by a Javelin, which earned the distinction of being the last aircraft to leave Perdiswell when it was transported to Elvington in the 1980s.

Spitfire LA198 was a long-term 'gate guard' at Perdiswell, although it is now long gone. (via Brian Ashley)

Today the airfield is part of Perdiswell Park, a large area of recreational land that incorporates a golf course and sports pitches. All that remains of the RAF's presence is Perdiswell Hall's old entrance gate pillars, and a couple of small patches of concrete where support buildings once stood. A driver training school now occupies the site where Clark Gable made his rather unorthodox arrival here, back in 1942.

Runways: 0 (grass field). *Hangars:* Blister (4). *Hardstandings:* 0. *Accommodation:* RAF: 18 Officers, 48 SNCOs, 80 ORs.

WREXHAM, Clwyd

Grid ref SJ362525, Lat 53:04:00N (53.0667) Lon 2:57:08W (-2.95223), 250ft asl. Off A5156, 1 mile NE of Wrexham

Construction of this airfield began in 1940, contracted to Sir Alfred McAlpine, and although the site was initially known as Borras, the RAF adopted the name of Wrexham when it opened in June 1941. The station was intended to be a fighter base, positioned directly under the route often used by the Luftwaffe on its missions towards the industrial areas of the North West, but the first unit to arrive here was an Anti-Aircraft Cooperation Flight from No 9 Group, equipped with Blenheims and Lysanders, which moved here from Speke in August 1941. No 96 Squadron was then based at Cranage, its operations often hampered by that airfield's poor landing field, which was often waterlogged; on 21 October the unit began to make the welcome transition to the new airfield at Wrexham, which was by then equipped with proper facilities and concrete runways. Two Hurricanes and fourteen Defiants arrived on that date and, although the squadron had been kept busy intercepting enemy bombers for some time, the Luftwaffe had started to shift its attention towards Russia and 96 Squadron enjoyed a less hectic time at Wrexham, using its stay to convert onto Beaufighters, operating a small number of Ansons and Blenheims to assist with the conversion process. Only one successful 'kill' was achieved during this period when a Defiant crew shot down a runaway barrage balloon.

The first Beaufighter Mk II arrived here on 2 May 1942, by which stage No 285 Squadron had arrived as a lodger unit. Defiants remained in use as a precautionary measure, operating patrols in the area, although Beaufighters took over this task during the summer of 1942. Beaufighters were used to mount fighter cover over the area on 16 July when High Ercall was visited by the King and Queen. Some weeks earlier in May, a display was mounted at Wrexham for the Royal Observer Corps and a variety of aircraft were despatched to the station for the event, including Spitfires and Hurricanes. A Mosquito from Sealand and a Wellington from Hawarden performed flying demonstrations for the assembled spectators.

As the Luftwaffe had clearly shifted its attention elsewhere by the summer of 1942, No 96 Squadron was moved to Honiley, although before the unit left one Beaufighter (together with its crew) was lost in a take-off accident. This left only 285 Squadron at Wrexham, a unit that had been formed from the AAC Flight, which had been here since the station opened. Now equipped with seven Hudsons, four Blenheims and six Lysanders, a small number of Defiants remained at Wrexham to provide target-towing facilities for this unit, some detachments being maintained by the unit at Honiley and Woodvale. On 29 October the unit's headquarters was moved to Honiley, but one Oxford and four Defiants remained at Wrexham.

The airfield was now virtually silent, visitors being uncommon, although a USAAF C-47 did appear here as part of an investigation into a crash of a similar aircraft type in the nearby hills. However, activity returned to Wrexham when the station was transferred to Flying Training Command in 1943, becoming a satellite field for Cranage, followed by Ternhill three weeks later. Some Masters from No 5 (P)AFU were detached to Wrexham until 4 May when the station was transferred to the control of Calveley. The large fleet (more than 170) of Miles Masters used by Calveley's No 17 (P)AFU quickly became a familiar site at Wrexham through 1943 until the unit's activities wound down the following year and the unit disbanded on 1 February 1944. Calveley then became the home of No 11 (P)AFU and Wrexham began to receive that unit's Oxfords, operated by B Flight. With more than 130 Oxfords spread between the two airfields, accidents were common. The most catastrophic took place on 26 July when HM748 and ED281 collided in midair over Cheshire, one aircraft surviving the collision despite being severely damaged.

In December 1944 No 11(P)AFU transferred to single-engine training and the Oxfords were replaced by the familiar Masters, although these were soon replaced by Harvards, four Flights being established at Wrexham. Flying activity continued with the Harvard until 21 June 1945, when the AFU disbanded and flying at Wrexham declined dramatically. No 5355 Airfield Construction Wing moved in, although a detachment from No 577 Squadron (formerly one of No 6 AACU's Flights) was still present with a handful of Oxfords and a few Spitfires. The unit had been at Wrexham as a lodger since the beginning of 1943, but by the end of 1945 the detachment had moved to Atcham and flying at Wrexham ended. The site was placed under Care and Maintenance and eventually sold off.

Significant portions of the airfield were eventually removed for hardcore and, although virtually all of the airfield buildings were bulldozed, some private flying continued for many years from the one runway that survived. Sadly, even this remaining feature was finally removed and today the former airfield and station is almost obliterated from the landscape. All that remains is a meagre patch of concrete that once formed the eastern threshold of the main runway, together with one hangar, now used for storage. The rest of the airfield, the runways, taxiways, hardstandings, dispersals, hangars, control tower, admin and domestic buildings are all gone, buried under a golf course and a sprawling quarry. From the tiny village of Borras, not even the slightest hint of the RAF's presence remains and the roar of the Harvard's piston engine has been replaced by the depressing sound of the quarry machinery.

Runways: 350 (1,350yd x 50yd) concrete, 050 (1,100yd x 50yd) concrete, 110 (1,560yd x 50yd) concrete. *Hangars:* Bellman (1), Blister (11). *Hardstandings:* 0. *Accommodation:* RAF: 90 Officers, 202 SNCOs, 612 ORs; WAAF: 8 Officers, 8 SNCOs, 240 ORs.

WYMESWOLD, Leicestershire

Grid ref SK586218, Lat 52:47:29N (52.79145) Lon 1:07:55W (-1.13194), 272ft asl. 1 mile SE of Hoton off A60

Opening on 16 May 1942, Wymeswold was assigned to No 7 Group, tasked with the training of bomber aircrew. The first unit to arrive was No 28 Operational Training Unit equipped with Wellingtons and Lysanders, although Halifaxes and Stirlings appear to have been used by the unit, as these were soon visible on the airfield. No 1521 BAT Flight also came to Wymeswold in 1943 with its fleet of Oxfords, remaining here until 1944. Bomber crew training continued without interruption from 1942 until 1944, many of the senior crews taking part in missions over Germany, including the famous 'Thousand Bomber' raids. By June 1944 the unit was equipped with a mixed fleet of Wellingtons, Hurricanes and Martinets but, with the need for new bomber crews diminishing quite rapidly, the unit's training task shifted towards the need for transport crews. On 15 October Wymeswold transferred to No 44 Group Transport Command and became the home of No 108 Operational Training Unit, converting former bomber crews onto the Douglas Dakota.

In August 1945 the Operational Training Unit became No 1382 Transport Support Conversion Unit, still equipped with Dakotas, but now part of No 4 Group Transport Command. The unit remained active at Wymeswold until 10 December 1947, when it moved to North Luffenham and Wymeswold was closed down. However, the station was to enjoy a second lease of life, and reopened on 3 May 1949 as part of No 12 Group, Fighter Command. No 504 (County of Nottingham) Squadron, Royal Auxiliary Air Force, transferred here from Hucknall, equipped with Spitfire Mk 22 aircraft, and swiftly converted onto the Meteor jet fighter, subsequently re-equipping with the Mk 4 variant and the Mk 8 in 1952.

In July 1954 No 1969 (Air Observation Post) Flight moved in from Desford as part of No 664 Squadron with Auster AOP6 and T7 aircraft, remaining here until March 1956, when the unit disbanded. More jet fighters arrived in August 1955 when No 56 Squadron moved here from Waterbeach to work up on the Hunter. When that unit returned to Waterbeach it was replaced by more Hunters, this time from Nos 257 and 263 Squadrons, which deployed to Wymeswold while the runways at their home base at Wattisham were being resurfaced. Many other aircraft types made occasional visits and air displays became an annual feature of life at Wymeswold, attracting types such as the F-86 Sabre, more Meteors, Canadian Bristol Freighters and USAF F-84 and B-45 jets.

No 56 Squadron's Hunters were amongst the last aircraft to operate from Wymeswold. They were also undoubtedly the noisiest! (Author's collection)

When the Royal Auxiliary Air Force was disbanded in 1957 No 504 Squadron ended operations on 12 February, after which Wymeswold became a satellite field for Syerston, and the resident No 2 FTS deployed regular detachments of Provosts to the airfield, these being exchanged for the Jet Provost in the 1960s.

Jim Broadwell remembers life near the airfield:

'I don't remember Wymeswold in any great detail now but I can certainly remember seeing the Hunters in particular and hearing them too, as they were pretty noisy especially on take-off. They often flew solo but sometimes pairs were also seen roaring off, and if you passed the airfield on the right day you could sometimes see groups of Hunters assembled on the readiness platform at the end of the runway. When the Hunters left, the airfield seemed almost deserted, although civil aircraft were still around for many years as well as some military types, but after the Hunters went it seemed almost like a different place. I've been back there on a couple of occasions to look around the old station and you can still visualise the aircraft there, but at the same time you have to pinch yourself to be sure that you're not imagining how it once was!'

Field Aircraft Services established a factory at the airfield and a wide variety of aircraft types were often seen at this facility, including RCAF F-86 Sabres and CF-100 Canucks, T-33s and US Navy C-54 and R5D-1 aircraft, although work gradually shifted towards the overhaul of civilian aircraft, including the Viscount, Viking, DC-4, DC-6, DC-7 and Marathon. When runway work was commenced at Hucknall, Rolls Royce exported its test flight operations to Wymeswold, and from January 1955 until February 1956 a strange mix of exotic aircraft types were operating from the airfield, sharing facilities with the resident RAF and RAuxAF units. In addition to Hunters and Canberras, the two Avro Ashton trials aircraft came here and became a familiar sight in the local area. With the departure of the RAuxAF and Rolls Royce aircraft, only the infrequent visits from Syerston's Jet Provosts maintained the RAF's presence here, but by the end of the 1960s they too hand gone and only Field Aircraft Services remained. When the company moved to Castle Donington, just a handful of aircraft remained on site awaiting completion of their overhauls. The last significant users of the airfield were six Harriers from No 1 Squadron, which deployed here from Wittering on exercise in May 1970. After this the airfield was largely abandoned, apart from occasional appearances by private aircraft.

A rare image of the short-lived Avro Ashton WB492, which operated from Wymeswold for some time. (Author's collection)

Today flying activities have ended but the airfield remains intact, the three runways still in good condition and the main runway, complete with fighter jet Operational Readiness Platforms at each end, looks more than capable of handling the arrival of more Hunters, if only the RAF still had any. Some of the hangars are still visible and the crumbling control tower is still standing. Many other buildings have survived too, although industrial development is slowly changing the shape of the former admin and technical sites. The runway is now used mostly for car racing although the local residents seem less than enthusiastic at the huge amount of noise nuisance that the racing cars generate. It is perhaps fortunate for them that the thunder of Hawker Hunters has long since faded into history.

Wymeswold seen from the air in August 2003. Although no longer used for flying, the airfield's runways are intact and in good condition. (via Richard E. Flagg)

Wymeswold's former watch office and fire tender building still stand but are slowly deteriorating. (Richard E. Flagg)

Runways: 198 (1,250yd x 50yd) concrete, 254 (2,000yd x 50yd) concrete, 312 (1,250yd x 50yd) concrete. *Hangars:* T2 (4), B1 (1). *Hardstandings:* Heavy Bomber (30). *Accommodation:* RAF: 190 Officers, 520 SNCOs, 1,226 ORs; WAAF: 10 Officers, 14 SNCOs, 411 ORs.

Index

Royal Flying Corps Squadrons/Units

Royal Navy Squadrons/Units

USAAF/USAF units

The Action Stations Revisited Series

Volume 1 Eastern England
9780859791459

Volume 2 Central England and the London Area
9780947554941

Volume 3 South East England
9780859791106

Volume 4 South West England
9780859791212

Volume 5 Wales and the Midlands
9780859791113

Volume 6 Northern England and Yorkshire
9780859791120

Volume 7 North East England, Scotland and Northern Ireland
9780859791441

Published by Crécy Publishing Ltd
1a Ringway Trading Estate
Shadowmoss Rd
Manchester M22 5LH
www.crecy.co.uk

Action Stations Revisited vol 1
East Anglia
Michael J F Bowyer

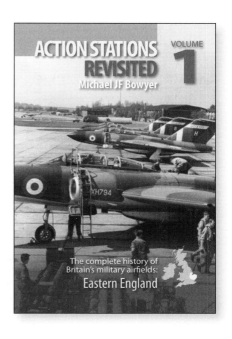

Nothing is forever, not even diamonds. Fundamental changes in international relations, changing threats and limited resources have led to a slim, overworked Royal Air Force, a modern, sleek equivalent of its earliest days and eastern England's elaborate airfields have a new role as home bases for expeditionary activities.

It has not always been like that. Cranwell was a naval base for much of WWI and Duxford, a 225-acre site, developed into a typical RAF fighter station of the 1920s and early 1930s. Fowlmere was too far from the Continent to allow its use as a starting point for offensive operations but its Spitfires tangled with Bf 109s in WWII. Lakenheath became a USAF Air Base with F-84Gs of the 508th Strategic Fighter Wing and Bentwaters accommodated F-16s and grisly green A-10s.

Michael JF Bowyer has drawn on over sixty years of personal recording, recollection and official sources to produce a definitive record of eastern England's airfields from today's major international airports and huge air bases down to tiny airstrips or disused remains. This fully revised second edition incorporates over 200 new photographs and much fresh information. *Action Stations Revisited – Eastern England* provides a vital record of the many advances witnessed in the region with Britain's busiest skies.

480 pages, hardback
234mm x 156mm
Over 400 photographs, maps and plans
9 780859 791458
£24.95

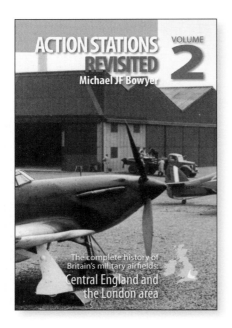

Action Stations Revisited vol 2
Central England and the London area
Michael J F Bowyer

The second volume in the highly successful Action Stations Revisited series updates the histories of over 140 airfields with military associations around the central England and London area. RAF Fighter Stations, training bases, contractor airfields such as those of De Havilland, Hawker and Vickers, plus the bases of the paratrooper units who played a large part in the D-Day landings all contributed to the aviation history of the area.

Included among the numerous well-known sites are Wittering, home of the Harrier; Benson, of photo reconnaissance fame; Brize Norton, now the RAF's in-flight refueller base; Cardington, still the departure point for airship voyages; Eastchurch, where naval aviation was pioneered and London Heathrow where the jet-set age was born. Legendary names from the Battle of Britain such as Biggin Hill, Kenley, Hornchurch and many others also lie among the plentiful stories recounted.

Action Stations Revisited No 2 Central England and the London Area contains over 280 photographs, most previously unpublished. The depth of research and the wealth of personal insight make the Action Station Revisited series a major contribution to aviation literature.

416 pages, hardback
234mm x 156mm
Over 280 photographs, maps and plans
9 780947 554941
£24.95

Action Stations Revisited vol 3
South East England
David Lee

The military airfields of the south east of England including those in Kent, Sussex, Hampshire and Wiltshire are all in the third volume of the new 'Action Stations Revisited' series.

These are the airfields from which the flimsy biplanes and blimps of World War One rose to defend Britain from Zeppelins and U-boats, the airfields from which Hurricanes and Spitfires took on the Luftwaffe in the Battle of Britain and which later took the fight to the enemy's home territory. Airfields from which the RAF stood ready at the most dangerous moments of the Cold War and which have become household names in more recent conflicts.

Within these pages well-known airfields such as Manston, Hawkinge, Odiham, Tangmere, Lee-on-Solent, Greenham Common, Thorney Island, Farnborough and Wroughton mingle with the almost-forgotten Bekesbourne, Welford, Grain, Hartford Bridge, Throwley, Ramsbury and Woodchurch.

The relics of the Sound Mirrors, Britain's early warning system before radar, is also covered amongst the many previously unpublished accounts and photographs which illustrate this comprehensive coverage of Britain's front line airfields.

Arranged in alphabetical order with maps and map references, directions, plus a comprehensive index, Action Stations Revisited No 3 South East England provides a fascinating wealth of information on south-east England's aviation heritage.

344 pages, hardback
234mm x 156mm
Over 150 photographs, maps and plans
9 780859 791106
£24.95

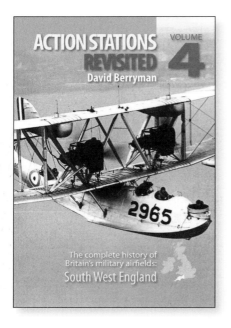

Action Stations Revisited vol 4 South West England

David Berryman

Over 120 military airfields of the south west are the subject of the latest volume of the new Action Stations Revisited series. The area covered includes most of the counties of Gloucestershire, Hampshire and Wiltshire, along with those of Dorset, Somerset, Devon, Cornwall, the Isles of Scilly and the Channel Islands.

The whole of British aviation history is reflected from the birth of military aviation at Larkhill, flying training at Old Sarum during the First World War and at Upavon during the 1930s, to fighter operations from Charmy Down during the Second World War. Postwar developments at Filton and Boscombe Down are supplemented by recent activities at Culdrose, St.Mawgan, Yeovilton and Lyneham.

Detailed accounts of the construction and operational use of the stations, with the aircraft types flown and units involved are copiously illustrated by over 340 photographs, many of them previously unpublished.

Fully indexed, this volume contains a wealth of information for any airfield visitor, modeller or aviation historian.

368 pages, hardback
234mm x 156mm
Over 150 photographs, maps and plans
9 780859 791212
£24.95